Trust, Organizations and Social Interaction

Trust, Organizations and Social Interaction

Studying Trust as Process within and between Organizations

Edited by

Søren Jagd

Professor, Department of Social Sciences and Business, Roskilde University, Denmark

Lars Fuglsang

Professor, Department of Social Sciences and Business, Roskilde University, Denmark

 Edward Elgar
PUBLISHING

Cheltenham, UK • Northampton, MA, USA

Published by
Edward Elgar Publishing Limited
The Lypiatts
15 Lansdown Road
Cheltenham
Glos GL50 2JA
UK

Edward Elgar Publishing, Inc.
William Pratt House
9 Dewey Court
Northampton
Massachusetts 01060
USA

A catalogue record for this book
is available from the British Library

Library of Congress Control Number: 2015959655

This book is available electronically in the Elgaronline
Business subject collection
DOI 10.4337/9781783476206

MIX
Paper from
responsible sources
FSC
www.fsc.org   FSC® C013604

ISBN 978 1 78347 619 0 (cased)
ISBN 978 1 78347 620 6 (eBook)

Typeset by Columns Design XML Ltd, Reading
Printed and bound by CPI Group (UK) Ltd, Croydon, CR0 4YY

Contents

Figures

Tables

Contributors

Jens Allwood is Professor of Linguistics at the University of Gothenburg, Sweden. He is also Director of the interdisciplinary center SCCIIL. His research primarily includes work in linguistics, communication and cognitive science. In linguistics, he has mainly worked on semantics and pragmatics. He has investigated face-to-face interaction from several perspectives, for example corpus linguistics, computer modelling of dialogue as well as multimodal and intercultural communication. Presently he heads projects concerned with multimodal communication, cultural variation in communication and the influence of social activity on spoken language.

Nataliya Berbyuk Lindström has a PhD in General Linguistics from the University of Gothenburg, Sweden. She is currently an Assistant Professor in the Department of Applied Information Technology, Chalmers University of Technology and University of Gothenburg. She is Program Director for the international Master in Communication programme. Her research interests comprise international/intercultural communication/ cross-cultural research, doctor–patient communication, multimodal communication, rhetoric, and technologies for e-learning.

Maria Bosse is a management consultant at Implement Consulting Group. Maria is a former PhD candidate at Roskilde University. Her research concerned management and board governance in start-up companies from the perspective of venture capitalists. Her research was anchored in the school of sociological pragmatism, and focused on micro processes of human interaction in organizations. Maria currently focuses on helping organizations to change routines and mindsets, to enhance trustful partnerships and collaboration. She has experience as a management consultant with clients and projects across the public and private sector. She has worked specifically with interdisciplinary challenges between venture-capitalists and start-up companies, as well as municipalities and hospitals.

May-Britt Ellingsen is senior researcher at Norut, Northern Research Institute, Tromsø, Norway and earned her Dr Philos. degree at UiT The Arctic University of Norway. She is an organizational sociologist and her research focuses on trust, innovation and organizational change. Her recent works are on business collaboration, trust and innovation in clusters. As researcher in applied social science, Ellingsen has a long experience in participatory research and dialogue-based evaluations of collaboration and development processes in the public sector.

Bjarne Espedal is Professor of Leadership and Organizational Theory at NHH – Norwegian School of Economics. He is Editor-in-Chief of *Beta. Scandinavian Journal of Business Research*. He has published numerous articles in journals such as *Human Resource Management*, *British Journal of Management*, *Journal of Applied Behavioral Science*, *Leadership*, *Journal of Organizational Change Management*, *Journal of Leadership & Organizational Studies*, *European Journal of International Management*, *Journal of Change Management*, *Advances in Developing Human Resources* and *Human Resource Development Review*.

Morten Frederiksen is Assistant Professor at the Centre for Comparative Welfare Studies, Department of Political Science, Aalborg University and holds a PhD in Sociology. He conducts research on social policy, welfare states, civil society and volunteering, values and values change, welfare attitudes and trust. His main theoretical interests lie within the sociology of valuation and evaluation and in investigating the cultural foundations of judgement.

Lars Fuglsang is Professor at Roskilde University. His main research interest is how institutional and organizational frameworks are created to deal with the impact of innovation, technology and other forms of change on business and society. His current research is focusing on a practice-based understanding of the innovation process. He has published his work in journals such as *European Urban and Regional Studies*, *Science, Technology, & Human Values*, *Scandinavian Journal of Management*, *Service Industries Journal* and *Organization*.

Anne H. Gausdal is Associate Professor at University College of Southeast Norway. She earned her PhD in Business Economics at Bodø Graduate School of Business, University of Nordland, Norway. Professor Gausdal has been involved in network development in the Norwegian industry since 2001. Her scientific production covers three main areas: methods for innovation, inter-organizational trust-building and network management, composition and outcome. She has published in journals that include the *Journal of Trust Research, Entrepreneurship & Regional Development, International Journal of Action Research, BETA, Scandinavian Journal of Business Research, Systemic Practice and Action Research,* and *Journal of the Knowledge Economy*.

Kjell Grønhaug is Professor Emeritus at the Norwegian School of Economics and Business Administration, Bergen. He holds an MBA and a PhD in marketing from the School, an MS in sociology from the University of Bergen, and carried out his postgraduate study in quantitative methods at the University of Washington. He has been Visiting Professor at several American and European universities. He has also been an Adjunct Professor at the Helsinki School of Economics and is associated with universities in Stavanger, Tromsø and Nordland. He is Honorary Doctor at Turku School of Economics and Business Administration, Stockholm School of Economics and the University of Gothenburg, and the recipient of the prize for excellence in research at his own institution awarded every fifth year. He has been involved in a number of research projects related to a variety of marketing problems, corporate strategy, industry studies and multiple evaluation studies. His publications include 18 authored and co-authored books, and numerous articles in leading American and European journals and contributions to many international conference proceedings.

Uffe Kjærgaard Hansen is a PhD candidate at Roskilde University. His research and teaching revolves around philosophy of science, problem-oriented project work, organizing and trust. He is currently studying how the practices of shop stewards, including organizing and establishing trusting relations at the workplace, are affected by goal-oriented development initiated at the union level. The research is conducted as qualitative studies at both the union and workplace level and within the frame of symbolic interactionism.

Mirjami Ikonen, PhD, is a Senior Lecturer in Management and Leadership at the UEF Business School, University of Eastern Finland. Her primary research focus is in interpersonal trust development and leadership issues from a process perspective. Her current research interests include organizational trust and communication, cultural issues and new qualitative methods.

Søren Jagd is Professor of Trust-Based Leadership at Roskilde University, Denmark. He holds a PhD from Copenhagen Business School. His main areas of research include leadership and trust, trust and control and process perspectives on trust. His work has appeared in journals such as *Current Sociology*, *Society and Business Review*, *European Journal of Social Theory* and *Organization*.

Svein Tvedt Johansen is Associate Professor, School of Business and Economics at UiT The Artic University of Norway. He holds a PhD in organizational behaviour from the Norwegian School of Economics

(NHH) in Bergen, Norway. In his research Johansen looks at the formation and development of interpersonal trust in organizational settings and the interaction between situational characteristics, goals and trust. Another research interest relates to hybrid organizations and management within hybrid organizations. Johansen has published in journals that include the *Journal of Business Ethics*, *Management Decision*, *Journal of Applied Social Psychology*, *Journal of Change Management* and *Public Opinion Quarterly*. Johansen's teaching experience includes courses on leadership, organization theory and HRM and strategic management. He is currently an associate editor of the *Scandinavian Journal of Business Research*.

Inga-Lill Johansson, Associate Professor, has a PhD in Business Administration from the University of Gothenburg, Sweden. Her research is focused on the relationship between accountability and trust. It involves studies of organizational practices and communication among professionals in business and public-sector organizations. She has published in journals such as *Journal of Organizational Transformation & Social Change*, *Qualitative Research in Accounting & Management*, *Management Accounting Research* and *Scandinavian Journal of Management*. She has co-edited a special issue of *International Journal of Public Sector Management* and is the co-editor of *An Actor's Approach to Management: Conceptual Framework and Company Practices* (DJØF Publishing, 2011) and *Värdet av Förtroende* (*The Value of Trust*) (Studentlitteratur, 2006).

Kirsti Malkamäki is PhD candidate in the UEF Business School, University of Eastern Finland. She graduated in Economics from the University of Eastern Finland in 2011. She has extensive experience in the field of trade organization at different levels of supervisory and management positions. Her current research focus is multilevel development of trust in organizations.

Kirsten Mogensen is Associate Professor, Roskilde University, Denmark. Mogensen was Chief Press, Information and Protocol Officer for Aceh Monitoring Mission 2005–2006, and has participated in a number of international election observation missions, most recently for the Carter Center in Myanmar. She has a background in professional journalism and has been Associate Professor in Journalism since 1989 at the Danish School of Journalism and since 1999 at Roskilde University. Mogensen has been affiliated with Stanford University (2010), Louisiana State University (2001–2002), and University of Minnesota (1975–76), either as a student or as a visiting scholar. Her research interests are in the area of public diplomacy and international trust building. Her research has appeared in journals such as *International Communication Gazette* and *Media, War & Conflict*.

Lovisa Näslund is Assistant Professor at the Stockholm School of Economics. She received her PhD in business administration in 2012 from the same school. Her research has focused on processes of trust creation in project groups and markets for professional services and organic goods, particularly focusing on how context shapes the conditions and means of the development of trust and distrust. Her research has been published in journals such as *Human Relations* and has been highlighted in *The Economist*.

Margit Neisig is Assistant Professor, Business Administration, Roskilde University, Denmark. She has a PhD in socio-technological planning, and has many years of practical experience in management of change/ transition in organizations. She has held positions as head of divisions in TDC (a Danish telecom company), the County of Funen and the Municipality of Fredensborg. She has been a consultant for several organizations and taught at several universities. Her main focus is on leadership and human resource management.

Kevin Anthony Perry is a Postdoc researcher in inclusion at the Department of Learning & Philosophy, Aalborg University, Copenhagen, Denmark. Currently, he is researching what promotes and hinders 'inclusion' in Danish Schools from the perspectives of children and young people. He has a BA (Hons) degree in European Social Work from Portsmouth University and a Master's of Science in Social Work from Aalborg University. He has a diverse background and has experience working in different occupations such as soldier, taxi driver, door-to-door sales, doorman, residential social worker and street youth worker. Prior to his PhD studies, he worked for the Regional Authority of Bornholm in Denmark from 2001 to 2008, working primarily with crime reduction in the local community. Kevin undertook his PhD at Roskilde University in Denmark. His doctoral thesis centres on the relationships between a group of young men with ethnic minority backgrounds and diverse frontline public sector employees whom they regularly encounter. The study carefully explores these relationships from both the perspectives of the young men with ethnic minority backgrounds and the professionals, and contributes towards understanding the micro processes at play in distrust and trust building processes.

Mette Apollo Rasmussen is a PhD fellow at Roskilde University. Her research and teaching centres round organization, leadership and trust studied from a micro process perspective. She is currently studying processes making participation in business networks valuable in collaboration with a Danish municipality. Her research is based on ethnographic fieldwork within a theoretical frame of symbolic interactionism. Generally, her research designs are based on qualitative data within a theoretical frame of symbolic interactionism and interpretations.

Taina Savolainen is Professor of Management and Leadership and leader of the research group of 'Trust within Organizations' at the University of Eastern Finland, Business School. She is a trust educator and trainer for enhancing workplace trust-building skills. She is an active researcher and author on trust publishing in academic and business forums with a specific focus on trust development in intra-organizational work relationships. Her current focus is in the process approach to trust research. She is a contributor to the three books published by TRUST Inc. in the Trust Across America–Trust Around the World Alliance network where she was named as one of the 100 Top Thought Leaders in Trust 2015, and is also involved in other international networks for promoting trust.

Marcus Selart is Professor of Leadership and Organizational Behavior at the Norwegian School of Economics (NHH). His areas of interest include how leadership and communication systems influence risk taking, trust, ethical behaviour and change acceptance. He has been a member of the Nordic research network on trust in and between organizations for several years. His central activities involve advising managers, teams and organizations. He also has experience of negotiations, change management, decision implementation, risk governance, and human resource selection.

Anna Swärd is Post-doctoral Researcher at the Centre for the Construction Industry at the Norwegian Business School BI in Oslo. Her main research is on trust processes in alliances and project based organizations focusing on the nature of trust, trust-formation processes, and the dynamics of trust. Her recent work focuses on practices, organizing and coordination in project-based organizations. Her research has appeared in journals such as *Journal of Purchasing and Supply Management* and *International Journal of Business Alliances.*

Niels Thygesen is Associate Professor at the Department of Management, Politics and Philosophy, Copenhagen Business School (CBS). His research focuses on trust, technology and temporality in public sector organizations. He is the Program Director of the Master of Public Administration at CBS. His research develops a poststructuralist and discursive approach to public sector management and includes continental philosophy, discourse theory, narrative theory and systems theory. His has published more than 20 articles and chapters on public sector management in international and Danish journals and two Danish books on trust management. He also is a member of the government initiative: The Panel of Center for Public Innovation.

Steen Vallentin is Associate Professor of CSR (corporate social responsibility) at the Department of Management, Politics and Philosophy, Copenhagen Business School (CBS). Apart from doing research in the field of trust and leadership in relation to public sector reform, his research focuses on the political aspects of CSR, including the role of government, the emergence of new modes of governance and the impact of media and public opinion on corporate communication and action. His work is published in numerous journals and books.

Foreword

'So how do you define trust?' From the way the question was put to me, I could sense that this social scientist was not asking out of friendly curiosity in a casual conversation but just lying in wait to catch something he could tear apart. This was in the early 2000s when I was a doctoral candidate in a phase when you know that you should be able to answer such a question but when you are still nervous to do so. 'Well, first of all, trust is a process', was how I started my somewhat tentative reply and, to my surprise, my inquisitor's face lit up and he became very favourably disposed to everything else I mentioned such as uncertainty, vulnerability, interpretation, expectation and even the leap of faith. This was the first time that I realized that a process view of trust is not just sensible for various reasons but also renders the concept highly compatible with other fields of social science.

However, when trust research took off during the 1990s and after, few scholars cared to investigate trust as a process, although foundational contributions from earlier decades should have led them to do so. Instead, much effort went into identifying different types of trust(worthiness) and devising cross-sectional measurements and models of trust. This is why I was delighted when I learned that the 'Nordic Research Network on Trust in and between Organizations' (Nordic Trust Network) had been created in Scandinavia in October 2010 and, more to the point, that this network combined a focus on trust in a Nordic context explicitly with process perspectives on trust. I was fortunate to be invited to give a keynote speech at the second network seminar in Roskilde, Denmark, in November 2011 where I met many like-minded researchers who were digging deeper into what it means to explicitly, or just implicitly, define and analyse trust as process (see: trust.ruc.dk).

The Nordic Trust Network's hard work is now paying off most evidently in this collection of chapters edited by Søren Jagd and Lars Fuglsang. Each contribution to the volume has found its own way of adopting a process view of trust, but reading the chapters, one can also sense the intense exchange of ideas that has taken place between the authors at the network seminars and at various other occasions when discussing their work over the past years. The overall coherence is maintained by studying the processes that shape trust as well as how trust shapes those processes, which makes perfect sense from a process perspective that points to an encompassing 'trust process'. This notion of entangled and embedded processes also matches the 'flat' ontology of process theory which frowns upon the terminology of 'micro' and 'macro' that some chapters in this book still use, though mostly in a very fluid and dynamic sense.

As reader, you can look forward to a book that stays true to its emphasis on process while accommodating 'weak' and 'strong' process approaches. It is appropriate at the current development stage of trust research to stay inclusive and also recognize the research on trust as process that does not go all the way back and embrace pre-Socratic metaphysics. Some readers might actually suspect, and some hope, that a book on process with mostly Scandinavian authors would be full of impenetrable 'Whiteheadiana'. Not so for the chapters you are about to read. Instead, they offer accessible explorations of trust as process that are meaningful especially because they bring in complementary theoretical traditions such as phenomenology, social constructionism, symbolic interactionism or sensemaking, and because the authors consider, for example, imprinting as well as emergence. Ultimately, as I would infer from the editors' introduction and claims made across chapters, the contributors to this volume are united by their interest in dynamic social interaction.

Another remarkable feature of this volume is how it combines conceptually and theoretically challenging process views with a strong empirical focus and grounding. Readers will be excited to read about trust processes in such diverse contexts as healthcare, consulting, military conflict, innovation networks, hypermarkets, construction projects, youth work, investment management, sports teams, municipalities, homecare and savings banks. While all studies presented apply some form of qualitative method, which I appreciate, the range of techniques for gathering and interpreting data is broad and the contributors display a strong sense of reflexivity regarding the need for data that are suitable for understanding processes. The insights produced are very valuable and still it remains one of the great tasks for future research to get an empirical handle on the trust processes we are interested in, not least bearing in mind that we are likely to become entangled as researchers in those ongoing processes we study.

Readers will realize, at least after reading this book, how much potential lies in studying trust as a process and/or as part of larger social processes, how much a process view can change our understanding of trustors, trustees and their ongoing relationships, and how much work there is also left to be done. This impressive volume provides a fair bit of reassurance that when somebody asks us how we conceptualize and operationalize trust, we may reply: 'Well, first of all, trust is a process.'

Guido Möllering
Associate Professor of Organization and Management
EWE Chair of Economic Organization and Trust
Jacobs University Bremen
Bremen, Germany, June 2015

1. Studying trust as process within and between organizations

Søren Jagd and Lars Fuglsang

INTRODUCTION

The goal of this book is to bring forward new knowledge about trust and processes in an organizational context. We argue that there is a need, on the one hand, to explore how trust is formed through processes of social interactions in which social actors observe, reflect upon and make sense of trust behaviour and its meaning in an organizational and social context. On the other hand, we need to explore how trust forms a constitutive element in social processes more generally in organizations. The goal of this book is to explore these two aspects of the intertwining of trust and social processes within and between organizations.

Trust understood as 'confident positive expectations regarding another's conduct' (Lewicki et al., 1998, p. 439) is today often seen as a precondition for social and economic development. Further, trust is sometimes regarded as a phenomenon that can be found – but not created (for example Sabel, 1993). Research shows, however, that trust can be influenced and manipulated through both social institutions and social interaction. Institutional arrangements, such as regulations and norms, can enable trust-relations at the interpersonal and inter-organizational level (Bachmann, 2001; Bachmann and Inkpen, 2011). Interaction with third parties (Burt and Knez, 1995; Ferrin et al., 2006; Lau and Liden, 2008) or management systems (Mayer and Davis, 1999) can also facilitate trust. Finally, trust relies on social processes of sensemaking that allow actors to explore and make sense of the foundation of trust at the interpersonal and institutional level (Fuglsang and Jagd, 2015).

Together, these different insights show that while the basic propensity to trust may be difficult to impact, because it is formed in early childhood (Erikson, 1965), anchored in culture (Saunders et al., 2010) and probably relatively stable over time (Fleeson and Leicht, 2006), the specific trust-relations among social groups are dependent on micro-processes of negotiation, interpretation and sensemaking (Wright and Ehnert, 2010). Furthermore, these micro-processes, where actors come to reinterpret their mutual relations, can be framed by structures of management, interaction and governance (Gausdal, 2012) and trust processes may also contribute to the reproduction and change of institutions (Fuglsang and Jagd, 2015). Following this, the purpose of this book is to explore how trust is framed by and is framing processes and structures of management, interaction and governance in various contexts. The book will build on a series of qualitative case studies that illustrate the characteristics of trust-building processes. The focus of trust as process has been neglected in trust research for many years, but is beginning to receive more attention in recent years (Lyon et al., 2015). The book thus seeks to contribute to the process view of trust by providing case-analysis of trust-building processes.

Since Zand's (1972) model of the dynamics of trust in the early 1970s, a considerable body of literature on trust building, trust maintenance and trust repair in organizations has accumulated. There is now a widespread consensus that trust is a multifaceted process that develops over time, rather than consisting of a limited set of discrete events. Thus, there is a need for process views of trust in order to better analyse how trust formation takes place and how different trust processes affect the reproduction of organizations. The concept of 'process', which has lately been emphasized in research, is, however, not a very clear term, and it is difficult to define in a unitary way (see Chia and Langley, 2004; Hernes, 2008; Langley, 2007). Rather than discussing process theory in a general sense, the focus of this book is to distinguish and explore processes and practices of social interaction important to trust formation.

Although trust is commonly seen as being built and reproduced through dyadic interactions, taking an explicit ontological assumption of trust as process is still not usual in trust research. Nevertheless, notable exceptions may be found. An early contributor to conceptualizing trust in a process perspective may be the German sociologist Georg Simmel who, as demonstrated by Guido Möllering (2001, 2006), conceptualized trust as a process of interpretation leading to expectation supported by a 'leap of faith'. More recently, Fernando Flores and Robert C. Solomon (1998) argued that trust is a dynamic aspect of human interaction and human relationships:

> Trust is a dynamic aspect of human relationships. It is an ongoing process that must be initiated, maintained, sometimes restored and continuously authen-ticated. Trust is not a social substance or a mysterious entity; trust is a social

practice, defined by choices. It is always relational: A trusts B (to do C, D, E). We can say that A is 'trusting', but by that we mean that he or she has a disposition to readily trust people. Indeed, the very word 'trust' is misleading, in so far as it seems to point to an entity, a thing, some social 'stuff'. Although we will continue to use the word, it might better be thought of as 'trusting', an activity, a decision, a transitive verb, not a noun. (Flores and Solomon, 1998, p. 206)

Following Dmitry Khodyakov (2007), a definition of trust as process should explain 'how all three temporal properties (the past, present, and future) influence the creation, development, and maintenance of trust' (Khodyakov, 2007, p. 125). Thus, process studies can be thought of as both focusing a sequence of events (creation, development and maintenance) and as an ontology of temporal properties that influence these events. Yet little, if any, research exists that is based on such a theoretical perspective.

Though empirical studies applying an explicit process perspective still may be scarce, notable exceptions are found. Maguire et al. (2001) analyse trust development between pharmaceutical companies and HIV/AIDS community organizations in Canada, focusing on the dynamics of identification-based trust. The study shows that discursive activity generating new identities is crucial for generating and maintaining identification-based trust. Adobar (2005) studied trust creation as a process of sensemaking in which small cues are enlarged through the incremental accumulation of evidence. Thus, trust building in partnerships may be a sort of self-fulfilling prophecy in which initial expectations positively impact behaviour and trust building. Recently, Nikolova et al. (2015) studied how clients and consultants actively create and maintain trusting relations. Trust creation is conceptualized as 'a socio-cognitive-emotional process' consisting of three interrelated practices: (1) signalling ability and integrity; (2) defining, negotiating and aligning to clients' expectations to demonstrate benevolence; and (3) demonstrating likability and personal fit (Nikolova et al., 2015, pp. 241–3).

The need for an explicit process approach may be revealed by the inherent tension in much trust research between a general agreement that trust is somehow created and reproduced through interactive processes, but nevertheless returning to an ontological assumption of trust as something that can be studied as if it is relatively stable, often applying different variations of survey study approaches. If trust is created and reproduced through interactive processes we need to apply methods that are able to capture the processes involved in the creation and reproduction of trust, hence we cannot rely on surveys alone. Lewicki et al. (2006, p. 992) point out that although we have learned a great deal from '"snapshot" studies that measure trust at a single point in time and test its relationship with hypothesized variables of interest, they provide limited insight into the dynamic nature of the growth and decline of trust over time within interpersonal relationships.'

Therefore, according to Guido Möllering, trust should be studied and conceptualized as 'a continuous process of forming and reforming the attitudes static surveys have measured so far and, crucially, as part of larger social processes' (Möllering, 2013, p. 285).

Huang and Wilkinson (2013) also point out that because the majority of studies on trust have been largely a-historical, a-processual and a-contextual, 'the specific mechanisms and processes through which trust develops and changes – the dynamics of trust – are less well understood' (Huang and Wilkinson, 2013, p. 463). In order to address this gap Huang and Wilkinson propose to study how trust develops and evolves over time based on the interaction of various psychological, social and economic mechanisms. Jarratt and Ceric (2015) further stress the limits of much process theory that fails to acknowledge properly the continuing evolution of an individual's dispositional trust, the imperfect perceptions of dynamics of cognitive trust, and the fragility of trust. To address these limitations of existing process theories of trust, Jarratt and Ceric propose to draw on insights from complexity theory which may help capture the interacting, self-organizing and emergent properties of trust.

Following these perspectives, in this book we intend to contribute to the understanding of how such 'trusting' is initiated, maintained, restored, continuously authenticated, and repaired as an integral part of social practices.

WHAT IS A PROCESS VIEW?

Process studies address questions about 'how and why things emerge, develop, grow, or terminate over time, as distinct from variance approaches dealing with co-variation among dependent and independent variables' (Langley et al., 2013). Langley and Tsoukas (2010), in their introduction to process organization studies, point to three conceptual dualities, which in different ways inspire studies of processes in organizations: process vs. substance metaphysics; process vs. variance theorizing; and narrative vs. logico-scientific thinking (see Table 1.1).

Process studies of organizations are inspired by process metaphysics (Whitehead, 1929) stating that processes, rather than substances, are the basic form of the universe. Events, states, or entities are unpacked by

revealing the complex relations made among them that together reproduce patterns and structures over time (Hernes, 2014, p. x). Becoming,
change, flux and disruption are main themes of a process worldview.
Process metaphysics regards change as constitutive of the world. Process
theory demonstrates how patterns and structures are created and stabilized by processes and events rather than explaining how structures create
events.

Table 1.1   Features of process and variance approaches

Process approaches	Variance approaches
Process metaphysics Processes, rather than substances, are the basic form of the world. Events, states or entities are unpacked by revealing the complex activities and transactions that take place and contribute to their constitution.	**Substance metaphysics** Processes are explained in terms of substances: processes contingently *happen* to substances, but substances are essentially unchanging in character.
Process theorizing Process theories provide explanations in terms of patterns between events, activities and choices over time.	**Variance theorizing** Variance theories provide explanations of phenomena in terms of relationships among dependent and independent variables.
Narrative thinking Incorporates temporal linkages between experienced events over time. It is a form of knowing used to give meaning to particular events drawing on culturally embedded narrative structures.	**Logico-scientific thinking** In logico-scientific (or paradigmatic) knowing generalizations are made about causal influences among variables.

Source: Adapted from Langley and Tsoukas (2010).

The distinction between 'process' and 'variance' theories was introduced
by Mohr (1982). While process theories provide explanations in terms of
patterns made between events, activities and choices over time, variance
theories provide explanations in terms of relationships among dependent
and independent variables. Process models deal with events and their

interconnecting, rather than variables, and, in process models, time ordering among the antecedents is crucial for the outcome.

The distinction between narrative vs. logico-scientific thinking is another way to describe two different forms of knowing. While logico-scientific knowing provides propositions or rules that connect categories of behaviour to categories of actors and situations, narrative knowing places actors and situations in a temporal, contextualized form, thus capturing nuances dropped in the abstraction process that is characteristic of paradigmatic knowing (Langley and Tsoukas, 2010). Narrative knowing is a form of knowing used to give meaning to particular events drawing on culturally embedded narrative structures.

A distinction has further been made between 'weak' and 'strong' process approaches according to the degree to which a strong process ontology has been applied (Bakken and Hernes, 2006). Weak process approaches build on phase models describing stages of development. Stronger process approaches propose the generative mechanisms active in producing these temporal sequences (Welch and Paavilainen-Mäntymäki, 2014). The strongest process approaches are based on the assumption that process is constitutive of the world – and hence that the task of research is to demonstrate the processual nature of things (Hernes, 2014).

Welch and Paavilainen-Mäntymäki (2014), calling for revitalizing process studies of the internationalizations process of firms, have analyzed how a process dimension has been downplayed in recent studies of internationalization. This analysis points towards crucial aspects of the research process important for revitalizing process studies more generally.

First, it is important to pose the initial research question explicitly as a process related question. While we may pose questions about the building, maintenance and the destruction of trust (weak process perspective), we may also ask questions about how particular forms of trust are important for the constitution of particular forms of relations among organizational actors (stronger process perspective). Asking how trust is involved in the production and reproduction of organizations may show how different forms of trust are important for different forms of organizing. Finally, we may aim to demonstrate the processual nature of trust as such (strongest process perspective).

Second, in deciding on the nature of the data set it is important to collect process data. This point may seem obvious but collecting process data is time-consuming and may be difficult to obtain so we may be inclined to collect data that are more readily available, such as interview data, that only to a limited degree highlight how trust is important for organizational processes.

Third, when we have access to process data we should analyze the data processually by identifying generative mechanisms, studying processes instead of antecedents or outcomes, studying a chain of events rather than a single event, focusing on temporality in the analysis, and offering process-based models in the conclusion.

HOW TO STUDY TRUST AS PROCESS

What does it mean to take an explicit process approach to the study of trust? In the following we explore different suggestions regarding applying a process perspective to organizations more generally and to the phenomena of trust more specifically.

The concept of 'process' has been lately emphasized in organizational research by Tor Hernes (2008), who highlighted two basic assumptions in process perspectives on organizations (Hernes, 2008, p. 128). The first is the ontological assumption that the world exists as flows in which entities are in a state of becoming rather than as a final state of being.

As discussed above, although trust is commonly seen as being created and reproduced through interaction processes, taking the ontological assumption of trust as process is still rare in trust research (but see Dibben, 2000, 2004 for an exception). In this book we attempt to show how trust is created and reproduced through the formation of social interaction processes which are repeated over time. Methodologically we primarily apply qualitative studies of processes involved in the creation and reproduction of trust.

The second assumption in process approaches to organizations, according to Hernes (2008), relates to epistemology assuming that 'actors intervene in the world of flows equipped with their understandings of how it works, and equipped with models of how to bring some order, either by continuing doing what they are doing already or by attempting to stabilize the worlds that surround them into some intended pattern' (Hernes, 2008).

This assumption points to the importance of actors' understanding of how the interaction in which they are involved actually works. Learning from and reflecting upon past experiences of social interaction then becomes of utmost importance for actors' interventions in social interaction and understanding of how to proceed in their social practices.

Möllering (2013) distinguishes, as summarized in Table 1.2, between five process views on trusting, highlighting different mechanisms in trusting: (1) continuing; (2) processing; (3) learning; (4) becoming; and (5) constituting. They can be placed, he argues, on a continuum from moderate to pronounced views on trusting, from trust as processing to trust as a process in itself (Möllering, 2013).

Table 1.2   Five process views on trusting

Trusting as	Example research questions	Research emphasis
Continuing	How does trust change over time?	Longitudinal
Processing	How do trustors and trustees generate and 'process' information in order to produce the outcome of trust?	Interpretation
Learning	How does trust change as a result of learning?	Building-up
Becoming	How is trust involved in producing knowledge, social identities and relationships?	Identity
Constituting	How is trust involved in the production of social structures?	Practices

Source: Adapted from Möllering (2013).

We also suggest, however, that we may distinguish process views by exploring processes of social interaction in a more concrete and empirical way. For example, some processes may be characterized by individual interventions and others by collective interventions. Thus, this book has a more empirical focus, trying to explore and theorize through case studies how processes of formation of social interaction can affect trust formation and how trust can affect individual identities and the formation of social interaction.

Even if we have to assume the social world to be flat (Friedman, 2005) it may be helpful analytically to distinguish between different processes involving trust. These different processes are not in opposition but are intertwined in several ways. First, trust may be studied as mental processes. Researchers have investigated how trust produces a certain state of mind cognitively and affectively (for example Hardin, 1993;

McAllister, 1995). A key question is how 'individual actors develop and hold positive expectations in the face of uncertainty and vulnerability towards others' (Möllering, 2013).

Second, trust may be studied as social processes. Here we distinguish between three intertwined social processes: dyadic processes involving two actors, group/organizational processes, and societal processes. We can thus distinguish different ways in which actors observe, reflect upon and make sense of trust behaviour of others as a basis for social intervention. This can involve an individual's relation to others (an individual person observing and reflecting upon others' trust behaviour), and various forms of collective reflections on trust behaviour. These different forms of trust processes may be understood as simultaneously available or overlapping rather than as separate forms, that is, as dimensions in a social learning process (see Figure 1.1).

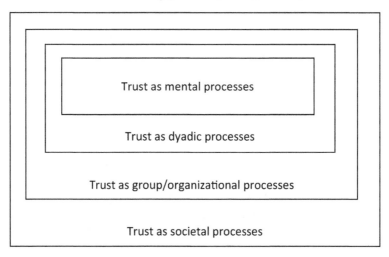

Figure 1.1   Trust as a multilevel phenomenon

- *Individual trust processes*: in this case trust/distrust is produced by individual actors observing and reflecting individually upon other relevant social actors' trust behaviour and its meaning. This may for example be a new employee in a company, who observes the behaviour of colleagues. From social interactions with these old-timers the employees must reflect on the meaning of the observed processes. Another example may be an employee observing a manager or a manager observing groups of employees – thus trying to figure out what the meanings and expectations in this social situation are.

- *Dyadic trust processes*: in this case, two people together observe and reflect upon the meaning of the trusting behaviour of others or themselves. It could be two colleagues in a company that are colleagues or friends. It could also be two managers who together are seeking to understand what kind of trusting behaviour is relevant in a giving context, thus adapting and applying the relevant trust repertoire themselves to the given situation.
- *Group trust processes*: group learning is when a group of people reflect mutually upon and discuss their own trust behaviour in relation to another group or a new situation. This may be both a formal group, such as a committee, or it may be more spontaneously gathered groups such as people exchanging views during a lunch break. Groups may be temporary or more permanent.

Furthermore, we can distinguish different distances to the observed reality that the social interaction process relates to. We use here Khodyakov's distinction between thick, thin and institutional trust (Khodyakov, 2007). The trustors may thus observe the trusting behaviours of others with whom there is a thick, thin or institutional relationship.

- *Thick interpersonal trust*: these are the strong ties between people who know each other well, like in close business relationships, family-based firms or groups of employees that know each other well. This may also be across firms in groups of facilitated networks where people build strong relationship to each other. In thick trust the basis for learning and exploring a common meaning of trust is strong due to repeated actions and the mutual moral obligations that can be present in such a community.
- *Thin interpersonal trust*: thin trust concerns the weaker ties between people who do not know each other well and will not come to know each other well. These relationships can also be learned by individual, dyadic, group or network-based learning processes. For example, two people can exchange experiences about the trust behaviour of a more distant third party and learn to adapt to this. This could be consumers in relation to providers of goods and services with whom they have no direct day-to-day contact.
- *Institutional trust*: this concerns trust based on institutions. Here too the social learning of trust can be seen as common exploration of meaning in social interaction. Confronted with, for example, the police, a citizen must make up his or her mind whether the police

are to be trusted and what behaviour to adapt vis-à-vis the police. There can be many differences and nuances in institutional trust across situations, authorities, countries and cultures that require continuous social learning.

We can conclude that trust can be seen as a process of formation of social interaction where social actors observe, reflect upon, make sense of and explore a common meaning of trust and intervene in social interaction. The social actors may be in a thick, thin or institutional relationship with each other. Social interaction may take place along different dimensions: individually, in dyadic relations, in groups or in networks. By looking more closely into these relationships the book contributes to: (1) clarifying what a process view may mean in trust research; (2) understanding how social interaction processes affects trust; and (3) theorizing trust as dependent on the exploration of a common meaning.

AN OVERVIEW OF THE BOOK

The book is structured in four parts: the first part focuses on how trust differs in various situations. The second part focuses on trust as action exploring the actor- and sensemaking-dimension in organizational trust by studying how actors are bound to make sense of the institutional and organizational environment in which they operate and how it impacts trust. The third part focuses on trust and time, exploring how trust becomes stabilized over time through ongoing efforts to frame trust-relations and create imprints of trust as well as distrust. The final part provides analyses of the complex interplay of different types of trust/distrust processes evolving over time within large organizations and between actors and organizations.

In the first part, the focus is on variations of trust in different situations. It is widely accepted that trust is a multiplex, dynamic phenomenon. Nevertheless, we still need to understand how the notions of trust and trusting actually differ in various situations. From a process perspective, we may ask what actually causes processes of trusting or of distrusting to develop in different ways, producing very different outcomes. This part contributes to trust as process research by exploring how various perspectives on variations of trust and distrust may help us understand different dynamics of trust processes.

In Chapter 2, Johansen, Espedal, Grønhaug and Selart argue that different situations call for different forms of adaptations that correspond to different forms of trust. Three different forms of trust are discussed:

trust as decision, trust as performance and trust as an uncontrollable force. In the chapter, the authors show how these three types of trust differ with respect to assumptions about trust, trustworthiness and agency as well as with respect to accompanying emotions. The chapter conclude by outlining a tentative process-model of trust and indicating questions for further research.

In Chapter 3, Frederiksen investigates the relationship between trust in institutions, trust in people and the interaction between these forms of trust from a phenomenological perspective. The analysis takes its point of departure in Luhmann's analysis of risk and danger as residing in different experiences of temporality. Building from the phenomenology of Løgstrup, the chapter argues that the experience of confidence belongs in the temporality of continuity – of stable contexts and dangers. Trust is in fact not a reaction to risk but a different phenomenological mode. Trust resides in a temporality of process and an unguarded attitude, whereas risk resides in a temporality of events, calculation and potential regrets. Institutions interact with trust in providing familiar handles on situations to determine when risk or trust seem appropriate. Frederiksen introduces the notions of trust compartments and risk compartments in order to describe the way people map social topographies of trust/process and risk/event from institutional embedding.

In Chapter 4, Allwood, Berbyuk Lindström and Johansson explore the enactment of accountability as a critical aspect of establishing and maintaining trust relationships. The chapter contributes to an understanding of trust as a dynamic relational process that varies with circumstances. Based on an analysis of a number of physician–patient consultations in a Swedish hospital, they show how the consultations lead to increased or decreased trust, and in some situations have no apparent effect. The consultations, and the accounts given in them, can possibly lead to trust if they correspond to the uncertainty or the needs the other party expresses, assuming willingness to collaborate and cooperate.

In the second part, the focus is on understanding trust as action and how institutional and organizational structures can enable and inspire trust-relations, yet the organizational context may often appear unstable, unfamiliar to the actors and ambiguous (Fuglsang and Jagd, 2015). People are bound to make sense of the institutional and organizational environment in which they operate, and how it affects trust. This part contributes to trust as process research by paying attention to the actor- and sensemaking-dimension in organizational trust, a perspective on institutional and organizational trust which appears to be underexplored in the literature.

In Chapter 5, Näslund argues that trust creation can be conceptualized as a process of interactional sensemaking between trustor and trustee. Empirically, the study is based on an interview study of Swedish management consultants and clients and the client–consultant relationship as it evolves during sales meetings and collaboration. It is shown that the trust-creating process relies on improvisational skills which require experience and it is facilitated by shared frames of reference, such as would be provided by a common habitus. The chapter demonstrates that by conceptualizing trust creation as an interactional process of sensemaking, enacted through improvisation, we can further our understanding of trust creation as process.

In Chapter 6, Mogensen analyses how two actors retrospectively made sense of the war and peace agreement in Aceh, Indonesia. With the purpose of adding to theories about the impact of macro-events on trusting at the micro level, this explorative study provides an analysis of seven episodes of trust which contributes to a sensemaking perspective on trust. They demonstrate that – in retrospect – trust and risk assessment has been an ongoing intersubjective process in which trust repertoires have been continually adapted, first throughout decades of war, and later during peace negotiations and decommission. The analysis of the seven episodes also gives indications of what bases of trust people rely on in high-risk situations. For example, there are indications that perceptions of the divine can provide an alternative framework for sensemaking during times when institutions cannot support trust.

In Chapter 7, Gausdal explores trust-building processes in networks, with particular emphasis on the link between practical intervention methods and trust-building processes. Based on a comparative case study with longitudinal data of three Norwegian regional networks, the chapter investigates dialogue-based methods that facilitate social learning of trust in networks. It argues that the participants must meet face-to-face to develop joint terms and understanding. Further, the participants should work together with reflection tasks organized in small, temporary, inter-organizational groups with time pressure, requiring all participants to be active by sharing, reflecting on, and having dialogues about experiences and challenges within the firms. The main contribution of the chapter is to increase the understanding of trust-building processes in networks as social learning processes at a practical micro level.

In Chapter 8, Malkamäki, Ikonen and Savolainen aim at improving the understanding of the trust-building process by an in-depth study of the implementation of a new management system (MS). The case study focuses on trust-building between two functional organizational units within a Finnish chain of hypermarkets. The study is based on qualitative interview-data gathered from actors at different organization levels. The chapter shows that the management system may play an important role in trust-building between organizational units by enabling a common understanding of a common goal, supporting a clarification of roles and responsibilities, and procedures for the basis for efficient cooperation.

In the third part, the focus is on how trust and distrust become stabilized over time through ongoing efforts to frame trust-relations and create imprints of trust as well as distrust. Trust in an inter-organizational context or in project teams relies partly on interpersonal relations. However, the relation between interpersonal trust and inter-organizational relationships or teamwork is an issue of great interest for trust studies. The chapters in this section contribute to this research from a process perspective and provide an analysis of trust and distrust as something that evolves over time.

In Chapter 9, Swärd explores the concept of imprinting in an inter-organizational context. Imprints are conditions or perceptions created during short, critical periods and remain stable over time. Despite the numerous studies on imprinting, the relation between imprinting and trust processes in inter-organizational relations remains to be further analysed. Insight about the imprinting process is gained from an explorative longitudinal study of two partners on a construction project that occurred in 2009–2013. The chapter offers insight into how we can understand imprinting in relation to trust – specifically, how trust imprints are created, how imprints persist, and why imprints change.

In Chapter 10, Perry applies the process perspective to a case study of the trust and distrust building between a group of young men with minority ethnic backgrounds, a team of youth workers, a job consultant and a police officer. The chapter deals with the frames used by the young men to organize the public sector employees, either as trusting or distrusting, along with some of the cultural tools used to construct these frames. The key question that the chapter deals with is: how can trust and distrust be understood as cultural frames? The case study reveals that both trust and distrust can be influenced and manipulated through social interaction over time and through the subsequent sensemaking processes in the context. The chapter contributes towards understanding the micro-processes at play in trust and distrust-building processes.

In Chapter 11, Hansen, Bosse and Rasmussen focus on how expectations are negotiated and changed. Symbolic interactionism is applied in the analysis of the ongoing and challenging relationship between an investment manager and an entrepreneurial team. The ethnographic narrative offers a rich description of how expectations are negotiated and changed as a part of trusting interactions. It provides the readers with insights into the relationship between expectations and trusting and how the developed framework based on symbolic interactions constitutes a productive framework for studying trusting in a process perspective.

In Chapter 12, Savolainen and Ikonen explore the development of trust as process in a team context, focusing on how the process of trust building emerges. The empirical study is conducted in two teams: a sports team and multi-professional team. By applying Kozlowski et al.'s theorizing of emergence (Kozlowski and Chao, 2012; Kozlowski et al., 2013), the purpose of this study is to produce empirically richer knowledge of the process of trust development by illuminating the way in which the process emerges in the team context.

The final part provides analyses of the complex interplay of different types of trust/distrust processes evolving over time within large organizations and between actors and organizations. The chapters in this section contribute to this research from a process perspective and provide analyses of complex interplay of different types of trust/distrust processes evolving over time.

In Chapter 13, Neisig applies Möllering's (2013) five process views of trusting: continuing, processing, learning, becoming, and constituting to an empirical study of a change process in a municipality in Denmark. By investigating a Danish free municipality trial in a job centre transforming from a New Public Management paradigm towards a New Public Governance paradigm, the chapter explores how the different stages of trusting in Möllering's framework may build on each other and how obstacles in trusting at lower stages might impose great difficulties in reaching good results in trusting at higher stages. These five process views are seen as layered or at least partly layered. Neisig finds that this layered understanding may explain major obstacles in change processes that involve changing trust relationships.

In Chapter 14, Vallentin and Thygesen explore a trust-based public sector reform from the point of view of the trust–control nexus. It is argued that trust reform in the public sector may be considered as a process that involves an interweaving of trusting and controlling mindsets and practices. Thus, the case is made for a complementary (as opposed to substitutive) view of trust and control. Vallentin and Thygesen argue that the role of trust in this context may be understood in lieu of the prevalence and interactions of different governance paradigms: the classical model of public administration, new public management (NPM) and new public governance (NPG). The empirical study focuses on reform efforts within home care in the Municipality of Copenhagen. Home care has been singled out as a low-skilled service area besieged by management control, documentation requirements and monitoring. However, instead of aiming to show how trust-based reform – in accordance with the ostensible benefits of trust promoted in the trust literature – can serve to liberate home care employees, the main concern is to showcase the intricate reconfiguration of social relationships that such reform gives rise to, in order to contribute to a more nuanced understanding of the trust–control nexus.

In Chapter 15 Elllingsen explores the relationship between trust and social change. The empirical example is a study of how changes in economic organization at the macro level – deregulation – can transform the trust relationship at the micro level – here between a savings bank and customers. The chapter presents a process view on trust based on interactionism and classic sociology combined with a grounded theory methodology. The perspective is that trust is a dynamic and multilevel process of social construction. Development and maintenance of trust is a dynamic process of sensemaking and social construction based on interplay between pre-contractual, relational and structural social bases. Mutual understanding is the trigger of the leap of faith, from doubt into trusting. The chapter analyses how deregulation transforms the social bases for trust between the savings bank and the customer and how trust is lost and then restored. The main finding is that social changes at the macro level influence trust relationships at the micro level and that social change is about changes in the social bases for trust.

REFERENCES

Adobar, H. 2005. 'Trust as sensemaking: The microdynamics of trust in interfirm alliances'. *Journal of Business Research* 58(3): 330–37.

Bachmann, R. 2001. 'Trust, power and control in trans-organizational relations'. *Organization Studies* 22(2): 337–65.

Bachmann, Reinhard and Andrew C. Inkpen. 2011. 'Understanding institutional-based trust building processes in inter-organizational relationships'. *Organization Studies* 32(2): 281–301.

Bakken, Tore and Tor Hernes. 2006. 'Organizing is both a verb and a noun: Weick meets Whitehead'. *Organization Studies* 27(11): 1599–616.

Burt, Ronald S. and Marc Knez. 1995. 'Kinds of third-party effects on trust'. *Rationality and Society* 7(3): 255–92.

Chia, Robert and Ann Langley. 2004. 'The first Organization Studies summer workshop: Theorizing process in organizational research (call for papers)'. *Organization Studies* 25(8): 1486.

Dibben, Mark R. 2000. *Exploring Interpersonal Trust in the Entrepreneurial Venture*. Basingstoke: Macmillan.

Dibben, Mark R. 2004. 'Exploring the processual nature of trust and cooperation in organisations: A Whiteheadian analysis'. *Philosophy of Management* 4(1): 25–39.

Erikson, E.H. 1965. *Childhood and Society.* Harmondsworth: Penguin.

Ferrin, Donald L., Kurt T. Dirks and Pri P. Shah. 2006. 'Direct and indirect effects of third-party relationships on interpersonal trust'. *Journal of Applied Psychology* 91(4): 870–83.

Fleeson, William and Christine Leicht. 2006. 'On delineating and integrating the study of variability and stability in personality psychology: Interpersonal trust as illustration'. *Journal of Research in Personality* 40: 5–20.

Flores, F. and R.C. Solomon. 1998. 'Creating trust'. *Business Ethics Quarterly* 8: 205–32.

Friedman, Thomas. 2005. *The World is Flat.* London: Allen Lane.

Fuglsang, Lars and Søren Jagd. 2015. 'Making sense of institutional trust in organizations: Bridging institutional context and trust'. *Organization* 22(1): 23–39.

Gausdal, A.H. 2012. 'Trust-building processes in the context of networks'. *Journal of Trust Research* 2(1): 7–30.

Hardin, R. 1993. 'The street level epistemology of trust'. *Politics and Society* 21: 505–31.

Hernes, Tor. 2008. *Understanding Organization as Process: Theory for a Tangled World.* Abingdon: Routledge.

Hernes, Tor. 2014. *A Process Theory of Organization.* Oxford: Oxford University Press.

Huang, Yimin and Ian F. Wilkinson. 2013. 'The dynamics and evolution of trust in business relationships'. *Industrial Marketing Management* 43: 455–65.

Jarratt, Denise and Arnela Ceric. 2015. 'The complexity of trust in business collaborations'. *Australian Marketing Journal* 23: 2–12.

Khodyakov, D. 2007. 'Trust as a process: A three-dimensional approach'. *Sociology* 41(1): 115–32.

Kozlowski, Steve W.J. and Georgia T. Chao. 2012. 'The dynamics of emergence: Cognition and cohesion in work teams'. *Managerial and Decision Economics* 33: 335–54.

Kozlowski, Steve W.J., Georgia T. Chao, James A. Grand, Michael T. Braun and Goran Kuljanin. 2013. 'Advancing multilevel research design: Capturing the dynamics of emergence'. *Organizational Research Methods* 16(4): 581–615.

Langley, Ann. 2007. 'Process thinking in strategic organization'. *Strategic Organization* 5(3): 271–82.

Langley, Ann and Haridimos Tsoukas. 2010. 'Introducing "Perspectives on Process Organization Studies"'. In Tor Hernes and Sally Maitlis (eds) *Process, Sensemaking, & Organizing.* Oxford: Oxford University Press, pp. 1–26.

Langley, Ann, Clive Smallman, Haridimos Tsoukas and Andrew H. Van de Ven. 2013. 'Process studies of change in organization and management: Unveiling temporality, activity, and flow'. *Academy of Management Journal* 56(1): 1–13.

Lau, Dora C. and Robert C. Liden. 2008. 'Antecedents of coworker trust: Leaders' blessings'. *Journal of Applied Psychology* 93(5): 1130–38.

Lewicki, R.J., D.J. McAllister and R.J. Bies. 1998. 'Trust and distrust: New relationships and realities'. *Academy of Management Review* 23(3): 438–58.

Lewicki, Roy J., Edward C. Tomlinson and Nicole Gillespie. 2006. 'Models of interpersonal trust development: Theoretical approaches, empirical evidence, and future directions'. *Journal of Management* 32(6): 991–1022.

Lyon, F., G. Möllering and M.N.K. Saunders. 2015. 'Introduction. Researching trust: The ongoing challenge of matching objectives and methods'. In F. Lyon, G. Möllering and M.N.K. Saunders (eds) *Handbook of Research Methods on Trust* (2nd edn). Cheltenham, UK and Northampton, MA, USA: Edward Elgar Publishing.

Maguire, Steve, Nelson Philips and Cynthia Hardy. 2001. 'When "silence = death", keep talking: Trust, control and the discursive construction of identity in the Canadian HIV/AIDS Treatment Domain'. *Organization Studies* 22(2): 285–310.

Mayer, Roger C. and James H. Davis. 1999. 'The effect of the performance appraisal system on trust for management: A field quasi-experiment'. *Journal of Applied Psychology* 84(1): 123–36.

McAllister, D.J. 1995. 'Affect- and cognition-based trust as a foundation for interpersonal cooperation in organizations'. *Academy of Management Journal* 38(1): 24–59.

Mohr, L.B. 1982. *Explaining Organizational Behavior: The Limits and Possibilities of Theory and Research*. San Francisco, CA: Jossey Bass.

Möllering, Guido. 2001. 'The nature of trust: From Georg Simmel to a theory of expectation, interpretation and suspension'. *Sociology* 35(2): 403–20.

Möllering, Guido. 2006. *Trust: Reason, Routine, Reflexivity*. Amsterdam: Elsevier.

Möllering, Guido. 2013. 'Process views of trusting and crises'. In Reinhard Bachmann and Akbar Zaheer (eds) *Handbook of Advances in Trust Research*. Cheltenham, UK and Northampton, MA, USA: Edward Elgar Publishing, pp. 285–305.

Nikolova, Natalia, Guido Möllering and Markus Reihlen. 2015. 'Trusting as a "leap of faith": Trust-building practices in client–consultant relationships'. *Scandinavian Journal of Management* 31(2): 232–45.

Sabel, Charles F. 1993. 'Studied trust: Building new forms of cooperation in a volatile economy'. *Human Relations* 46(9): 1133–70.

Saunders, Mark N.K., Denise Skinner, Graham Dietz, Nicole Gillespie and Roy J. Lewicki. 2010. *Organizational Trust. A Cultural Perspective*. Cambridge: Cambridge University Press.

Welch, Catherine and Eriikka Paavilainen-Mäntymäki. 2014. 'Putting process (back) in: Research on the internationalization process of the firm'. *International Journal of Management Reviews* 16: 2–23.

Whitehead, Alfred North. 1929. *Process and Reality: An Essay in Cosmology*. New York: Macmillan.

Wright, Alex and Ina Ehnert. 2010. 'Making sense of trust across cultural contexts'. In Mark N.K. Saunders, Denise Skinner, Graham Dietz, Nicole Gillespie and Roy J. Lewicki (eds) *Organizational Trust: A Cultural Perspective*. Cambridge University Press, pp. 107–26.

Zand, Dale E. (1972). 'Trust and managerial problem solving'. *Administrative Science Quarterly* 17(2): 229–39.

PART I

Variations of trust

2. Trusting as adapting

Svein Tvedt Johansen, Bjarne Espedal, Kjell Grønhaug and Marcus Selart

Trust both reflects and transforms a social reality. Whereas the trust literature has successfully described how trust reflects a social reality or how people make decisions to trust someone based on experience, we know little about how trust transforms social situations or how people trust other people without experience or obvious good reasons for trusting them (Möllering, 2006). We know even less about the relationship between the two: trust as a reflection of a social reality and trust as a force capable of transforming social reality. A process model of trust must accommodate both views as well as explaining how trust can move from merely reflecting to transforming a social world. To understand such shifts, we need to understand how people experience and understand trust. Situations here give meaning to trust and motivate behaviour that again shapes situations (Johansen et al., 2013). Importantly, a process view needs to account for changes in trust, including changes in the meaning that people ascribe to trust (Knee et al., 2003; Möllering, 2013).

In this chapter, we view trust in relation to people's adaptation to social situations involving uncertainty and vulnerability. Looking at trust through the prism of adaptation brings several advantages. First, adaptation is by definition context-dependent. Viewing trust in relation to adaptation compels us to consider how social situations and their structural features influence trust and behaviour. Adaptation thus directs our attention to the relationship between individual needs (for example for security) and the situation (dependency and uncertainty) and to the way in which people's experience of trust in turn may influence the situation through evocation, selection, manipulation or transformation (Buss, 1987; Kihlstrom, 2013). Viewing trust as adaptation also draws our attention to the existence of different forms of adaption and the fact that different situations afford or allow for different strategies (Balliet and Van Lange, 2013; Buss, 1987; Rusbult and Van Lange, 2003). Different adaptations correspond to what we will refer to as three different forms or metaphors of trust (Lakoff and Johnson, 2003): 'trust as a decision', 'trust as a performance' and 'trust as an uncontrollable force'. We argue that different situations afford and motivate different strategies for managing dependence and uncertainty in social relationships and are likely to activate different metaphors and implicit theories of trust that support and coordinate such strategies (Knee et al., 2003; Patrick and Lonsbary, 2003; Rusbult and Van Lange, 2003; Tamir et al., 2007).

Viewing trust as adaptation offers a framework for integrating different conceptualizations of trust across the literature, bridging the gap described above between trust as reflecting and trust as transforming social reality. Viewing trust as adaptation also squarely positions the actor in our theorizing on trust and is consistent with a more embodied view of trust. An embodied view of cognition sees cognition as taking place in very particular and often complex environments, serving practical ends while exploiting and manipulating external props as thinking aids (Anderson, 2003, p. 91; Chemero, 2013). Thinking reflects people's subjective experience of having a body and of being in the world as well as interacting with a physical and social world (Lakoff and Johnson, 1999). Trust here constitutes an integral part of adapting to a social situation, as opposed to a precursor or consequence of adapting: Trust is what we feel, think and experience while being in and seeking to understand and manage social situations involving interdependence and risk. Viewing trust as adaptation also connects to what Möllering (2013) refers to as trusting as becoming, in which trust refers not so much to something that people *have* as to something that people *live* or *are*. Trusting here is seen as part of 'the actor's continuous becoming' (Möllering, 2013, p. 293). People become who they are and assume their identities as a result of trusting other people (Wright and Ehnert, 2010).

In the rest of the chapter, we continue by examining existing conceptualizations of trust before presenting our own definition. We describe the structural features of social situations that influence people's adaptation to vulnerability and uncertainty and describe three forms of trust that correspond to different adaptive strategies. We present a tentative research model delineating the relationships between situations, trust and strategies for managing vulnerability. Finally, the last section reviews the contribution of the chapter and offers suggestions for further research. We variously refer to adaptation, strategies and in some cases adaptive strategies. The term 'adaptation' here refers to people's attempts to align themselves with a social situation. A strategy here refers to a set of coherent actions designed to ensure adaptation. A strategy may or may not be conscious, intended or successful.

DEFINING TRUST: TRUSTING AND ADAPTING

Trust has been defined in different ways, as a belief, an attitude, an intention or a choice. Whereas some definitions emphasize beliefs, others emphasize intentions or equal trust with manifest behaviour or cooperation (Kramer, 1999). A much-used definition integrates previous conceptualizations by describing trust as 'a psychological state comprising the intention to accept vulnerability based upon positive expectations of the intentions or behaviour of another' (Rousseau et al., 1998, p. 395). Common to these definitions is the assumption that trust reflects a set of expectations founded on knowledge or experience about a trustee or a specific situation (Burke et al., 2007; Kramer, 1999; Mayer et al., 1995; Rousseau et al., 1998). Mayer et al. (1995), in their seminal integrative model of trust, exemplify this position as seeing trust as reflective of people's beliefs, which again reflect experience and information accumulated over time. Trust interacts with perceived risk, influencing what Mayer et al. refer to as risk taking in relationships. Typologies of trust differentiate between different forms of trust based on the content or what trust is about (Das and Teng, 2004; Sheppard and Sherman, 1998) or the basis or foundation upon which trust is built. Thus, Lewicki and Bunker (1996) describe trust as undergoing a series of developmental stages in which trust changes from presumptive, calculative(or deterrence)-based trust to trust based on actual experience (knowledge-based) and to identity-based trust in which a trustor and a trustee come to identify with each other's needs and motives. Initial trust models portray initial trust as founded on a combination of institutional safeguards, normalcy beliefs, categorization processes and role enactment (McKnight and Chervany, 2006; McKnight et al., 1998; Meyerson et al., 1996).

Situational features, including the degree of interdependence (Sheppard and Sherman, 1998), social affiliation (Tyler and Degoey, 1996) or the degree of vulnerability (Kramer, 1996), have been found to influence the content of trust or what trust is about. However, while these contributions focus on how people's perception of the trustee changes, they stop short of investigating people's adaptations or strategies. The extant literature largely tends to focus on how people react to other people – based on the information that we have about other people, we either trust or do not trust them. The existing definitions of trust thus tend to emphasize the role of information and uncertainty reduction as bases for trust, yet such definitions at the same time exclude the potential importance of other strategies to people's experience of trust. Thus, managing vulnerability by seeking to influence a trustee to cooperate constitutes another, more proactive adaptation that is likely to influence people's experience of trust.

However, situations involving vulnerability in the form of unilateral dependence and conflicting interests (Rusbult and Van Lange, 2003, p. 363) have been found to trigger a series of highly involved and effortful responses – people, when confronted with new and potentially threatening information, seek more information about other people to be able to predict their behaviour or intentions or to seek to influence them (Fiske and Dépret, 1996; Johansen et al., 2013). People actively seek to influence their destiny and are acutely aware of and responsive to their own attempts to exert control (Bandura, 1989; Greenberger and Strasser, 1991; Scherer et al., 2001). People do not confine themselves merely to observing a trustee but actively seek to influence events (Rusbult and Van Lange, 2003).

The trust literature exemplifies the range of such adaptations. While Bacharach and Gambetta (2001) and Kramer (1996, 2006) describe trust as resulting from carefully evaluating signs or keeping scores of other people's behaviour, assuming the role of what Kramer refers to as 'intuitive auditors', Luhmann (1979) and Szerszynski (1999) suggest that trust can be seen as a form of 'altercasting' or 'performative act'. Flores and Solomon (1998, p. 205) see trust as 'social practices defined by our choices, to trust or not to trust'. Consistent with the view of trust as a performative act, Salamon and Robinson (2008) find in a study of a retail chain that employees' collective experience of being trusted by the management was associated with stronger responsibility norms and improved performance (sales and customer service).

While each of these contributions purports to offer a general description of trust, we suggest instead that they can be seen as representing context-dependent theories of trust and trusting. Such theories, as suggested by the examples above, are reflected in the research literature as well as in the often-implicit lay theories that people use when thinking about trust, social interaction and relationships (Dirks et al., 2009; Knee et al., 2003). Such theories are likely to reflect pragmatic adaptations to different social situations (Fiske, 1992b; Rusbult and Van Lange, 2003). Hence, people may be expected to invest more resources in developing trust in situations in which a relationship is seen as important and valuable (Lewicki and Bunker, 1996) and in which people see themselves as capable of exerting influence.

Like Rousseau et al. (1998), we see trust as a 'psychological state that comprises an intention to accept vulnerability'. Instead of linking trust directly to positive expectations, however, we suggest that the psychological state will be based on people's cognitive and affective experience of adapting to situations involving vulnerability. Such strategies do not in themselves constitute trust but are likely to shape how people experience trust. Strategies here include searching for, acquiring and assimilating information, but can also include more proactive attempts to influence the expectations and the behaviour of the trustee.

Thus, our revised definition defines trust as *a psychological state comprising the intention to accept vulnerability based on people's cognitive and affective experience of adapting to situations involving vulnerability and uncertainty*. This definition thus brings together trust and situational adaptation to vulnerability and situations. We suggest that different situations bring about different forms of adaptation and different types of trust, which in turn can reproduce, change or transform situations, which again can influence people's adaptation. The conventional view of trust as primarily reflecting people's appraisal of a trustee – through observations or third-party information – here constitutes one of several possible forms of adaptation in which a trustor seeks control through acquiring information (Skinner, 1996). Still other types of adaptation may include proactively seeking to influence the situation through giving and in return expecting trust. Here trust may be seen as constituting a performative act or a form of altercasting (Luhmann, 1979; Salamon and Robinson, 2008). Willingness to trust associated with such forms of adaptation will be distinct from traditional notions of trust yet still commensurate with the present definition. Such types of adaptations range from seeing trust as a performative act or altercasting, which influences other people and their trustworthiness (Luhmann, 1979), to more detached strategies of observing and responding to a trustee. Both types of strategy involve information processing, yet the focus and type of information processing are likely to be different. Thus, linking trust with people's subjective experience of adapting to vulnerability opens up a range of different types of trust reflecting different forms of adaptation to different situational contingencies. Common to these different forms of trust, however, is the common notion of adaptation and of a trustor seeking to adapt him- or herself to a social situation using the best of his or her resources. The effects of trust are likely to be influenced by the way in which people construe trust in specific situations – people are not merely passive receptacles of information but bring their own understanding of trust to social situations, which is likely to influence how they set about developing relationships as well as the amount of effort that they are willing to expend. The definition contributes to a better understanding of trust in at least three ways. First, viewing trust as an experience associated with adapting broadens the view of trust to include forms that were previously excluded. While including the forms captured in the existing definition, it also leaves room for other forms, in which trust constitutes a more active type of altercasting or performative act. Second, the definition, apart from being broader, also helps to explain trust by linking it as an experience with adaptation. Finally, by highlighting adaptation, the definition suggests a more agentic and embodied view of trust, which sees trust from the perspective of a trustor who acts in and on the world as opposed to observing and thinking about it passively (Anderson, 2003).

In the following, we present three forms of trust. To offer a better description of the forms and the differences between them, we present them as three metaphors for trust: trust as a decision, trust as a performance and trust as an uncontrollable force (Lakoff and Johnston, 1999; Schön, 1993). These metaphors link to implicit theories that include assumptions about the locus of control (who or what controls or influences the development of trust and the nature of a trustee's trustworthiness (fixed, malleable or ephemeral)) (Dweck and Leggett, 1988; Knee et al., 2003).

SITUATIONS, STRATEGIES AND TRUST: THREE FORMS OF TRUST

If different forms of trust represent adaptations to social situations, we first need to describe the situational features that are likely to influence how people adapt. We do so by drawing on interdependence theory (Kelley et al., 2003; Rusbult and Van Lange, 2003). According to Rusbult and Van Lange (2003, p. 353), the 'situation structure specifies the interpersonal reality that social cognitive activity is about, in that cognition is frequently oriented towards understanding (a) situations, or the unique problems and opportunities inherent in a given situation, ... and (b) persons, or a given interaction-partner's goals and motives'. Situations, argue Rusbult and Van Lange, afford 'the expression of some motivations and some personal qualities but not others'. Situations also differ with respect to which adaptive strategies are feasible. Thus, some situations may allow for extensive communication, while other situations leave little room (Rusbult and Van Lange, 2003).

Here we reduce structural properties to three main categories of situational features that we suggest are likely to influence the activation of different trust metaphors and corresponding strategies for managing uncertainty and vulnerability. The first dimension involves the degree to which the interests of the parties conflict or converge (Rusbult and Van Lange, 2003). Trust here has been found to be more important in situations involving larger as opposed to smaller degrees of conflicting interest (Balliet and Van Lange, 2013). Such situations or social dilemmas introduce greater risk as the parties cannot accommodate the interests of their partner without sacrificing some of their own interest. Thus, people become dependent on the goodwill or benevolence of the other person (Mayer et al., 1995). Interactions involving few conflicting interests are unlikely to raise issues of trust as the parties can pursue their self-interest with little or no harm to the other party.

The second feature, given that we see the trust as relevant, is value, or the extent to which people see potential for a constructive relationship with the trustee. This is likely to reflect the perceived value of outcomes, which can be accessed through the relationship or relationship-specific motives. Some relationships are more attractive than others because other people possess attributes or resources that we cannot easily obtain elsewhere or because we care about the relationship for a series of reasons (for example a coach might take pride in his or her team performing or people come to identify with the other party and the relationship). Thus, relationship-specific motives (the value of a relationship) are likely to influence how many resources people are willing to invest (or sacrifice) to preserve or build a particular relationship.

The third category, which we refer to as control, consists of situational features that influence a trustor's expectation that he or she can actually influence the views and motivations of a trustee and the situation (transforming a competitive situation into a more collaborative situation) (Skinner, 1996). Situations that involve an area of common interest, which extends over time, provide the trustor with ample information and allow free communication between the partners, thus suggesting greater potential for influencing a trustee and a relationship than situations that involve little common ground, are one-off encounters, provide the trustor with little or no information about his or her motives and provide little room for communication (Wildschut et al., 2003). Thus, communication has long been known to enhance cooperation in social dilemmas, with a stronger effect for face-to-face communication than written communication (Balliet, 2010). Similarly, the expectation of repeated (as opposed to single) interaction has been found to promote cooperation in social dilemmas (Van Lange et al., 2011). A common explanation is that repeated interaction allows the parties to sanction cooperation and non-cooperation (Axelrod, 1984; Van Lange et al., 2011). A similar argument, which also connects to the previous argument about the effects of communication, is that repeated interaction allows more room for communication (of which sanctioning is one form). Together, value and control correspond to the distinction in attitude models between valence, or the evaluation of an outcome as valuable or desired, and expectancy, or the belief that a behaviour will lead to a desired and intended outcome (Eagly and Chaiken, 1993; Fishbein and Ajzen, 1972).

Different appraisals of situations are likely to be associated with different forms of adaptation or coping strategies that reflect salient goals (such as how important a particular relationship is) as well as people's expectations about their ability to influence the outcomes or control (Skinner, 1996). Buss (1987) thus identifies three ways or strategies in which people can affect their environment: (1) evocation; (2) selection; and (3) behavioural manipulation. Evocation refers to the situation in which the presence of a person in an environment alters that environment. In some cases, individuals, by their very presence (such as standing out as the only man or woman in an otherwise all-female or all-male group), may alter the social dynamics within that group. Selection occurs when people make choices about which environments or relationships to enter. Manipulation occurs when people seek to change a chosen environment in a particular way. Kihlstrom adds a fourth strategy, which can be used in combination with the others: transformation, in which people, through covert mental activities, alter their mental representation of their subjective environment or their private experience of the environment (Kihlstrom, 2013). Associated with these different adaptive strategies, we argue that there are three different forms or metaphors for trust (Lakoff and Johnson, 2003) that represent three different experiences of trust (Rusbult and Van Lange, 2003). These forms constitute well-learned behavioural repertoires and schemas (Bargh and Ferguson, 2000) for managing dependence and uncertainty in social situations. Our primary interest here, however, is not in schemas or cognitive structures as such. Instead, we suggest that different situations naturally lend themselves to or afford different forms of adaptation and that our experience of trust in the continuation of this will reflect the situation. The metaphors and implicit theories can be seen as adaptive in that they prepare and facilitate adequate responses and reactions to specific situations (Fiske, 1992b; Rusbult and Van Lange, 2003). Thus, a 'trust as a performance' metaphor prepares people to shape and in some cases transform social situations when a relationship is seen as important and when such influence is seen as possible. A 'trust as a decision' metaphor suggests prudence and care in situations in which a trustor does not expect to see the trustee again and/or in situations in which a trustor is likely to have little influence over a trustee. A 'trust as an uncontrollable force' metaphor likewise can be adaptive in situations in which people have little or no control or information and need to align themselves with that situation.

We refer to the first form of trust as *trust as a decision*. This form of trust corresponds to what Buss refers to as selection. We adapt to vulnerability by selecting situations or selecting our exposure to vulnerability in that situation. Trust as a decision is likely to occur in situations that are seen as less important or consequential and/or in which communication is limited or difficult and there is little expectation of repeated encounters. To use Gambetta and Hamill's example of taxi drivers, a driver is unlikely to be able to reform a hardened criminal in a one-time encounter (Gambetta and Hamill, 2005). This could also be the case when trust is seen as inconsequential or easy and people as a result are less inclined to invest in costlier and more risky strategies, such as trying to influence a trustee through unilateral displays of trust (trust as a performance) (Weber et al., 2005). Here trust is essentially seen as a reflection of properties of the benefactor of trust, the trustee. Developing trust here involves the task of unpacking a 'true and assumed unchanging' identity of the trustee as either trustworthy or not. This is likely to involve a second, more basic metaphor that sees trustworthiness as a hidden, fixed quality of the trustor (Molden and Dweck, 2006). Trust here is often seen as developing over time, 'largely as a function of the parties having a history of interaction that allows them to develop a generalized expectancy that the other's behavior is predictable and that he or she will act trustworthily' (Lewicki and Bunker, 1996, p. 121). This first view of trust is expressed in the question: to what extent can I trust him? Because outcomes (trust) according to this metaphor are seen as being caused by the trustee, trust here is likely to be associated with other-directed emotions that include gratitude or anger (Weiner, 1985). The 'trust as a decision metaphor' is also likely to influence people's reactions to trust in that there is likely to be a close correspondence between people's construal of the other as trustworthy or not and their behaviour towards the trustee. Because trustworthiness is seen as a fixed quality of the trustee, the trustor is likely to see little reason to repair broken relationships. Thus, for the 'trust as a decision' metaphor, the trustee, not the trustor, drives the formation and development of trust. The trustor has moderate control – the trustor can decide whether or not to expose him or herself, but cannot influence the trustworthiness of the trustee. Trust here is accompanied by other-directed emotions (directed towards the trustee), including gratefulness or (if trust is breached) anger. We refer to the second form as *trust as a performance*. This form corresponds to what Buss refers to as manipulation, as well as to what Kihlstrom refers to as transformation (Kihlstrom, 2013). We adapt to vulnerability and uncertainty by seeking to influence other people's trustworthiness through our own behaviour and communication of norms and expectations (Luhmann, 1979; Salamon and Robinson, 2008; Szerszynski, 1999). The trust as a performance form sees trust as a performative act that involves effort and perseverance (Szerszynski, 1999). Unlike the former case, in which trust is seen as reflecting a hidden given property of the trustee, trust is seen here as resulting from a process that the trustor initiates and supports. People here hold a stronger interest in the relationship and hold more opportunities to influence a trustee through multiple encounters. As shown in the literature, trust in people we know, or seek to get to know, invokes a very different and more emotional form of trust (Rempel et al., 1985). The 'trust as a performance' metaphor thus has very different implications for how people approach the formation of trust. Unlike in the trust as a decision metaphor, trust is seen here as an emerging quantity and at least partially as a reflection of the trustor's efforts. In showing trust and offering to cooperate first, a trustor may shape the trustee's perception of the relationship, communicate a set of common norms, limit the range of acceptable choices and increase the likelihood of cooperation and hence the trustworthiness of the trustee. Hence, this second metaphor highlights the agency of the trustor and the consequences of showing trust (and particularly of not trusting) as opposed to the consequences of being right or wrong about a trustee. Emphasis here is likely to be on impact – a trustor's ability to influence the trustee through the demonstration of trust and faith (Salamon and Robinson, 2008). This suggests a greater emphasis on direct and close contact even when this contact is likely to bias the trustor's impression of the trustee. Thus, this second view of trust is captured in the question: how can I trust her? Trust as a performance is likely to involve different sentiments from the first metaphor. Thus, the prominent emotions associated with this second trust metaphor may include self-directed emotions, including pride or shame, as the experience of trust reflects back on the trustor and the trustor's initiatives and performance in the relationship (Weiner, 1985). In terms of reactions to trust, trust associated with this second metaphor would suggest self-conscious monitoring of both the experience of trust and the trustor's behaviour based upon whether these reactions are seen as furthering the relationship or not. Breaches of trust are less likely to be seen as fatal as the trustor sees trust as an incremental emerging quality of the relationship that can be influenced by his or her actions. Breaches of trust are thus likely to be associated with intensified attempts to repair trust, reflecting an expectation that breaches can be mended and that such efforts can even strengthen a relationship (Knee et al., 2003). In the trust as performance metaphor, the locus of trust lies with the trustor – trust reflects a decision or effort on the part of the trustor. The trustor constitutes the causal agent that drives the formation and development of trust. The trustor has considerable control, including the capacity to influence the motivations and actions of the trustee. Trust here is associated with self-directed emotions, including pride or shame (when trust fails).

Finally, in other situations, people may have little or no experience of interacting with a trustee (for example a distant leader) or people may have little prior experience of a specific type of situation. In such situations, in which people neither have much prior experience to use to evaluate the accuracy or quality of information (trust as a decision) nor see themselves as incapable of influencing the situation or the trustee, people may resort to using basic affective reactions as information (Forgas, 1995; Schwarz and Clore, 1983). The third form thus sees *trust as an uncontrollable force* – in which the trustor has little or no control over or insight into why he or she trusts someone. This third metaphor is less easily classified in Buss's (1987) framework but may correspond to evocation in that trust results not as much from choice or actions but from being present and receptive. This third form finds expression in statements like 'I cannot help but trust him', 'you just have to trust her' or, at the opposite end of the spectrum, 'I just don't trust him or her'. Trust here is attributed to psychological processes that are only partially open to introspection, a force to be reckoned with or for which trustors will need to take precautions, but that otherwise leave the trustor with little choice or opportunity for agency. This can be likened to similar metaphors for creativity, in which people see creativity as a divine revelation that cannot be forced (Runco and Albert, 2010). The essence of this perspective can be expressed in the question 'how do I feel about trusting him?' The 'trust as an uncontrollable force' metaphor also has different implications for people's reactions to trust. Since trust as an uncontrollable force cannot be controlled or even forecasted, the third metaphor suggests a preoccupation with the here and now of trust in a relationship. People respond to their experience of trust in the present. Because trust is seen as uncontrollable and without a clear locus, we expect trust here to be associated with general and non-specific emotions, like contentment or anxiety (Weiner, 1985). Because trust as an uncontrollable force introduces an element of randomness, it is less likely to generate substantial investments in a relationship. Because people see themselves as exercising little control, breaches of trust may be fatal as people see themselves as unable to restore trust once it is seen as lost. For the 'trust as an uncontrollable force' metaphor, the locus of trust is seen as existing outside both the trustor and the trustee, and the trustor possesses little control over the development of trust (Tamir et al., 2007).

Table 2.1 summarizes the differences between the three trust forms. Different situations, described through the dimensions of value and control, here elicit different trust forms (trust as a decision, a perform- ance and an uncontrollable force). These differ with respect to assump- tions about locus or what influences the development of trust (the trustee, the trustor or neither), as well as assumptions about the trustee's trustworthiness, such as whether the trustworthiness of the trustee is assumed to be constant or entity-like, incremental and susceptible to influence (Dweck and Leggett, 1988) or ephemeral. Finally, we suggest that different forms of trust are likely to be accompanied by different sets of emotions.

Table 2.1   Characteristics of different forms of trust

Situation Value/control	Trust form	Locus of control	View of the trustees' trustworthiness	Accompanying emotions
Low to moderate/low to moderate	'Trust as a decision'	Trustee	Entity	Gratitude/anger (other-directed)
High/high	'Trust as a performance'	Trustor or joint trustor and trustee	Incremental	Pride/shame (self-directed)
Low to moderate/low	'Trust as an uncontrollable force'	Neither	Ephemeral	Contentment/ anxiety (non-specific)

As shown in Table 2.1, in the 'trust as a decision' metaphor, trust reflects an innate quality of the trustee. The trustor has control to the extent that he or she has knowledge and can predict the likely outcome of engaging in a relationship with the trustee, but the trustor cannot change the trustworthiness of the trustee (which is assumed to have a fixed, entity-like quality). Accompanying emotions are directed outwardly towards the trustee (gratitude or anger). In the 'trust as a performance' metaphor, the trustor initiates trust by showing trust. Control is high as trust as a performative act is seen as capable of influencing the trustworthiness of the trustee. In contrast to the 'trust as a decision' metaphor, the trustworthiness of the trustee is seen as malleable – people can be made trustworthy. The accompanying emotions are self-directed (pride, shame). Finally, in the 'trust as an uncontrollable force' metaphor, the locus of control lies neither with the trustor nor with the trustee. The trustor's experience of control is at its lowest as the trustor has little insight into why he or she trusts or on what basis, and is unable to influence the trustee in any significant way. The accompanying emotions are non-specific (contentment or anxiety).

A TENTATIVE TRUST PROCESS MODEL

Figure 2.1 describes the relationships between situations, trust and strategies. Different situations here afford and motivate different strategies and lead people to activate different trust metaphors that help them to coordinate and make sense of actions and strategies for managing uncertainty and vulnerability. The relationship between situations, metaphors and strategies, however, is not one-directional. Metaphors and strategies also influence how people see and understand social situations. Thus, the 'trust as a performance' metaphor, once activated, is likely to influence how people see the trustee and social situations, increasing the salience of metaphor-consistent situational features over non-consistent features (Sedikides and Skowronski, 1991). Moreover, the experience of engaging in a specific adaptive strategy reinforces people's understanding of a specific situation, hence reinforcing the activated metaphor. Failure to fit a strategy to a specific situation, on the other hand, may weaken the activated metaphor, causing people to question its underlying assumptions. Trust as a psychological state comprising an intention to accept vulnerability is seen here as influencing and being influenced by the specific strategies that people use to manage and deal with uncertainty and vulnerability, hence the bidirectional arrows. People's willingness to accept risk will reflect their adaptation and affective and cognitive experiences associated with adapting. Performing a given strategy (for example seeking information or seeking to influence a trustee) is likely to influence how people feel about the strategy as people are likely to search out information that is consistent with or reinforces a chosen strategy (Gollwitzer, 1990).

The relationship between a given situation and the activation of different strategies and trust metaphors are also likely to be moderated by personal and cultural traits and personality differences. People first tend to understand and see situations differently. They bring their capacities, traits and experiences to the situation. According to Mischel and Shoda (1995), personality traits can be seen as tendencies to interpret and respond to ambiguous situations in specific ways. Thus, people may attach different values to social interaction and affiliation (Mikulincer and Selinger, 2001) or see themselves as being more or less capable of influencing a specific situation (Skinner, 1996). Some may be more prone to seeing trust as an uncontrollable force or emotion, something that they simply feel (Tamir et al., 2007), whereas others may tend to see trust as a choice or ambition (Baier, 1986).

In the same way that different people may respond differently to situations, we also suggest that cultural norms, values or assumptions affect how people conceive of and manage social situations involving vulnerability and uncertainty. This also follows a view of trusting as an embodied and situated activity involving interaction with and manipulation of external props (Anderson, 2003; Wilson, 2002). How people feel and think about trust at a given point thus may rely heavily on their interaction with other people and objects and associated cultural scripts and schemas. Dependency and vulnerability constitute core features of any community and strategies for handling such uncertainty and vulnerability; hence, they are likely to become features of common cultural scripts and schemas in most cultures (Fiske, 1992a; Keesing, 1974; Taras et al., 2010). The forms of trust described here also potentially offer a better understanding of the way in which culture and cultural scripts influence people's experience of trust, not only regarding how trust is produced but even with respect to how people understand and experience trust in different situations.

Over time, people's adaptations are likely to influence the perceptions and actions of other people and hence shape the structural conditions that gave rise to the initial reaction in the first place. Based on this, we can think of different trajectories. One trajectory described in the literature (Lewicki and Bunker, 1996) is for people over time to learn to know the other party as well as to come to identify with the other person and the relationship. Here the value of the relationship has increased (we wish for the relationship to continue), as has control (we no longer see ourselves as capable just of understanding, but also of influencing the trustee). Hence, people's views of trust, we argue, are likely to shift from the 'trust as a decision' metaphor to a 'trust as a performance' metaphor. Linking trust to different strategies and metaphors of trust presents us with the tools to conceptualize how such changes occur. The model is shown in Figure 2.1.

Here situations described in structural terms (conflicting interests, value and control) lead people to adopt different adaptive strategies, accompanied by different forms of trust. We suggest that a person's view and experience of trust in a given situation are likely to reflect a given strategy. Whereas partially conflicting interests, moderate interests or stakes in the relationship and low or moderate control would be expected to be associated with the 'trust as a decision' form, a greater interest in the relationship when combined with greater control would be expected

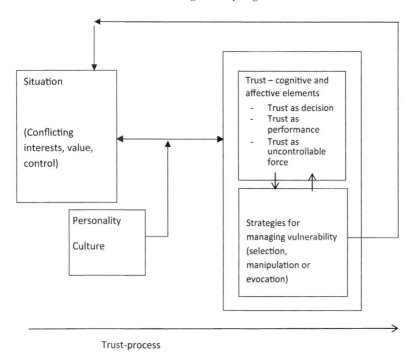

Trust-process

Figure 2.1 A tentative process model of trust

to be associated with the 'trust as a performance' form. The activation of different strategies is likely to occur automatically as situations tend to favour one strategy over others and as people are highly trained and socialized into adapting to social situations (Bargh and Ferguson, 2000).

The framework presented here is not complete. A more complete framework should include the effects of actual experience and describe how experience and the activation of different forms of trust interact. Favourable experience with a trustee, for instance, may increase a trustor's motivation to pursue a relationship as well as raising his or her expectation of being capable of influencing the trustee, hence causing a trustor to adopt the 'trust as a performance' form. A more active form of trust (trust as a performance), by inviting a trustee to cooperate, may become a self-fulfilling prophecy initiating a virtuous cycle of trusting and trustworthy behaviour. The model, we believe, is therefore consistent with Lewicki and Bunker's (1996) stage model of trust, in which trust is seen as progressing through a series of stages from calculative to knowledge- and identity-based trust. However, in contrast to Lewicki and

Bunker's model, trust in our model is seen to be influenced not only by what happens within the relationship but also by factors outside the relationship. Thus, a number of factors external to the relationship could make a relationship more valuable (for example career changes may make a particular relationship more important or a shift in status may make someone more likely to exert control in a relationship). More generally, the model adds explanatory power by enabling us to describe outcomes that are not otherwise captured by the existing trust models. Thus, we can think of two individuals who are both experiencing strong trust in a trustee, yet because one sees trust as a decision and the other sees it as a performance, the two individuals may still respond differently to the trustee. For instance, a person who sees trust as a performance may be expected to pursue opportunities for trust building more actively than another person who sees trust as a decision.

CONCLUDING COMMENTS

In this chapter we have presented what could be described as an embodied and situated perspective of trust, suggesting that trust is understood better when viewed in relation to people's attempts to deal with vulnerability and uncertainty in social interaction. We set out to show how different situations motivate and allow for different forms of trust and described and explained three forms of trust that have different implications for the ways in which people see, interact and invest in relationships.

   The definition and framework described here, we believe, thus contribute to a better understanding of trust and trust as a process in several ways. First, an embodied perspective of trust highlights the role of the trustor as an active, purposeful agent, with goals and plans that respond not only to information in the form of experience, institutional safeguards or third-party opinions, but also to his or her experience of acting in and on a social world, striving to manage relationships and attain valued outcomes. We believe that an embodied view of trust presents us with a richer and more realistic representation of how people actually experience trust and forms a better basis for understanding trust processes (Anderson, 2003; Chemero, 2013). Related to this, the framework also offers a different take on the relationship between trust defined as a psychological state and behaviour and strategies. Rather than seeing trust as an attitude or intention that precedes adaptation, we see the experience of trust as an integral part of adapting to social dependence and vulnerability in social situations. People's understanding and experience of trusting guides and supports their attempts to deal with specific situations. Thus, people's experience of trust is seen here not merely as a basis for making decisions, but as helping to orchestrate and support a chosen strategy (Ferguson and Bargh, 2004).

Finally, the model describes the relationships between structural features of social situations, trust metaphors and strategies. The theories presented here expand our understanding of trust beyond the existing distinctions, such as resilient or fragile (Ring, 1996), cognitive or affective (McAllister, 1995) or calculative, knowledge-based or identity-based trust (Lewicki and Bunker, 1996). Viewing trust as a performance, we believe, offers insights into how trust forms under less than ideal circumstances and how people in some cases are capable of transforming social situations through unilateral displays and communications of trust. Rather than trust merely reflecting a social world, trust here may instead help to create or transform the social world.

The model raises new questions that need to be addressed. While we have focused on people's understandings of trust, we have said little about how different trust metaphors interact with experience. A performative view of trust ('trust as a performance'), for instance, may be more resilient in the face of ambiguous or even negative information in the early stages of a relationship deemed to be potentially valuable by a trustor. The 'trust as a decision' metaphor, on the other hand, may be better suited to detecting uncooperative and untrustworthy individuals in situations that warrant vigilance but are less conducive to forming new relationships (Murray et al., 2008).

Trust, as is often pointed out, is a relational phenomenon (Lewis and Weigert, 1985). Whereas the focus here has been on individual trustors' reactions to social situations, people's understanding of trust is also likely to be influenced by the way in which other people understand and experience trust. People's experience of trust as a result is likely to take on emergent properties that cannot easily be attributed to one individual trustor. A more relational and emergent perspective on trust is likely to add complexity, yet it does not negate the underlying insight that people's experience of trust is likely to reflect their experience of adapting to situations involving vulnerability and uncertainty.

Seeing trust as linked to adaptation may conflict with the way in which people normally think of trust, as a comparatively stable psychological state that changes only slowly and gradually over time and with experience (Kramer, 2006; Lewicki and Bunker, 1996). One way to reconcile these different views may be to differentiate between a more basic and stable type of trust based on a common history and experience of interaction and a more variable, situationally contingent form of trust.

Here the first, more basic form of trust would form a foundation for the second type (Gill et al., 2005). A view of trust as stable and invariant, however, may also reflect a (Western) preference for consistency and coherence in our attitudes towards other people across situations (Leising, 2011; Suh, 2002). Hence, in hindsight, people may overestimate the consistency of their attitudes, including trust in other people.

Future studies will need to begin by describing people's implicit theories of trust and trusting. To our knowledge, no such studies exist yet. Not only should future studies seek to describe such theories, but they should also seek to describe the origin of such theories, their use as well as their consequences (including in combination) for social interaction and relationships (Tidwell et al., 1996). Research of this kind, we believe, offers substantial rewards but will require rich, unfiltered and preferably longitudinal data. Since people may often be unaware of their implicit theories, enabling participants to think aloud and reason about trust in real-life situations is likely to be important. Possible research designs here include time-series data in the form of scheduled interviews, diaries (Bolger et al., 2003) or forms of thinking-aloud procedures (Someren et al., 1994).

REFERENCES

Anderson, M.L. (2003) Embodied cognition: A field guide. *Artificial Intelligence*, 149 (1), 91–130.

Axelrod, R.M. (1984) *The Evolution of Cooperation*. New York: Basic Books.

Bacharach, M. and Gambetta, D. (2001) Trust in signs. In: Cook, K. (ed.), *Trust and Society*. New York: Russell Sage Foundation, pp. 148–94.

Baier, A. (1986) Trust and antitrust. *Ethics*, 96 (2), 231–60.

Balliet, D. (2010) Communication and cooperation in social dilemmas: A meta-analytic review. *Journal of Conflict Resolution*, 54 (1), 39–57.

Balliet, D. and Van Lange, P.A.M. (2013) Trust, conflict and cooperation: A meta-analysis. *Psychological Bulletin*, 139 (5), 1090–112.

Bandura, A. (1989) Human agency in social cognitive theory. *American Psychologist*, 44 (9), 1175–84.

Bargh, J.A. and Ferguson, M.L. (2000) Beyond behaviorism: On the automaticity of higher mental processes. *Psychological Bulletin*, 126 (6), 925–45.

Bolger, N., Davis, A. and Rafaeli, E. (2003) Diary methods: Capturing life as it is lived. *Annual Review of Psychology*, 54, 579–616.

Burke, C.S., Sims, D.E., Lazzara, E.H. and Salas, E. (2007) Trust in leadership: A multi-level review and integration. *Leadership Quarterly*, 18 (6), 606–32.

Buss, D.M. (1987) Selection, evocation, and manipulation. *Journal of Personality and Social Psychology*, 53 (6), 1214–21.

Chemero, A. (2013) Radical embodied cognitive science. *Review of General Psychology*, 17 (2), 145–50.

Das, T.K. and Teng, B.S. (2004) The risk-based view of trust: A conceptual framework. *Journal of Business and Psychology*, 19 (1), 85–116.

Dirks, K.T., Lewicki, R.J. and Zaheer, A. (2009) Repairing relationships within and between organizations: Building a conceptual foundation. *Academy of Management Review*, 34 (1), 68–84.

Dweck, C. and Leggett, E.L. (1988) A social-cognitive approach to motivation and personality. *Psychological Review*, 95 (2), 256–73.

Eagly, A.H. and Chaiken, S. (1993) *The Psychology of Attitudes*. Fort Worth, TX: Harcourt, Brace, Jovanovich College Publishers.

Ferguson, M.J. and Bargh, J.A. (2004) Liking is for doing: Effects of goal proximity on automatic evaluation. *Journal of Personality and Social Psychology*, 87 (5), 557–72.

Fishbein, M. and Ajzen, I. (1972) Attitudes and opinions. *Annual Review of Psychology*, 23, 487–544.

Fiske, A.P. (1992a) The 4 elementary forms of sociality: Framework for a unified theory of social-relations. *Psychological Review*, 99 (4), 689–723.

Fiske, S.T. (1992b) Thinking is for doing: Portraits of social cognition from daguerreotype to laserphoto. *Journal of Personality and Social Psychology*, 63 (6), 877–89.

Fiske, S.T. and Dépret, E. (1996) Control, interdependence and power: Understanding social cognition in its social context. *European Review of Social Psychology*, 7 (1), 31–61.

Flores, F. and Solomon, R.C. (1998) Creating trust. *Business Ethics Quarterly*, 8 (2), 205–32.

Forgas, J.P. (1995) Mood and judgment: The Affect Infusion Model (AIM). *Psychological Bulletin*, 117 (1), 39–66.

Gambetta, D. and Hamill, H. (2005) *Streetwise: How Taxi Drivers Establish Customers' Trustworthiness*. New York: Russell Sage Foundation.

Gill, H., Boies, K., Finegan, J.E. and McNally, J. (2005) Antecedents of trust: Establishing a boundary condition for the relation between propensity to trust and intention to trust. *Journal of Business and Psychology*, 19 (3), 287–302.

Gollwitzer, P.M. (1990) Action phases and mind-sets. In: Higgins, E.T. and Sorrentino, R.M. (eds), *Handbook of Motivation and Cognition: Foundations of Social Behavior*, Vol. 2. New York: Guilford Press, pp. 53–92.

Greenberger, D.B. and Strasser, S. (1991) The role of situational and dispositional factors in the enhancement of personal control in organizations. In: Cummings, L.L. and Staw, B.M. (eds), *Research in Organizational Behavior*, Vol. 13. Greenwich, CN: JAI Press.

Johansen, S.T., Selart, M. and Grønhaug, K. (2013) The effects of risk on initial trust formation. *Journal of Applied Social Psychology*, 43 (6), 1185–99.

Keesing, R.M. (1974) Theories of culture. *Annual Review of Anthropology*, 3, 73–97.

Kelley, H.H., Holmes, J.G., Kerr, N.L., Reis, H.T., Rusbult, C.E. and Van Lange, P.A.M. (2003) *An Atlas of Interpersonal Situations*. New York: Cambridge University Press.

Kihlstrom, J.F. (2013) The person–situation interaction. In: Carlston, D.E. (ed.), *Oxford Handbook of Social Cognition* (a volume in the *Oxford Library of Psychology*). Oxford: Oxford University Press, pp. 786–803.

Knee, C.R., Patrick, H. and Lonsbary, C. (2003) Implicit theories of relationships: Orientations toward evaluation and cultivation. *Personality and Social Psychology Review*, 7 (1), 41–55.

Kramer, R.M. (1996) Divergent realities and convergent disappointments in the hierarchic relation: Trust and the intuitive auditor at work. In: Kramer, R.M. and Tyler, T.R. (eds), *Trust in Organizations: Frontiers of Theory and Research*. Thousand Oaks, CA: Sage, pp. 216–46.

Kramer, R.M. (1999) Trust and distrust in organizations: Emerging perspectives, enduring questions. *Annual Review of Psychology*, 50, 569–98.

Kramer, R.M. (2006) Trust as situated cognition. An ecological perspective on trust decisions. In: Bachmann, R. and Zaheer, A. (eds), *Handbook of Trust Research*. Cheltenham, UK and Northampton, MA, USA: Edward Elgar Publishing, pp. 68–84.

Lakoff, G. and Johnson, M. (1999) *Philosophy in the Flesh: The Embodied Mind and its Challenge to Western Thought*. New York: Basic Books.

Lakoff, G. and Johnson, M. (2003) *Metaphors We Live By*. Chicago, IL: University of Chicago Press.

Leising, D. (2011) The consistency bias in judgments of one's interpersonal behavior: Two possible sources. *Journal of Individual Differences*, 32 (3), 137–43.

Lewicki, R.J. and Bunker, B.B. (1996) Developing and maintaining trust in work relationships. In: Kramer, R.M. and Tyler, T.R. (eds), *Trust in Organizations: Frontiers of Theory and Research*. Thousand Oaks, CA: Sage, pp. 114–39.

Lewis, J.D. and Weigert, A. (1985) Trust as a social reality. *Social Forces*, 63 (4), 967–85.

Luhmann, N. (1979) *Trust and Power*. Chichester: Wiley.

Mayer, R.C., Davis, J.H. and Schoorman, F.D. (1995) An integrative model of organizational trust. *Academy of Management Review*, 20 (3), 709–34.

McAllister, D. (1995) Affect- and cognition-based trust as foundations for interpersonal cooperation in organizations. *Academy of Management Journal*, 38 (1), 24–59.

McKnight, D.H. and Chervany, N.L. (2006) Reflections on an initial trust-building model. In: Bachmann, R. and Zaheer, A. (eds), *Handbook of Trust Research*. Cheltenham, UK and Northampton, MA, USA: Edward Elgar Publishing, pp. 29–51.

McKnight, D.H., Cummings, L.L. and Chervany, N.L. (1998) Initial trust formation in new organizational relationships. *Academy of Management Review*, 23 (3), 473–90.

Meyerson, D., Weick, K.E. and Kramer, R.M. (1996) Swift trust and temporary groups. In: Kramer, R.M. and Tyler, T.R. (eds), *Trust in Organizations: Frontiers of Theory and Research*. Thousand Oaks, CA: Sage, pp. 166–95.

Mikulincer, M. and Selinger, M. (2001) The interplay between attachment and affiliation systems in adolescents' same-sex friendships: The role of attachment style. *Journal of Social and Personal Relationships*, 18 (1), 81–106.

Mischel, W. and Shoda, Y. (1995) A cognitive-affective system theory of personality: Reconceptualizing situations, dispositions, dynamics and invariance in personality structure. *Psychological Review*, 102 (2), 246–68.

Molden, D.C. and Dweck, C.S. (2006) Finding 'meaning' in psychology: A lay theories approach. *American Psychologist*, 61 (3), 192–203.

Möllering, G. (2006) *Trust: Reason, Routine, Reflexivity.* Oxford, UK and Amsterdam, the Netherlands: Elsevier.

Möllering, G. (2013) Process views of trusting and crises. In: Bachmann, R. and Zaheer, A. (eds), *Handbook of Advances in Trust Research.* Cheltenham, UK and Northampton, MA, USA: Edward Elgar Publishing, pp. 227–306.

Murray, S.L., Derrick, J.L., Leder, S. and Holmes, J.G. (2008) Balancing connectedness and self-protection goals in close relationships: A levels of processing perspective on risk regulation. *Journal of Personality and Social Psychology*, 94 (3), 429–59.

Rempel, J.K., Holmes, J.G. and Zanna, M.P. (1985) Trust in close relationships. *Journal of Personality and Social Psychology*, 49 (1), 95–112.

Ring, K. (1996) Fragile and resilient trust and their roles in economic exchange. *Business and Society*, 35 (2), 148–75.

Rousseau, D.M., Sitkin, S.B., Burt, R.S. and Camerer, C. (1998) Not so different after all: A cross-discipline view of trust. *Academy of Management Review*, 23 (3), 393–404.

Runco, M.A. and Albert, R.S. (2010) Creativity research: A historical view. In: Kaufman, J.C. and Sternberg, R.J. (eds), *The Cambridge Handbook of Creativity.* New York: Cambridge University Press, pp. 3–19.

Rusbult, C.E. and Van Lange, P.A.M. (2003) Interdependence, interaction, and relationships. *Annual Review of Psychology*, 54, 351–75.

Salamon, S.D. and Robinson, S.L. (2008) Trust that binds: The impact of collective felt trust on organizational performance. *Journal of Applied Psychology*, 93 (3), 593–601.

Scherer, K.R., Schorr, A. and Johnstone, T. (eds) (2001) *Appraisal Processes in Emotion: Theory, Methods, Research.* Canary, NC: Oxford University Press.

Schön, D. (1993) Generative metaphor: A perspective on problem-setting in social policy. In: Ortony, A. (ed.), *Metaphor and Thought.* Cambridge: Cambridge University Press, pp. 137–63.

Schwarz, N. and Clore, G.L. (1983) Mood, misattribution, and judgments of well-being: Informative and directive functions of affective states. *Journal of Personality and Social Psychology*, 45 (3), 513–23.

Sedikides, C. and Skowronski, J.J. (1991) The law of cognitive structure activation. *Psychological Inquiry*, 2 (2), 169–84.

Sheppard, B.H. and Sherman, D.M. (1998) The grammars of trust: A model and general implications. *Academy of Management Review*, 23 (3), 422–37.

Skinner, E.A. (1996) A guide to constructs of control. *Journal of Personality and Social Psychology*, 71 (3), 549–70.

Someren, M.W., Barnard, Y.F. and Sandberg, J.A.C. (1994) *The Think Aloud Method: A Practical Guide to Modelling Cognitive Processes.* London: Academic Press.

Suh, E.M. (2002) Culture, identity, consistency, and subjective well-being. *Journal of Personality and Social Psychology*, 83 (6), 1378–91.

Szerszynski, B. (1999) Risk and trust: The performative dimension. *Environmental Values*, 8 (2), 239–52.

Tamir, M., John, O.P., Srivastava, S. and Gross, J.J. (2007) Implicit theories of emotion: Affective and social outcomes across a major life transition. *Journal of Personality and Social Psychology*, 92 (4), 731–44.

Taras, V., Kirkman, B.L. and Steel, P. (2010) Examining the impact of culture's consequences: A three-decade multilevel, meta-analytic review of Hofstede's cultural value dimension, *Journal of Applied Social Psychology*, 95 (5), 405–39.

Tidwell, M., Reis, H.T. and Shaver, P.R. (1996) Attachment, attractiveness, and social interaction: A diary study. *Journal of Personality and Social Psychology*, 71 (4), 729–45.

Tyler, T.R. and Degoey, P. (1996) Trust in organizational authorities: The influence of motive attributions on willingness to accept decisions. In: Kramer, R.M. and Tyler, T.R. (eds), *Trust in Organizations: Frontiers of Theory and Research*, Beverly Hills, CA: Sage Publications, pp. 331–56.

Van Lange, P.A.M., Klapwijk, A. and Van Munster, L.M. (2011) How the shadow of the future might promote cooperation. *Group Processes and Intergroup Relations*, 14 (6), 857–70.

Weber, J.M., Malhotra, D. and Murnighan, J.K. (2005) Normal acts of irrational trust: Motivated attributions and the trust development process. *Research in Organizational Behavior*, 25, 75–101.

Weiner, B. (1985) An attributional theory of achievement motivation and emotion. *Psychological Review*, 92 (4), 548–73.

Wildschut, T., Pinter, B., Vevea, J.L., Insko, C.A. and Schopler, J. (2003) Beyond the group mind: A quantitative review of the interindividual–intergroup discontinuity effect. *Psychological Bulletin*, 129 (5), 698–722.

Wilson, M. (2002) Six views of embodied cognition. *Psychonomic Bulletin and Review*, 9 (4), 625–36.

Wright, A. and Ehnert, I. (2010) Making sense of trust across cultural contexts. In: Saunders, M.N.K., Skinner, D., Dietz, G., Gillespie, N. and Lewicki, R.J. (eds), *Organizational Trust: A Cultural Perspective*. Cambridge: Cambridge University Press, pp. 107–216.

3. Divided uncertainty: a phenomenology of trust, risk and confidence

Morten Frederiksen

According to contemporary research, trust may be given both to people and institutions. Trust may in itself be an institution, and the influence of institutions may affect both trust in people and trust in other institutions. This chapter seeks conceptually to clarify the relationship between trust, interpersonal relationships, and institutions by comparing and developing Niklas Luhmann's theoretical investigation system for trust and confidence with Knud E. Løgstrup's phenomenology of trust. The chapter contributes to trust research by:

- Making a phenomenological distinction between risk and trust which is tenable at the level of subjective experience rather than objectivizing analysis. This distinction defines trust as a process and risk as a disruption of process.
- Theorizing the relationships between trust in people, and confidence in institutions, as mutually reinforcing because they are fundamentally different and deal with different types of uncertainty, rather than being hyphenated versions of the same fundamental category of human experience.

Historically, trust researchers have often discussed the role of institutions. De Tocqueville (2000 [1835]) explained the trust that Americans have in each other through their involvement in the institutions of civil society, and in contrast to the European preference for trust in governmental institutions. Simmel (1990) sought to explain the rise of money systems as an institutionalization of expectations and trust. Parsons (1967) considered trust in the mutuality of the normative social order to be a prerequisite for social interaction. Fukuyama (1996) presents a powerful narrative within political science which posits that trust in political, financial, legal and administrative institutions is a prerequisite for a peaceful and prosperous society. These and similar research agendas can easily be identified in the trust literature now being produced in abundance within both business studies and social science. However, the entire trust discussion is becoming something of a mess because of the complex subject–institution relationship. Trust is a concept employed to describe trust in people (Frederiksen, 2012a), trust in institutions (Rothstein and Uslaner, 2005), trust in systems (Simmel, 1990), trust as an institution (Uslaner, 2002), trust in people grounded in institutions (Coleman, 1982) and trust in one institution, organization or system caused by another institution, organization or system (Warren, 1999). This messiness is not a problem in itself and seems to reflect the multiple vernacular uses of the trust word. However, it is clearly a scientific problem to indiscriminately employ a concept which seems to conflate so many different types of human experience. Trusting in the cooperativeness of a colleague, trusting the currency system because of the central banking system, and trusting a friend to be sympathetic and emphatic to your personal problems are decidedly different experiences. No number of hyphenated trust conceptualizations will justify grouping these experiences within the same category. While there are numerous distinctions between different types of trust (for example Misztal, 1996), the number of hyphenations and subcategories seems to indicate that the master concept – trust – is being stretched to breaking point. One has to question whether these subconcepts do in fact share something which defines them as versions of trust.

In this chapter I seek to untangle the relationship between trust in people and trust in institutions by returning to the issue of uncertainty, which is what links all these different notions of trust together. Trust – whether in institutions or people – involves actions or decisions in the face of uncertainty: uncertainty about the intentions of the other and uncertainty about the actions and operations of systems and organizations. Many researchers seem to treat trust as a 'leap of faith' (Möllering, 2001), acceptance of vulnerability (Misztal, 2011), weak inductive knowledge (Simmel, 1950), or a specific level of acceptable risk probability (Coleman, 1990). All these approaches somehow address the absence of certainty regarding outcomes or events: they concern uncertainty. Similar arguments have been made by numerous researchers, including Lewis and Weigert (1985), Nooteboom (2007), James Jr (2014), Reich-Graefe (2014), as well as Möllering (2006). In the following analysis the relationship between trust and uncertainty will be a focal point.

While we may, arguably, consider trust as a way of dealing with uncertainty, it is by no means the only way of dealing with uncertainty. Specific probabilistic ways of dealing with uncertainty – such as gambling – tend to set it apart from trust as chance, risk taking, or sometimes magical thinking. Similarly, people coping with unfathomably complex issues of uncertainty, or holding obviously unjustified expectations are seen to have faith, rather than trust. Finally, when uncertainty appears to be very low we prefer to speak of certainty, not trust. The argument that I pursue in this chapter is that the trust concept is employed too readily with regard to all uncertainty, and that it is helpful to distinguish between different forms or levels of uncertainty and different ways of dealing with them. Similar arguments, albeit with different theoretical approaches, can be found in Williamson (1993) and Karpik (2014).

While trust research has engaged the trust–uncertainty relationship in many fruitful ways, there has been no real discussion of which forms of uncertainty trust relates to – with the exception of Luhmann's (1979) work on trust. In the following I seek to contribute to a more differentiated notion of uncertainty by conceptually separating the uncertainty related to institutions from the uncertainty related to interpersonal relations. This somewhat trivial distinction, I argue, allows us to separately analyse ways of dealing with these forms of uncertainty and, furthermore, to investigate the relationship between these different levels.

First, I outline some theoretical issues involved in the connection between institutions and interpersonal relations in trusting. Secondly, I present Luhmann's analysis of trust and confidence and situate institutions within this framework. Thirdly, I employ Løgstrup's phenomenology of trust in a critique of Luhmann's framework. Fourthly, I propose trust compartments as a phenomenological concept describing the impact of institutional uncertainty on interpersonal uncertainty, thus bridging the two frameworks. Finally, I summarize and draw conclusions from the analysis.

TRUST IN INSTITUTIONS, TRUST IN PEOPLE

The multilevelled structure of trust is part of almost any empirical or theoretical analysis of trust at the interpersonal level, and the complex relationships between systems, institutions and interpersonal interaction have led researchers to propose rather different conceptualizations of multilevelled trust dynamics. Seligman (1997) and Williamson (1993) argue that trust only becomes a cogent concept if no institutional structures or systems provide a common set of references – akin to the thick and thin trust arguments presented in Chapter 1. Trust, according to these authors, describes a type of expectation in situations where uncertainty cannot be reduced by knowledge, interpretation or calculation. Conversely, Barber (1983) and Möllering (2006) consider trust to be grounded in expectations of stable and pervasive social institutionalizations – akin to the institutional trust presented in Chapter 1.

Barber, on the one hand, argues that trust without institutional structure is impossible, because a shared backdrop of social structures – formalized or otherwise – provides the system of roles and expectations relevant in any specific instance. To Barber and likeminded authors (Rose-Ackerman, 2001; Uslaner, 2002; Rothstein, 1998), this latter type of argument assumes that both institutional frames of reference and explicit trust in formalized institutions effectively regulate interpersonal relations. Möllering (2006), on the other hand, argues that institutions form part of the shared life worlds of people who interact, providing shared structures of meaning and interpretation helpful in establishing trust as expectation. Life world institutions provide familiar sets of expectations and interpretative repertoires in interpersonal encounters. In some sense this connects the argument back to a thick trust argument. The issue of sequence has been of some interest to trust scholars. Evolutionary theories of trust (Lewicki and Bunker, 1996) hold that intersubjective trust within and between organizations develops from trust in the other's competence within institutionalized roles towards more genuinely trusting the other. The reverse position is held by authors such as Giddens (1991) and Garfinkel (1963), who suggest that trust is fundamentally intersubjective, and that trusting institutions and organizations requires experience with representatives from those institutions, building a level of familiarity able to sustain and guide expectations and eventually leading to trust in the institution or system. Möllering's (2005) argument would support this idea to some degree, since life worlds develop from interaction and experience. Recent research on trust in and between organizations suggests a similar approach to trust as being inherently intersubjective (Dietz and Den Hartog, 2006).

Looking at the general pattern, there seem to be two prevailing positions. On the one hand, there is an *assurance* argument underscoring the institutional regulation of interaction through ready-made categories of expectation and interpretation. On the other hand, there is an *interpretation* argument positing that people's accumulated experience with people and institutions is pivotal in assessing new situations. This argument comes in a *calculativeness* version which emphasizes that people objectively calculate probabilities based on experience with people and institutions, and a *familiarity* version emphasizing that people assess new situations based on habitual, taken-for-granted categories of classification. These debates have proven fruitful in investigating the complexity of trust, but are bogged down by the search for a causal configuration of institutional and intersubjective trust. My suggestion is that some of these differences are produced by disagreement about where to draw the line between the substance and the context of interpersonal trust. Consequently, further clarification of the relationship between interpersonal trust and the institutional context would prove valuable in developing our conceptualization of trust.

A number of theories encourage a more thorough investigation of the distinction between institutions and people with regard to trust (Hardin, 1992; Luhmann, 1988; Løgstrup, 1997). According to these authors, uncertainty works in different ways when dealing with institutions and subjects, and overcoming uncertainty or not has quite different consequences at the different levels in terms of actions and experiences. In the following, these differences are investigated within both Luhmann's and Løgstrup's theories of trust, seeking a point of convergence. However, first I will briefly sketch the institutional concept employed in this chapter. While only a crude outline, it will suffice for the conceptual purposes at hand.

Trusting people always takes place within some sort of institutional context and is more often than not embedded within symbolic or material systems of one form or another. Trusting my banker involves trusting the bank institution and both the credit and the money systems. The reverse, in contrast, is not necessarily true: I may very well trust the money system without trusting my banker, or any banker for that matter. Should my trust in the money system falter, any trust I have in my banker will be of little use to me. Institutions, however, are a more complex matter than systems. Institutions are often, but not necessarily, imbedded in either organizations or systems, or both. They involve roles, expectations, norms and so forth which are more or less explicitly codified and enforceable. The human resource management organization within a corporation exemplifies this. This type of organization is subject to codified institutions such as policies and procedures linked to and embedded in legislative systems, but it is also subject to informal institutions such as voluntary consent and enforcement. Some institutions, such as the informal rules of conversation, are pervasive since they are essentially involved in all forms of interaction, while others, such as corporate cultures, are limited to a very specific context.

LUHMANN: TRUST, RISK AND UNCERTAINTY

Niklas Luhmann (1979) analyses trust as a response to specific socio-temporal experiences of uncertainty. According to Luhmann, uncertainty is not the same as not knowing, having forgotten, or failing to calculate. Uncertainty has rather to do with the unknowable aspect of the future: contingency. Contingency is the space of potentiality describing the multitude of 'future presents': all the possible presents that may eventually emerge as an actual present. Which of the future, potential presents eventually become *the* present depends on social processes in the previous presents. While one course of events may be more probable, likely or usual than another, complex social processes involve an element of unpredictability and volatility ultimately grounded in contingency. To Luhmann, this describes the fundamental flow of socio-temporality in which the complex contingency field of potentiality is an ever narrower funnel until only one present is ultimately realized (Figure 3.1).

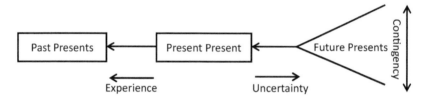

Note: *The arrows from future presents to past presents denote the experience of the temporal flow, whereas experience and uncertainty denote how past and future are made relevant to the present.

*Figure 3.1   Temporal flow and relevance in the present**

In Luhmann's (1979) application, which I subscribe to in the following, uncertainty is defined as the phenomenological experience of contingency within the socio-temporal flow. While uncertainty is partial, compared to contingency, it is still overwhelming and requires people to reduce the complexity involved in interaction. Experience, as a fundamental mode of complexity reduction, works to reduce uncertainty by laying out the foundations of expectation as familiarity, according to Luhmann. Familiarity describes the taken-for-granted character of the social and natural world as it emerges in a situation. Familiarity stems from embodied experience allowing people to take institutional structures, expectations, roles, strategies and so on for granted because they are usual within a given situation. Familiarity allows people to tacitly identify the kind of situation they are dealing with. The infinite possible outcomes of a specific situation are reduced by familiarity to expecting the probable, the usual or the habitual outcomes. Fundamentally, this is the familiarity version of the interpretation argument presented above.

The onslaught of complex modernity wears away familiarity, making scarce those domains of social relations that are sufficiently familiar to sustain expectations (Luhmann, 1979). As a result, complexity – and consequently uncertainty – cannot be reduced by familiarity, Luhmann argues. Instead of drawing on life worlds and familiarity, people must seek recourse in social systems and formal institutions to underpin expectations. Interpersonal experience therefore must be increasingly complemented, augmented or even substituted by experience with, and reliance on, systems and formal institutions. Fundamentally, this is the assurance argument presented above.

As modernity reduces familiarity, interpersonal relationships – romantic or otherwise – come to rely on the explicit communication of trustworthiness: one has to enact trustworthiness in order for the other to interpret their intentions, according to Luhmann. Such intentions can no longer be taken for granted, and must – in situations where there are no institutional or system assurances, such as romantic relationships – instead be deduced through a process of reflexive interpretation. Fundamentally, I would argue, this is the calculativeness version of the interpretation argument presented above.

Depending on the social character of a situation, contingency is experienced differently and complexity reduction takes different forms accordingly. Luhmann (1979, 1988) describes two different types of socio-temporal ascriptions of causality associated with systems/institutions and people respectively: continuity and events. These describe fundamentally different ways of experiencing contingency and complexity and, consequently, different forms of uncertainty. To Luhmann, these represent the evolution of modernity, continuity being primordial time, and events the time which emerged as part of modernity.

Uncertainty within the Socio-temporality of Events and Continuity

The first type of uncertainty is nested within an experience of time as continuity (Figure 3.2). Continuity, in Luhmann's application, refers to the experience of things as fixed in time, unaltered, reliable, and most of all stable, regardless of passing time. This is the character of the physical environment, institutions and systems, as well as of the traditions and roles of pre-modern society (Luhmann, 1979, 1988). These stable features of continuity are ruled by an inner, inaccessible logic which makes the institution or system appear and behave tomorrow as it did yesterday.

This type of social ascription produces a 'reversible time' where the future mirrors the past: natural catastrophes, tax audits, elections, the value of money, and the existence of public transport are taken to be equally dependable features for the future as they were in the past. Here uncertainty is experienced as the danger of familiar events which take place regardless of the subject's actions. One may seek to avoid such events by getting out of harm's way but no one has any real influence on them or ability to predict them.

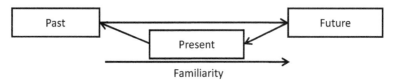

Figure 3.2   Temporal flow of continuity and danger

Luhmann's second mode of experiencing uncertainty is nested within the temporality of events (Figure 3.3). This is the socio-temporal experience of linear time, in which events are initially potential futures, then manifested as actual events in the present and, finally, recede into the past, becoming experience. The linearity of time means that the past is not mirrored in the future and, consequently, expectations require the subject to reflect on the past and extrapolate to the future. Within this socio-temporality, uncertainty does not have exterior characteristics within continuity. Rather, event temporality involves agency and the double-contingency of intersubjective relations. The phenomenological form of uncertainty within the event temporality is risk (Luhmann, 1988, 1993). Whereas danger involves external, future threats, independent of agency, risk involves undesirable future events brought about by one's own actions. The risk form of uncertainty is at its most demanding when people try to take the actions and reactions of others into account in deciding on a strategic course of action. In the following I will subscribe to Luhmann's definition of risk and danger.

Consequently, the phenomenological difference between these socio-temporalities has to do with attribution (Luhmann, 1993). In the continuity form of uncertainty, danger is attributed to the socio-material environment and bad outcomes are interpreted as bad luck, unfavourable gods or malicious institutional structures. This connects back to the assurance argument that outside forces are what drive actual events, and depending on the nature of those forces, trust may or may not appear justified. In the event form of uncertainty, risk is attributed to agency and bad outcomes are interpreted as a result of one's bad decisions: risk is

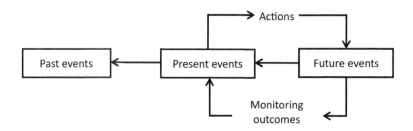

Figure 3.3   Temporal flow of events and risk

associated with regret. This connects back to the calculativeness version of the interpretation argument. To Luhmann, however, risk is not the probability of a potential future event, but rather the state of mind in the event temporality. Consequently, calculativeness is not an assessment of risk, but rather the product of risk.

Luhmann's analysis of trust, risk and uncertainty builds from Knight's (1921) seminal insight, but reconfigures the relationship between the concepts. Knight separates risk and uncertainty to describe the calculable knowable, and incalculable unknowable, respectively. Luhmann builds from the notion of contingency, making every event at least in part unknowable and incalculable. Uncertainty describes the state of not being able to know anything with certainty – risk describes one way of dealing with this experience – a state of mind in which one separates situations into operational, calculable parts and tries to devise strategies taking these into account. To Luhmann, however, calculation within risk is a fiction, since contingency always makes complexity much greater than calculativeness can handle.

Trust and Confidence

Returning to the point of departure, it is now possible to be more specific in analysing how trust is related to *different forms* of uncertainty. The answer that Luhmann provides is that it is not. Rather, in order to be of any analytical use, the concept of trust must be linked to only one type of uncertainty. Luhmann (1979) argues that trust describes a way of dealing with uncertainty within the event temporality, and proposes the confidence concept to describe dealing with uncertainty within the continuity temporality. Confidence is based in familiarity: the reversible time of continuity allows us to expect the future to mirror an unthreatening past and we can assume stability in a taken-for-granted manner. Luhmann perceives trust, in contrast, as the risky endeavour of acting on expectations that are not fully based on knowledge or experience – to accept the possibility of regret.

This distinction between trust and confidence as relating to different forms of uncertainty does not mean that no other strategies exist: mistrust is another way of dealing with event-uncertainty just as fear is a way of dealing with continuity uncertainty. What is interesting about the distinction between trust and confidence is that these are the complexity-reducing phenomenological forms. Mistrust and fear involve the full burden of risk and danger, respectively, requiring the subject to carefully consider and calculate actions, perceptions and probabilities, or else to flee and hide. Trust and confidence, however, do away with uncertainty and allow subjects to act as if contingency was reduced or non-existent. The phenomenological forms of trust and confidence may 'functionally' do somewhat similar things, but are phenomenologically distinct since one is intimately linked to agency and alterity and the other to naturalization and exteriority.

The relationship between the two is, according to Luhmann (1988), one of substitution: as we are increasingly incapable of trusting because the Other is becoming increasingly unfamiliar, we substitute interpersonal trust with confidence in systems and formal institutions. My trust in my banker is of little consequence to my actions if I have fundamental confidence in the banking system and the formal institutions of control and accountability in which our interaction is embedded. Trust, according to Luhmann, is left for our few close interpersonal relationships, and increasingly confidence takes over.

While there is both logic and beauty to Luhmann's argument of a transition from trust to confidence, it appears to be fundamentally flawed from a phenomenological point of view. The increasing reliance on formal institutions and systems seems beyond dispute, but the substitution effect between trust and confidence seems rather implausible. If I distrust my banker, my trust in the banking systems and formal institutions will hardly stop me from acquiring another banker or taking my business to another bank. Similarly, I may trust my son's teacher and I may have confidence in the school system. However, whereas a lack of confidence in the system may be substituted with trust in the specific teacher, the reverse is hardly the case. Luhmann falls on the side of the assurance argument mentioned at the beginning, disregarding the issue of the continued process of social learning and extrapolation from the interpersonal to the institutional – the familiarity version of the interpretation argument. Fundamentally, Luhmann's interest was non-phenomenological and in the end his investigation abandons trust and turns towards the analysis of risk.

Luhmann suggests that trust is a complexity reduction necessary to manage the overwhelming complexity of the social. Nonetheless, he argues that in order to trust, the subjects need to assess the relevant norms and action systems, experience, and the characteristics and signals of the other. This makes the argument rather unconvincing, since complexity is hardly reduced by trust if trust in turn requires a highly complex process of assessment: in reflexivity complexity re-emerges internally as a response to external complexity.

In order to further pursue the phenomenology of a trust–confidence relationship and the complexity-reducing nature of trust, we must turn to phenomenology proper.

LØGSTRUP: TRUST, SITUATIONS AND SPONTANEITY

The most coherent exposition on trust within phenomenological research is found in the works of the Danish philosopher and theologian K.E. Løgstrup (1905–80). In his masterpiece *The Ethical Demand*, originally published in 1956 (1997), he describes trust as a fundamental, inter-subjective relationship stemming from the shared humanity of all subjects. His works have played no role in the social scientific conversation on trust (see, however, Frederiksen, 2014a), but have made a more significant contribution within phenomenological philosophy (Grøn, 2010; Niekerk, 2007). Løgstrup studied with Heidegger, Bergson, Merleau-Ponty and Lipps, and drew inspiration from Kirkegaard, Husserl and Scheler in his work.

Like Luhmann, Løgstrup (1997) connects trust to the fundamental human characteristic of agency, defining trust as intersubjective. Løgstrup, in contrast to Luhmann, defines trust as a spontaneous attitude that requires little previous justification. This conceptualization positions trust as an alternative to calculation rather than as the end product of calculation, which is where Luhmann ends. Løgstrup's conceptualization of trust consequently accounts for any complexity-reducing functions of trust more convincingly than Luhmann's.

Løgstrup writes of trust:

> The basic character of trust is revealed in yet another way. In love and sympathy there is no impulse to investigate the other person's character. [...] Of ourselves we make no conscious effort, for the simple reason that there has been nothing about the other to raise our suspicion. If, on the other hand, we are not in sympathy with the other person, or if there is a certain tension between us and the other because of something about the other regarding

which we are uncertain or against which we react with irritation, dissatisfac-
tion, or antipathy, then we begin to form a picture of the other's character. We
then begin to see in him or her a variety of dispositions because we are on our
guard. (Løgstrup, 1997: 13)

Løgstrup's argument is that we trust unless made suspicious by something particular, and only then is suspicion raised, making us consider the
potential consequences of our actions – what Luhmann would describe as
a shift into risk and the event temporality. Løgstrup defines these dual
modes of experience as the sovereign expressions of life and the
obsessive, respectively. While these types are not exhausted by trust and
mistrust, we may for simplicity's sake disregard other forms such as love
and jealousy.

To Løgstrup these forms are ways of 'being-in-the-world' in the
Heideggerian sense, describing the different ways people are in internal,
involved relationships with the world (Niekerk, 2007). Rather than a
Cartesian subject–object relationship, the relationship between humans
and the worlds to which they belong is mutually constitutive. In this
sense, Løgstrup was decades ahead of the current interest in trust as
process (Möllering, 2013, Chapter 1). The obsessive and the sovereign
expressions of life characterize different fundamental ways of perceiving,
experiencing and making sense of the world. In the obsessive, people are
in a self-enclosed and self-sustained state trying to make sense of a
particular person or situation by interpreting, analysing and doubting.
Here the Cartesian subject–object separation emerges in a way quite
similar to Luhmann's notion of risk as a state of mind. A sovereign
expression of life, in contrast, 'draws content from the specific situation
and the relation to the other, which is to say, from my conception of that
situation and relation, of their actual circumstances and history' (Løgstrup, 2007: 52f). Characteristic of the obsessive are actions driven by
strategies developed through a distanced, objectivizing relationship to the
situation. In contrast, the sovereign emerges as non-Cartesian spontaneity
from the way activity and interaction unfold in a situation. This spontaneity characterizes the process of, for example, trust, which takes hold of
the situation and carries people away without reservations and strategy.
Within Luhmann's analysis we find no parallel to this spontaneity in
terms of temporality or uncertainty.

We may understand Løgstrup's notion of life as interdependent and in
process: unless we guard ourselves we are in constant interaction and it is
from the situated process of interaction that we as subjects emerge
(Frederiksen, 2014a). Consequently, situations are fundamental to Løgstrup's analysis, as the space of unfolding relationships, perceptions and

identities; however, the obsessive presents an alternative mode in which we strive to tear ourselves out of the processual flow of the situation in order to make it the object of our interpretation. While this is essentially impossible, the obsessive disrupts the processual flow and turns the unfolding of social relationships into a laboured, conflicted endeavour (Fink and MacIntyre, 1997). The obsessive is in many regards similar to Luhmann's notion of risk. More surprisingly, however, Luhmann's notion of trust also seems to fall within Løgstrup's classification of the obsessive.

The sovereign expressions of life are potentiality and enforcement. On the one hand, trust as potentiality immanent in interaction must be allowed to emerge: guards must initially be lowered. On the other hand, trust as enforcement unfolds in a situation by making sense of the situation, rather than the other way around (Grøn, 2005: 28; Løgstrup, 1997).

Where Luhmann fails to account for trust as complexity reduction, substituting exterior complexity of situations with interior complexity of decisions and risk, Løgstrup does so more convincingly: trust is not a calculated, deliberate action but a sweeping processual flow constituting both situations and subjects. To Løgstrup, trust suspends the need for second guessing, reflexive decision making and the obsessiveness of risks. Trusting means that the direction and momentum of the situation make sense without requiring further justification. In this sense, Løgstrup radicalizes the familiarity version of the interpretation argument, making trust the very process of situated meaning, rather than its outcome. This, however, raises the question of when, and under which circumstances, trust may enforce itself on a situation. While Løgstrup argues that trust is the default attitude, this by no means entails that trust is always, or even in most cases, a given. In order to answer the question we need to revisit the issue of temporalities.

Løgstrup's Theory of Temporality

While also inspired by Husserl, Løgstrup's Augustinian analysis of time diverges from Luhmann's and consequently, the focus of the analysis is placed elsewhere (Løgstrup, 2008). Løgstrup (2008) argues that the temporal flow of future, present and past is linked to anticipations grounded in the situation. Contrary to Luhmann's notion of an event temporality which perceives the present from a future point of view, Løgstrup suggests that the future is present as a potentiality, and anticipation in the present, rather than in an analysis of the future. The present is not merely a point in time but rather has duration, and consequently it is possible to conceive of present presents – to elaborate on Luhmann's terminology (Løgstrup, 2008: 43). The anticipation of development and direction within the present, rather than directed at the future, is the fundamental temporality of situated process. This process of the present constitutes a third temporal mode distinct from both continuity and event.

Within this process, temporality trust and spontaneity emerge as direction without calculation and deliberation, because it is inseparable from the flow of the situation – the inertia of the present presents – unlike the calculative distinction between present action and future events. Løgstrup addresses the interaction between temporal modes, which Luhmann ignores. Løgstrup draws a distinction between temporal objects and a-temporal 'things' (Løgstrup, 2008). Whereas temporal objects emerge and decay within the experience of the temporal flow, a-temporal things include all that has no origin or decay in immediate experience and is consequently experienced as outside the temporal flow. The notion of a-temporal things constitutes a temporality similar to Luhmann's continuity temporality: the stable, naturalized permanence of institutions, systems and the natural environment. The notion of temporal objects connects conceptually both to the event temporality of calculation and the process temporality of anticipation.

Whereas Luhmann treats event and continuity temporalities as fundamentally separate, Løgstrup considers them co-constitutive. The transitivity and irreversible destruction of any temporal object is only experienced in contrast to the permanence and indestructible character of a-temporal things, and vice versa. Following Løgstrup, the temporality of trust is a process of the present constituted in continuous contrast to the stability of the things surrounding and permeating the situation. Contrary to Luhmann, Løgstrup's analysis of time underscores the interdependencies of event and continuity as well as the distinction itself. Løgstrup's analysis of the temporal objects fails to distinguish, however, between the temporality of the obsessive and the temporality of the sovereign expressions of life. I nonetheless suggest that the sovereign fits into the flow of present presents within the situation, extending tacit anticipations of directedness from the contents of the situation. The obsessive, however, disrupts the continuous flow of processual time through a Cartesian, iterative sequence of strategic actions and calculation of consequences: the event temporality of risk.

In the following section I will draw on both Luhmann's and Løgstrup's theories of trust and time in recasting the differentiation between trust, risk and confidence.

TRUST, RISK AND CONFIDENCE

Fundamentally, confidence and continuity stem from a form of familiarity. Institutions, systems and socio-natural environments are regulated by erratic or predictable 'clockwork' of which we usually have a superficial understanding but with which we are often familiar. The more predictable institutions and systems take on a naturalized stability, whereas the more erratic appear random in nature. Whether erratic or predictable, according to Løgstrup (2008) they constitute the non-temporal things which supply the environment of any situation. To be in a state of confidence means that institutions and the systems which permeate a specific situation are familiar and not seen as dangerous (Luhmann, 1988). Consequently, uncertainty is reduced by confidence to a naturalized expectation of continuity. Phenomenologically, this state is characterized by feeling competent, knowing and empowered, since the subject familiarity is grounded in use and experience: the subject is in well-known territory (Løgstrup, 1995: 255f). An illustration of this is the difference between the first day at a job in a new organization and the first day of work after a year in the same position. The systems, routines, expectations, requirements, rituals and so forth which characterize the organization create an overwhelmingly complex and uncertain experience in the first case, but usually not in the second. We become habituated, routinized, and 'at home' in the environment of systems and institutions through processes of social learning and, consequently, uncertainty is greatly reduced by familiarity.

This does not mean that all familiar situations underpin confidence if they are successfully identified, since some situations and the institutions, objects and roles they involve may be familiar as dangerous, and better avoided. If, however, the situation appears familiar as unthreatening, confidence is established and people may engage with situations without the evasive and defensive strategies associated with danger.

Within this reified social world of familiarity, confidence and danger we encounter the only truly unpredictable co-inhabitants: other people (Luhmann, 1979; Grøn, 2005). Agency is the engine of contingency and complexity and, consequently, the fundamental source of uncertainty. While never truly accessible or interpretable, other people are endowed with agency, motives, interests, misconceptions and so forth, as are we. Thus we know what they are capable of, but not what they specifically intend. Like us, they are capable of interpretation, strategy and calculation, taking our actions into account. If we feel compelled to scrutinize their intentions, strategies and incentives, we are in a state of risk and in the obsessive; however, if we assume that no adverse intentions or outcomes are involved, the sovereign expression of life may unfold and trust takes hold of the situation.

According to Løgstrup (1997), trust itself is not derived from familiarity and confidence, which are essentially extensions of the past into the present. Rather, trust is derived from and constitutive of the present process. Familiarity may stabilize the situation through confidence, thus suppressing suspicion, risk and the obsessive, but nonetheless, when trust falters and suspicion is raised, it is directed at the other and sudden uncertainty as to the intentions and reactions of the other – even if this is a result of failing confidence in the institutions stabilizing the situation.

The calculative mental mode of risk, as defined by Luhmann, is obsessed with actions, decisions and consequences, similar to Løgstrup's notion of the obsessive. Trust, in Løgstrup's definition, is a mode of spontaneity which supersedes calculation and caution, allowing interaction to flow freely and unguarded. Thus by defining trust and risk as respectively sovereign and obsessive, a third temporal mode of process is added to Luhmann's dual temporalities (Figure 3.4). This is the temporality of sovereign expressions of life drawing its form and direction from the flow of the present, rather than recollected past (continuity) or calculated future projections (risk). The process of the present presents is the temporal experience of being engrossed and immersed in the immediate interactions and relationships, the sustained present of the situation.

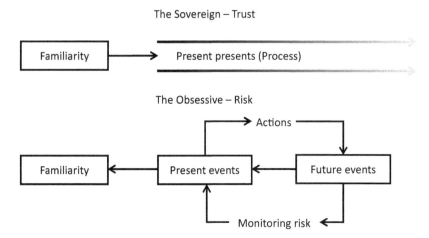

Figure 3.4   Temporal flow of sovereign trust and obsessive risk

Luhmann's (1993) notion of risk is perfectly able to account for what he earlier defined as trust (1979), and it is entirely plausible that this conceptual overlap between trust and risk is the reason he abandoned the trust concepts after developing the risk concept. Løgstrup's (1997) notion of trust, however, adds a third element to the theory which is fundamentally different from both confidence and risk. Accordingly, the combined theory of Løgstrup and Luhmann suggests that trust emerges as a spontaneous unguardedness within the present(s) if nothing unsettles the situation and prompts one to consider alternatives and potential regret. If, however, something spurs one to show caution and to be on guard, then the situation becomes one of risk and obsession. Given this conceptual constellation, we may enquire when and under which circumstances confidence works to engender trust or risk.

A PHENOMENOLOGY OF THE TRUST–CONFIDENCE LINK

Confidence based on familiarity is the foundation of getting involved in a situation whether characterized by risk or trust, because the alternative – danger – would involve defensive and evasive action in one way or another. The substantial character of the confidence involved in situations of trust and in situations of risk differs substantially, however. Confidence as an antecedent to trust is a general trusting orientation – the familiar expectation that nothing untoward may be afoot. Confidence antecedent to risk is strategic – the familiar expectation that in this situation something potentially untoward *is* afoot, requiring strategic action (Frederiksen, 2014b).

This idea of a general trusting orientation is put forward by Grøn (2010) in his interpretation of Løgstrup's theory of trust. The general trusting orientation which originates in confidence is a prerequisite for trusting: for trust to be able to unfold and take charge of the situation, an unguarded approach to the world is required, because apprehensiveness unleashes uncertainty, making people raise their guard (Andersen, 2005; Løgstrup, 1995). We may, however, venture a more precise specification of the conditions necessary for confidence to take the form of a trusting orientation. To put it briefly, it does so if the institutional environment is: (1) experienced as free of danger; (2) sufficiently familiar to support the feeling of competence; and (3) linked to a situation which may involve trust. Fundamentally, this contradicts the cognitivist proposition that institutions and systems underpin trust by giving some form of assurance (Inkpen and Currall, 2004; Bachmann and Inkpen, 2011; Shapiro,

1987) – a notion to which Luhmann also subscribes. Conversely, Løg-strup's analysis of the unguarded transition into the spontaneity of trust suggests that no assurance is needed since the need itself would indicate a cautious, calculated and obsessive conception of the situation. The suggestion is that confidence underpins trust simply by making notions of danger, incompetence and disempoweredness irrelevant in the mind of the trustor.

The impact of confidence on a specific situation is not that it defines outcomes, but that it is the result of a tacit, familiar classification of the situation based on experience. The situation appears as a specific type of situation with which the would-be trustor is confidently familiar, assuming the stable, continuous presence of specific systems and institutions. Consequently, confidence gives a sense of direction to the processes of the situation: the familiar expectation of a more or less wide array of possible process trajectories relevant to that specific situation. This tacit, situational classification serves as a frame or compartment defining in advance both the situation and the mindset of the potential trustor as one of either spontaneity, unguardedness and trust or obsession, calculative-ness and risk (Frederiksen, 2014a, 2014c, 2012a; Frederiksen and Heinskou, forthcoming).

A trust compartment emerges if confidence in the institutional back-drop of the situation suggests an array of possible futures, none of which prompts caution, risk or the obsessive. Conversely, in risk compartments confidence suggests an array of possible futures which require the reflexive monitoring of potential future outcomes of present actions. Such compartments work as a heuristic classification within the map of social venues and situations, defining them in advance as either riskily uncertain or not. In Løgstrup's vocabulary, we can think of these two types of compartments as different types of contrasts or relationships between the temporal objects of social interaction and the a-temporal things of unchanging context. The phenomenology of the trust compart-ment is the general trusting orientation in which the continuity of the institutional context allows the trustor to follow the processual flow of the situation without resistance. The phenomenology of the risk compart-ment is a complex, uncertain structure of rules and forces which increases the obsessive, calculative orientation towards the intentions and sincerity of the other and potential strategies taking these intentions into account. In Luhmann's vocabulary we may think of them as familiar structures of continuity. In the vocabulary of Möllering (2006), Vaitkus (1990) and Brown (2009), we may think of these compartments as a phenomenological expression of life world structures.

It is important not to see this as an oversimplification: compartments are abstract and may dynamically interact: the familiar streets of a neighbourhood may belong to very different compartments in daylight and by night. The complete trust between siblings may become irrelevant once an inheritance dispute pushes them into the risk compartment of self-interest. A transaction with a taxi driver may be carried out in trust in one country and risk in another, regardless of the actual trustworthiness of the taxi drivers. Compartments work as default or 'etcetera-' assumptions which are taken for granted unless they are drawn into question by conflicting impressions and interpretations which may raise suspicion, as in the quote from Løgstrup above. The trusting orientations associated with trust compartments are, moreover, variable entities. The array of process trajectories, that familiarity suggests as conceivable in a given situation, defines the parameters of trust. Rarely, if ever, is trust in everyone about everything (Hardin, 2006; Frederiksen, 2012b). Familiarity with the institutional and system context of a situation not only assists in confidently classifying the situation, but also in classifying the trajectories of interaction relevant to that situation. Confidence, consequently, helps build assumptions about the range of potential processes and the scope of issues to which trust may pertain. Trusting colleagues, for instance, involves fewer and more specified issues subject to more formal institutional limitations than trusting your spouse (Frederiksen, 2012b). Shifting between different compartments may both entail shifting between wider and narrower scopes of trust and shifting between trust and risk compartments. Using the institutional and system topography of social relationships as a familiar heuristic of trust scopes will shift part of the burden of uncertainty in intersubjective relationships on to the shoulders of confidence.

It is furthermore important to notice that this does not take the impact of the particular other into account. The subject of this chapter is the impact of institutions and systems on intersubjective trust, but the notion of compartments works the other way as well: if the particular other encountered within a familiar situation acts in ways which question the trustor's conception of the situation then caution is raised and the situation shifts into a compartment of risk.

CONCLUSION

The above analysis and the proposed concepts of risk and trust compartments seek to rethink the Luhmannian framework within Løgstrup's temporal phenomenology. What Luhmann defined as a modern and a pre-modern way of trusting in other people is here recast as respectively risk and trust, which coexist as two different ways of experiencing socio-temporality. Løgstrup's contribution to the analysis is that uncertainty and contingency are never dealt with in their totality and not always in obsessive contemplation of consequences. Situations sustain expectations of only a limited set of potential actions and encounters unless something pushes one to doubt these expectations. The true impact of Løgstrup's phenomenology on the Luhmannian framework is to be found 'within' the compartments. Luhmann considered institutions and systems as sources of assurance with regard to the actions and intentions of the other, and consequently as part of a process of interpretation of the intentions of the other. Following Løgstrup, the proposition in this chapter is the reverse: because of confidence in the institutions and systems involved in a specific situation, the complexity and contingency of the situation is reduced and people are less likely to be prompted to suspicion. In such situations, they remain off-guard and need not interpret the intentions of the other. The point is that trust as spontaneity can only emerge and take sovereign control of a situation if no one reserves or guards themself: if the Cartesian subject–object distance of risk does not hamper spontaneity. Confidence not only limits uncertainty and reduces complexity, it can negate risk and the issue of vulnerability. This is not always the case because, as previously mentioned, some situations, such as strategic decision making, may be associated with risk. However, in situations in which familiarly comprises unthreatening process trajectories, confidence may sustain a trust compartment, making risk and the need to guard oneself irrelevant. The importance of this insight, compared to the Luhmannian idea of interpretation and signalling, is that it accounts for trust's powerful capacity for generating cooperation, relationships and common goals. Trust is not the outcome of a process of interpretation or calculation, but is a sovereign form of interaction which is unleashed when guards are down. Confidence, whether in institutions, systems or other non-temporal things involved in the situation, is what allows us to lower our guard in situations which are familiarly supportive of trust. Confidence is a principal component in unleashing trust.

This proposition has profound implications for the issue of the trust–control nexus and in general for trust building within organizations and other strongly institutionalized contexts. The mainstream notion of assurance (Barber, 1983; Luhmann, 1979; Rose-Ackerman, 2001; Zucker, 1986) suggests that institutions which create assurance in interpersonal relationships will support the development of trust in those relationships. If trustor and trustee are submitted to institutionalized incentives, sanctions and regulative norms, then they will behave trustworthily by observing the norms, pursuing the incentives, and avoiding the sanctions. If these institutionalized structures emphasize the potential adverse outcomes in a situation in which norms are breached, however, then the situation is in advance compartmentalized as risk. Consequently, it becomes necessary to be cognizant of the intentions of the other and to take account of adverse outcomes of present actions. Control, sanctions and incentives will in many situations push people into the obsessive, analysing the situation from the perspective of self-interest and outcomes. If institutionalizations are imbued with shared meaning, however, making sense of situations, purposes, roles and goals without nudging people into strategic and cautious agency, the array of futures which emerges from the situation will in most cases be cooperative and supportive of trust. Control and regulative norms on one hand emphasize the individual purpose within the situation, and meaning shared by interacting, on the other hand, emphasizes shared identities, purposes and potentialities of the interaction.

Taking the interpretation position (Giddens, 1990; Garfinkel, 1963; Brownlie and Howson, 2005), institutions are trusted because people gather intersubjective experiences supporting trust in those institutions, more or less reflexively extrapolating from interaction to the institution and system structures involved in interaction. From Løgstrup's point of view, this confuses the a-temporal things with the temporal objects. While these are co-constitutive of the phenomenological experience of any situation, they are so by contrast, not by similarity. Whatever confident familiarity one has with a specific institutional setting, it derives from experience with the institution and not with the agency and uncertainty associated with the people encountered. Within any familiar institutional setting or system, however, environment confidence involves potential situation trajectories: the interactive flows habitually relevant in this institutional context. Regardless of the actual level of confidence, experience may suggest that a situation is one of risk or one of trust. Consequently, the interpretation position, I argue, is correct in that accumulation of experience with the trustworthiness of other people is important. However, it is wrong to claim that trust is based on experience. Confidence and experience are not important for trusting but rather are important for the classification of situations and the relevant trajectories of interaction: the general trusting orientation conducive to trusting or the general strategic orientation conducive to risk (Frederiksen and Heinskou, forthcoming). Consequently, experience with other people, and trusting them, is important in developing the heuristics of familiarity used in identifying when strategy or unguardedness is called for. Trust, however, emerges from a spontaneity within the flow of interaction, making confidence and the trusting orientation conducive to trust, but not the foundations of trust. Even within situations highly conducive to trust, trust may fail due to disruptions in the flow of interaction.

The distinction between trust in people and confidence in systems and institutions is helpful because it prevents us from conflating what are distinct levels of uncertainty and different ways of managing it. While these are mutually interdependent and co-constitutive, they are not the same. In order to understand how confidence in democracy or corporate policies underpins trust in a local MP or executive, it is vital to realize that 'trust' in institutions or people is not transitive. Confidence as a trusting orientation instead clears the path for potential trust given specific familiar assumptions built from previous experiences of trust and confidence. Confidence does so, not by suggesting that trust is justified, but by supporting strong assumptions about the process flow of inter-action suppressing the question of trust justification. It is when we feel confidently familiar with a situation, and the need for strategic projections of the future is absent, that we may immerse ourselves in the flow of present presents and be carried away into trust.

REFERENCES

Andersen, S. (2005), Erfaringsbeskrivelse: Løgstrup og fænomenologien. In: D. Bugge, P.R. Böwadt and P.A. Sørensen, eds, *Løgstrups Mange Ansigter.* Copenhagen: Forlaget ANIS, pp. 13–26.
Bachmann, R. and Inkpen, A.C. (2011), Understanding institutional-based trust building processes in inter-organizational relationships. *Organization Studies,* **32**(2), pp. 281–301.
Barber, B. (1983), *The Logic and Limits of Trust.* New Brunswick, NJ: Rutgers.
Brown, P.R. (2009), The phenomenology of trust: A Schutzian analysis of the social construction of knowledge by gynae-oncology patients. *Health, Risk and Society,* **11**(5), pp. 391–407.
Brownlie, J. and Howson, A. (2005), 'Leaps of Faith' and MMR: An empirical study of trust. *Sociology,* **39**(2), pp. 221–39.
Coleman, J.S. (1982), Systems of trust. A rough theoretical framework. *Angewandte Sozialforschung,* **10**(3), pp. 277–99.
Coleman, J.S. (1990), *Foundations of Social Theory.* Cambridge, MA: The Belknap Press of Harvard University Press.
Dietz, G. and Den Hartog, D.N. (2006), Measuring trust inside organisations. *Personnel Review,* **35**(5), pp. 557–88.
Fink, H. and MacIntyre, A. (1997), Introduction. In: *The Ethical Demand.* Notre Dame, IN: University of Notre Dame Press.
Frederiksen, M. (2012a), *Suspending the Unknown: The Foundations, Limits, and Variability of Intersubjective Trust,* Published PhD thesis, Dept of Sociology, Copenhagen University.

Divided uncertainty 65

Frederiksen, M. (2012b), Dimensions of trust: An empirical revisit to Simmel's formal sociology of intersubjective trust. *Current Sociology*, **60**(6), pp. 733–50.

Frederiksen, M. (2014a), Calculativeness and trust: A view from phenomenology. *Journal of Trust Research*, **4**(1), pp. 34–43.

Frederiksen, M. (2014b), Relational trust: Outline of a Bourdieusian theory of interpersonal trust. *Journal of Trust Research*, **4**(2), pp. 1–26.

Frederiksen, M. (2014c), Trust in the face of uncertainty: A qualitative study of intersubjective trust and risk. *International Review of Sociology*, **24**(1), pp. 1–15.

Frederiksen, M. and Heinskou, M.B. (forthcoming), Trusting the other or taking a chance? An investigation of chance and trust temporalities. *Time and Society* (published online ahead of print).

Fukuyama, F. (1996), *Trust.* Harmondsworth: Penguin.

Garfinkel, H. (1963), A conception of and experiments with 'trust' as a condition of stable concerted actions. In: O.J. Harvey, ed., *Motivation and Social Interaction.* New York: Ronald Press, pp. 187–238.

Giddens, A. (1990), *The Consequences of Modernity.* Cambridge: Polity Press.

Giddens, A. (1991), *Modernity and Self-identity.* Cambridge: Polity Press.

Grøn, A. (2005), Livsytrin, person, situation: Løgstrup og subjektiviteten. In: D. Bugge, P.R. Böwadt and P.A. Sørensen, eds, *Løgstrups Mange Ansigter.* Copenhagen: Forlaget Anis, pp. 27–42.

Grøn, A. (2010), Trust, sociality and selfhood. In: A. Grøn and C. Welz, eds, *Trust, Sociality and Selfhood.* Tübingen: Mohr Siebeck.

Hardin, R. (1992), The street-level epistemology of trust. *Analyse & Kritik*, **14**(2), pp. 152–76.

Hardin, R. (2006), *Trust.* Cambridge: Blackwell Publishers.

Inkpen, A.C. and Currall, S.C. (2004), The coevolution of trust, control, and learning in joint ventures. *Organization Science*, **15**(5), pp. 586–99.

James Jr, H.S. (2014), You can have your trust and calculativeness, too: Uncertainty, trustworthiness and the Williamson thesis. *Journal of Trust Research*, **4**(1), pp. 57–65.

Karpik, L. (2014), Trust: Reality or illusion? A critical examination of Williamson. *Journal of Trust Research*, **4**(1), pp. 22–33.

Knight, F.H. (1921), *Risk, Uncertainty and Profit.* New York: Hart, Schaffner and Marx.

Lewicki, R.J. and Bunker, B.B. (1996), Developing and maintaining trust in work relationships. In: R.M. Kramer and T.R. Tyler, eds, *Trust in Organizations: Frontiers of Theory and Research.* London: Sage, pp. 114–39.

Lewis, J.D. and Weigert, A. (1985), Trust as a social reality. *Social Forces*, **63**(4), pp. 967–85.

Løgstrup, K.E. (1995), *Ophav og Omgivelse. [Meta fysik 3].* Copenhagen: Gyldendal.

Løgstrup, K.E. (1997), *The Ethical Demand.* Notre Dame, IN: University of Notre Dame Press.

Løgstrup, K.E. (2007), The ethical demand. In: K.V.K. Niekerk, ed., *Beyond the Ethical Demand.* Notre Dame, IN: University of Notre Dame Press.

Løgstrup, K.E. (2008), *Skabelse og Tilintetgørelse: Religionsfilosofiske Betragt-ninger (Metafysik IV)*. Copenhagen: Gyldendal.
Luhmann, N. (1979), *Trust and Power: Two Works by Niklas Luhmann*. New York: John Wiley and Sons.
Luhmann, N. (1988), Familiarity, confidence, trust: Problems and alternatives. In: D. Gambetta, ed., *Trust: Making and Breaking Cooperative Relations*. Oxford: Basil Blackwell, pp. 94–108.
Luhmann, N. (1993), *Risk, a Sociological Theory*. Berlin: Walter de Gruyter.
Misztal, B. (2011), Trust: Acceptance of, precaution against and cause of vulnerability. *Comparative Sociology*, **10**(2), pp. 358–79.
Misztal, B.A. (1996), *Trust in Modern Societies*. Cambridge: Polity Press.
Möllering, G. (2001), The nature of trust: From Georg Simmel to a theory of expectation, interpretation and suspension. *Sociology*, **35**(2), pp. 403–20.
Möllering, G. (2005), Rational, institutional, and active trust: just do it!? In: K. Bijlsma-Frankema and R.K. Woolthuis, eds, *Trust under Pressure: Empirical Investigations of Trust and Trust Building in Uncertain ˙Circumstances*. Cheltenham, UK and Northampton, MA, USA: Edward Elgar Publishing, pp. 17–36.
Möllering, G. (2006), *Trust: Reason, Routine, Reflexivity*. Oxford: Elsevier.
Möllering, G. (2013), Process views of trusting and crises. In: R. Bachmann and A. Zaheer, eds, *Handbook of Advances in Trust Research*. Cheltenham, UK and Northampton, MA, USA: Edward Elgar Publishing, pp. 285–305.
Niekerk, K.V.K. (2007), Introduction. In: K.V.K. Niekerk, ed., *Beyond the Ethical Demand*. Notre Dame, IN: University of Notre Dame Press, pp. ix–xxxi.
Nooteboom, B. (2007), Social capital, institutions and trust. *Review of Social Economy*, **65**(1), 29–53.
Parsons, T. (1967), *Sociological Theory and Modern Society*. New York: Free Press.
Reich-Graefe, R. (2014), Calculative trust: Oxymoron or tautology? *Journal of Trust Research*, **4**(1), pp. 66–82.
Rose-Ackerman, S. (2001), Trust, honesty, and corruption: Reflection on the state-building process. *European Journal of Sociology*, **42**(3), pp. 526–70.
Rothstein, B. (1998), *Just Institutions Matter*. Cambridge: Cambridge University Press.
Rothstein, B. and Uslaner, E.M. (2005), All for all: Equality, corruption, and social trust. *World Politics*, **58**(1), pp. 41–72.
Seligman, A. (1997), *The Problem of Trust*. Princeton, NJ: Princeton University Press.
Shapiro, S.P. (1987), The social control of impersonal trust. *American Journal of Sociology*, **93**(3), pp. 623–58.
Simmel, G. (1950), The secret and the secret society. In: K.H. Wolff, ed., *The Sociology of Georg Simmel*. London: The Free Press of Glencoe.
Simmel, G. (1990), *The Philosophy of Money*. London: Routledge.
Tocqueville, A. de (2000), *Democracy in America*. Chicago, IL: The University of Chicago Press.
Uslaner, E.M. (2002), *The Moral Foundations of Trust*. Cambridge: Cambridge University Press.

Vaitkus, S. (1990), The crisis as a bankruptcy of trust: The fiduciary attitude, human nature and ethical science. *International Sociology*, **5**(3), pp. 287–98.

Warren, M.E. (1999), *Democracy and Trust*. Cambridge: Cambridge University Press.

Williamson, O.E. (1993), Calculativeness, trust, and economic organization. *Journal of Law and Economics*, **36**(1, Part 2, John M. Olin Centennial Conference in Law and Economics at the University of Chicago), pp. 453–86.

Zucker, L.G. (1986), Production of trust: Institutional sources of economic structure, 1840–1920. *Research in Organizational Behavior*, **8**, pp. 53–111.

4. Trusting and distrusting in dialogue: a study of authentic medical consultations

Jens Allwood, Nataliya Berbyuk Lindström and Inga-Lill Johansson

In this chapter, we will illustrate how trusting and distrusting are expressed in dialogue in a Swedish organizational context – public health care. In doing so, we will point to the enactment of accountability as a critical aspect of establishing and maintaining or not maintaining trust relationships. Specifically, we will analyse and discuss how the requesting and giving of accounts influence trusting and distrusting with the purpose of contributing to the understanding of trusting as a dynamic relational process that can vary with circumstances.

Trust can be built or lost through experience. Our trusting or distrusting of another person depends on our evaluation of the actual actions and accounts of actions given by this person and/or other persons. Accounts provide an opportunity to assess the extent to which the actions of a person are understandable and acceptable with regard to different criteria, such as legal, financial, ethical and so on. Accounts can be understandable and believable without, for example, being ethically acceptable. Thus, besides performing acceptable actions, giving acceptable accounts of our actions is a way in which we can make other persons trust us, avoid potential distrust and even counteract manifest distrust. Conversely, non-acceptable actions and non-acceptable accounts can lead to distrust.

Though accounts are instruments for repairing distrust and building trust, there is no guarantee that an accepted account will increase trust, as successfully meeting the requirements of accountability may not be sufficient for this. However, if we do trust another person, it probably holds that he/she has provided acceptable actions and accounts regarding the aspects of behaviour that we trust. An empirical question for us concerns the role of provided accounts in situations in which earlier experiences of interlocutors create uncertainty for account recipients about the expected positive/optimal function of current actions by the account giver. Does the account lead to increased or decreased trust or is it irrelevant?

BACKGROUND AND REVIEW

Many definitions have been given of trust; a fairly representative definition is provided by Khodyakov:

> Trust is a process of constant imaginative anticipation of the reliability of the other party's actions based on (1) the reputation of the partner and the actor, (2) the evaluation of current circumstances of action, (3) assumptions about the partner's actions, and (4) the belief in the honesty and morality of the other side. (Khodyakov, 2007: p. 126)

To be able to grasp the interactional and dialogical dimensions of trusting/distrusting, we turn to Möllering (2001, 2006, 2013). Inspired by Simmel, Möllering suggests that trust processes involve three elements: *interpretation* of experiences, which gives 'good reasons' to trust (distrust), and *suspension* of doubt about the expected effects of earlier actions, which enables the movement from interpretation to *expectation*, the final stage of the process. Suspension of doubt and *a leap of faith* are considered to be characteristic aspects of trust.

We combine Möllering's view of trust processes with the following definition of trust (Allwood, 2014: p. 193):

> Trust = socio-emotional epistemic attitude involving belief/faith/reliance in the expected positive/optimal function/behaviour of whom/what is trusted.

This gives us an understanding of both the process and the function of trust. The process can be studied by considering how the different aspects of trust suggested by Allwood (2014) vary in interpersonal relationships.

1. basic trust, that is, reliance on interlocutors having normal perception, understanding and linguistic competence;
2. collaborative trust, that is, a belief that interlocutors will adopt and collaborate toward a joint purpose;
3. cooperative trust, that is, the belief that interlocutors will take you into ethical consideration;[1]
4. trust with respect to commitments and obligations;
5. trust with respect to competence, that is, the interlocutor's specific

competence in a particular area, for example medicine, law or economics.

The functions of trust can be brought out by comparing our definition with the definition of Khodyakov. As can be seen, our definition is similar to Khodyakov's, but it is broader and more precise. We have 'belief in the expected positive/optimal function/behaviour of whom/ what is trusted', whereas Khodyakov has 'imaginative anticipation of the reliability of the other party's actions'. Our definition is also more precise regarding the features of interaction influencing trust; we have five such features or aspects, whereas Khodyakov really only has one, namely 'the belief in the honesty and morality of the other side'.

Our definitions of trust and of the different aspects of trust thus provide a basis for both a static and a dynamic understanding of trust (trusting), involving trust as a process that can both increase and decrease in strength and extent in relation to the five aspects distinguished. In this way, trust (trusting) is seen as a dynamic relation, that is, a process that can vary with circumstances. The static side of trust is given by the definition of trust: *socio-emotional epistemic attitude involving belief/ faith/reliance in the expected positive/optimal function/behaviour of whom/what is trusted*. This holds true independently of the strength and extent of the trusting relation. If there is no element of 'belief/faith/ reliance in the expected positive/optimal function/behaviour of whom/ what is trusted', there is no trust.

According to Scott and Lyman (1968: p. 46), an account is 'a statement made by a social actor to explain unanticipated or untoward behavior – whether that behavior is his own or that of others, and whether the proximate cause for the statement arises from the actor himself or from someone else'. However, accountability and accounts may be viewed as phenomena with a much wider scope. According to Garfinkel (1967[1984]: p. 2), accounts of everyday activities are used as 'prescriptions with which to locate, to identify, to analyze, to classify, to make recognizable, or to find one's way around in comparable occasions'. This implies that accounts are expected from all of us continuously, in all parts of our lives, private as well as professional. Thus, being a patient may involve requests for accounts ('Have you taken your medication according to the instructions?') and requests from patients for accounts from care professionals ('Why do I have to take this medication?'). Being a professional involves being exposed to requests for accounts from beneficiaries (like patients) and from managers, authorities and so on.

To support our analysis of the relation between accountability and trust, we will assume the following definitions of *accounting for (giving an account for)* and *accountability* (Allwood et al., 2015):

Account for = report, describe in a comprehensible and acceptable way.

Accountability = reification of the ability and obligation to give an account, often combined with expectations/assumptions concerning account giving, encompassing reporting and explaining actions.

The concept of 'accountability' as distinct from 'account' thus includes expectations/assumptions concerning account giving that nearly always involve expectations about socially acceptable behaviour and responsibility. Satisfying such expectations is often crucial for whether a person is trusted or not.

Health care consultation is a type of social activity that often involves an asymmetrical power relationship. A patient often does not possess enough knowledge about medicine and has few options but to trust the physician's medical knowledge and professional skills to solve health problems (trust with respect to competence mentioned above). 'Patients tend to think of their doctors as nearly godlike in their capabilities and loyalty to patients' (Hill and O'Hara, 2005: p. 1723), and we could view their beliefs as 'overtrusting' in the sense that doctors are human too. The trust of patients in their physicians probably normally implies all the aspects of trust distinguished above, that is, basic, collaborative, cooperative trust combined with reliance on the physician's commitments and competence. This means that the patient believes that the physician will understand, take care of and help him/her and treat him/her with fairness, justice, consistency, reliability and competence. If the physician does not live up to these requirements, for example regarding competence or reliability, distrust may start to develop and be expressed by a patient holding the physician accountable for treatments. As physicians have come to expect trust from patients as a default condition, any demands for accounts from patients may be perceived as questioning their competence. Health care researchers have for some time called for more research on the new relationships between patients and physicians (and other care professionals) to increase the knowledge about the role of trust (see, for example, Rowe and Calnan, 2006; Skirbekk et al., 2011).

METHOD

In this section, we present our empirical studies and methods for analysis.

Our data consist of video-recorded and transcribed interactions: physician–patient consultations in a Swedish hospital (surgery). The illustrations in this chapter consist of 22 minutes of recording time. The recordings were made after obtaining written consent from everyone involved. The consent form presented the purpose of the study, the data collection, confidentiality issues and the possibility to withdraw from participation at any time as well as information about the benefits and risks involved. No researcher was present during the recordings.

In operationalizing trusting behaviour, we were inspired by Möllering, who suggests that *suspension of doubt* can be identified empirically by the use of words like 'everything will be fine', 'no need to worry' or 'just go ahead' (Möllering, 2001: p. 414) or by words indicating ambivalence, due to an understanding of one's own vulnerability, like 'despite', 'although', 'as if' and 'nevertheless' (Möllering, 2006: p. 6). The opposite, *no suspension*, is assumed to be expressed explicitly by questions, demands for information and so on. In both cases, what is implicitly communicated needs to be taken into consideration since the role of the implicit (cf. Skirbekk, 2009; Skirbekk et al., 2011) is assumed to be more important in displaying trust and distrust than in displaying other socio-emotional epistemic attitudes, for example happiness or irritation (see also Grossen and Salazar Orvig, 2014).

Jokinen and Allwood (2010) suggest that cues to uncertainty (and similar phenomena such as hesitation, doubt, lack of knowledge and ignorance) may be found for example in body gestures like shoulder shrugging, which can, however, have different interpretations in different cultural contexts. Any empirical analysis of how trusting is displayed in dialogue thus requires multimodal dimensions of communication to be taken into consideration (such as prosody/phonology, vocabulary, grammar, facial gestures, manual gestures, body movements and posture). Interestingly, facial cues have been found to be superior to acoustic cues in trustworthiness information (cf. Tsankova et al., 2013). The validity of the analysis of trusting behaviour may be enhanced by self-confrontation playback interviews during which explanations of behaviour involving the interpretation of the experiences as well as the expectations created are given by the recorded parties. Due to limitations of time and resources, we were only able to annotate a subset of these features. This means, for example, that we were not able to annotate prosody and communicative gestures. The conventions used for the transcription of the recordings are shown in Table 4.1.

In line with Garfinkel (1967[1984]), we investigated the role of accountability and accounts in trusting (distrusting) by identifying sequences in the dialogues that implicitly or explicitly could challenge what is taken for granted by the interacting parties. A challenge is something that may have serious consequences for immediate and future cooperation (cf. Flanagan, 1954, on the critical incident technique). For our purposes, we identified communicative features whereby demanding or giving accounts can be related to such challenges.

In the following section, we will present two illustrations from health care, each one with the analysis interwoven, and a summary of the findings. In the excerpts, we will comment on mood when it is possible to identify it in the recordings.

Table 4.1   Transcription conventions

Symbol	Explanation
P, D, F, D	Participants (e.g. patient, physician)
[ ]	Overlap brackets; numbers used to indicate the overlapped parts
( )	Transcriber's uncertain interpretation of what is being said
I, II, III	A short, intermediate and long pause, respectively
+	An incomplete word, a pause within a word
CAPITALS	Contrastive stress
:	Lengthening
< >, @ < >	Comments about non-verbal behaviour, comments on standard orthography, other actions, clarifications, intonation

TRUSTING AND DISTRUSTING IN MEDICAL CONSULTATIONS

In this section, we will see how trusting and distrusting are shown between people who do not know each other very well – two different patients meeting their physicians for a check-up. The material is taken from a previous investigation of the influence of cultural differences on communication in health care (cf. Berbyuk Lindström, 2008). The choice of example depends on what was available in the material and is incidental concerning the ethnicity of the physician.

Illustration I. Patient Trusting Physician?

A Swedish female cancer patient is meeting a female Iranian physician for a check-up. The physician asks her about the side-effects of the treatment. The patient replies that she is experiencing no side-effects and mentions that she is worried about this (see Box 4.1).

BOX 4.1   EXCERPT 1

D = doctor (physician)
P = patient

Original (Swedish)	English Translation
D1: nähä inga biverkningar [1 elle nånting annat]1 / inga [2 andra besvär]2	D1: No really no side-effects [1 or anything else]1 / no [2 other problems]2
P1: [1 nä / inte va ja vet]1	P1: [1 no / not that I know of]1
D2: [2 nä]2	D2: [2 no]2
D3: magen sköte sej [3 väl å]3	D3: Stomach is [3 fine and]3
P2: [3 ja]3	P2: [3 yes]3
D4: inga illamående [4 å]4	D4: No nausea [4 or]4
P4: [4 nä]4 nä nåt // annat < ska de vara så >	P4: [4 No]4 no // something else < should it be like that >
@ < mood: worried, intonation: rising >	
D5: < ja: de e ju / > klart att de e så	D5: < Yeah it is of course /> it is so
@ < mood: hesitant >	
P5: jo för att eh / e / ja / ja // ja ha den uppfattningen liksom att / ju sämre man mår efteråt < > ju bättre verkan ha de	P5: Well because eh / eh / I / I // have this belief like that the worse you feel afterwards < > the better effect it has
@ < after the treatment >	
D6: ja de e den gamla uppfattningen // många patienter tror dä å tidiare många läkare också trodde att de de skulle vara så / men de e inte /	D6: Well that is the old view // many patients believe in it and earlier many physicians also believed that it should be like that / but it is not /
P6: < de har [5 ingen betydelse]5 >	P6: < It does not [5 matter]5 >
@ < intonation: rising >	
D7: [5 nä]5 de e bara biverkningar som man får av re så att slippe man biverkningar så e de dess bättre	D7: [5 No]5 / it is only side-effects you get from it so if you can escape side-effects it is better
P7: ja ha faktist inte känt nånting däremot så fick ja en väldi hosta	P7: Actually I have not felt anything but I have got a formidable cough

---

The physician asks the patient about any side-effects of her cancer treatment (D1–D3) and the patient reports experiencing none (P1–P4). The patient indirectly expresses worries: 'should it be like that?' (P4). The hesitant tone of the physician (D5) indicates her difficulties in responding. It may be related to her Swedish language competence, that is, difficulties in understanding the patient or expressing herself. Noticing the physician's hesitation, the patient explains that she believes that 'the worse you feel afterwards the better effect it has' (P5). The patient voices a view concerning the effects of treatment that she implicitly wants to be evaluated by the physician. The physician provides this evaluation: 'that is the old view' (D6) and 'if you can escape side-effects it is better' (D7). However, the patient continues to express worries by eliciting confirmation of her conclusion – 'it does not matter' (P6) – and bringing up new symptoms – 'I have got a formidable cough' (P7). Later in the interaction, the physician claims that the coughing is not a side-effect. At the end of the consultation, the patient returns to the discussion of her concerns (see Box 4.2).

The patient is explicit about her worries concerning the treatment. She wants to know whether the tumour 'disappears or if it can be kept under control' (P1) and attempts to make this clear to the physician by twice seeking confirmation from the physician that her worries have been understood: 'do you understand what I mean?' (P1, P2). One reason could be that she is not satisfied with the physician's evaluation in Excerpt 1 (D6, D7). Another reason could be difficulties in accepting the message from the physician or a suspicion about the physician having problems understanding her. The physician provides responses such as 'we will try to do the best we can of course' (D1) and 'I said that that the chance to be able to cure decreases the more treatments we have given it is not zero of course' (D2), which indicates the seriousness of the situation. Later in the interaction, the physician and the patient are planning the treatment (see Box 4.3).

The physician explains that 'we will give the treatment in the same dose as last time' and again assures the patient that 'you shouldn't be worried about having no side-effects that it won't help it will do just as much' (D1). The patient does not seem convinced when she responds 'It will' (P2).

When the patient reveals that she suspects that the physician does not understand her, this illustrates a potential lack of basic trust in the physician's Swedish language competence, which may influence the physician's understanding of what the patient says. At the same time, it illustrates a potential lack of trust concerning the physician's collaboration in establishing joint understanding. It is difficult to say whether the

BOX 4.2   EXCERPT 2

Original (Swedish)	English Translation
P1: mm de e ju den hä ständia oron liksom att // om de försvinner eller om de kan hållas i schack förstå du va ja menar	P1: Mm it is this constant worry somehow // if it disappears or if it can be kept under control do you understand what I mean
D1: mm // vi / vi ska försöka göra de bästa vi kan // förstås // e så att e / de va de här förhöjda // tumörmarkören som vi hade // [1 så att]1 de ///	D1: Mm // we / we will try to do the best we can //of course // eh so that / it was those increased tumour markers // which we had // [1 so that they]1 ///
P2: [1 mm]1	P2: [1 mm]1
P3: tycker att de e så konstit att ja kan må så bra å ändå vara sjuk / < förstå du va ja menar >	P3: Think it is strange that I can feel so good and still be ill / < do you understand what I mean >
@ < intonation: rising >	
D2: m / m / m // ä / ja: men e/ de e / de e ju / de här själva de här tumören de / de kan va en / (allså) bara en sån liten börda va så att de/ man man kan aldri säga att att / att att vi / aldri kan bota dej men de / ja ja sa att att att chansen för å kunna bota minskar ju ju fler behanlingar vi ha gett å så va / [2 men]2 e de e inte noll < fårstås > så så att de/ vi försöke så gott vi [3 kan så]3 få vi se	D2: m / m / m // er / yeah: but er / it is / it is well / this this tumour itself / it can be / (only) such a small burden so that / one can never say / that that we / can never cure you/ I I said that that the chance to be able to cure decreases the more treatments we have given / [2 but]2 er it is not zero < of course > so so because / we try the best we [3 can]3 so we will see
@ < förstås >	
P4: [3 m]3	P4: [3 m]3

BOX 4.3   EXCERPT 3

Original (Swedish)	English Translation
D1: då så då då ska vi ge behandlingen i samma e dos som förra gången // [1 så]1 ska du inte vara orolig att att du inte ha du inte biverkningar så att de inte ska hjälpa / de gör de / lika / mycke	D1: Well then we will give the treatment in the same dose as last time // [1 then]1 you should not be worried about having no side-effects that it won't help / it will / just as much
P1: [1 jaha]1	P1: [1 I see]1
P2: de gö de	P2: It will
D2: ja	D2: Yes

patient has a lack of trust in the physician's cooperation or in the commitments and obligations of the physician. The patient does not explicitly question the efforts of the physician and the other care professionals, but continues to be worried, which may indicate a certain lack of trust in the physician's professional competence. There is research showing that some Swedish patients are suspicious and lack trust in the professional competence of physicians educated outside the EU/ EEA (cf. Berbyuk Lindström, 2008). In any case, the patient's worries do not seem to have been suspended, perhaps related to an insight that she may die. There are no clear indications of trust or distrust in the patient from the side of the physician.

We conclude that it is difficult to decide whether this situation can be seen as an illustration of the processes of trusting or distrusting. The patient seems to accept the physician's accounts and agrees to continue the treatment at the end of the interaction. This could indicate trusting but can also be seen as a more or less polite acceptance without any relevance to trusting or, if reluctant, indicating distrusting. The excerpts illustrate that accounts are crucial communicative instruments in influencing the trust process. The accounts need to be comprehensible, clear, confirmative and at the same time considerate, respectful and truthful. Balancing these requirements demands a lot from the physician, even more so when cultural differences are involved.

Illustration II. Patient Distrusting the Physician and Vice Versa

A middle-aged Swedish male patient comes to see a middle-aged male Iranian surgeon who has treated him before. The patient has a bullet in his shoulder and is in constant pain. He believes that the bullet has split into small fragments, causing the symptoms (see Box 4.4).

The physician starts by stating, 'I know everything about you' (D1), to which the patient replies sceptically, 'is that so' (P1), indicating that he doubts that the physician knows everything and that there may be a problem concerning trust from the very beginning. The consultation continues, and after asking a number of questions and conducting a physical examination, the physician concludes that an X-ray and a consultation with an orthopaedist are needed to evaluate the problem better. However, the patient insists on removing the bullet immediately, claiming that he has had four X-rays already and that he sees any delay in removing the bullet as unnecessary and unacceptable. In Excerpt 5, the patient argues that the Swedish Poisons Information Centre informed him that it is dangerous to have a bullet in the body due to an increased risk of lead poisoning (see Box 4.5).

BOX 4.4   EXCERPT 4

Original (Swedish)	English Translation
D1: per-oskar / vi känner varandra och e vi har ju behandlat dej på avdelningen och e ja vet allting om dej då	D1: Per-Oskar / we know each other and eh we've treated you and eh I know everything about you then
P1: < jaha >	P1: < Is that so >
@ < mood: sceptical >	
D2: så ja vill gärna veta hur du mår ida	D2: I would like to know how you feel today
P2: ja mår inte bra	P2: I do not feel well

BOX 4.5   EXCERPT 5

Original (Swedish)	English Translation
P1: så kan de gå väldit fort sa dom på giftcentralen till mej	P1: It can develop very fast they told me at the Poisons Information Centre
D1: m [1 nej nej nej]1 de e ju dom har fel [2 de e]2 inte hundra procent på de sättet va	D1: No [1 no no no]1 it is they you know are wrong [2 it is]2 not a hundred percent in that way right
P2: [1 (…)]1 P3: [2 jaha]2	P2: [1 (…)]1 P3: [2 is that so]2

The patient implicitly criticizes the surgeon, by referring to another authority, when he says, 'It can develop very fast they told me at the Poisons Information Centre' (P1). The physician takes up the challenge from the patient by claiming, 'it is they you know are wrong' (D1). Again, the patient responds with 'is that so' (P3), which is a sign of disbelief in the physician. The mere fact that the patient turned to the Swedish Poisons Information Centre to ask for information indicates a potential lack of trust in the physician, since the physician has not provided him with the information about the risk. The physician then continues by explaining the actions to be taken (see Box 4.6).

BOX 4.6   EXCERPT 6

Original (Swedish)	English Translation
D1: då gör vi så per-oskar ja kommer skriva remissen prata me dom å sen så vi kollar de här om vi	D1: Then we will do it like this Per-Oskar I will write a referral talk to them and we check this if we
P1: ja å ganska omgående för att ja vet att de de tjuåttonde december [1 (...) det ja]1 // å (...) ja ja skulle vart här för	P1: Yes and fairly promptly because I know that it is December twenty-eighth [1 (..) it yes]1 // and (...) I should have been here for
D2: [1 m]1	D2: [1 m]1
D3: ja har ju tat ut kulan på folk efter tre år utan någon liksom problem	D3: You know I have removed the bullet from people after three years without any like problems
P3: ja men då har de vart helkapslade å så inkapslade så att	P3: Yes but then they have been totally enclosed and so encapsulated that
D4: att de e ju de finns ju såna saker de finns ju men e vi sätter igång så snart som möjlit jättebra ja tittar en gång till på bilderna själv	D4: There are things like that you know there are but we start as soon as possible very good I will look at the pictures once more myself
P4: ja	P4: Yes

The physician attempts to convince the patient by referring to his professional experience: 'I removed the bullet from people after three years without any like problems' (D3). The patient argues that the bullets 'have been totally enclosed' (P3). The surgeon explains that he will start the procedure as soon as possible and states, 'I will look at the pictures once more myself' (D4). After the patient has requested copies of his X-rays and has insisted on being hospitalized directly, the physician responds as in Excerpt 7 (see Box 4.7).

Again, the physician attempts to use his position of authority to claim trust: 'we are the ones who should judge if you trust us working as physician' (D1) to persuade the patient. The response from the patient – 'so what's the problem, cut it out and remove it' (P2) – shows that the argument apparently does not have any effect. The physician tries to calm (and thereby rebuild trust in) the patient by describing the actions to be taken by health care professionals, including himself: 'we X-ray you we talk to the orthopaedist' (D2). The patient continues to be worried about the delay and asks 'how long will this take' (P3). Realizing that the

BOX 4.7   EXCERPT 7

Original (Swedish)	English Translation
D1: per-oskar de går inte de e så här inte fungerar hälsovården // de är ju inte så att du kommer å säger att ja vill bli inlagd va / de e ju de e ju vi som ska bedöma om du litar på oss arbetar som doktor ja säger att de bästa för dej de e ju som ja gör va // men om du vill liksom påverka själv // då de en helt annan sak ja förstår att du har ont / [1 de]1 e därför ja reagerar annars skulle 2[(...)]2	D1: Per-oskar it does not work it's like this health care does not function // you know it's not like you come and say that I want to be hospitalized right / you know you know we are the ones who should judge if you trust us working as physician I say that the best for you it's of course what I do right // but if you want to kind of influence yourself // then it's a quite different thing I understand that you're in pain / [1 that is] 1 why I react otherwise I would 2[(...)]2
P1: [1 ja]1	P1: [1 yeah]1
P2: [2 jo jo]2 ja fattar vidden att // varför ja ska hållas (...) nu // du har konstaterat att ja har kula i axeln / så va e problemet skär bort den å ta bort den	P2: [2 well well]2 I understand the extent that // why I should be kept (...) now // you have determined that I have a bullet in my shoulder / so what's the problem, cut it out and remove it
D2: e lyssna på mej // vi röntgar dej / vi pratar me ortopeden / sen vi diskuterar va vi ska göra // fortsätt me den här medicineringen tills du kommer till ortopeden // okej	D2: E listen to me // we X-ray you / we talk to the orthopaedist / then we discuss what we should do // continue with this medication until you get to the orthopaedist / / okay
P3: a hur lång tid tar detta då	P3: How long will this take
D3: e ja vet inte // vi försöker och agera den som ska göras så snart som möjlit	D3: Eh I do not know // we will try to act what needs to be done as soon as possible
P4: ja	P4: Yeah

patient disagrees with his suggestions, the physician's patience seems to be strained (see Box 4.8).

The patient seems to listen to the physician, but when the physician leaves the room, he explodes, talking to a nurse (N) (see Box 4.9).

The patient's comments 'scam and trickery' and 'the hospital saves money' (P1) indicate that he is suspicious about the arguments of the physician and probably does not trust him. The accounts given by the physician have thus not had the effect of raising trust; rather, the distrust of the patient has remained and possibly been strengthened.

BOX 4.8 EXCERPT 8

Original (Swedish)	English Translation
D1: du vill inte bli påtittad utav en ortoped du vill [1 inte]1	D1: You do not want the orthopaedic surgeon to check you you [1 don't]1
P1: [1 ortoped]1 titta på mej alla tittar på mej ja har blivit röntgad å röntgad å röntgad / så att e	P1: [1 Orthopaedic surgeon]1 looks at me all look at me I have been X-rayed and X-rayed / so that er
D2: kanske behöver ingen röntgen kan skicka liksom kan referera den här röntgen du har gjort å dom ska titta å bedöma det igen då // men frågan e ju att om dom här kulorna dom här fragmenten har flyttat på sej // har dom fastnat i nån muskulatur har dom kommit nära leden [2 de]2 e massor av saker ska man tänka å du tänker inte på såna saker // å tyvärr ja har inte tid å liksom diskutera så här va MEN låt oss // skicka till ortopeden en remiss titta på de de e ju VÄRT va // ja lovar dej garanti sätt foten utanför sverige ingen vill alls titta på de här // jo om du [3 kommer]3 till ett amerikanskt sjukhus eller ett sånt	D2: Maybe do not need X-ray can send and can reference this X-ray you've done and they will look at and judge it again then // but the question is that if these bullets those fragments have moved // have they got stuck in some muscle have they come close to the joint [2 there]2 are lots of things you should think and you do not think about things like that // yes unfortunately I do not have time to like discuss this huh BUT let's // send to the orthopaedist a referral look at it it is WORTH while isn't it // I promise you I guarantee put your foot outside Sweden no one wants to look at it at all // yes if you [3 come]3 to a U.S. hospital or a place like
P2: [2 ja]2	P2: [2 yeah]2
P3: [3 jo]3	P3: [3 yeah]3

BOX 4.9 EXCERPT 9

Original (Swedish)	English Translation
P1: bluff å båg va // då hinner man väl dö här e // blyförgiftning // va sparar sjukhuset pengar // (…) / skrämmande // ortopeda mej hit å ortopeda mej dit // bara röntgen (…) // men skulle ja dö utav blyförgiftning i såna fall inspelat på band att ja har krävt å bli opererad så att (…) // va fan ska ja här å göra ///	P1: Scam and trickery // you can die here of // lead poisoning // the hospital saves money // (…) / scary // orthopede me here and orthopede me there // only x-ray (…) // but should I die of lead poisoning in that case it is recorded on the tape that I have required to be operated so that (…) // what the devil am I doing here ///
N1: hur går de per-oskar	N1: How is it going Per-Oskar
P2: jodå // ja står å biktar mej bara	P2: Well // I am confessing only

This situation illustrates the patient's and the physician's mutual lack of both collaborative and cooperative trust. To start with collaborative trust, the physician and the patient do not work towards a joint purpose. The patient wants surgery immediately, while the physician will not offer it, defending his decision by referring to hospital procedures and stating that he does not consider the patient's problems to require immediate action. The patient may feel that the physician does not care about his opinions and problems, while the physician may experience that the patient does not believe him and his suggestions (lack of cooperative trust). Further, the patient may think that the physician did not provide him with information about potential lead poisoning on purpose, to avoid surgery and to save money for the hospital, which may also show a lack of trust with respect to commitments and obligations.

The situation further illustrates the patient's lack of trust in the physician's competence. The physician refers to his professional authority and experience without any apparent effect, probably due to cultural differences. In Iran, physicians are often viewed as absolute authorities, and their words are rarely questioned (Behjati-Sabet and Chambers, 2005; Berbyuk Lindström, 2008), while in Sweden, patients expect explanations based on facts. In addition, similar to the case with the Iranian female physician, some lack of trust may be due to the physician being educated outside the EU/EEA. In addition, there are concerns about basic trust. When the physician terminates the interaction, it may indicate that he does not believe that the upset and stressed patient can listen to and perceive what he is talking about. Whatever the physician now tries to communicate, his accounts (justifications of actions taken/not taken) will not be found to be acceptable by the patient.

We conclude that this illustration is a clear case of a process of distrust. The patient is implicitly and explicitly questioning the collaboration and cooperation of the physician, and he is evaluating his trust with respect to the physician's commitments, obligations and competence. From the physician's point of view, it is not as evident that he is distrusting, although there are indications at the end.

The role of the accounts is important in this situation, as in the previous illustration with the cancer patient. The patient is afraid of developing lead poisoning and suspicious about the effectiveness of the health care system, possibly due to earlier experiences. To provide accounts that can lead to the suspension of doubts following such a start may be extremely difficult, not to say impossible. It may be necessary to meet again several times to earn an increasing amount of trust to repair the damage.

DISCUSSION AND CONCLUSIONS

In this chapter we have presented examples of health care dialogues to illustrate processes in which trust relations are challenged. We have also shown how accounts are provided in these situations to attempt to maintain trust. We have analysed the situations with regard to whether the accounts led to increased or decreased trust or had no apparent effect.

In summary, we have found that although *basic trust* can often be assumed to be the default, in medical encounters basic trust is perhaps challenged by the lack of linguistic competence of one of the physicians and may in this case be added to other reasons for doubts that the patient may have. In addition, the patients' difficulties in perceiving information may challenge the physicians' trust in the basic capabilities of the patients.

Collaborative trust (that is, a belief that interlocutors will adopt and collaborate toward a joint purpose), by and large, seems to be present. In our medical encounters, parties share the purpose of communicating and carrying out the consultancy. However, there is disagreement about particular tasks (surgery to remove a bullet) when the physician does not comply with the patient's demands and the patient does not comply with the physician's advice. We can say that there is a kind of partial collaborative distrust, which is seen in the demands for accounts and the attempts to provide responsive accounts.

When it comes to *cooperative trust* (that is, the belief that interlocutors take one into ethical consideration), the issues are more complex. There is some evidence of distrust. The patient with a bullet in his shoulder and his physician both show evidence of being threatened with regard to their freedom of action. Since losing freedom and being uncertain about the correctness of information are unpleasant, the ethical dimension of pain and pleasure becomes involved as well.

Cooperative/collaborative trust is also linked to trustworthiness, reliability and dependability with regard to *commitments and obligations* in general, but here it is specifically related to the activities that the parties are pursuing together. There is disagreement about the arguments for not providing surgery and about the obligations of the physician and the hospital.

Finally, *trust with respect to competence* is very much at stake in situations during which the patient has a different opinion about the medical treatment from the physician. Our data show that cultural differences may explain the extent to which patients have default trust in their health professionals.

In general, we can see that trusting and distrusting are complex phenomena. In our analysis, we found that accountability and account giving come to have a crucial role in the process of increasing or decreasing trust, since this is one of the main ways in which we can obtain information concerning the five types of behavioural features that we suggested are essential for trust. We have shown that accounts can lead to trusting (Illustration I). A necessary condition is that they correspond to the uncertainty that the other party expresses, assuming willingness to collaborate and cooperate. Having analysed authentic interactions, we can claim that it is more complicated to identify trusting than distrusting. Part of the explanation is that, although it may be possible to identify suspension of doubt, it is quite complicated to observe the leap of faith (cf. Möllering, 2006). In our illustrations, it was possible to some extent to identify suspension of doubt, but not the leap of faith. Further, accounts should be presented in an understandable way assuming both basic and area-specific competence (Illustration I). Cultural difference (Illustrations I and II) is an aspect of significance here. Finally, accounts should confirm commitments and obligations. We have shown that accounts can lead to distrusting if they do not meet these conditions.

We have found that it is complicated to counteract distrusting using accounts. This is especially true when it becomes unexpectedly necessary in an ongoing interaction (Illustration II). It requires both an awareness of the role of trust and knowledge about how trust problems are communicated, that is, realizing that the other party is uncertain about, or doubting, something that one has said or done (or not said or not done). In addition, it requires communicative skills and knowledge about how to express oneself in a careful and nuanced way. This is of course difficult when exposed to open distrust from another person face to face.

Perhaps actions taken (not taken) may be more important for trusting (distrusting) than accounts (Illustration II). The role of accounts in situations of distrusting actions is most likely to differ from the role of accounts in situations of distrusting talk. This, together with the challenges involved in analysing the leap of faith in dialogue, calls for further research, taking multimodal means of communication into consideration.

NOTE

1. This involves behaviour in accordance with the so-called 'golden rule', with specific consequences such as do not hurt – give pleasure; do not coerce/force – give freedom; do not lie/mislead – give correct information.

REFERENCES

Allwood, J. (2014) Trust as a communicative and epistemic simplifier and facilitator. In: Linell, P. and Markova, I. (eds), *Dialogical Approaches to Trust in Communication*. A volume in *Advances in Cultural Psychology: Constructing Human Development*. Charlotte, NC: Information Age Publishing, pp. 189–211.

Allwood, J., Johansson, I-L., Olsson, L-E. and Tuna, G. (2015) On the need for an ethical understanding of health care accountability. *Journal of Organizational Transformation and Social Change*, 12 (2), pp. 121–37.

Behjati-Sabet, A. and Chambers, N.A. (2005) People of Iranian descent. In: Waxler-Morrison, N., Anderson, J.M., Richardson, E. and Chambers, N.A. (eds), *Cross-Cultural Caring: A Handbook for Health Professionals*. 2nd edn. Toronto: UBC Press, pp. 127–62.

Berbyuk Lindström, N. (2008) *Intercultural Communication in Health Care. Non-Swedish Physicians in Sweden*. PhD. Gothenburg, Department of Philosophy, Linguistics and Theory of Science, University of Gothenburg.

Flanagan, G.C. (1954) The critical incident technique. *Psychological Bulletin*, 51 (4), 327–58.

Garfinkel, H. (1967[1984]) *Studies in Ethnomethodology*. Cambridge: Polity Press.

Grossen, M. and Salazar Orvig, A. (2014) Forms of trust/distrust and dialogicality in focus-group discussions about medical confidentiality. In: Linell, P. and Markova, I. (eds), *Dialogical Approaches to Trust in Communication*. A volume in *Advances in Cultural Psychology: Constructing Human Development*. Charlotte, NC: Information Age Publishing, pp. 3–27.

Hill, C.A. and O'Hara, E.A. (2005) A cognitive theory of trust. *Washington University Law Review*, paper 55, 1717–70.

Jokinen, K. and Allwood, J. (2010) Hesitation in intercultural communication: Some observations and analysis on interpreting shoulder shrugging. In: Ishida, T. (ed.), *Culture and Computing*. LNCS 6259. Berlin and Heidelberg: Springer-Verlag, pp. 55–70.

Khodyakov, D. (2007) Trust as a process: A three-dimensional approach. *Sociology*, 41 (1), 115–32.

Möllering, G. (2001) The nature of trust: From Georg Simmel to a theory of expectation, interpretation and suspension. *Sociology*, 35 (2), 403–20.

Möllering, G. (2006) *Trust: Reason, Routine, Reflexivity*. Oxford: Elsevier.

Möllering, G. (2013) Process views of trusting and crises. In: Bachmann, R. and Zaheer, A. (eds), *Handbook of Advances in Trust Research*. Cheltenham, UK and Northampton, MA, USA: Edward Elgar Publishing, pp. 285–305.

Rowe, R. and Calnan, M. (2006) Trust relations in health care – The new agenda. *European Journal of Public Health*, 16 (1), 4–6.

Scott, M.B. and Lyman, S.M. (1968) Accounts. *American Sociological Review*, 33 (1), 46–62.

Skirbekk, H. (2009) Negotiated or taken-for-granted-trust? Explicit and implicit interpretations of trust in the medical setting. *Medicine, Health Care & Philosophy*, 12 (1), 3–7.

Skirbekk, H., Middlethon, A-L., Hjortdal, P. and Finset, A. (2011) Mandates of trust in the doctor–patient relationship. *Qualitative Health Research*, 21 (9), 1182–90.

Tsankova, E., Aubrey, A.J., Krumhube, E., Möllering, G., Kappas, A., Marshall, D. and Rosin, P.L. (2013) Facial and vocal cues in perceptions of trustworthiness. In: Park, J.I. and Kim, J. (eds), *ACCV Workshops, Part II*. LNCS 7729. Berlin: Springer, pp. 308–19.

PART II

Trust-building and sensemaking

5. Playing by ear: trust creation as improvisation and sensemaking

Lovisa Näslund

Selling complex services may also be described in terms of creating trust. The reason for this is the highly uncertain nature of consulting services, in terms of predictability of the outcomes, which in turn is caused by the co-creational nature of services, which means that neither seller nor buyer can know beforehand exactly what the result of the delivered service will be (cf. Von Nordenflycht, 2010). As both parties will be involved in the production, it follows that neither buyer nor seller will be able to control the process entirely, which leads to a measure of unpredictability as to the outcomes, which cannot be standardized beforehand as each interaction and each client will be somewhat different (Clark, 1995; Løwendahl, 2005; Sturdy, 1997). This is especially true for smaller, more process-oriented consulting companies, who do not use standardized methods and models, but instead tailor each project to the client's needs. Typically, these consulting companies rely heavily on interpersonal relationships to obtain clients, as high levels of uncertainty encourage clients to choose suppliers based either on first-hand, personal knowledge, or, if that fails, recommendations from trusted others such as colleagues or close business acquaintances (Glückler and Armbrüster, 2003; Näslund, 2012). Buying and selling these consulting services is thus largely based on thick interpersonal trust based on familiarity and strong interpersonal ties. If these are not available, then clients will likely rely on thin interpersonal trust, using intermediaries or guardians of trust to gather information on the consultants, and then, based on those recommendations, try to build thick trust (Khodyakhov, 2007).

The process leading up to the purchase of consulting services may also be described in terms of a trust-building process, where the agreement to form a working relationship and embark on a project may also be conceptualized in terms of the client deciding to make a leap of faith, acting as if it were certain that the project would be successful.

Trust creation has been widely discussed in research, often described in terms of creating trustworthiness, and the qualities in the trustee that are perceived to convey this (Dietz, 2011; Mayer et al., 1995). In this chapter, the focus is less on the qualities that constitute trustworthiness, and more on the nature of the interactions that constitute this trust-building process. The chapter aims to contribute to the development of a process-oriented perspective on trust and trust creation, by analysing the interactional and co-creational aspect of trust creation. It is argued that by conceptualizing trust creation as an interactional process of sensemaking, enacted through improvisation, we can further our understanding of the mechanisms of trust creation as an interactional process, beyond the trustor's assessment of trustee trustworthiness. From a professional service perspective, it will be shown how, in the interaction between client and consultant, the process of co-creation of trust runs parallel, and is intertwined, with the co-creation of the service.

In order to study this, interviews with clients and management consultants in Sweden were undertaken, with a focus on how their relationship evolved as a consequence of their collaboration, and how such working relationships were begun, strengthened or aborted. The consulting companies studied were small to middle-sized, worked mainly with a process-oriented approach (Schein, 1969), and mainly employed senior consultants on projects that were small in terms of the number of consultants involved, but which would often go on for an extended period of time, focusing on change management and HR, rather than strategic analysis. The clients were large companies in a variety of industries, and represented in the study by the CEO or HR manager.

In the following, we will discuss the theoretical framework in terms of trust, sensemaking and improvisation, before we return to the empirical part of the study and the analysis. The chapter concludes with a discussion of these findings.

TRUST, SENSEMAKING AND IMPROVISATION

As stated above, trust is here viewed essentially as a leap of faith (Möllering, 2006), a process situated in time, where the interpretation of the past and expectation of the future bring the trustor to make a leap of faith in the present. Trust thus bridges the unknown, a gap made smaller through interpretation and expectation, based on the trustor's perception of the trustee and the situation at hand. However, while the leap of faith is the essence of trust, it does not equal trust. Rather, trust is a process consisting of three elements: interpretation of the present, suspension of disbelief as demonstrated in the leap of faith, and expectations of the future, as shown in Figure 5.1.

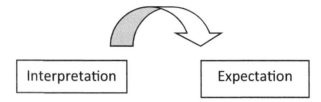

| Interpretation | | Expectation |

Source: Adapted from Möllering (2006).

Figure 5.1   The three elements of trust

The figurative distance between the interpretation of what has been, and the prediction of what may be expected to come if a certain action is taken, makes for uncertainty, which then has to be overcome by a leap of faith, by suspension of disbelief. It is important to note that the leap of faith cannot be seen in isolation: it is the combination of all three components which constitutes trust. While the leap of faith is the essence of trust, it is only part of the trusting process, which has cognitive as well as emotional or affective aspects (Jones, 1996). While trust is often defined in terms of a psychological state (see the standard definition of trust in Rousseau et al., 1998 for a well-known example), this more sociologically-inspired conceptualization by comparison offers a more process-oriented view of trust.

The description of the leap of faith in terms of commitment and decision making is not incidental, for while not all processes of trusting are necessarily on the scale of important decisions, the decision point constitutes an instant where trust becomes visible. When making a decision requires a leap of faith, then such a decision in effect constitutes trust. The moment of choice, in this case the instant when the client decides to move forward with a certain consultant and a certain consulting project, therefore provides a suitable case for a study of the process of trust building. In other words, we here focus on trust-as-choice, serving as an exchange mode and active choice of commitment, rather than trust-as-attitude, the passive and non-committal evaluation of trustworthiness (Li, 2007). The leap of faith is made at the moment the choice is made, but it is a moment which has been preceded by a process of information gathering and presentation on both sides, making it, as we have seen, a temporally and contextually embedded phenomenon, as the 'now' of the leap of faith will soon turn into the 'then' of interpretation of the past, and thereby become input in the process leading up to the choice to dare or not dare another leap of faith when the next project comes along. The outcome of one leap of faith, whether the trust is honoured or deceived, is thus likely to influence and possibly shift the frames of reference of the trustor, influencing how cues will be interpreted for the next leap of faith (Möllering, 2013).

A further implication of this conceptualization of trust is that it is temporally and socially embedded, rather than an isolated phenomenon (Buskens and Weesie, 2000). It therefore follows that any attempt to understand how trust is created also necessitates a focus on the temporal and social contexts within which it comes about – what lies before and after making the choice to trust – and the social structures that surround it (Saunders et al., 2010). It also follows from this perspective that trust may be viewed as a process of sensemaking, as it is through sensemaking that interpretation of the present and expectations of the future are formed. Trusting is therefore to a large extent to be regarded as a process of sensemaking, where trustors incrementally gather evidence of the other's behaviour, looking for cues as to what can be expected from the other's behaviour, and how they have behaved in the past, which are then interpreted and categorized in the light of earlier frames of references and experiences (Adobor, 2005; Weick, 1995).

The social embeddedness of trust in this conceptualization is twofold: first, the trustee is not just the passive recipient of trust – rather, trust creation is an interactive process between the two parties, as the trustee, wanting to be trusted, will try and influence the interpretation and expectation of the trustor, so as to make the leap of faith more likely. Consequently, when trust is created between consultants and clients, it is not a matter of the trustee, the consultant in this case, being passively assessed, hoping that this evaluation will lead to the trustor coming to the conclusion that they are indeed trustworthy, and that a leap of faith would therefore be advisable. Instead, it is an interactional process, where the consultant will actively seek to learn what fears and threats the clients perceives, and then seek to act in a manner so as to reduce these threats, for example by showing benevolent consideration, or by reflecting an understanding of the client's stance (Williams, 2007). In a crisis situation, for example if either or both parties feels threatened or scared, the emotional involvement is also likely to affect the sensemaking process, which should not be seen as a detached cognitive game of assigning meaning to events, but rather as a process which becomes most acute in times of high emotional involvement, which is also likely to skew or otherwise influence the frames used (Maitlis and Sonenshein, 2010). It is a process which will be influenced by the social context, in a more implicit way by the labels and categories used in sensemaking, and more explicitly through attempts at sensegiving, where others actively try to influence the sensemaking process in a particular direction (Gioia and Chittipeddi, 1991; Weick et al., 2005). The trust-building process thereby becomes a process of sensemaking and sensegiving, where the trustor is looking for cues, and the trustee is trying to influence this process in order for it to reach a favourable outcome. Trust creation on professional service markets is therefore fundamentally an interactional process, which engages the trustee as much as the trustor.

Trust is also socially embedded because the interpretation of the past draws on the social context – in making an interpretation of the offer at hand from a seller, the buyer will draw on the knowledge they have of the problem at hand. Similarly, when making an expectation of the future, such as the likelihood that a specific consultant will be able to deliver the required service, the trustor also draws on knowledge of the trustee, of the industry, on past experiences of that particular consultant, and of other consulting projects. This knowledge creates schemata or frames which act as data reduction devices, enabling actors to make sense of organizational complexity (Lockett et al., 2014). Through sensemaking, we are able to bring order to the flux of organizing, ordering and labelling the stream of experience, thereby making it comprehensible and possible to act on (Näslund and Pemer, 2012). If the sensemaking process fails to bring coherence, then action and trust also become impossible, or at least unappealing, as uncertainty will then become a chasm that cannot be overcome (Weick, 1993). If it succeeds, then shared trust histories can be created, which will then provide an interpretative frame for coming events, and provide a basis for continued trust (Möllering, 2013). Collective sensemaking enables collective action, which in turn is necessary in order to co-create a professional service (Maitlis, 2005). To some extent, these schemata are created in the immediate social context, through negotiation, whereby existing frames may be challenged or altered, but group membership is not a sufficient source to account for the schemata an individual will employ. The sensemaking process will most likely differ between two members of the same organization, or two participants of the same meeting, as frames are not only locally constructed in dialogue, but also stem from the actor's social position and lived experience: personal history and background. These frames, shaped by experience, can be understood in terms of Bourdieu's notion of *habitus*, an incorporated system of dispositions that allows people to act, think and orient themselves in the social space they are in, in short the incorporated values of the field in which someone feels at home (Bourdieu, 1990; Broady, 1990; Lockett et al., 2014). The habitus is the social order that we carry with us at all times; it provides us with a room of possibilities, and determines what we see as reasonable courses of action and reaction in a given situation. Every time we react to others, we thus recreate that incorporated structure, causing the structure to reproduce itself. This does not mean that people are to be seen as automatons, mindlessly reproducing the structures we inhabit. Rather than dictating an action, the habitus provides the means for practice – the habitus is thus both 'structuring structure' and 'structured structure', providing the nexus where agency and structure may interact, a 'capacity for structured improvisation' (Postone et al., 1993, p. 4).

From a sensemaking perspective, the interaction between consultant and client which allows them to build trust is a process of paying attention to cues that are interpreted and given meaning by frames. These frames are to some extent socially negotiated in interaction between the two parties, trustor and trustee, but both parties will enter the interaction with frames formed by earlier experiences, by their habitus. The habitus thus determines what interpretations seem plausible, but does not necessarily provide a fixed meaning: there will always be some room for negotiation, for challenging frames, for shifting meanings. This is a process in which the trustor and trustee are mutually involved, whereby they co-create trust, but where neither party has the ability to unilaterally determine meaning and interpretation, but engages in a struggle to make collective sense (Colville et al., 2013).

The process of creating trust is interlinked with processes of sensemaking and sensegiving, where both parties provide cues and interpretative frames, which calls for structure as well as improvisation (Barrett and Peplowski, 1998). In a sales meeting between consultant and client, as considered here, the consultant has to instantaneously determine what response is appropriate given the situation, so as to be able to engage in sensegiving, and make the trustor, in this case the client, arrive at an interpretation of past knowledge and experience, and of expectations of the outcomes that make the leap of faith feasible. As it is not possible to know beforehand exactly how the meetings will unfold, however, and new information is added as the client explains more about their situation and the problem at hand, these attempts at sensegiving can be prepared, but not planned in detail, as a consequence of the co-creational nature of these services.

While improvisation certainly requires creativity and is decided on the spur of the moment, it does not mean that it can be anything, or that it is entirely unpredictable. The improvisation has to adhere to the 'non-negotiable framework that constrains what the soloist can play' (Barrett and Peplowski, 1998, p. 558). In terms of sensemaking and habitus, earlier experience gives us a basis upon which to improvise, and thus both limits and enables understanding and action (Lockett et al., 2014; Weick et al., 2005). A more exhaustive study of what jazz musicians actually do when they improvise reveals that improvisations are in fact rarely completely improvised, but are rather based on pre-prepared sketch plans, which outline the features of upcoming passages. When the improvisations are then performed, musicians, as predicted by Weick (1995; Weick et al., 2005), are calling on well-learned ideas from memory, a firm grasp of harmony and melody, and bearing in mind and repeating earlier sections of the song (Norgaard, 2011). Successful improvisation, it would seem, is just as much the result of careful preparation and a good memory, than of spur-of-the-moment inspiration. Not altogether surprisingly, improvisation skills have been shown to improve with training and experience (Vera and Crossan, 2004). Organizational improvisations are obviously not solos, but are created through interaction with others – thus, they require not only playing by the rules of the situation, but also a keen eye for the responses and reactions of the others (Kamoche et al., 2003). It is such continuous coordination which allows for interaction to be co-constituting, playing off each other and reflecting on what the other is saying, thereby opening and shifting meaning, rather than iterating an established pattern, which disables variation, and sets rather than shifts meaning. If meanings are set, then the dialogue ceases to be transformational (Gergen et al., 2001). Closer studies of improvisations in business settings, such as negotiations, stress this social aspect of improvisation and reveal that exchange partners strive towards quickly coordinating a shared logic of exchange, and then adhere to this logic throughout their interaction, a process made easier if there are pre-existing social ties between the participants. If the interaction runs into difficulties, the participants use the same methods to encourage the interaction to run smoothly again, rather than turning to improvisation (McGinn and Keros, 2002). A controlled process allows for more controlled sensemaking, while a more animated exchange, with a higher degree of improvisation, by nature also holds more transformative potential in terms of sensemaking, and shifting frames, while being less likely to produce unitary accounts. A controlled process, with a higher degree of sensegiving, therefore has a more predictable outcome (Maitlis, 2005).

Improvisational skills thus become necessary when engaging in the trust-building process if the trustee is to be able to successfully engage in sensegiving, thereby enabling the trustor's leap of faith. This will be especially salient in the context of the sales process of management consulting, as there will probably be only a limited amount of interaction prior to a project being decided upon, and every cue then carries comparatively more weight in the overall assessment of the other's intentions and capabilities, and the feasibility of the project. In the following, we will look further into this, by way of analysing client–consultant interaction in sales meetings.

RESEARCH DESIGN

The study is based on interviews with 19 management consultants and HR directors in Stockholm and Gothenburg. The HR directors were chosen from a variety of industries, but all from larger companies with more than 500 employees, and most had ties to several suppliers. The consultants came from smaller consulting companies, working with organizational change and development, and were organized as expert houses rather than talent factories. In other words, they were consulting firms that may be regarded as networks of senior consultants, rather than hierarchical pyramids, where very few junior consultants are employed, and where all consultants are directly involved in sales, and all are responsible for finding projects and clients (Werr and Schilling, 2011). This type of consulting company was chosen in order to maximize the uncertainty of the outcome of the service provided, and thereby the need for trust, as trust was based on them as individuals rather than on the organization of the consulting company, such as may be the case with larger, global consulting companies such as BCG or McKinsey. All interviewed consultants were senior, with direct responsibility for client accounts, and were expected to create and develop their own accounts. The respondents were asked about their interactions with the other party (consultants or clients, respectively), about the process leading up to the agreement to do business together, and to give details of previous collaborations that had been successful and not so successful. In addition to these accounts, they were also asked in more general terms what they thought was important for this process, and what had made them more or less successful in terms of the service provided and the relationship created. The interviews lasted between 45 minutes and 1 hour 25 minutes, were digitally recorded, and later transcribed. The transcribed interviews were then analysed using N-Vivo software, where common themes in the interviews where picked out and then used to categorize the content of the interviews, thus allowing for detailed comparisons of descriptions, and accounts of similar events and occurrences in different interviews.

IMPROVISATIONAL TANGO: CONSULTANT–CLIENT INTERACTION

In the following analysis, we will see that whilst consulting certainly calls for improvisation, it would seem that these improvisations should follow expected conventions if they are to be conducive to trust building. A consulting project is commonly preceded by a series of sales meetings, which potentially lead to the client signing a contract and giving the project a green light. Especially in a new relationship, these meetings are thus the arena where trust can be created or absent, leading to collaboration or parted ways. Since a client meeting can only be prepared up to a point, this means that ultimately, the consultant has to rely largely on improvisation to create a favourable impression, which may then serve as a basis for trust creation.

As discussed above, it would seem that when studied in practice, improvisation is a paradoxical notion: on the one hand, the essence of improvisation is free flights of fancy, acting on the inspiration of the moment – on the other hand, when taking a closer look at these flights, they seem based on and put together from carefully prepared and memorized patterns, from information on structures and genres, and from what has been performed before. This latter might also be seen in terms of knowledge of industry norms, and the specifics of the client organization, what they take for granted, and how they interpret events – their frames of references, and the categories and labels they use in their sensemaking process. This knowledge provides room for improvisation, and the ability to present an impromptu response or solution that fits the situation and the audience. This is of course more easily done if the consultant shares the same background and incorporated norms, the same habitus, as the client. Sharing the same norms and experiences as the client will make successful improvisation decidedly easier, and facilitate a sense of mutual understanding, since both parties can rely on their social instinct, their 'gut reaction' so to speak, to make choices. The significance of having a similar frame of mind for trust development in a relationship can be exemplified in this mutual description by a consultant and a client of the beginning of a very long client/consultant relationship, first from the client's side, and then from the consultant's:

> And so we met Peter. And he is as only he can be, very confidence-inspiring, he really inspires confidence. You can see that he understands our business exactly, and many of the other consultants, they haven't the faintest. They don't come from [our industry], so they don't know. They speak in these very

> general terms which I'm sure are perfectly suited at Ericsson, but which we don't understand.

> I just can't bear working in some organizations. [...] For example, we work with [government body], and some parts of Ericsson, and it's so bloody slow, it doesn't suit me at all. [...] And then we change consultants, there are others who are better suited to that. In the same way we throw in some of our consultants at [HR manager's company], where you have a rapid-fire mentality some days. I love being there, for me it's the best there is. [...] It matters a great deal what you've done before, where you feel at home.

Feeling at home with the other party makes their behaviour seem so much more reasonable and understandable, which in turn will make the parties more likely to trust enough to choose each other – as happened in this particular case. The significance of 'feeling at home' becomes even more apparent if you consider the case of moving outside the economic field altogether – one consultant described beginning a project at the Church of Sweden, which turned out most unfortunately. The aim of the project was to find a solution to the dwindling numbers of members and attendants in the church, but reaching a common understanding of how the problem should be addressed proved very difficult. As it turned out, the client was offended by the consultant's insistence that they must analyse the market and decide which segment should be their targeted clientele. 'But the church must be there for everyone! The Lord's house is for all of His people!' they protested, and felt that the consultant did not understand them in the least. The consultant, on the other hand, thought that this was a hopeless case – if a client cannot even grasp the simple concept of market segmentation, there is little hope for them. Although it may seem merely an amusing anecdote, this episode can also be seen as an example of what might happen when clients and consultants do not share the same habitus, and how this discrepancy will disrupt attempts at trust creation. The clergyman and the consultant evidently had differing frames of reference, and thus logics of action: they had different evaluations of the purpose of an organization, and as a consequence seem incomprehensible or even incompetent to each other. Of course, one might argue that the consultant might have realized this before the meeting, read up on the values of the church, and thus escaped causing offence; however, even if they had done so, they may not have been able to improvise answers in the meeting in a manner that was conducive to trust. Responding in concurrence to a logic that is not their own, people will inevitably also be less graceful in their actions. This is not to say that it cannot be done, only that it tends to be more arduous, as one consultant explained:

We say that we work with people, and they're not industry-specific, that is, getting people to change what they know, how they behave and what they accomplish, and in that sense, we're not limited to specific industries. But for my own part, if I work in an industrial firm, I think it's easier for me, because there I feel at home. Not everyone thinks so, but to me it's an advantage if you really know the client's industry.

Experience and incorporated norms – the habitus – thus form the basis on which to improvise, but there remains the improvisation itself, which requires skill and experience. It would appear that selling consulting services requires being able to strike a fine balance: on the one hand, the interviewed consultants stress how important it is to listen, to be well-informed about the prospective client and adapt to what they need. Several of the interviewed clients emphasize the importance of the consultants really listening to their needs, not so much because they perceive themselves as essentially different from everyone else, but because they nevertheless have a unique set of conditions and predicaments.

Of course we are special in our own way, but then all companies have their special uniqueness. And I don't think it matters, irrespective of that it's very important that you are met by someone who listens and understands what needs we are expressing. [...] what I mean is that they should understand what we're saying, and counter that somehow, saying that I hear what you say, but still, we see it like this. And if you don't do that, then I'm missing a dimension. [...] It should be challenging, but you should do it from the viewpoint of having tried to understand what it is that we do. That you have a clear image of the problem. Not too hasty in conclusions, not too quick in analyses, but really listen first, and then, based on that, show that you have given it some thought.

You have to be able to think on your feet, as one consultant described it, listening to what people have to say and adapting to it instantaneously – but the listening, as we saw in the above quote, always precedes the improvisation. The trust-creating process seems essentially collaborative, at least in this context, based not only on the assessment of the qualities of the other, but also on their responsiveness and attentiveness, and ability to combine integrity with adaptability. Without listening, a consultant cannot memorize the structures and patterns of the client's organization, and is therefore also less likely to be convincing in improvisation. Such improvisation, it would appear, can only take place in interactive dialogue. On the other hand, clients are less likely to be interested in consultants who uncritically accept whatever the client company proposes, as one HR manager explained:

It's quite common with consultants that they just say 'Oh, but we'll adapt to what you want'. Sure as heck they'll do that, but you need a certain competence to be able to determine exactly what kind of leadership is needed, for example, and if we knew that, then maybe we wouldn't have to buy it. [...] maybe at some level you need them as a discussion partner to get it [the leadership training] down, but if they just say 'Oh, we'll adapt!', and you don't get any kind of ... Well, then we've just hired a teacher, and frankly, we might as well do it by ourselves then.

This notion is echoed by a consultant, explaining how they have to be 'a bit stubborn, daring to contradict. That's our role.' Striking the balance between being obnoxious and overtly compliant requires a certain amount of tact on the part of the consultant. Presumably, there are certain areas where contradictions are welcome and others where people are perceived as stubborn or inflexible. With a similar understanding of the organization and industry at hand, discerning between the two is likely to become easier. People will be more likely to instinctively make the right choices, and improvise in a manner that is appealing to the client, inducing confidence and thus making the 'as-if'-thinking necessary for trust seem more enticing. It is, however, also something which is likely to improve with experience and practice, as described by some more experienced consultants who had strategies for how to interact success- fully with the client during initial meetings, which of course would make improvisation easier, since they could then depend on ready-made templates, rather than innovation of the moment. Presumably, having such templates at their disposal is also likely to make it easier for consultants to listen attentively to the client, rather than being pre- occupied with deciding on what to say themselves, as in these two examples from experienced consultants:

There are two techniques; the first is to be a little like the sun, making people feel comfortable, and then they open up more and more. The second is being the northern wind, blowing their jacket off, and then they become a little ... And men in senior positions often feel more comfortable with that second approach. That is, if you show some muscle, that you can be a bit dangerous, then they feel more at ease. 'Oh, that's good', kind of 'Aha, we're a little bit alike, then!'

It's a method of asking questions. This is always sensitive; it's like talking to the parents of troubled children. What I do, is start by saying 'There's a lot that's good here, where does that come from? Who has inspired all these people, that it has become so good?' 'Well, that would be me, then.' 'Ok, but these not-so-good things then, where do they come from?' 'Yes, that's what I'd like to know, where the heck does that come from?' 'Mmn, who recruited all of these people?' *coughs* 'Yeees, right ...' So this is ... It's a deeply rooted human instinct. And it's always a balance, how tough you're allowed to be.

As one consultant put it, 'you develop a kind of experience and skill for what … in which direction you should take the discussion', and thus with experience, consultants seem to put their foot in their mouth with decreasing frequency, partly because they learn the importance of preparation, and learning as much as possible about the client and their organization beforehand:

> You have to know and understand something of the department of the person you're talking to, how that part of the organization works, otherwise you'll make a mistake. I've made them myself, once we went to a person responsible for competence development, trying to sell the outsourcing of competence development, but 'Hey, that's my job exactly!' Then you realize that, maybe, this was a stupid idea. We hadn't really done our homework then.
>
> *How do you do that?*
>
> You've got to ask a lot of questions, and then adapt the message as you go. A lot of research in order to try and understand – if you can somehow find out about the client, that is. Either through contacts, others who have been in contact with this company before, try and ask around, and get a picture of what they might need. But then also when you're there, ask questions.

It would seem that a mixture of templates, and information gained from listening to the client, their needs and wants, ameliorated by a common understanding, will together provide a basis for improvisation. It should be noted that improvisation in this context is not a matter of playing a solo, but rather of listening carefully to the response an improvisation elicits in its audience, and responding to that.

DISCUSSION

The process of trust creation between consultant and client is, as we have seen, essentially an interactive process, which this chapter has sought to unpack. It is less a cognitive process of interpretation performed by the trustor as the assessment of trustworthiness, but one where both parties are attentive to cues, both those they provide for the other, and those the other provides for them. In order to produce a 'trust story', a unified interpretation that both parties find plausible, the consultant seeks to be aware of the frames of the trustor, and to provide cues that would make sense given the interpretative frames of the other (Maitlis, 2005; Möllering, 2013). This capacity for adaptation only goes so far, however – if consultant and client share the same habitus, then their frames will be similar, and improvisation will come more effortlessly. If their references are too dissonant, then improvisation becomes not only difficult, but nigh impossible, as the habitus limits what frames are available or even understandable. Through social negotiation, consultants and clients may shift frames, but they cannot seem to reinvent the frames provided by their lived experiences and the context where they have gained their experience. Imagination does not run free, but rather is circumscribed and constricted by habitus and interpretative frames (Weick, 1995).

The emotional or affective aspect of trust also influences the sensemaking process, and the possibilities and conditions for sensegiving, such as suspicion of deceit or perceived lack of benevolent understanding, which is likely to make one interpretative frame seem more plausible than another (Maitlis and Sonenshein, 2010). To be able to successfully engage in sensegiving, a consultant needs a certain amount of tact, which is to some extent dependent on experience – experience that provides the consultant with more frames with which to interpret the situation, so as to be able to make an interpretation similar to the client – but also on common background and similar habitus, without which it will be difficult to access the client's frames. Since frames can be negotiated but rarely overthrown, as the likely outcome of a perception of incompatible interpretations of the situation at hand and the shared experience of interaction, seems to be the interpretation that the other is incompetent and/or deceitful (rather than adapting radically different interpretative frames) and thus cannot be expected to behave trustworthily in the future. Whilst improvisation is thus to some extent a professional skill that can be learnt, this skill has its limits, as improvisational possibilities are circumscribed by habitus.

If we regard trust creation in terms of improvisation and sensemaking, we are thus also able to highlight the interactional nature of the trust-building process. Improvisation is not possible without careful listening, since by reacting to the other, providing development of and reflections on the cues that they give, meanings can be shifted (Gergen et al., 2001; Kamoche et al., 2003). Effective sensegiving is therefore only possible if the interpretations suggested are coherent with the interpretative frames of the counterpart, which either requires an awareness of the other's frames, or shared frames. Trust creation between client and consultant is thus dialogic in nature, and requires an ear not only for cues, but also for the frames that the other uses to interpret them. In order to appear trustworthy, the consultant cannot seem too strategic or compliant in the cues they provide, as such behaviour may be interpreted as devious, signalling not benevolence and integrity, but rather self-interest and opportunism. In other words, as an improvisational partner, the consultant needs to listen and follow, but not to the extent that their independence and integrity seems forgone.

CONCLUSION

In conclusion, this study has sought to shed more light on the process that leads up to trust between client and consultant by arguing that it can be understood in terms of sharing a frame of references and improvising in concordance with this affinity. In order for the parties to hazard the leap into the uncertain that embarking on a consulting project will inherently be, it is crucial that they are able to close this gap as much as possible, so to speak, by feeding into the sensemaking process that creates the interpretation of the past and expectations of future outcomes. Sharing the same interpretative schemata and habitus means that this belief will seem easier to form, as the parties will then experience each other as predictable and trustworthy, thus allowing thick interpersonal trust to form and develop.

Whilst consulting certainly calls for improvisation, these improvisations should follow the expected conventions. If the consultant's answers seem irrelevant or completely ignorant, this will be noticed, and likely be perceived as a sign of untrustworthiness. Sharing a frame of reference with a client will not automatically guarantee earning their trust, but it will most likely help. If your intuition is right, then you will at least be improvising in the right genre, metaphorically speaking: the improvisation has to be recognizable within the industry and organizational logic in order to be successful. Of course, much may still go awry, as consultants still need to master the skills of improvising, but with a common habitus, at least you know when it sounds right or wrong, and what it should sound like, to continue the jazz metaphor. Incorporating the right values and a sense of what is appropriate and important will mean a head start compared to a consultant who enters from a different field altogether, and will make attempts at sensegiving more likely to be successful. As relational contracts, such as the embedded client–consultant relationships studied here, are more resilient to volatility than to ambiguity, it seems reasonable to assume that an underlying common understanding that decreases ambiguity is conducive to a durable relationship (Carson et al., 2006).

By analysing the interaction between consultants and their clients in terms of improvisation, sensemaking and trust building, we are able to unpack the process of trusting as improvisation based on templates and frames. These frames and templates may well be, and are often, negotiated in the present, as part of the interaction between client and consultant, but it is a negotiation of existing frames, provided by the social context, and the individual habitus of the actors involved. The process of trust building runs as an undercurrent in sales meetings and consulting projects, and thus it is not a matter of either having or not having trust, but rather the result of ongoing interpretation of cues and negotiation of frames. Trust enables consulting projects to take place, and once they are taking place, the experiences of one project feed into the expectations of the next. For consultants and other service providers, due to the co-creational nature of professional services such as these, trust building is an integral part of work. Improvisation is then a skill that can be used to help actively build trust, as it allows for attempts at sensegiving. If a common meaning can be created or is present from the beginning, this improvisation becomes considerably less arduous, as successful improvisation relies on a combination of good knowledge of the rules of the genre, access to templates of action, quick adaptation to the response of the other, and the development of the meeting or the project. Trust, similarly to improvisation, relies on the combination of the known and the uncertain. If everything is uncertain, trust is impossible, and if everything is known, trust is unnecessary.

REFERENCES

Adobor, H. (2005). Trust as sensemaking: the microdynamics of trust in interfirm alliances. *Journal of Business Research*, *58*, 330–37.

Barrett, F.J. and Peplowski, K. (1998). Minimal structures within a song: an analysis of 'All of Me'. *Organization Science*, *9*(5), 558–60.

Bourdieu, P. (1990). *The Logic of Practice*. Cambridge: Polity Press.

Broady, D. (1990). *Sociologi och Epistemologi: om Pierre Bourdieus för-fattarskap och den Historiska Epistemologin*. Stockholm: Högskolan för Lärarutbildning.

Buskens, V. and Weesie, J. (2000). An experiment on the effects of embeddedness in trust situations: buying a used car. *Rationality and Society*, *12*(2), 227–53.

Carson, S.J., Madhok, A. and Wu, T. (2006). Uncertainty, opportunism, and governance: the effects of volatility and ambiguity on formal and relational contracting. *The Academy of Management Journal*, *49*(5), 1058–77.

Clark, T. (1995). *Managing Consultants. Consultancy as the Management of Impressions*. Buckingham: Open University Press.

Colville, I., Pye, A. and Carter, M. (2013). Organizing counter terrorism: sensemaking amidst dynamic complexity. *Human Relations*, *66*(9), 1201–23.

Dietz, G. (2011). Going back to the source: why do people trust each other? *Journal of Trust Research*, *1*(2), 215–22.

Gergen, K.J., McNamee, S. and Barrett, F.J. (2001). Toward transformative dialogue. *International Journal of Public Administration*, *24*(7&8), 679–707.

Gioia, D.A. and Chittipeddi, K. (1991). Sensegiving and sensemaking in strategic change initiation. *Strategic Management Journal*, *12*(6), 433–48.

Glückler, J. and Armbrüster, T. (2003). Bridging uncertainty in management consulting: the mechanisms of trust and networked reputation. *Organization Studies*, *24*(2), 269–97.

Jones, K. (1996). Trust as an affective attitude. *Ethics*, *107*(1), 4–25.

Kamoche, K., Pina e Cunha, M. and Vieira da Cunha, J. (2003). Towards a theory of organizational improvisation: looking beyond the jazz metaphor. *Journal of Management Studies*, *40*(8), 2023–51.

Khodyakhov, D. (2007). Trust as a process: a three-dimensional approach. *Sociology*, *41*(1), 115–32.

Li, P.P. (2007). Towards an interdisciplinary conceptualization of trust: a typological approach. *Management and Organization Review*, *3*(3), 421–45.

Lockett, A., Currie, G., Finn, R., Martin, G. and Waring, J. (2014). The influence of social position on sensemaking about organizational change. *Academy of Management Journal*, *57*(4), 1102–29.

Løwendahl, B.R. (2005). *Strategic Management of Professional Service Firms* (3rd edn). Copenhagen: Copenhagen Business School Press.

Maitlis, S. (2005). The social processes of organizational sensemaking. *Academy of Management Journal*, *48*(1), 21–49.

Maitlis, S. and Sonenshein, S. (2010). Sensemaking in crisis and change: inspiration and insights from Weick (1988). *Journal of Management Studies*, *47*(3), 551–68.

Mayer, R.C., Davis, J.H. and Schoorman, F.D. (1995). An integrative model of organizational trust. *Academy of Management Review*, *20*(3), 709–34.

McGinn, K. and Keros, A.T. (2002). Improvisatin and the logic of exchange in socially embedded transactions. *Administrative Science Quarterly*, *47*(3), 442–73.

Möllering, G. (2006). *Trust: Reason, Routine, Reflexitivity*. Oxford: Elsevier.

Möllering, G. (2013). Process views of trusting and crises. In R. Bachmann and A. Zaheer (eds), *Handbook of Advances in Trust Research*. Cheltenham, UK and Northampton, MA, USA: Edward Elgar Publishing.

Näslund, L. (2012). *The Leap of Faith. Creating Trust on Professional Service Markets.* (PhD), Stockholm: Stockholm School of Economics.

Näslund, L. and Pemer, F. (2012). The appropriated language: dominant stories as a source of organizational inertia. *Human Relations*, *65*(1), 89–110.

Norgaard, M. (2011). Descriptions of improvisational thinking by artist-level jazz musicians. *Journal of Research in Music Education*, *59*(2), 109–27.

Postone, M., LiPuma, E. and Calhoun, C. (1993). Introduction: Bourdieu and social theory. In C. Calhoun, E. LiPuma and M. Postone (eds), *Bourdieu: Critical Perspectives*. Cambridge: Polity Press.

Rousseau, D.M., Sitkin, S.B., Burt, R.S. and Camerer, C. (1998). Not so different after all: a cross-discipline view of trust. *Academy of Management Review*, *23*(3), 393–404.

Saunders, M.N.K., Skinner, D., Dietz, G., Gillespie, N. and Lewicki, R.J. (eds) (2010). *Organizational Trust: A Cultural Perspective*. Cambridge: Cambridge University Press.

Schein, E.H. (1969). *Process Consultation: Its Role in Organizations' Development*. Reading, MA: Addison-Wesley.

Sturdy, A. (1997). The consultancy process: an insecure business? *Journal of Management Studies*, *34*(3), 389–413.

Vera, D. and Crossan, M. (2004). Theatrical improvisation: lessons for organizations. *Organization Studies*, *25*(5), 727–49.

Von Nordenflycht, A. (2010). What is a professional service firm? Toward a theory and taxonomy of knowledge-intensive firms. *Academy of Management Review*, *35*(1), 155–74.

Weick, K.E. (1993). The collapse of sensemaking in organizations: the Mann Gulch disaster. *Administrative Science Quarterly*, *38*(4), 628–52.

Weick, K.E. (1995). *Sensemaking in Organizations*. London: Sage Publications.

Weick, K.E., Sutcliffe, K.M. and Obstfeld, D. (2005). Organizing and the process of sensemaking. *Organization Science*, *16*(4), 409–21.

Werr, A. and Schilling, A. (2011). 'Talent factories' and 'expert houses': patterns of human resource management in professional service firms. In IPOB (ed.), *The Future of Knowledge-intensive Service Work: Theory and Practice of Managing Human and Organizational Resources* (pp. 127–52). Marburg: Metropolis.

Williams, M. (2007). Building genuine trust through interpersonal emotion management: a threat regulation model of trust and collaboration across boundaries. *Academy of Management Review*, *32*(2), 595–621.

6. Making sense of war and peace: from extreme distrust to institutional trust in Aceh, Indonesia

Kirsten Mogensen

At the end of every violent conflict, leaders must help citizens make sense of the human suffering and economic hardship that they have endured and thereby help create a foundation for trust between former enemies so that they can live peacefully together.

That was also the challenge leaders faced when the civil war in Aceh, Indonesia, came to an end in 2005.

Representatives of the two conflicting groups chose to tell stories in which life was perceived as better after the war than it had been before, because new institutions would secure the dignity of people. That way they not only made sense of the suffering, but also saved the dignity of fighters, which previous research has found important for trust after a war.

This explorative study contributes to research in trust as a process with analyses of seven episodes extracted from an interview with a government representative and a speech by a rebel spokesman. In these episodes, actors made sense of how they found different bases for trust production throughout decades of war and, later, during peace negotiations and the decommissioning process. In retrospect, it seems as if trust and risk assessment were an ongoing intersubjective process in which trust repertoires were continually adapted.

Analyses of their stories also allow us to discover bases of trust that make sense to people who have experienced high-risk situations. For example, there are indications that religion, faith and spiritual trust may help powerless people deal with the horrors and insecurity caused by civil war. That way, religion can provide an alternative framework for sensemaking during times when institutions cannot support trust.

CREATING MEANING

People who have lived through war often feel a need to discuss and reflect on their experiences (Knorr-Cetina, 1981; Neal, 1998; Schok et al., 2010), and every day people around the world try to make sense of war and reconciliation in interpersonal discussions, academic writing and public speeches. This reasoning is affected by factors such as personal knowledge (Stapel and Marx, 2007), self-esteem, optimism and perceived control (Schok et al., 2010) and nightmares (Grayman et al., 2009), and by literature such as Leo Tolstoy's *War and Peace* (1869). Schok et al. (2010) found in a study of 1561 Dutch veterans that they tried to incorporate their military experiences into a meaningful, coherent life narrative, and that social approval after homecoming made that process easier. When threatening events are interpreted as meaningful, veterans tend to experience more trust and less distrust.

Frankl ([1946] 2004, p. 105) wrote that 'Man's search for meaning is the primary motivation in his life', and 'meanings materialize' when we communicate, according to Weick et al. (2005). In retrospect, people strive to create convincing narratives of what has happened based on a selection of previously bracketed observations. The narrative is not an objective account: it is adapted to the communication context and it is constantly redrafted 'so that it becomes more comprehensive, incorporates more of the observed data, and is more resilient in the face of criticism' (Weick et al., 2005). Swidler (1986, p. 284) writes that 'culture provides a repertoire of capacities from which varying strategies of action may be constructed'. The retention from sensemaking is 'used as a source of guidance for further action and interpretation' (Weick et al., 2005), including perception of relevant trust repertoires (Fuglsang and Jagd, 2015).

BASES OF TRUST

In this chapter, trust is understood as 'confidence in one's own expectations' (Luhmann, 1979, p. 4) that the trustee will behave in accordance with positive expectations (Lewicki et al., 1998). The term 'trust form' is used to denote different bases of trust. Referring to Schütz (1962) and Garfinkel (1963), Zucker (1986) writes that trust has two major components: (1) background expectations, including shared symbols and shared interpretive frames; and (2) constitutive expectations, including intersubjective meaning and independence from self-interest; and she suggests that trust be measured in terms of indicators, for example indicators associated with characteristic, process and institutional-based modes of trust production.

The first two are based on reciprocity (Douglas Creed and Miles, 1996; Zucker, 1986). Trust based on characteristic involves a sense of belonging to a social group with shared characteristics, for example ethnicity, and an expectation that others within the group will behave in accordance with certain familiar norms. This form of trust is indicated in the narratives when informants distinguish between social groups. Process-based trust develops best in smaller, homogeneous communities where people interact repeatedly over a long time and in that process develop mutual expectations. It was widespread in preindustrial societies and it is indicated when, for example, informants mention once taken-for-granted social exchange processes in villages, or how a limited number of individuals were successfully involved in negotiations over a shorter period of time. In families and small villages where people have lived together all their lives, expectations are based on familiarity (Luhmann, 1979). Violation of positive expectations produces a 'sense of disruption of trust, of profound confusion' (Zucker, 1986). However, breach of trust will only lead to distrust if the trustor expects such violations to be intentional and to continue (Luhmann, 1979; Zucker, 1986). Interpersonal trust (or distrust) is indicated in the narratives when informants describe personal relationships.

In industrial societies where people interact outside their own social community, institutional trust substitutes or supplements process-based trust (Zucker, 1986). It is tied to formal social structures such as bureaucracy, regulations and professional accreditation. Institutional-based trust is indicated in the narratives when formal structures are a pre-condition for trusting behaviour. Research indicates that where the institutional framework is weak, actors tend to rely on personal power in inter-organizational relationships, while in a strong institutional environment they might choose trust (Bachmann, 2001).

Islam plays a very important role in Aceh and also in the analysed narratives. The term 'religion' refers here to the institutions and dogmas related to faith. Surveys indicate that where political and governmental institutions are not considered trustworthy, actors look to religious leaders for trustworthy advice (Gilani, 2013; Ferrett, 2005), and recent research suggests that especially poor, powerless people, who have experienced extreme hardship, tend to use a religious framework in their meaning-making (Hyndman, 2009; Oishi and Diener, 2014; Stephens et al., 2013). Faith is, according to Kvanvig (2016, p. 12), 'a disposition to act in service of an ideal'. To practise a religion and be faithful does not necessarily require trust, but faithful people will try to follow commands, and if a command is to trust or distrust other people, including strangers and enemies, the faithful do so. Spiritual trust is willingness to trust supernatural advice and it is based on an inner knowing, which mystics refer to as intuition (Bailey, 1951; Helminski, 1999). Kvanvig (2016, p. 20) writes that some spiritual practices may be linked to trust, for example Stoic apatheia: 'Such an attitude toward the universe as a whole can display one's trust in the created order and in whomever or whatever is responsible for that order.' Peters (2003) compares apatheia with the Sufi tradition *tawakkul*. Sufism emphasizes the importance of trust in God and His plan, including 'trust in greater guidance' (Helminski, 1999). The term 'spiritual trust' is borrowed from Bailey (2013), who writes that in ancient Africa it included people's 'trust in their capability to arrive at the truth'. Spiritual trust is indicated in the narratives when informants specifically refer to the perception of supernatural advice in a vulnerable situation where trusting is linked to serious risk.

When faced with risky situations, actors can choose between different trust repertoires, according to Mizrachi et al. (2007, p. 144). They suggest that the practice of trusting is shaped by three interrelated dimensions: (1) social actors' ability to 'choose and apply strategies of trust in different social contexts'; (2) a cultural 'repertoire of symbols and practices from which forms of trust are selected, composed, and applied'; and (3) 'power and the political context, which shapes both the choice and the meaning attached to a particular form of trust'.

During a national crisis, people often do not know whom to trust and what to believe (Neal, 1998). Such lack of confidence in expectations can be paralysing (Luhmann, 1979). Bachmann and Inkpen (2011) write that when the breakdown in trust has been at macro-level, the repair work must take place at macro-level in order to capture the core problem. From this perspective, organizations can build or repair trust relations by using institutional structures that reduce 'the risk of misplaced trust' (p. 285). Examples of such structures are legal regulations and community norms, structures and procedures. Bachmann and Inkpen (2011, p. 285) write:

> [I]nstitutions help to establish ... shared explicit and tacit knowledge between the trustor and the trustee. In these circumstances, an individual or collective actor finds good reasons to trust another actor, individual or collective, because institutional arrangements are ... capable of *reducing* – which is not the same as eliminating! – the risk that a trustee will behave untrustworthily, allowing the trustor to actually make a leap of faith and invest trust in the relationship.

Govier and Verwoerd (2002) suggest that post-conflict reconciliation 'may be understood as involving centrally the building or rebuilding of trust'. Maintaining a working relationship is per definition an ongoing process.

METHODOLOGY

Life stories are constantly evolving products. Each time people tell their stories, the elements and interpretations may change to match new circumstances. In this study, two people – who used to speak on behalf of conflicting parties in the 30-year war in Aceh – have tried to make sense of the peace process for an international audience. In doing so, they used their own life experiences to create narratives which indicate changing forms of trust and trust repertoire. Circumstances have required that the informants exercise a larger span of trust repertoire in their lives than most people do and their stories are therefore especially useful for an explorative study of trust and sensemaking in a war and reconciliation context. The two informants are:

1. Free Aceh Movement (GAM) Representative Irwandi Yusuf, born in Aceh in 1960 and with a Master's degree in veterinary science from Oregon State University, USA. In the analyses, I use quotes from his speech at the final decommissioning ceremony in Banda Aceh in December, 2005 (Yusuf, 2005). The speech was written with both the Acehnese and the international audience in mind.
2. Senior Representative for the Government of Indonesia to Aceh, Minister Sofyan Djalil. Djalil was born in Aceh in 1953 and has a PhD from The Fletcher School of Law and Diplomacy, Tufts University, USA. He was interviewed in his office in Jakarta, Indonesia on 1 February 2006. The interview was recorded and transcribed by me. Interviewing with me was Professor Emeritus Scott Thompson, Tufts University, who knew Djalil from his time in the USA. We drafted a news story that was never published, but our manuscript is used as a foundation for the case descriptions in this chapter because it is the best possible evidence of how we perceived Djalil to have made sense of the war and peace process at the beginning of 2006. The transcribed interview has been consulted in order to qualify the interpretations.

During the implementation of the peace process in the autumn of 2005, I was chief press officer for the Aceh Monitoring Mission (AMM), an organization created at the request of the conflicting parties in order to monitor and facilitate the peace process. I participated on a regular basis in meetings with both parties and drafted some of the official documents. In the analyses I will draw on my observations.

Process studies are usually longitudinal and can be 'approached as situated sequences of activities' (Langeley and Tsoukas, 2010). This case study is divided into three temporal sections: 1953–75, 1976–2004 and 2005. Each section starts with a short description of the situation seen from a macro-perspective, followed by one or more micro-level descriptions and my interpretation of which trust forms are indicated. Inspired by the methodology used by Fuglsang and Jagd (2015), the trust repertoires are interpreted on the basis of the described enactment and selection in each case description.

FAITHFUL VILLAGE LIFE: 1953–76

Aceh is an old sultanate that for centuries has fought for its autonomy, first in struggles with colonial powers and then with various Indonesian governments. Islamic religious leaders traditionally play important roles in the Acehnese society, and they primarily want autonomy in the fields of religion, customary law and education. In the 1950s and 1960s, different groups were involved in guerrilla wars against the Indonesian government, including the Islamic Armed Forces of Indonesia, Darum Islam, which was supported by Aceh's political and religious elites (Hillman, 2012). It is assumed that the rebels at one time were in control of most of the countryside in Aceh, while cities were controlled by the Indonesian government. Looking back to this period of time, Minister Sofyan Djalil had fond memories of a childhood in a small Acehnese village, where he grew up as the youngest of five siblings.

Episode 1

> The family lived in a wooden house built on poles so animals from the jungle could not enter the living room. Poultry lived under the house, and on the outskirts of the village were the rice fields, of which a small part belonged to the family.

> His father was the imam in the *meunasah* – a house where men in the villages in Aceh traditionally meet to recite the Qur'an – and every night the village kids would gather in his home where his mother would teach them to read the Qur'an. 'I was very close with my mom. She is very smart, wise, and I never experienced my mother scolded me.' He went to school with his three years older brother, and both were later trained as religious teachers.

Some of the Darum Islam rebels lived in Djalil's village, but they moved out when the military came, and Djalil says that the conflict did not torment him during his childhood because the parties did not fight directly in the village. What was the most frightening for him as a child was when a tiger from the jungle killed the family dog. 'I had a very happy childhood,' he recalls.

The description implies that faith was important for the peasants in the village and that life was structured around religious practices. The Darum Islam fighters that claimed to be in control of the countryside wanted obedience to the Sharia, and at micro-level Djalil's parents played important roles in teaching the religious dogma. Village life was also regulated by mutual expectations based on established processes: for example, the rebels routinely left the village when the military arrived to avoid fighting within the village. The villagers were vulnerable in the conflict, and it was risky to trust the rebels.

The withdrawal can be interpreted as a 'gift' to the villagers in exchange for inclusion in the community. Characteristics were important in deciding whom to trust. Rebels belonged to the community, while the soldiers came from outside. The surrounding jungle – home to wild animals as well as fighters – was not a safe place for children to wander in. Trustworthy, then, was everything familiar within the village border, and the evil came from outside. On an interpersonal level, Djalil was especially close to his mother and the brother who was closest to him in age. These two people play important roles as (dis)trustees throughout Djalil's war and peace narrative. Whenever there is reference to a brother below, it is this brother.

ERUPTION OF TRUST: 1976–2004

Dispute over the distribution of oil revenues triggered GAM's violent uprising in 1976, and in order to crush the movement, the Indonesian government used very heavy-handed military reprisals against villagers suspected to be supporters of GAM. Generations of Acehnese children grew up in fear of going to work in the rice fields, and of kidnapping, rape and extortion by either GAM or the Indonesian National Armed Forces (Jeffery, 2012; Hillman, 2012; Sindre, 2013). The number of deaths caused by the conflict is not known, but sources estimate 10 000–33 000 lives (Amnesty International, 2013; Jeffery, 2012). Attempted peace talks failed, partly due to mutual distrust (Schiff, 2014). For long periods families were separated, and foreigners were advised not to travel to Aceh because it was too dangerous. Almost every family in Djalil's childhood district became affected by the military crackdown on the rebels, and the popular support for GAM grew. Djalil's brother joined the rebels and later fled with his family because he was wanted by the Indonesian counterinsurgency. At this time, Djalil was a graduate student in the USA, and he did not know that his brother had joined GAM until he received a phone call from Malaysia in 1990.

Episode 2

Djalil:

I heard his voice – he talked to me in such a different way – at that time he was very radical and believed in what he fought for. He would only speak to me in the Acehnese language, and I would only speak to him in Indonesian. That showed our political differences.

I do not support the idea of tribal or national attachment. Before I went to school, I knew I was part of a village. Then I learned that my village was part of Aceh and in school I learned that Aceh is part of Indonesia. Later I learned that Indonesia is part of the world, and I see myself as part of the world community.

This is an example of how a phone conversation can transform interpersonal trust into distrust. Because trust is linked to perception, Djalil continued to trust his brother until he learned about his links to GAM and realized that they belonged to conflicting groups in the civil war, so that it could be life threatening to trust.

Years later, trust in his childhood village was also disrupted. It was 2003 and Djalil was back in Indonesia. One day he attended an anniversary at a factory three hours from the village, and on the way back he decided to visit his mother whom he had not visited for five years. He was accompanied by the driver and one guard.

Episode 3

When they were only one kilometre from his village, the driver refused to turn down the village road. He said that he did not feel good about it. Shortly after, the driver stopped and asked if he should continue to the village despite his feelings.

Djalil:

'I said: No! If you do not feel good about it, then we will not visit my village and my mom. The guy who accompanied me was so angry with the driver, because we passed the road. I said no, it is okay.'

They drove on, and when they shortly afterwards came to a larger town on the road, Djalil received information that his mother had tried to warn him not to go to his village because somebody had been kidnapped in the area the night before. A few days later, a journalist and a cameraman were kidnapped and kept for one year. At this time, GAM was a well organized movement and GAM activists were moved from one area to another, so in Djalil's childhood village now lived many who did not know him.

Djalil:

'If I had turned, I would most certainly have been kidnapped. I believe it was an intervention of supernatural power that prevented us from driving to the village. If I had turned right, they would have taken me, and then I would not have been minister.'

As a student in Boston in the 1990s, Djalil had adopted a Sufi perspective on the world.

Djalil:

'Sufi wisdom says that what you achieve is because of God's will alone. We are like people thrown into the river. Our job is to make us flow. If you are suddenly thrown into one place, then do your best.'

Fighters from other areas had settled in the village, and these immigrants disrupted the old process-based trust in the village. This interpretation is in line with Zucker's (1986) observation that immigration of people with diverse cultures had a disrupting effect on process-based trust in rural America in the 1800s. Djalil's mother – who used to play an important role in the village – no longer trusted her fellow citizens enough to risk her son's visit, which implies a decline in her status. Such sensemaking at micro-level reinforced the perception of internal armed conflict (ICRC, 2012) at macro-level.

It was a high-risk situation: they were vulnerable. Djalil received advice from two co-travellers with different opinions, and was faced with the dilemma of whom to rely on. Mayer et al. (1995) describe three factors influencing the perception of trustworthiness: ability, benevolence and integrity. However, the narrative provides no clues to Djalil's perception of his co-travellers on these three parameters, which indicates that they were not important in the retrospective sensemaking. He chose to listen to the driver, and the determining argument – as recalled by Djalil three years later – was the driver's expression of his intuitive negative feeling. The guard was frustrated with the driver's lack of obedience, but if Djalil had chosen to rely on the guard instead of the driver, their lives would have been in danger.

The driver may have had any number of reasons – some of which had nothing to do with spirituality – for saying that he did not feel good about driving to the village. The important information here is that Djalil interpreted it as a sign of supernatural interference, because such an interpretation requires trust in the ability and willingness of supernatural powers to engage in human lives. This example shows that just as in other vulnerable situations where trusting is risky, spiritual trust is based on an instant cognitive evaluation of a complex situation. It is neither a question of faithfully following commands, nor of referring to religious leaders and scriptures.

This case is different from one discussed by Mayer et al. (1995) about a farmer and the weather. In their opinion, a farmer cannot trust the weather 'because there is no relationship with an identifiable "other party" to which the farmer would make himself or herself vulnerable'. The difference between the supernatural and the weather as described in these cases is that the supernatural is perceived as intending to interfere in the lives of individual humans, while the weather is not. That also means that the supernatural in this case can be perceived as trustworthy or not using Mayer et al.'s criteria of ability, benevolence and integrity, while the weather cannot. We know from studies of religions that people have different perceptions of the ontology of divine and supernatural phenomena. Trust is always based on the perception of the trustor, and in this case Djalil perceived the supernatural as an entity with the ability to guide and a willingness to help him. A hint of determinism was added because he mentioned that he could not have taken part in the peace process as a minister had he been kidnapped.

The rebels felt that they had good reason to fight with heavy tools. Looking at a collection of automatic rifles, GAM representative Irwandi Yusuf said in 2005:

Episode 4

> When we in GAM started the fight for the better life and dignity for Acehnese, we needed heavy tools such as the weapons here. Those were years of hardship, and our weapons have served their purposes of bringing up Acehnese to this position, a dignified one.

People who are perceived as threatening one's dignity are not considered trustworthy (British Council, 2012), and GAM did not trust institutions to secure their dignity, so they chose to rely on hard power. This sensemaking reflects Bachmann's (2001) findings that if there are no strong institutions to support trust in trans-organizational relations, then people tend to rely more on their own power. From a reconciliation perspective, it seems important that Yusuf recognized the value of GAM's fight. If

Acehnese veterans reacted similarly to Dutch veterans, such recognition may have made them less distrustful towards the peace process (Schok et al., 2010).

RECONCILIATION: 2005

Peace talks started in the autumn of 2004. At that time Yusuf was a political prisoner in Banda Aceh, but when the Indian Ocean tsunami claimed an estimated 168 000 Acehnese lives in December 2004, he managed to escape (Hillman, 2012). At that time, international humanitarian help was badly needed, and the government feared that if any of the foreign aid workers were kidnapped, all the foreign aid workers would leave the region, so peace talks were intensified. Former Finnish President Martti Ahtisaari, Chairman of the Board of Directors of the Crisis Management Initiative, was asked to facilitate the negotiations. Djalil was part of the five-man Indonesian delegation, and he recounts how trust gradually developed during the months of negotiations in Helsinki.

Episode 5

'The first meeting was actually nothing but expressions of anger. That was to be predicted when you meet for the first time after 30 years of conflict. All dirty words were used. We were prepared for that and had agreed to keep quiet.'

As negotiations progressed, social manners improved, according to Djalil.

'After negotiations we often had coffee together; during prayer and lunchtime we kept talking to them. Being an Acehnese had some plusses and some minuses in the negotiation talks. On one hand, it was much easier for me to talk with GAM representatives because we were attached to the area, talked the same dialect and had similar cultural background. On the other hand, people would think that I was partial.'

Djalil summarized the lessons learned from the negotiations:

'First, the approach in negotiations must be dignity to all. We never said: "surrender or we beat you." Dignity is very important to Acehnese; we must respect the person. Second, there must be a professional facilitator. Third, it is very important to be eye-to-eye in one room so that you learn how the other party feels and what is important to them. And you must be patient – continue to communicate.'

This text implies that key actors in the peace process consciously co-created bases for trusting, including institutional, process, characteristic and interpersonal. The institutional framework for the peace process was backed by international hard power such as security around the negotiations, disaster relief, technical skills and expertise in many fields, as well as international soft power. This institutional framework was an umbrella for the other bases of trust production that were equally important for the success, but which could not have evolved without the pressure and guarantees provided by a powerful international community. The process contributed to a trusting environment. The chairman allowed, for example, GAM representatives to express their anger over and over again; the Indonesian government representatives had decided not to retaliate, and Finland provided security. To allow people to express themselves verbally without fear can be perceived as respect for their dignity, and both informants stress that dignity is very important for the Acehnese.

Djalil was Acehnese and therefore belonged to the same ethnicity as GAM representatives. He spoke Acehnese, understood the body language, had grown up within the same religion and was familiar with the cultural frames of interpretation. Furthermore, a number of key people involved in the peace process, including Djalil and the GAM leadership, were well educated and had spent years in Western countries, so they shared many characteristics. The actors were eye to eye in the room, so they could get to know each other, and the breaks also provided an opportunity for development of interpersonal trust.

The peace process strategy was to gradually build confidence and trust between GAM and the Indonesian government (Schiff, 2014). In August 2005, a Memorandum of Understanding was signed. In the following months, GAM handed over 840 weapons for decommissioning, while the government withdrew non-organic police and troops from the province. Djalil's brother was among the exiled GAM activists who returned home. The following is my eyewitness account from one of several weapon collections that took place throughout Aceh in the autumn of 2005.

Episode 6

The young men came voluntarily from the jungle to hand in their weapons and see them destroyed.

The scene was the football field in a small village in Aceh surrounded by cacao trees and coconut palms, jungle and streams. Here were women with colourful scarves and men wearing Acehnese hats with beautiful embroidery.

The jungle drums had carried the message to the nearby villages, and hundreds of onlookers lined up to witness the former guerrilla fighters hand their weapons over to the international staff of the Aceh Monitoring Mission, who then checked, registered and cut the weapons into pieces.

Djalil was in the field talking with the national media, the former guerrilla fighters, and the monitors from ASEAN and the EU. Afterwards, when the helicopter with VIPs left the scene, he instinctively helped the monitors hold onto the decommissioning tent, so it did not blow away. He was not going with the helicopter; he would sleep in a small wooden house in his childhood village.

That day, the rice field was transformed into a meeting place for people who used to fear each other and, by showing up, they all demonstrated trust. The rebels who handed in their weapons dared to do so – even though that made them vulnerable – because they trusted the institutional framework. A key element in that was transparency; that is to say, the weapons were cut by international monitors in public to avoid rumours about what happened to them, and Djalil demonstrated respect for the monitors by helping with practical tasks like holding on to a tent pole. In the crowd were many villagers who had for years not dared to leave their homes but who now found it safe to face the rebels and the soldiers from a short distance. The presence of high-level representatives for the different parties at each weapon collection not only signalled the overall power behind the institution, but their behaviour towards each other – that they cooperated and talked casually – also signalled cooperation. The image of reconciliation was broadcast around Aceh and the rest of the world, because there were generally dozens of journalists present at decommissioning sites.

Djalil also demonstrated recovered trust in the villagers by sleeping there. Djalil later said that when he returned to his village after the peace agreement, he was heartily received. Numerous well-wishers came to see him. He is not sure if it was because of the peace agreement or simply because he was a village boy returning to the village as a minister.

To celebrate the completion of the decommissioning process, a cere-mony was organized at Blang Padang Sports Field in Banda Aceh in December 2005. Former GAM fighters and international monitors were lined up, the rebels' last weapons were cut to pieces and, in Aceh, families had gathered around their radios to listen to the VIP speeches. Yusuf made an effort to explain why, on one hand, the suffering endured through 30 years of civil war was meaningful, and why, on the other hand, reconciliation now made more sense. He did so by referring to the process of crafting traditional Aceh furniture. He said:

Episode 7

> I know a craftsman who makes beautiful chairs for the sitting room. They are
> made of wood which is carved to fit the eyes and cushioned to provide
> comfort to the body. A number of different tools are used to make such a
> wonderful Acehnese chair.
>
>   First, the craftsman must cut the tree and it requires a strong saw,
> preferably a machine saw. It is hard work. But as the process continues and
> tree has become a chair, the big saw is no longer an appropriate tool. Using a
> strong machine saw on the fine woodcutting of the chair is not advisable
> because it will destroy the beauty of the chair. In this phase, the craftsman
> needs lighter tools. In the end, the craftsman only needs fine sandpaper and
> oil to polish the chair.
>
> We can compare the creation of such a chair with the creating of a good
> society here in Aceh.

In Yusuf's tale, the machine saw was later compared to the heavy
weapons used by GAM fighters. They had been necessary, but they had
done their work and it was time for these 'heroes' to retire. Now it was
time for political tools and democracy to replace them. Yusuf was later
elected governor of the Indonesian Province of Aceh (2007–12), which
indicates that the Acehnese trusted him.

   It is worth noting that Yusuf introduced the crafting of Acehnese
furniture as a metaphor in retrospective sensemaking. GAM's strategy
seems to have emerged as events happened over the years (Sindre, 2013),
but by the end of 2005 it was possible, with a 'retrospective attention', to
describe the process as a logical line of events.

CONCLUSION AND DISCUSSION

Acehnese peasants of the 1950s and 1960s could base trust on familiarity
with the characteristics and norms of the group to which they belonged.
The civil war between GAM and the Indonesian government disrupted
these traditional forms of trust for a number of reasons, such that
members supported conflicting parties and that fighters moved around. It
may be argued that process- and characteristic-based trust was recreated
in new communities, such as among GAM fighters and among soldiers.
However, for civil society, the creation of institutional structures backed
by international hard power was paramount for recreation of trust.

   In this study, trustors were constantly forced to make new evaluations,
which shows that trust and risk assessment is an ongoing intersubjective
process. The case studies support Fuglsang and Jagd's (2015) finding that

trust is a dynamic phenomenon in the sense that trust repertoires change when the population faces dramatic events at macro-level. In Aceh, events at macro-level – such as the upstart of extraction of natural resources and the tsunami – impacted patterns of trusting at micro-level. Micro-level risk and trust assessments were what gradually changed the perception at macro-level. Analysis of seven episodes demonstrates how trust repertoires from one period were carried into the next, where they were often experienced as inadequate, which caused frustration. In the years 1976 to 2004, trust-related frustrations were caused by violations of positive expectations, while unfounded distrust had to be overcome in the peace process. However, trust repertoires from each situation were remembered and could be re-enacted when situations at macro-level again made them relevant, such as Djalil's trusting behaviour in dealing with villagers. This seems to indicate that an individual will store trust repertoires from situations experienced throughout life so that the treasure chest will contain a wide variety of trust repertoires reflecting a person's life experiences.

It appears from the case study that when strong institutions were missing and therefore could not support trusting, religion and trust in a divine order could provide an alternative base for sensemaking and trust among poor, powerless people, which seems to be in accordance with the previous findings (Ferrett, 2005; Gilani, 2013; Oishi and Diener, 2014; Stephens et al., 2013). While the inferences of spiritual trust vary for different cultures and individuals, in general, religion, faith and spiritual trust may reduce complexity and help people deal with the anxiety of chaotic circumstances at the macro-level. We will need more empirical studies that explore the role of spirituality in relation to trusting because a better understanding of the links between institutional trust, spiritual trust and hard power may be useful for international post-conflict work.

The analyses of the peace process in 2005 show that it was possible to consciously build institutions that supported trust. However, the success depended on the ability of the leaders to persuade their followers to support the peace process, and in Aceh both parties were fortunate to have key people with communication skills. The successful narratives told citizens that life was better after than before the war. That way they made sense of the suffering and saved the dignity of fighters. Other empirical studies may help determine whether the creation of convincing narratives generally can be used as a tool in trust repair efforts.

ACKNOWLEDGEMENT

I am grateful to Dr Sofyan Djalil for sharing his insights; Professor Scott Thompson for research cooperation; Dr Poul Bitsch Olsen for suggestions related to the analyses; the editors and anonymous reviewers for their constructive comments. A previous version was presented to the 8th FINT/EIASM Conference on Trust Within and Between Organizations, Coventry, UK, 2014, and I thank everyone who contributed with reviews and suggestions in that context.

REFERENCES

Amnesty International (2013). Time to face the past: justice for past abuses in Indonesia's Aceh Province. [Online] Available from: http://www.amnesty.org/en/library/asset/ASA21/001/2013/en/5a7956bb-be04-494a-85e20c02d555b58e/asa210012013en.pdf (accessed 2 June 2014).

Bachmann, R. (2001). Trust, power and control in trans-organizational relations. *Organization Studies*, 22 (2), 337–65.

Bachmann, R. and Inkpen, A.C. (2011). Understanding institutional-based trust building process in inter-organizational relationships. *Organization Studies*, 32 (2), 281–301.

Bailey, A.A. (1951). *Initiation, Human and Solar*. New York: Lucis Press.

Bailey, J.A. (2013). Spiritual trust. [Online] Available from: http://www.blackvoice news.com/columnists/joseph-a-bailey-ii-md/48928-spiritual-trust.html (accessed 24 May 2014).

British Council (2012). *Trust Pays: How International Cultural Relationships build Trust in the UK and Underpin the Success of the UK Economy*. London: British Council.

Douglas Creed, W.E. and Miles, R.E. (1996). A conceptual framework linking organizational forms, managerial philosophies, and the opportunity costs of control. In: Kramer, R.M. and Tyler, T.R. (eds), *Trust in Organizations: Frontiers of Theory and Research*. Thousand Oaks, CA: Sage Publications, pp. 16–38.

Ferrett, G. (2005). Africans trust religious leaders. [Online] Available from: http://news.bbc.co.uk/2/hi/africa/4246754.stm (accessed 24 May 2014).

Frankl, V.E. ([1946] 2004). *Man's Search for Meaning*. London: Rider.

Fuglsang, L. and Jagd, S. (2015). Making sense of institutional trust in organizations: bridging institutional context and trust. *Organization*, 22 (1), 23–39.

Garfinkel, H. (1963). A conception of and experiments with 'trust' as a condition of stable concerted actions. In: Harvey, O.J. (ed.), *Motivation and Social Interaction: Cognitive Determinants*. New York: Ronald Press, pp. 187–239.

Gilani (2013). Trust and Confidence Index 2013: Religious Leaders, Educational Institutions and Media Enjoy High Trust from the Public, NGOs Rank Low.

Gilani Poll/Gallup Pakistan. [Online] Available from: http://site. gilanifoundation. com/?p=1719 (accessed 24 May 2014).

Govier, T. and Verwoerd, W. (2002). Trust and the problem of national reconciliation. *Philosophy of the Social Sciences*, 32 (2), 178.

Grayman, J.H., Good, M.D. and Good, B.J. (2009). Conflict nightmares and trauma in Aceh. *Culture, Medicine & Psychiatry*, 33 (2), 290–312.

Helminski, K. (1999). *The Knowing Heart: A Sufi Path of Transformation.* Boston, MA: Shambhala.

Hillman, B. (2012). Power-sharing and political party engineering in conflict-prone societies: the Indonesian experiment in Aceh. *Conflict, Security and Development*, 12 (2), 149–69.

Hyndman, J. (2009). Siting conflict and peace in post-tsunami Sri Lanka and Aceh, Indonesia. *Norwegian Journal of Geography*, 63 (1), 89–96.

ICRC (2012). Internal conflicts or other situations of violence – what is the difference for victims? [Online] Available from: http://www.icrc.org/eng/ resources/documents/interview/2012/12-10-niac-non-international-armed-conflict.htm (accessed 7 May 2014).

Jeffery, R. (2012). Amnesty and accountability: the price of peace in Aceh, Indonesia. *International Journal of Transitional Justice*, 6 (1), 60–82.

Knorr-Cetina, K. (1981). Introduction: the micro-sociological challenge of macro-sociology: towards a reconstruction of social theory and methodology. In: Knorr-Cetina, K. and Cicourel, A.V. (eds), *Advances in Social Theory and Methodology: Towards an Integration of Micro- and Macro-Sociologies.* Boston, MA: Routledge & Kegan Paul, pp. 1–48.

Kvanvig, J.L. (2016). The idea of faith as trust: lessons in noncognitivist approaches to faith. In: Bergmann, M. and Brower, J. (eds), *Reason and Faith: Themes from Richard Swinburne*. Oxford: Oxford University Press.

Langeley, A. and Tsoukas, H. (2010). Introducing perspectives on process organization studies. In: Hernes, T. and Maitlis, S. (eds), *Process, Sense-making and Organization*. Oxford: Oxford University Press, pp. 1–26.

Lewicki, R., McAllister, D. and Bies, R. (1998). Trust and distrust: new relationships and realities. *Academy of Management Review*, 23 (3), 438–58.

Luhmann, N. (1979). *Trust and Power: Two Works by Niklas Luhmann. With Introduction by Gianfranco Poggi*. Chichester: John Wiley & Sons.

Mayer, R.C., Davis, J.H. and Schoorman, F.D. (1995). An integrative model of organizational trust. *The Academy of Management Review*, 20 (3), 709–34.

Mizrachi, N., Drori, I. and Anspach, R.R. (2007). Repertoires of trust: the practice of trust in a multinational organization amid political conflict. *American Sociological Review*, 72 (1), 143–65.

Neal, A.G. (1998). *National Trauma & Collective Memory: Major Events in the American Century*. New York: M.E. Sharpe.

Oishi, S. and Diener, E. (2014). Residents of poor nations have a greater sense of meaning in life than residents of wealthy nations. *Psychological Science*, 25 (2), 422–30.

Peters, F.E. (2003). *Islam: A Guide for Jews and Christians*. Princeton, NJ: Princeton University Press.

Schiff, A. (2014). Reaching a mutual agreement: readiness theory and coalition building in the Aceh peace process. *Negotiation and Conflict Management Research*, 7 (1), 57–82.

Schok, M.L., Kleber, R.J. and Lensvelt-Mulders, G. (2010). A model of resilience and meaning after military deployment: personal resources in making sense of war and peacekeeping experiences. *Aging & Mental Health*, 14 (3), 328–38.

Schütz, A. (1962). On multiple realities. In: Natanson, M. (ed.), *Collected Papers, 1: The Problem of Social Reality*. The Hague: Martinus Nijhoff, pp. 207–59.

Sindre, G.M. (2013). Rebels and aid in the context of peacebuilding and humanitarian disaster: a comparison of the Free Aceh Movement (GAM) and the Tamil Tigers (LTTE). *Forum for Development Studies*, 41 (1), 1–21.

Stapel, D.A. and Marx, D.M. (2007). Making sense of war: using the interpretation comparison model to understand the Iraq conflict. *European Journal of Social Psychology*, 37 (3), 401–20.

Stephens, N.M., Fryberg, S.A., Markus, H.R. and Hamedani, M.G. (2013). Who explains Hurricane Katrina and the Chilean Earthquake as an Act of God? The experience of extreme hardship predicts religious meaning-making. *Journal of Cross-Cultural Psychology*, 44 (4), 606–19.

Swidler, A. (1986). Culture in action: symbols and strategies. *American Sociological Review*, 51 (2), 273–86.

Tolstoy, L. (1869). *War and Peace*. New York: Random House.

Weick, K.E., Sutcliffe, K.M. and Obstfeld, D. (2005). Organizing and the process of sensemaking. *Organization Science*, 16 (4), 409–21.

Yusuf, I. (2005). Final Decommissioning Ceremony: Speech by GAM Representative, Mr Irwandi Yusuf. [Online] Available from: http://www.aceh-mm.org/download/ english/Speech%20by%20Irwandi.pdf (accessed 5 May 2014).

Zucker, L.G. (1986). Production of trust: institutional sources of economic structure, 1840–1920. *Research in Organizational Behavior*, 8, 53–111.

7. Trust-building in networks as practical social learning processes

Anne H. Gausdal

Trust is considered essential for innovative networks that involve the creation and the sharing of knowledge (Hatak and Roessl, 2010; Newell and Swan, 2000) in a reciprocal way, as it is a significant factor in both sharing and absorbing tacit knowledge (Von Krogh et al., 2000, p. 45). The sharing of tacit knowledge is crucial for knowledge creation (Chung and Jackson, 2011; Nonaka et al., 2000) and when trust runs low, people become more preoccupied with explicit, provable knowledge (Von Krogh, 1998). As trust grows, network participants are increasingly willing to put themselves at risk, for example through intimate disclosure, reliance on the counterpart's promises, or sacrificing present rewards for future gains (Parkhe, 1993). Trust is positively correlated with cooperation and reduced conflict levels; it leads to more cooperative negotiation behaviours and more integrative negotiation outcomes in interpersonal and intergroup negotiations (Lewicki et al., 2003; Ross and LaCroix, 1996). Trust is also crucial for reducing complexity (Luhmann, 1979) and for enriching the participant's opportunities and access to resources (Uzzi, 1997). Trust is therefore a significant governance mechanism in long-term relationships such as networks (Hatak and Roessl, 2010). An important issue is therefore whether – and how – trust can be built or learned in general and in networks in particular. The aim of this chapter is thus to identify trust-building processes in networks, with particular emphasis on practice and the link between intervention methods and such processes.

Within trust research, two traditions of building interpersonal trust exist: the behavioural and the psychological (Lewicki et al., 2006). This study addresses mainly the psychological tradition, which focuses on different factors and characteristics. Personal qualities of the trustor and trustee may induce trust, for example ability, benevolence, integrity (Mayer et al., 1995), sincerity, tactfulness and confidentiality (Moorman et al., 1993). Characteristics of the form of the relationship, past relationships between the parties and their communication processes influence trust-building (Lewicki et al., 2006). Structural parameters that govern the relationship between the parties, for example third parties, may also build trust (Burt, 2001; Ferrin et al., 2006). Trust is created by human interaction (Hardwick et al., 2013), social learning processes (Möllering, 2013) and cooperation (Dirks and Ferrin, 2002; Hardin, 2002; Ross and LaCroix, 1996). Moreover, some defined actions, denoted as trust-builders (Abrams et al., 2003) and trust-building processes in the context of networks (Gausdal, 2012) have been identified. This literature shows that interpersonal trust can be influenced and manipulated through social qualities, characteristics, institutions and interaction. The main focus in this chapter is on social interaction and in particular on practical dialogue-based methods.

The chapter presents and discusses three dialogue-based methods expected to facilitate interpersonal trust through social learning (Möllering, 2013) and interactions as practical activity. Particular emphasis is directed towards what happens when the network participants meet and how the interventions or practices are carried out. The research question is: what are the core practical interventions in dialogue-based methods that facilitate social learning of trust in networks?

The main contribution of the chapter is to increase the understanding of trust-building processes in networks as social learning processes at a practical micro level. There is a need for further studies in complex field settings that assess the change in trust and 'longitudinal qualitative techniques are particularly well suited' (Lewicki et al., 2006, p. 1015). Therefore, to answer the research question, a comparative study with longitudinal data from three Norwegian regional networks has been undertaken.

This chapter is organized as follows: first, the five trust-building processes and three dialogue-based methods are presented. Second, the research method is explained and the findings are laid out. Third and finally, there is a discussion followed by a concluding section.

TRUST-BUILDING PROCESSES AND DIALOGUE-BASED METHODS

Trust is the willingness to be vulnerable to the actions of another, irrespective of the ability to monitor or control that other party (Mayer et al., 1995). Individual learning processes are cognitive or social. Cognitive learning processes are internal, whereas social learning processes happen among individuals in an interactive and performative process in which they observe, reflect upon, make sense of and give feedback to others. Several dialogue-based methods, such as network reflection, network IGP (an acronym for individual, group and plenary reflections) and foresight may contribute to trust because they hold some of the trust-building and social learning processes: connection, communication, direction, temporary groups and resource sharing (Gausdal, 2012).

Connection

Most trust-building processes presuppose that people are connected and in networks the participants involved rarely meet accidentally. Connections may be facilitated actively, for instance they can be set up through group work or by someone playing the procuress role by interviewing people and then connecting them (Wenger et al., 2002). The optimal context for stimulating personal connections and having people learn to trust each other is in small groups (Von Krogh et al., 2000).

Communication

Frequent, rich and collaborative communication is important in building trust. Frequent communication increases the exchange of information in order to assess each other's abilities, intentions and behaviour; hence it 'increase[s] trust in one another's competence' (Abrams et al., 2003, p. 68). The quality of the communication is also important in building trust. Abrams et al. (2003) emphasize the value of face-to-face contact – making interactions meaningful and memorable – as well as the development of close relationships. Collaborative communication – which requires a combination of sharing, inquiring and listening – increases interpersonal trust (Abrams et al., 2003; Gausdal, 2012). The quality of the communication also requires people to be involved and to participate actively when they meet (Gausdal, 2012).

Direction

Shared vision and language seem to increase trust in networks (Abrams et al., 2003; Argyres, 1999; Tsai and Ghoshal, 1998). Language differences are a basic barrier to communication as they affect both the richness and the collectiveness of communication (Wenger et al., 2002). Shared vision and language are reinforced by setting common goals for the network from early on and by utilizing opportunities to learn common terminology and ways of thinking, while at the same time being aware of misunderstandings due to different jargons and thoughts

(Abrams et al., 2003). Groups with common goals develop interdependence among members, which results in the group becoming a
'whole', with an intrinsic tension among the members directed at
reaching the goals (Lewin, 1935). This feeling of wholeness and unity
creates emotional bonding and relationships (Johnsen and Johnsen,
1994).

Temporary Groups

In projects in which each party is dependent on the other, creating
vulnerability, uncertainty and risk, 'the trust necessary to act in the face
of vulnerability will be there quickly' (Meyerson et al., 1996, p. 183).
Trust may thus be learned swiftly over short, intense periods of interaction in temporary groups with time pressure (Meyerson et al., 1996).
Furthermore, to build trust swiftly, stable and standardized roles and
clearly defined tasks are required (Möllering, 2006).

Resource Sharing

Someone who receives trust and good faith usually wishes to be trusting,
loyal and generous in return. Resource sharing, or social exchange, is
distinguished from a strictly economic exchange by its inherent unspeci-
fied obligations, as well as by the fact that it both requires and promotes
trust (Blau, 1986). Taking risks in sharing expertise and tacit or experimental knowledge, giving people access to limited or sensitive resources
when appropriate and being willing to let others access one's personal
network contacts also promotes interpersonal trust (Abrams et al., 2003).

Network Reflection

Network reflection is a method for inter-organizational management
education that is close to Mintzberg's (2004) experienced reflection
(Gausdal, 2008). Experienced reflection is a method for management
education that, in addition to short lectures, seminars and presentations,
includes reflection tasks. During these tasks, the participants reflect on
their practice on their own, collectively in small groups and during class.
The facilitating role here is to prepare the right context (Schön, 1987);
the pedagogy therefore helps to facilitate (Mintzberg and Gosling, 2006).
The network part of this method consists of several network interventions; these may be recruiting participants from a network, a planned ad
hoc lunch intervention in temporary groups at the first seminar, seminars
involving firm presentations, plant visits and network news, as well as

inter-organizational presentations dealing with challenges within the firms, tailoring the content and pedagogy to the participants' expectations and providing participants with the same concepts, literature and lectures as mutual backdrops for communication. Reflection tasks are organized in temporary inter-organizational groups, different for each seminar (Gausdal, 2008). Table 7.1 presents the activities involved in network reflection and relates the activities to their respective trust-building processes.

Table 7.1   Connecting network reflection activities with trust-building processes

Network reflection activity	Trust-building learning process
• Participants meet face to face at several seminars over several months • Reflection tasks organized in temporary inter-organizational groups • Lunch intervention organized in temporary inter-organizational groups • Presentations organized in temporary inter-organizational groups	Connection
• Participants meet face to face at several seminars over several months • Seminars held at various locations, some including plant visits • Lunch intervention organized in temporary inter-organizational groups and requiring participants to work together on non-work topics/issues and share non-work competences and creative ideas • Reflection tasks organized in small temporary inter-organizational groups • Reflection tasks at each seminar requiring reflection and discussion of experience and challenges within the firms, as well as theoretical frameworks • Inter-organizational presentations – dealing with practical challenges within the firms • Presentations organized in temporary inter-organizational groups • Social mingling at informal moments, e.g. breaks and plant visits • Joint meals at seminars • One seminar with overnight stay at a retreat	Communication

Table 7.1 (continued)

Network reflection activity	Trust-building learning process
• Tailoring the content and pedagogy to the participants' expectations, discussed and mapped out at the first seminar • Providing participants with the same concepts, literature and lectures as mutual backdrops for communication by participating in the same class • Firm presentations and network news • Emails to follow up, prepare and motivate for each seminar • Recruiting participants from a cluster network with people from the same industry and the same region, who practise some of the same professions	Direction
• A planned ad hoc intervention at the first seminar on a safe project with a clearly defined target: preparing lunch • Reflection tasks that demand reflection alone or collectively in small groups and during class at a given point in time • Inter-organizational presentations – dealing with practical challenges within the firms	Temporary groups
• Reflection tasks at each seminar requiring sharing, reflection and discussion of experience and challenges within the firms, as well as theoretical frameworks • Lunch intervention requiring participants to work together on non-work topics/issues and share non-work competences and creative ideas	Resource-sharing

As shown in Table 7.1, network reflection appears to include the trust-building learning processes of connection, communication, direction, temporary groups and resource sharing.

Network IGP

Network IGP is developed to support the organic development of network relationships with a sufficient level of trust and to initiate knowledge mobility (Gausdal, 2013). Network IGP is deduced from network reflection (Gausdal, 2008) and inspired by dialogic conferences (Gustavsen, 1992), cooperative learning (Johnsen and Johnsen, 1994) and reflection (Schön, 1983). Network IGP entails a combination of individual and collective reflections on a given topic, problem or question. It consists of four phases: preparation process, individual reflection, group reflection and plenary reflection. First, the participants are divided into inter-organizational groups of three to six and start out with a short

Trust-building in networks as social learning processes

preparation process, including stating their names and their primary task at work, as well as sharing some safe personal information, for example where they live, their favourite leisure activity or their best summer memory. Second, the *individual reflection* is carried out in a given time (for example 3 minutes) on a given topic, problem or question. Third, a collective *group reflection* ensues, which is time-controlled (for example 20 minutes). The collective group reflection starts with talking rounds, in which all the participants share their ideas and suggestions from their individual reflection one by one with limited talking time (1–2 minutes). It continues with normal discussion, perhaps prioritizing answers, and finally the answer to the given topic, problem or question is arrived at. Fourth, the *plenary reflection* consists of short presentations (for example 2 minutes) of the answers from each group, followed by a plenary prioritization and/or discussion. The method therefore includes the trust-building processes of connection, communication, temporary groups and resource sharing. If the method is used to develop visions and goals, it may also entail the process of direction (Gausdal, 2013).

Regional Foresight

Regional foresight is a tailored, participant-based method to promote the understanding of future challenges. The method may be used to generate support for a regional agenda towards R&D and innovation (RCN, 2013). The paramount objective of this support mechanism is to strengthen the region's readiness for the future, including enabling colleges and research institutes to play a part in regional innovation. The objectives pertaining to the different processes will vary, but all the processes should aim at strengthening the quality of the regional cooperation and the regional innovation system and contributing to consensus on the main development tasks (RCN, 2013). It is also common to use foresight to develop joint vision and goals, for example in networks, which is the case in this study. Regional foresight covers a series of process-oriented techniques, that is scenario analyses, brainstorming, consensus conferences, strategy workshops and Delphi surveys. Professional facilitators should assist in the organization and implementation of the method. Regional foresight therefore comprises the trust-building processes of connection, communication, direction and temporary groups. Moreover, if it is used to share tacit knowledge, personal contacts, advice and tips for example, it may also entail the process of resource sharing. As noted above, the three methods comprise several of the trust-building social learning processes. Table 7.2 gives an outline of the methods and their trust-building processes.

Table 7.2   Methods and trust-building processes

Method	Trust-building processes
Network reflection	Connection Communication Direction Temporary groups Resource sharing
Network IGP	Connection Communication (Direction) Temporary groups Resource sharing
Foresight	Connection Communication Temporary groups (Resource sharing) Direction

METHOD

The empirical part of this study contains three longitudinal, mostly qualitative and process-orientated cases. Case study is useful here because the issues examined are very much linked to their contexts (Hartley, 2004). Primary data were collected through in-depth interviews, participatory observation, network facilitation, document studies, long conversations and a survey. The longitudinal data were obtained through the close monitoring of the development processes of the networks by means of participatory observation and action research. Data collection was carried out with informed consent and all transcribed interviews were approved by the informants. In reporting the results, the informants and firms have been made anonymous.

In Arena Healthinnovation (AH), approximately 135 hours were spent on planning and facilitating three interventions, observation and participation in meetings, seminars, 'innovation lunches', foresight workshops and product development workshops. Five in-depth interviews with key informants – CEOs, middle managers and the board – and five long conversations with the AH manager were undertaken. The data collection period lasted five years – from 2008 to 2012.

In Electronic Coast (EC), approximately 732 hours were spent on planning and facilitating the interventions (2001–2002), observation and participation in 44 network meetings (2001–2006), 42 telephone interviews (2004), three personal group interviews (2005) and five personal in-depth interviews (2006). The interviewees for the telephone interviews were programme participants, whereas those for the group interviews were programme participants and management groups in two of the participants' firms and at University College, a total of seven people in all. The data collection period lasted five years, from 2001 to 2006.

In Clean Water Norway (CWN), approximately 540 hours were spent on planning and facilitating several network IGP interventions, observation and participation in team, network and board meetings (2007–2011) and two foresight workshops (2010–2011). In all, 27 telephone interviews and 10 in-depth interviews with 16 informants were undertaken in the period 2008–2012.

In AH and CWN, a group interview with the network board was carried out in late 2011 and a survey was conducted during May to August 2012. In the survey, the current level of trust and whether the firms trusted each other more at that time than they did three years previously were measured on a scale from 1 to 7, where 1 = completely disagree, 4 = neither agree nor disagree and 7 = completely agree. The survey was carried out through an electronic questionnaire addressed to the contact person in all the 12 AH firms and all the 36 CWN firms. From AH, eight answers were received, hence the response rate was 66.7 per cent. From CWN, 21 answers were received, yielding a response rate of 58.3 per cent.

FINDINGS

Three cases illustrate how the dialogue-based methods have been used in practice and show the effects of trust on social learning.

Electronic Coast

Electronic Coast (EC) is committed to arena and network building, with the aim of promoting growth and innovation in the region's electronics-based firms. The electronics firms are mostly classified as small and medium enterprises (SMEs), most of which are sub-suppliers and some are also competitors. The network reflection pedagogy was developed and applied in a management education programme in collaboration between EC and Vestfold University College in 2001–2002. It was a part-time programme (15 ECTS), financed by a participant fee and lasted nine months. The programme consisted of eight seminars, most of which were held during the daytime, although one seminar involved an overnight stay at a retreat. At the first seminar, after just two hours, the *lunch intervention* was enacted; as one participant (representative of others) explained during interviews four years later:

> It worked out well because it was a way of becoming acquainted that did not necessarily depend on who you were in a sense. Consequently, you were not known according to your title or profession, but rather you were just you.

The seminars were held in various locations, including some plant visits, and at each of them firm presentations and network news were agenda items. The main lecturer was present at all the seminars and facilitated the interventions. Attendance at the seminars was high and a sign of the development of affective trust is expressed in the following quotation:

> Gradually, the confidence became so high because you had been working in teams with all the others, you were among friends.

It also seems that the participants found that the building of relationships and trust during the programme was faster than expected. As one of them put it 'I felt that I very quickly got in contact with several of the others'.

Four years after the programme ended, the participants started to cooperate on trust-demanding activities, such as the joint development of products, quality management systems and using each other as mentors, as well as on two regional communities of practice. The 27 participating managers from 14 firms, who at the outset were mostly strangers to each other, increased their cooperation considerably, both during the programme and later on. They established strong and stable communities, presenting high levels of learning and trust, and developed systems to coordinate actions aimed at confronting common problems. The network reflection pedagogy therefore seems to have had a trust-building effect among strangers.

Arena Healthinnovation

Arena Healthinnovation (AH) aims to develop technical solutions covering the future needs for health services, with an emphasis on health promotion and traditional health and care services in private homes or at the place in which the user is currently staying. To develop AH as a network comprising 12 private technology firms, the municipality, the regional university and the regional hospital, five foresight workshops with an overnight stay were organized in 2009 and 2010. The mission was to connect the participants, develop a common vision and strategy, define common unique knowledge and common opportunities, strengthen the sense of connectedness and finally develop joint projects. During the foresight process, activities were mainly carried out in temporary groups. Each group consisted of participants from the different stakeholders and the groups were reorganized at each workshop. The merging of the different stakeholders and logics was a challenge, as reflected in the following comments by one of the firms' CEOs about the first workshop:

> It was very unsettling to be together with the municipality, ergo representatives from a demanding customer. Moreover, suddenly someone from the university was sitting there. What on earth? What are we actually a part of?

Another CEO stated in the early phase:

> We are not really on the same planet as academia. I do not always understand what they want, it is completely different. The cultural gap is huge.

The participants and the network manager all emphasized the importance of the informal social interaction to build relations, such as dining together in the evening.

The results from the foresight workshops are visible above all in greater openness and transparency between the firms, also with respect to their technological platforms. The actors have defined common unique knowledge, common opportunities, common goals and strategies, and common innovation projects. In one of the innovation projects, eight firms are jointly developing new technology in the 16 planned senior citizen housing units in the municipality. In 2012, the private firms established their joint marketing organization. Moreover, according to the manager, 'An insane trust capital has developed among the participants'. In the 2012 survey, the level of trust had a mean value of 6.1 and a mode value of 6 and 7; whether the firms trusted each other more than they did three years previously had a mean value of 6.6 and a mode value of 7 (on a scale of 1–7). One of the firm representatives described the experience in the following manner:

> The process which has been going on to get this all started and to set up some framework and so on ... it is because we have met up, and also partly because we have been sitting in groups and discussing, and partly because we have eaten and drunk together, that we have gotten to know each other a bit and feel we can trust each other to some extent.

Furthermore, one CEO in the AH board declared:

> The trust we have developed allows us to open up the technology process. I
> work in an IT company and we take special care to protect such things, but
> here it is possible to open up and cooperate more than is usual.

During the foresight workshops, several social learning processes among
the participants from different types of stakeholders and cultures took
place. As illustrated above, these processes have contributed to trust
building.

Clean Water Norway

Clean Water Norway (CWN) is a public–private regional network in the
water cleansing industry. Its main aim is to strengthen the value creation
in the network, be a strong supplier to the water and drain industry on a
national scale and become a global actor (CWN, 2011). CWN covers the
value chain from sub-suppliers to systems suppliers, consultants, research
organizations and demanding customers (CWN, 2011). The customer
base covers public sewer plants, public water cleansing plants, construction firms, different kinds of industries producing waste water, shipping
firms and relief organizations. Before CWN was established in 2007,
there was relatively little interaction between the firms (Gausdal and
Hildrum, 2012).

Network IGP was introduced at the first ordinary network meeting in
October 2007 to determine what the main topic at the next meeting
should be. The alternative 'Learning from the Electronic Coast' was
chosen. Therefore, at the next network meeting three representatives from
EC shared their experiences and gave CWN a lot of advice based on their
efforts, gains, pitfalls and successful activities. Subsequently, the EC and
the CWN participants worked together in temporary groups, using
network IGP, to consider how the water firms could utilize CWN in their
value creation. One of the conclusions in the plenary session was that
'network teams must be organized ASAP'. Thus, at the next network
meeting, potential CWN teams were selected and started. Immediately
afterwards, the initial team meetings were organized as a part of the
network meeting, applying network IGP with external trained facilitators.
One informant described this process as follows:

> We were almost forced to sit down in groups and try to get it going, and I
> think probably it was a precondition. If you did not do it that way, I do not
> think we had been sitting with the teams today.

In 2010 the network was in need of a new strategy process. Such a
process was therefore initiated and completed in the spring of 2011,

managed as a light version of foresight, with network IGP as the method for all the group work. To sum up, network IGP was applied 20 times at network and board meetings from 2007 to 2012, each time lasting from 10 to 75 minutes (Gausdal, 2013).

The importance of trust among the network participants seems to have been learned at an early stage, as is also emphasized by one of the CEOs:

> Trust is the keyword. The road to achieving such a high level of trust among us, allowing us to share business ideas and future plans, is long. In CWN we trust that what we tell each other will not be misused. We can therefore utilize each other's competence without negative implications for the firms. This level of trust is the most important result of CWN (RCN, 2010, p. 4).

From 2007 to 2008, the participants showed a great deal of trust-dependent behaviour. CEOs and middle managers contributed actively by sharing their knowledge in temporary groups at network meetings and started to work actively together in network teams. The firms carried out their first joint recruitment campaigns, offered each other the use of their laboratory facilities and started contacting each other to discuss joint customer projects. From 2009 onwards, they also started sharing R&D ideas and challenges, as well as collaborating in several joint R&D projects; for instance, two – partly competitive – firms collaborated with researchers on an R&D project to use new enabling technology, BioMEMS, to identify and measure water pathogens. Furthermore, the firms cooperated in several joint customer projects and one firm invited all the other CWN participants to use their newly established Egypt office (www.vannklyngen.no, 2009). In the 2012 survey, the level of trust had a mean value of 5.3 and mode value of 6; whether the firms trusted each other more than they did three years previously had a mean value of 5.7 and a mode value of 7. The predominant dialogue-based method for developing CWN was network IGP and to a certain degree also foresight. It is reasonable to assume that these processes have contributed to the social learning of trust within CWN.

Comparing the Three Cases

An overview of the context according to relevant theoretical dimensions and how the three cases do (or do not) vary accordingly, is provided in Table 7.3.

Table 7.3   The three cases (networks) and their dimensions

Network/ dimension	Electronic Coast	Arena Healthinnovation	Clean Water Norway
Size (number of participating firms)	14	12	36
Participants	Technology firms (SMEs) Regional university	Technology firms (SMEs) Municipality (customers) Regional university Regional hospital	Technology firms (SMEs) Municipality (customers) Regional university R&D institutions
Main industry	Electronics and micro-technology	Health technology	Water cleansing
Methods applied	Network Reflection	Foresight	Foresight Network IGP
Trust now (2012)		6.1	5.3
Trust each other more than three years ago		6.6	5.7

The three cases differ in the application and management of the dialogue-based methods and in the social learning of trust. In Electronic Coast, network reflection was carried out over a period of nine months, while in Arena Healthinnovation the foresight method was applied through five two-day workshops over the course of one year. In Clean Water Norway, network IGP was employed 20 times in the space of five years and foresight was applied by means of two 2-day workshops over the course of three months. The slightly lower level of trust in CWN compared to AH could be explained by network size. By number of members, CWN is three times larger than AH and because the best context for learning trust is small groups, the disposition to trust a few network partners in a small network is higher than in larger networks.

DISCUSSION AND CONCLUSION

Trust seems to have been learned in all the three cases and it is likely that the dialogue-based methods, network reflection, network IGP and foresight have contributed to the social learning processes of trust. What is still not clear is what the core interventions are which contribute to the social learning of trust in these practical methods. To find out, it may be useful to break the methods down into their practical interventions and compare them, which is done in Table 7.4.

Table 7.4   The practical interventions of the three methods

Practical interventions	Network reflection	Network IGP	Foresight
Recruiting participants from a network with people from the same industry and the same region, who practise some of the same professions	X	X	X
Participants meet face to face	X	X	X
– at several seminars over several months	X	X	X
– also invited to share some personal information		X	
Reflection tasks organized in small temporary	X	X	X
inter-organizational groups under time pressure	X	X	X
– demanding reflection alone and/or collectively	X	X	X
in small groups	X	X	
– requiring sharing, reflections and dialogues of experience and challenges within the firms			
– requiring all participants to be active			
Developing joint visions and goals	X	X	X
Developing joint terms and understanding			X
Lunch intervention organized in temporary	X		
inter-organizational groups	X		
– requiring participants to work together on non-work topics/issues and share non-work competences and creative ideas			
Seminars comprising	X	X	X
– social mingling at informal moments, e.g.	X	X	X
breaks and plant visits	X	X	X
– joint meals	X		X
– overnight stay at a retreat	X		X
– various localities, some including plant visits			
– firm presentations and network news			
Theoretical anchoring	X		
– providing participants with the same concepts, literature and lectures as mutual backdrops for communication	X		
– discussing practical use of theoretical frameworks			
Presentations organized in temporary inter-organizational groups dealing with practical challenges within the firms	X		
External facilitator of the processes	X	X	X

As shown in Table 7.4, the joint interventions in all three methods are: recruiting participants from a network with people from the same industry and the same region, who practise some of the same professions; letting the participants meet face to face at several seminars over several months and develop joint terms and understanding; having them work together on reflection tasks organized in small, temporary, inter-organizational groups, requiring all participants to be active by sharing, reflecting and engaging in dialogue on experiences and challenges within the firms; furthermore, organizing seminars in various locations with joint meals and social mingling at informal moments, for example breaks and plant visits. Finally, an external facilitator facilitates the interventions in all three methods.

A particularly interesting element for the analysis of the potential ability of these joint social interventions to contribute to the social learning of trust is their content in terms of trust-building processes or other trust-building mechanisms. Recruiting participants from a network with people from the same industry and the same region, who practise some of the same professions, contributes to building institution-based trust (Williamson, 1996). It is also significant that many of the participants have a common background or a similar demographic profile, something that influences trust-building (Levin et al., 2006). External facilitators represent a joint third-party relationship, which also contributes to building trust (Burt, 2001; Ferrin et al., 2006). These types of trust-building, however, do not require interpersonal contact and are therefore not dependent on social learning.

The joint interventions address different trust-building processes. All the three methods are linked to the trust-building processes in Table 7.2, but for the purpose of this study – analysing the core practical interventions – these links are too simplistic and their content needs to be explicated or unwrapped. All the methods entail the face-to-face meeting of participants at seminars through social mingling and joint meals, both of which represent core parts of the trust-building process of connection. The face-to-face communication and dialogue in small groups and that at different locations contributes to the quality of the trust-building process of communication. Having the participants meet at several seminars over time at formal and informal moments and insisting on their active involvement (a common trait for the methods described here) contributes to the frequency of the trust-building process of communication. The development of joint terms and understanding contributes to moulding the language aspect of the trust-building process of direction. Working together in small, inter-organizational groups under time pressure contributes to the trust-building process of temporary groups. The sharing of experiences and challenges within the firms, with the ensuing reflections, contributes to the trust-building process of resource sharing. To sum up this discussion, Table 7.5 links the joint interventions to their corresponding trust-building processes.

Table 7.5 Linking joint interventions and trust-building processes

Joint practical interventions	Trust-building processes
Recruiting participants from a network with people from the same industry and the same region, who practise some of the same professions	(Institution-based trust)
Participants meet face to face – at several seminars over several months	Connection Communication
Reflection tasks organized in small temporary inter-organizational groups under time pressure – requiring all participants to be active	Communication Temporary groups Resource sharing
Developing joint terms and understanding	Direction
Seminars with – social mingling at informal moments, e.g. breaks and plant visits – joint meals – various localities, some including plant visits	Connection Communication
External facilitator of the processes	(Third-party relationship)

According to Möllering (2013: 291),

> It has been an interesting but unduly peripheral question in trust research to what extent the learning process of trust can be started without a trust basis but with the aim to develop trust. In other words, will actors engage in interaction in order to gain experience with others, thus 'testing' if trust might be developed?

In all the three cases here, the methods of network reflection, network IGP and foresight have been applied with participants from different organizations from their very first meeting. As they were all from the same nation and working in the same region, some kind of characteristic-based trust (Zucker, 1986) might already have existed among them. Because most participants were strangers when the methods were introduced and some of them represented different types of stakeholders, such as private firms, public plants, the public sector and academia, my assumption is that their trust basis was very weak at the outset. They nevertheless engaged in social interaction to gain experience with others. These methods are therefore appropriate to 'test' if trust might be developed in a given setting. I argue that this may happen because these methods entail the social learning and trust-building processes of connection, communication, direction, temporary groups and resource sharing.

Based on the findings presented in this section, we can conclude that the answer to the research question, 'What are the core practical interventions in dialogue-based methods that facilitate social learning of trust in networks?', is to let the participants meet face to face at several seminars over several months and develop joint terms and understanding. Furthermore, the participants should work together on reflection tasks organized in small, temporary, inter-organizational groups under time pressure, requiring all participants to be active by sharing, reflecting on and having dialogues about experiences and challenges within the firms. Moreover, seminars could be arranged in various locations with joint meals and social mingling at informal moments, for example during breaks and plant visits. These interventions seem to have the potential to facilitate the social learning of trust in networks in general and seem also to work at very early stages with weak or absent trust bases among participants.

This study naturally has several limitations. Longitudinal real-life cases represent complex settings with several activities that may influence the results. The isolation of the phenomenon studied is almost impossible to achieve and other factors may therefore have influenced the results. In the selected cases, the composition of the participant sample and their predisposition for trust, the type of participants and the basic level of trust in the different contexts may also have exerted some influence. The fact that Norway is a high-trust society (Newton, 2001) may have influenced the results; it would therefore be of interest to test the interventions in other national contexts.

This study makes both theoretical and practical contributions. The theoretical contributions constitute the presentation and discussion of the three dialogue-based methods – network reflection, network IGP and foresight – as well as breaking the methods down to their practical interventions and comparing them to identify the joint interventions that seem to contribute to the social learning of trust in networks. Another theoretical contribution is the linking of the practical interventions with trust-building processes in networks and other types of trust-building activity. This contributes to the emerging psychological tradition of research on how to manage trust-building in general and in networks in particular. More precisely, it contributes to how human interaction processes, communication and cooperation influence trust-building. The practical contributions are the outlining and the description of the methods and the interventions which may influence the social learning processes of trust in networks. This may be of interest to managers, network managers, consultants and policy makers.

REFERENCES

Abrams, L.C., Cross, R., Lesser, E. and Levin, D.Z. (2003) Nurturing inter-personal trust in knowledge-sharing networks. *Academy of Management Executive*, 17 (4), 64–77.

Argyres, N.S. (1999) The impact of information technology on coordination: Evidence from the B-2 'Stealth' bomber. *Organization Science*, 10 (2), 162–80.

Blau, P.M. (1986) *Exchange and Power in Social Life*. New Brunswick, NJ: Transaction Publishers.

Burt, R.S. (2001) Bandwidth and echo: Trust, information, and gossip in social networks. In: Casella, A. and Rauch, E. (eds) *Networks and Markets. Contributions from Economics and Sociology*. New York: Sage, pp. 30–74.

Chung, Y. and Jackson, S.E. (2011) Co-worker trust and knowledge creation: A multilevel analysis. *Journal of Trust Research*, 1 (1), 65–83.

CWN (2011) *Application to the Arena Program*. Tonsberg: CWN.

Dirks, K.T. and Ferrin, D. (2002) The role of trust in organizational setting. *Organization Science*, 12, 450–67.

Ferrin, D., Dirks, K.T. and Shah, P.P. (2006) Direct and indirect effects of third-party relationships on interpersonal trust. *Journal of Applied Psychology*, 91 (4), 870–83.

Gausdal, A.H. (2008) Developing regional communities of practice by network reflection: The case of the Norwegian electronics industry. *Entrepreneurship and Regional Development*, 20 (3), 209–35.

Gausdal, A.H. (2012) Trust-building processes in the context of networks. *Journal of Trust Research*, 2 (1), 7–30.

Gausdal, A.H. (2013) Methods for developing innovative SME networks. *Journal of the Knowledge Economy*, 25 (1), 15–38.

Gausdal, A.H. and Hildrum, J. (2012) Facilitating trust building in networks: A study from the water technology industry. *Systemic Practice and Action Research*, 25 (1), 15–38.

Gustavsen, B. (1992) *Dialogue and Development*. Maastricht: Van Gorcum.

Hardin, R. (2002) *Trust and Trustworthiness*. New York: Russell Sage Foundation.

Hardwick, J., Anderson, A.R. and Cruickshank, D. (2013) Trust formation processes in innovative collaborations: Networking as knowledge building practices. *European Journal of Innovation Management*, 16 (1), 4–21.

Hartley, J. (2004) Case study research. In: Cassel, C. and Symon, G. (eds) *Essential Guide to Qualitative Methods in Organizational Research*. London: Sage, pp. 323–33.

Hatak, I. and Roessl, D. (2010) Trust within interfirm cooperation: A conceptualization. *Our Economy*, 56 (5–6), 3–10.

Johnsen, D.W. and Johnsen, R.T. (1994) *Learning Together and Alone. Cooperative, Competitive, and Individualistic Learning.* 4th edn. Boston, MA: Allyn and Bacon.

Levin, D.Z., Whithener, E.M. and Cross, R. (2006) Perceived trustworthiness of knowledge sources: The moderating impact of relationship length. *Journal of Applied Psychology*, 91 (5), 1163–71.

Lewicki, R.J., Tomlinson, E.C. and Gillespie, N. (2006) Models of interpersonal trust development: Theoretical approaches, empirical evidence, and future directions. *Journal of Management*, 32 (6), 991–1022.

Lewicki, R.J., Saunders, D.M., Minton, J.W. and Barry, B. (2003) *Negotiation: Readings, Exercises, and Cases.* 4th edn. Boston, MA: McGraw-Hill/Irwin.

Lewin, K. (1935) *A Dynamic Theory of Personality.* New York: McGraw-Hill.

Luhmann, N. (1979) *Trust and Power.* Chichester: John Wiley.

Mayer, R.C., Davis, J.H. and Schoorman, F.D. (1995) An integrative model of organizational trust. *Academy of Management Review*, 20 (3), 709–34.

Meyerson, D., Weick, K.E. and Kramer, R.M. (1996) Swift trust and temporary groups. In: Kramer, R.M. and Tyler, T.R. (eds) *Trust in Organizations: Frontiers of Theory and Research.* Thousand Oaks, CA: Sage Publications, pp. 166–195.

Mintzberg, H. (2004) *Managers not MBAs.* Harlow: Pearson Education.

Mintzberg, H. and Gosling, J. (2006) Management education as if both matter. *Management Learning*, 37 (4), 419–28.

Möllering, G. (2006) *Trust: Reason, Routine, Reflexivity.* Oxford: Elsevier.

Möllering, G. (2013) Process views on trusting and crises. In: Bachmann, R. and Zaheer, A. (eds) *Handbook of Advances in Trust Research.* Cheltenham, UK and Northampton, MA, USA: Edward Elgar Publishing, pp. 285–305.

Moorman, C., Deshpandé, R. and Zaltman, G. (1993) Factors affecting trust in market research relationships. *Journal of Marketing*, 29 (1), 81–101.

Newell, S. and Swan, J. (2000) Trust and inter-organizational networking. *Human Relations*, 53 (10), 1287–328.

Newton, K. (2001) Trust, social capital, civil society, and democracy. *International Political Science Review*, 22 (2), 201–14.

Nonaka, I., Toyama, R. and Konno, N. (2000) SECI, Ba and leadership: A unified model of dynamic knowledge creation. *Long Range Planning*, 33 (1), 5–34.

Parkhe, A. (1993) Strategic alliance structuring: A game theoretic and transaction cost examination of interfirm cooperation. *Academy of Management Journal*, 36, 794–829.

RCN (2010) *Innovation through Cooperation.* Oslo: Research Council Norway.

RCN (2013) Dialogue methods. [Online] Available from: http://www.forskningsradet.no/prognett-vri/Dialogmetoder/1253953597902 (accessed 10 May 2014).

Ross, W.H. and LaCroix, J. (1996) Multiple meanings of trust in negotiation theory and research: A literature review and integrative model. *The International Journal of Conflict Management*, 7, 314–60.

Schön, D.A. (1983) *The Reflective Practitioner: How Professionals Think in Action.* New York: Basic Books.

Schön, D.A. (1987) *Educating the Reflective Practitioner.* San Francisco, CA: Jossey-Bass.

Tsai, W.P. and Ghoshal, S. (1998) Social capital and value creation: The role of intrafirm networks. *Academy of Management Journal,* 41 (4), 464–76.

Uzzi, B. (1997) Social structure and competition in interfirm networks: The paradox of embeddedness. *Administrative Science Quarterly,* 42 (1), 35–67.

Von Krogh, G. (1998) Care in knowledge creation. *California Management Review,* 40 (3), 133–53.

Von Krogh, G., Ichijo, K. and Nonaka, I. (2000) *Enabling Knowledge Creation: How to Unlock the Mystery of Tacit Knowledge and Release the Power of Innovation.* Oxford: Oxford University Press.

Wenger, E.C., McDermott, R. and Snyder, W.M. (2002) *Cultivating Communities of Practice: A Guide to Managing Knowledge.* Boston, MA: Harvard Business School Press.

Williamson, O.E. (1996) *The Mechanisms of Governance.* New York: Oxford University Press.

Zucker, L.G. (1986) Production of trust: Institutional sources of economic structure, 1840–1920. *Research in Organizational Behavior,* 8, 53–111.

8. Process of trust building: a case study in the management system context

Kirsti Malkamäki, Mirjami Ikonen and Taina Savolainen

The importance of trust in leadership has been widely recognized both in the literature and in practice. Trust is examined as an antecedent and intangible resource for improved organizational performance and competitiveness (Savolainen and López-Fresno, 2013). Trust is also seen as a potential challenge to the principles of control. Nowadays technology and e-leadership provide transparency and new ways of cooperating in organizations, as well as new means of control. Building trust is also listed as one of the elements and tasks of leaders because the performance of an organization is a result of leadership and management systems (Yukl, 2010). Trust-based management is directed towards accessing and leveraging intangible resources, such as employee commitment and learning behaviours (Bijlsma-Frankema and Koopman, 2004).

Interpersonal trust has been the focus of several studies (Mayer et al., 1995; Lewicki and Tomlinson, 2003). On the other hand, interpersonal trust is also seen as being too limited to describe the holistic view of trust in business (Kramer, 1999; McEvily and Tortoriello, 2011). In addition, Bachmann (2011) has stated that we have assumed for too long that trust cannot be managed and that it should be seen as a micro-level phenomenon that emerges between two individuals. Thus, researchers have pointed out that trust should be examined at both the macro level and the micro level within an organization (McEvily et al., 2003). Moreover, the question of the interrelationship between trust and control at the interpersonal level and the macro level has been studied much less and has not been incorporated widely in academic discussion. Our study concerning the trust-building process in the management system context will ultimately inform both researchers and practitioners on this fundamental process in organizations. This study offers new, empirically grounded insights into the processes of trust building, as well as into the complex relationship between trust and control.

The research questions in this qualitative case study are related to the understanding of the case: what the case is about and what can be learned in its context (Eriksson and Kovalainen, 2008). The purpose is to shed more light on the following research question: how does the management system contribute to trust-building processes in the organization?

TRUST AND CONTROL WITHIN THE MANAGEMENT SYSTEM

Although several theoretical traditions have recognized the importance of trust in economic exchange, scholars have also called for provision of a clearer understanding of the elements and factors affecting managers in acting (or not acting) to promote organizational trust (Sitkin and George, 2005). Furthermore, 'the literature on trust in organizations suggests that managers who invoke and draw attention to their appropriate use of a wide variety of controls can engender greater trust' (Sitkin and George, 2005). This underscores the importance of trust building by management in organizations and reveals the nature and role of the management system, thus contributing to the growing body of practice-orientated scholarship (Feldman and Orlikowski, 2011).

Trust creates a foundation for cooperation, facilitating or hindering interaction between teams and individuals, as well as in business networks and partnerships (Ring and Van de Ven, 1994; Rousseau et al., 1998; Tyler, 2003; Savolainen et al., 2014). Trust has been shown to have an influence on processes such as the effectiveness of communication, cooperation, information sharing and improved organizational performance (Burke et al., 2007). The vast majority of trust definitions across different levels and different referents include two key dimensions: (1) positive expectations of trustworthiness; and (2) willingness to accept vulnerability (Fulmer and Gelfand, 2012). Trust is defined as 'the willingness of a party to be vulnerable to the actions of another party based on the expectation that the other will perform a particular action important to the party' (Mayer et al., 1995: 712). Therefore, the relational definition is 'applicable to our study as the definition is applicable to both individuals and organizations' (Schilke and Cook, 2013). In this chapter, the theoretical discussion and empirical study draw on the relational view of trust (Mayer et al., 1995) and a process view of trust building; in other words, the question of how interactions between actors contribute to change is taken into account to provide knowledge about the process (Langley et al., 2013).

According to Bachmann (2011), trust can either appear in the form of (1) interaction-based trust, or as (2) institutional-based trust. Interaction-based trust refers to interpersonal trust, whereas institutional-based trust (confidence) is seen as more systematic, viewed as trust in institutions and abstract systems, in which relationships between actors are indirect, systemic and impersonal (Seligman, 1999). 'Management systems encompass both the management of an organization and the leadership of those working for it' (Laamanen and Tinnilä, 2009). For this reason, researchers and practitioners alike are interested in identifying the mechanisms through which trust in leadership can be developed, as well as those factors which moderate this relationship (for example Gillespie and Mann, 2004).

Strategy execution and operations are usually tightly linked in a management system. Thus, the management system is a managerial toolkit with which to execute the strategy and operations. It comprises strategy development, objectives and initiatives, the operational plan to attain objectives and initiatives for assessing the data and monitoring the effectiveness of the plan (Kaplan and Norton, 2008). Furthermore, the performance monitoring and evaluation process included in the management system covers the essential task of ensuring that the organization's strategic aims in terms of customer relationship management (CRM) are delivered to an appropriate and acceptable standard and that the basis for future improvement is established (Payne and Frow, 2005).

Laamanen and Tinnilä (2009: 12) define a management system as 'the entity comprised of the organizational structures, operating principles, methods, processes and resources as well as the performance indicators that form an organization's measurement system that are needed to achieve the organization's goals'. Some previous research (Das and Teng, 1998; Das, 2002; Möllering, 2005; Weibel, 2007) on trust and control has already moved towards perspectives that allow for complex interconnections between the two concepts. However, too little research addresses both concepts at the same time, notwithstanding the possibility of a positive relationship between trust and control (Möllering, 2005; Sitkin and George, 2005).

Generally, trust and control are seen as interlinked processes, complementary or supplementary. Commonly, they are regarded as key to attaining effectiveness in inter- and intra-organizational relations (Costa and Bijlsma-Frankema, 2007). Both trust on the one hand and precise control mechanisms on the other are meant to be useful in enhancing the perceived probability of desired behaviour (Das and Teng, 1998). Furthermore, 'the literature on trust in organizations suggests that managers who invoke and draw attention to their appropriate use of a wide variety of controls can engender greater trust' (Sitkin and George, 2005: 308). Also, Möllering (2005: 300) states that 'trust does not exist without control and it is not possible fully to explain the one without the other'. Thereby, trust can also flourish in the control process.

The management system of the current case organization covers the description of the roles of the units in the internal CRM process, as well as objectives and key standards and indicators of quantitative and qualitative performance, for example, written defined procedures and performance-monitoring based on metrics and observation aimed at improving cooperation and trust development in practice. The performance monitoring and assessment processes cover the essential task of ensuring that the organization's strategic aims in terms of CRM are being delivered to an appropriate and acceptable standard and that a basis for future improvement is established (Payne and Frow, 2005).

EMPIRICAL STUDY

Case Company

This empirical case study is based on qualitative data (Malkamäki, 2010), gathered from a chain of hypermarkets, a highly valued listed trading sector company in Finland. The total number of employees was around 3500 in 2010. The case organization covers two functional units – a central unit and a store function unit (69 hypermarkets). The central unit consists of a number of units (for example purchasing, marketing, financial management and concept design), which administer the activities of the entire chain. In this case study, the focus is on the purchasing and store function units.

A new management system was implemented in 2009, clearly based on feedback from a field inquiry from the organization. The new management system includes a complete enterprise resource planning (ERP) system, including structural solutions, indicators, management procedures, resource planning mechanisms and support systems (for example databases for financial administration and the utilization of these databases in directing business management). Thus performance monitoring is possible by the managers and supervisors responsible for performance using the intranet. In particular, the management system is a 'toolkit' in CRM process management – steering and monitoring the management of sales, profits and capital, as well as marketing and human resource costs and the behaviour of employees.

Before 2009 there was wider operational freedom for managers of both units concerning autonomy in decisions and operations. Therefore, the range in the managers' performance rates in the units was high. In addition, the roles, rights and responsibilities of the units were not clearly defined. Hence the operations between the units at that time were partly overlapping, generating ambiguity and a lack of trust. In contrast, the roles and tasks and the responsibilities and rights of the units are clearly defined and described in the new management system. The purchasing unit is responsible for selection management, pricing, marketing, giving instructions for product display and controlling capital management in stores. The store function unit is responsible for fulfilling the customer promise: the practical implementation of marketing, the display of products, and human resources and customer service activities. In addition, there are defined written procedures according to the roles of the units. Accordingly, the final customer value is based on the cooperation and performance of these two organizational units.

Data collection and analysis

In this study, a qualitative approach is adopted as the interpretive approach seeks descriptions of the phenomena studied and aims to gain understanding of the perceptions of actors in their own, real-life contexts. The purpose is to study the process of trust building holistically, aiming to gain a profound understanding of the complex nature of trust building and subtle distinctions that are critical for understanding a particular situation in an organization (Ikonen, 2013). In particular, trust is considered inherently context-dependent (McEvily and Tortoriello, 2011).

Conducting a case study requires a researcher's profound knowledge and understanding of the phenomenon in the chosen case and access to the key informants. The data for the study were collected by the researcher, who is an experienced manager, having been a member of the case organization for more than 30 years in different organizational supervisory positions. In 2009, the researcher, together with 21 department store managers, was made redundant. However, she was encouraged to conduct a study and collect data in the organization for her Master's thesis and dissertation work.

On the one hand, this experience enables access to the organization and knowledge concerning the best experts to interview, as well as a deep understanding of the case, the language, the cultural norms and the circumstances of the organizational actors (Eriksson and Kovalainen, 2008). On the other hand, an outsider position may provide a better opportunity to be increasingly analytical (Eriksson and Kovalainen, 2008). In this study, the criticality of analysis is increased by co-authors. Moreover, the researcher was highly conscious of the need to be aware of her prior understanding during the research process and when reporting the findings. In a qualitative study, in which the empirical materials are derived through interacting with the informants, the data and interpretations can be more 'representative of social worlds' than would otherwise be the case.

The data were gathered in face-to-face interviews during 2010. The data consist of interviews with six supervisors/leaders at different levels in middle or lower management positions. The informants were chosen based on their hierarchical position in the CRM process at the time and tenure (2–20 years) in the case organization. Based on the number of employees in the units, two managers were chosen from the purchasing unit (PU) and four managers from the store functions unit (SFU). Three of the interviewees were known to the interviewer beforehand, having met the researcher previously, and three of them were new acquaintances.

The data were collected through thematic interviews according to the themes of leadership, interaction and trust. The themes were based on both theoretical themes and the existing practical themes in the organization. The interviews varied from 30 to 75 minutes in length as a result of additional questions which arose during the discussion. The data constitute 89 pages of text in Finnish, translated into English in the course of the re-analysis. The content of the transcribed data was analysed using thematic content analysis and the interpretation was theory-driven.

Findings

In this section, the findings from the qualitative study are described according to the following three dimensions, based on the empirical framework of the study: (1) common goal and roles; (2) cooperation and procedures; (3) leadership and interaction.

Common goal and roles

According to an interviewee, the cooperation of the units is based on the common goal and the structure of the organization. The units are responsible for different management processes in the CRM process to guarantee the economic success of the company. The roles, rights and responsibilities of the units are different and are clearly defined. Both parties are dependent on each other, which creates a need for reciprocity and motivation for collaboration:

> We are all working here for one reason: so that we can guarantee the financial perspective of the company and we're working together for that purpose. Yes, for sure we're not a separate unit and neither are they. We have our own duties, but still we're working together. You know, we can't do things without the others and their staff, and so they can't either. (PU1)

The setting and sharing of common goals by means of a supportive management system are the basic strengthening elements of trust at the organizational level. Managers monitor goal-setting and performance at the unit level and by persons in charge on the intranet. Transparency and a clear measurement system enable monitoring of one another's performance. Transparency is perceived as pressure to achieve goals and follow the agreed upon procedures:

> Of course, it's now organized so that there are clear responsibilities, aims, and indicators, yes, and also measurement is transparent now. So we can also see in store functions that it's not only our figures but also the figures of purchasing ... by the persons in charge we can see their area of responsibility and how they are related to their objectives. (SFU6)

It seems that there are fewer conflicts now due to transparency resulting from having similar rules set for everyone to be followed in the units. The next excerpt describes the interviewee's feeling of justice as an outcome of transparency and control through the equal management system manifested. For example, attempts to take unanticipated risks or unplanned trials are not permitted and not even in friendship-like relationships:

> There are no more conflicts in the organization like before because hiding places are destroyed through the transparency of the system. Everything is so transparent; you can find all the figures in SAP ... So you can see that everyone has to participate. ... It's trustworthiness and so on. Our systems have made it possible. There are no hiding places any more. ... If you think about how it used to be ... now you know that there won't be surprises. (SFU5)

Professional competences and results facilitate trust development over time. Common success affects the attitudes of employees and their commitment to the organization and gives support to and increases faith in the management system driving development. Further learning to collaborate and success in reaching the goals supports trust building. Experiences of success create confidence regarding the functioning of the prevailing system. In addition, the following excerpt illustrates that ability and competence are appreciated by leaders in both functional units:

> People in the purchasing unit show their workmanship and abilities, and vice versa, as they can see we are able to manage the product display and other activities. ... Trust is built by doing, I believe. As if you had to deserve it through deeds. (SFU6)

In summary, pursuing goal achievement, the operational units share a common goal and roles are clarified. This makes the units dependent on one another. Showing competence and skills builds trust between the units. In addition, the intranet is open and transparent to all working in managerial positions. Everyone may follow how the performance goals are met.

Cooperation and procedures

Based on the findings, the procedures are clearly defined and available through the intranet for everyone. The documented procedures, as well as the rights and responsibilities, provide useful and understandable guidelines for the operations. An informant in the study described the roles and procedures as follows:

> So, we have our own duties here and all the units have theirs. Right now, we've got a lot of new and more precise procedures on how things are to be done and led systematically by a certain policy and principle. They are all written down and available to everyone, and they are clear. So everyone can understand what his or her role is. (PU2)

Everyone is expected to operate according to the procedures, which can be seen as a driving force for organizational justice and equality. Traditionally, performance in the organizational units has varied considerably and the implementation and building of 'best practices' was previously challenging:

> Well, we have these procedures, we have management policy and everything is documented. These are also monitored so that everything is done according to them and everyone is expected to follow the rules. Before, it was like the decision was one way or another, and each one made it a bit different, but now we are doing it in the same way. (PU2)

According to the informant, the systematic documentation of procedures is a 'buttress' and support for supervisors in their work. Supervisors at every organizational level are aware of the control system and they are strongly expected to follow the defined procedures. Moreover, discussion stays at the level of fact, based on defined procedures rather than purely based on the opinion of a sole actor or supervisor:

> Well, this sort of systematic documentation is helpful. On the other hand, in a way it also forces one to follow it. Operations are checked now and if supervisors aren't operating by them [documented procedures], there's intervention. It applies to all. It applies to all at every level. ... I think this is the right direction. And we can talk about things by their real names, so that it's not only about opinions or lip service. (SFU6)

The informant remarked that the performance of the purchasing unit has significantly improved because procedures that are defined and written down oblige everyone to operate according to instructions, justifying the expectations and monitoring according to the procedures.

> I must say that now when there are these rules, well, as ridiculous as it is – clear rules – I think that it's much clearer now. For example, the amount of emails from the product line has notably diminished, and I think that a kind of assertiveness has taken place a lot. (SFU3)

When actions are planned in the long term and challenges and problems are addressed through cooperation and coordinated at the chain level, it improves predictability. According to the data, predictability has improved since the procedures of the new management system have brought consistency to the overall functional coordination. This supports the knowledge-based stage in Lewicki and Bunker's (1996) model of trust development, which is based on the predictability of the other party. The informant describes the current cooperation and operations as follows: 'So, the rules are not changed now, you know, but when we have these defined procedures and if change is needed, that could be possible in a systematic way. Not by reacting too quickly' (SFU6).

The management system is seen as a cornerstone for managers in operative management as the performance has improved. Sitkin and George (2005) suggest that managers may promote trust through the perceptions of individuals and institutional legitimacy because an employee is more likely to trust the decision of a manager if there are easy-to-recognize markers of the legitimacy of the manager, the decision and the organization. As the informant describes it, 'But in this management model, it leads little by little to more efficient results ... as the management is done better now' (SFU6).

In sum, everyone is expected to follow the documented procedures based on the management system. Thus, the management system is seen as a backrest for equal, consistent, predictable management.

Leadership and interaction

Well-organized interaction and information channels are key elements for cooperation as communication between units is nowadays based on email and the intranet. Trust building seems to be enhanced when communication between the units is clear, consistent and coherent, with specified information channels, timing and content of the information. As an informant stated, 'I mean there is lot of information in general. We are living with this terrible information flow. What is essential for the store, what is so important that really needs to be forwarded ...?' (PU1).

Clear and understandable communication and information enables the receiver to understand and operate effectively. It seems that at its best, the timing and content of the message are carefully considered. In addition, it is important that support services are as flawless as possible to avoid disappointments in customer service in stores, for example caused by mistakes made by the purchasing unit in product information.

> Trust towards the chain unit is better now, as it seems that it's clearer now there. And ... perhaps the information to stores has been clearer as well, and there are days when you're informed of certain issues ... so in a way, you don't have to worry about that much ... it's nicer to work here at the store when there aren't as many mistakes or customer disappointments now. (SFU3)

Previously, the collection, giving and receiving of feedback was mostly oral, or occasionally by email. The implementation of the management system has established a systematic procedure, a channel for feedback that is transparent and available to all actors. Coordinated and organized forums for interaction have diminished interruptions by telephone calls and emails and have increased overall efficiency. Different forums for interaction (for example meetings) are needed to gain common understanding:

> Before, we used to have talks with the department manager and purchasing manager. I think that sort of communication has decreased a little, but it's also because we've got these procedures for everyday life, so you really don't need to take a phone call in every case. ... Well, I mean that I believe no one would mind that this sort of communication has decreased. ... But these general district meetings have also been very important, as sessions about making us understand each other much better. (PU1)

Consistency and reasoning regarding decisions are important. If decisions are not well-reasoned, experiences of disappointments and surprise are common; far from strengthening trust development, this comes across rather as a lack of appreciation. This seems to be related to inefficiency and low commitment. These findings emphasize the importance of clear decision-making rules and procedures:

> Our opinions and comments are asked for, and the decision arrives on how we are going to do things afterwards, but reasons are forgotten. It has happened once or twice, so I'd like to know the reasons why. ... It came to my mind that it's more like at will, I mean like 'shut up, that's how we'll proceed'. (SFU5)

A well-organized, flexible, real-time and equally participatory system for feedback enables broad information-sharing between partners. Feedback-based development makes operations more effective and is also a way of appreciating the other party, enhancing cooperation and trust through the experience of being able to have an impact on current issues in the organization. A new feedback channel and systematic procedure for collecting feedback from the retail unit and routing it to the purchasing unit was recently implemented. Feedback is collected in different ways depending on the purpose. An informant described the current situation as follows: 'Well, now we have a model for that [feedback], I mean they give feedback from the field in that "efficiency office", and then we read it and give answers if it's marked "response desired", so we'll give responses' (PU2).

Cooperation has new modes due to the new MS. For example, representatives from the other units regularly attend each other's meetings. The main plans are made in cooperation, which provides a fruitful basis for problem solving and enhancing understanding on the issues affecting efficiency and success in general. One informant remarked: 'There are, for example, sales managers from product lines who participate in the store function unit meetings so that we can discuss operations – for example, what is needed for seasonal campaigns' (SFU6).

In summary, procedures and practices of interaction, including communication and meetings, are described. It is expected that everyone will follow the procedures. This makes it possible to receive the same kind of information and discuss and give feedback. As a consequence, collaboration and problem solving improve.

SUMMARY OF FINDINGS

The findings show that the management system is seen as a foundation for the CRM process and coordination in the trust-building process between the organizational units. The trust-building and development process between the functional units seems to be based first on structural factors of the management system: (1) a common goal and the roles of the organizational units in the CRM process; (2) defined procedures; (3) transparency; (4) control; (5) interaction procedures. However, these are not separate functions but rather interlinked actions (see Table 8.1).

A common goal, the clear allocation of roles and responsibilities, defined policies and procedures, as well as indicators and an intranet information system, form the basis for leadership and cooperation. Thus structural and operational issues based on the management system seem to have a significant role in trust development. Therefore, it appears that reciprocity and especially competences are the essential elements of trust building in the case studied. Moreover, transparency, control and inter-action seem to be the core elements of the trust-building process between organizational units. Providing and receiving feedback and the meeting procedures, as well as knowledge sharing and the cooperative development of functions operate as the glue between partners. Thus organized, coherent, direct and indirect interaction and communication procedures are practices that manifest trust building in the organization. The management system is a guiding frame and a set of means for streamlining the operational procedures of the company. It involves transparency, bringing the issue of trust and control into focus.

CONCLUSION AND DISCUSSION

In this case study, leaders' perceptions and experiences of trust development were examined between two organization units. The data consist of six interviews. All supervisors interviewed were in middle or lower management positions. Based on the results of this study, it seems that a well-structured and functioning management system and appropriate degree of control and monitoring could be seen as antecedents of trust in this case. On the other hand, the management system is also seen as a 'tool' of change management, or more precisely, the change in management culture (referring in practice to behaviour) according to defined procedures in this case.

Table 8.1   Summary of findings

Management system	Practical actions	Meanings of trust and cooperation
Organizational factors	Roles and job descriptions in CRM process. Clear allocation of rights and responsibilities.	Coherent understanding of the rights and responsibilities and different roles in the CRM process in order to achieve the common goal. Awareness of the dependency on each other. Transparency, reciprocity and consistency of management and operations.
Leadership model	Meeting practices and reporting system.	Leading according to top management decisions throughout the organization. Support for supervisor in management operations.
Defined Procedures	Documented, clearly defined procedures available in the intranet. Rules (e.g. meeting practices).	Procedures and expected operations not questioned. Consistency. Systematization. Improved performance. Reciprocity.
Control	Operations and behaviour monitored and controlled. Expectations to operate according to procedures and regulations.	Consistency of management and controlling. Predictability. Transparency. Feeling of justice and equality.
Transparency	Data, results and measures available for leaders on the intranet.	Everyone is expected to operate according to objectives and procedures. Everyone is able to monitor operations of supervisors. Equality and fairness. Predictability. Fewer conflicts.
Interaction	Transparent communication and information channels. Meeting practices: Face-to-face interaction and communication.	Equal communication and information channels for everyone on the intranet. Efficiency. Learning and possibility to communicate and give feedback. Discussion based on facts and on a business-like level. Knowledge sharing and common understanding. Competence in action planning and problem-solving together.

The functional structure in the organization provides a framework for collaboration between the organizational units. A clear division of rights and responsibilities and the procedures defined in the management system form a foundation and framework for consistent management and operations. When operations and behaviour are consistently controlled according to the procedures and demanded equally from every organizational level, it seems to produce trust towards the organization and at the interpersonal level. Therefore, a clear and transparent management system is also the basis of a leader–follower relationship, a 'buttress', or a frame for all operations. Thus, organizational trust is created and strengthened by consistent management throughout the organization, from the top level to the 'floor'.

Transparency and control have been facilitated by the management system. In this study, controlling and monitoring are seen as supportive elements for the consistency of management. As supervisors are expected to operate according to the procedures, they are also able to monitor that other supervisors are operating according to the targets, which engenders a feeling of justice and equality. From a practical point of view, it is expected that the procedures embedded in the system will be followed; for this purpose, monitoring is essential because in an organization with an old and strong corporate culture, this kind of obedience fluctuates. It follows that the role of the management system also seems to be that of a control mechanism which provides strictly defined rules, directing supervision at all organizational levels. This is in line with Das and Teng (2001). The implementation of control in business organizations requires a certain level of trust; without such trust, it will be difficult to accept outcome measurements, to follow specified behavioural patterns and to share values (Das and Teng, 2001). Transparency and control have been facilitated by the management system, so it seems that trust and control are unequivocally intertwined.

The functional units are dependent on each other, so collaboration is based on interaction and reciprocity. Thus interaction, providing and receiving feedback and the meeting procedures are practices that manifest trust building in the organization. Communication, knowledge sharing and the cooperative development of functions operate as the glue between partners. In addition, the findings suggest that success and trustworthiness, especially competences and integrity, are the essential elements of trust building in the case studied here. In other words, actors learn and realize that constructive communication and factual feedback enhance the improvement of performance and cooperation.

Moreover, the common goal encourages both sides to listen to each other and provide support for collaboration to succeed, which in turn gives rise to a sense of appreciation and provides for an open discussion. In this kind of large organization, interpersonal interactions are rare between the organizational actors of the units and a considerable amount of information is available on the intranet. Hence, trust seems to be built first in the organization due to the lack of interpersonal contacts. This is in line with the model of Lewicki and Bunker (1996). They state that in the first stage of trust development, calculative trust is not based on interpersonal trust but on transaction.

In conclusion, on the basis of the data, we may conclude that the management system is seen as a foundation for cooperation, as a 'toolkit' for supervisors to enhance intra-organizational trust and success to fulfil the customer promise. Thus, in this case company, it seems that trust relies on neither interpersonal relationships nor human characteristics, but is strongly related to the management system, the structures and processes. In this case, the process of trust development is seen as an ongoing process over time, based on experiences of cooperation framed by the management system. Therefore, the role of the management system in trust building is to shape structures for cooperation as trust in management develops according to the value the actors accord the system as an enabler of success in their own tasks. This study offers new, empirically grounded insights into the processes of trust building and also into the complex relationship between trust and control.

Theoretical Implications

These findings suggest important avenues for the role of a management system in trust building. The first contribution of this research emerges from the understanding that trust and the structural issues based on the management system are intertwined: organizational structure, clear roles, rights and responsibilities, indicators and transparency. Second, the management structure framework provides new theoretical insight into the relationship of trust and control. It provides a theoretical foundation for understanding the positive trust–control relationship. Generally, trust and control are seen as complementary or supplementary (Costa and Bijlsma-Frankema, 2007). The dynamics of the justification of the management system and its legitimacy by defined procedures that everyone is expected to follow for cooperation with a partner unit transcend trust between the functional units. These findings are supported by Zaheer et al. (1998), who argue that the institutionalized practices and routines transcended by a boundary spanner have an influence on trust building in inter-organizational cooperation. Third, the study provides a conceptual contribution, revealing some features of the trust-building process and interaction procedures. In a large organization, both face-to-face and 'in-line' interactions are important in the trust-building process, including coordinated and organized feedback and meeting procedures, as well as forums for planning and problem solving together.

To sum up, it seems that the development of trust is multilevel: trust develops both towards the organization and between the actors. Structural and operational issues play a significant role in trust development, both at the interpersonal and organizational level. The results suggest that institutionalized practices and routines for dealing with a partner unit, as captured by inter-unit trust, transcend the influence of the individual boundary spanner. Finally, the findings imply that this currently under-researched area of the trust-development process needs to be considered more carefully and understood more deeply as trust operates at multiple levels (Rousseau et al., 1998) and relationships may be multiplex. For further research, we also suggest studying trust development at multiple levels in complex real-life business relationships, both in terms of process and context (Savolainen, 2011; Ikonen, 2013).

Practical Implications

Our findings imply that there are several important practical insights for managers in terms of how trust is generated in the management system context. Both structural and operational issues need to be taken into account when applying the tools for improving and sustaining successful cooperation in the internal CRM process. In the trust-building process, there are three key elements for managers to consider: first, the clear definition of roles and tasks in the CRM process; second, consistent and logical management involving control and monitoring, based on policies and procedures; third, giving and receiving feedback and acting according to feedback. As interpersonal interaction in general is limited in a large company, communication can be enhanced by well-organized procedures and practices for making interactive participation possible for all personnel. Finally, within the management system, the fundamental question is how an organization creates value for the customer in fulfilling the promises given, which lays the ground for competitive advantage and success.

REFERENCES

Bachmann, R. 2011. At the crossroads: Future directions in trust research, *Journal of Trust Research*, vol. 1, no. 2, pp. 213–30.

Bijlsma-Frankema, K. and Koopman, P. 2004. The oxymoron of control in an era of globalisation, *Journal of Managerial Psychology*, vol. 19, no. 3, pp. 204–17.

Burke, C.S., Sims, D.E., Lazzara, E.H. and Salas, E. 2007. Trust in leadership: A multilevel review and integration, *The Leadership Quarterly*, vol. 18, no. 6, pp. 606–32.

Costa, A.C. and Bijlsma-Frankema, K. 2007. Trust and control interrelations: New perspectives on the trust–control nexus, *Group & Organization Management*, vol. 32, no. 4, pp. 392–406.

Das, T.K. 2002. The dynamics of alliance conditions in the alliance development process, *Journal of Management Studies*, vol. 39, no. 5, pp. 725–46.

Das, T.K. and Teng, B. 1998. Between trust and control: Developing confidence in partner cooperation in alliances, *Academy of Management Review*, vol. 23, no. 3, pp. 491–512.

Das, T.K. and Teng, B.S. 2001. Trust, control, and risk in strategic alliances: An integrated framework, *Organization Studies*, vol. 22, no. 2, pp. 251–83.

Eriksson, P. and Kovalainen, A. 2008. *Qualitative Methods in Business Research*, London: Sage Publications.

Feldman, M.S. and Orlikowski, W.J. 2011. Theorizing practice and practicing theory, *Organization Science*, vol. 22, no. 5, pp. 1240–53.

Fulmer, C.A. and Gelfand, M.J. 2012. At what level (and in whom) we trust: Trust across multiple organizational levels, *Journal of Management*, vol. 38, no. 4, pp. 1167–230.

Gillespie, N. and Mann, L. 2004. Transformational leadership and shared values: The building blocks of trust, *Journal of Managerial Psychology*, vol. 19, no. 6, pp. 588–607.

Ikonen, M. 2013. Trust development and dynamics at dyadic level. A narrative approach to studying process of interpersonal trust in leader–follower relationships. Publications of the University of Eastern Finland Dissertations in Social Sciences and Business Studies No. 53.

Kaplan, R.S. and Norton, D.P. 2008. Mastering the management system, *Harvard Business Review*, January, pp. 63–77.

Kramer, R.M. 1999. Trust and distrust in organizations: Emerging perspectives, enduring questions, *Annual Review of Psychology*, vol. 50, no. 2, pp. 569–98.

Laamanen, K. and Tinnilä, M. 2009. *Prosessijohtamisen Käsitteet – Terms and Concepts in Business Process Management*, 4th edn, Espoo: Teknologiateollisuus Oy/Teknologiainfo Teknova Oy.

Langley, A., Smallman, C., Tsoukas, H. and Van de Ven, A.H. 2013. Process studies of change in organization and management: Unveiling temporality, activity, and flow, *Academy of Management Journal*, vol. 56, no. 1, pp. 1–13.

Lewicki, R.J. and Bunker, B.B. 1996. Developing and maintaining trust in work relationships, in A. Zaheer and R. Bachman (eds), *Landmark Papers on Trust, Vol. II*, Cheltenham, UK and Northampton, MA, USA: Edward Elgar Publishing, pp. 388–413.

Lewicki, R.J. and Tomlinson, E.C. 2003. Trust and trust building, in G. Burgess and H. Burgess (eds), *Beyond Intractability*. Conflict Information Consortium, Boulder, CO: University of Colorado.

Malkamäki, K. 2010. *Luottamuksen Rakentuminen Sisäisessä Asiakkuudessa: Tapaustutkimus kaupan alan yrityksen kahdesta toimintayksiköstä. [Trust Building in Internal Customer Relationship Management: A Case Study in the Two Operating Units of the Trade Organization].* Master's thesis, Joensuu: University of Eastern Finland, Department of Business.

Mayer, R.C., Davis, J.H. and Schoorman, D.F. 1995. An integrative model of organizational trust, *Academy of Management Review*, vol. 20, no. 3, pp. 709–34.

McEvily, B. and Tortoriello, M. 2011. Measuring trust in organizational research: Review and recommendations, *Journal of Trust Research*, vol. 1, no. 1, pp. 23–63.

McEvily, B., Perrone, V. and Zaheer, A. 2003. Trust as an organizing principle, *Organization Science*, vol. 14, no. 1, pp. 91–103.

Möllering, G. 2005. The trust/control duality: An integrative perspective on positive expectations of others, *International Sociology*, vol. 20, no. 3, pp. 283–305.

Payne, A. and Frow, P. 2005. A strategic framework for customer relationship management, *Journal of Marketing*, vol. 69, October, pp. 167–76.

Ring, P.S. and Van de Ven, A.H. 1994. Developmental processes of cooperation in interorganizational relations, *Academy of Management Review*, vol. 19, no. 1, pp. 90–118.

Rousseau, D.M., Sitkin, S.B., Burt, R.S. and Camerer, C. 1998. Not so different after all: A cross-discipline view of trust, *Academy of Management Review*, vol. 23, no. 3, pp. 393–404.

Savolainen, T. 2011. Inter-personal trust development between actors within organizations: From linearity to multiplicity, paper presented at The First Seminar of the Nordic Trust Research Network on Trust Within and Between Organizations, May, Joensuu, University of Eastern Finland.

Savolainen, T. and López-Fresno, P. 2013. Trust as intangible asset: Enabling intellectual capital development by leadership for vitality and innovativeness. *Electronic Journal of Knowledge Management*, vol. 11, no. 3, pp. 244–55.

Savolainen, T., Lopez-Fresno, P. and Ikonen, M. 2014. Trust–communication dyad in inter-personal workplace relationships: Dynamics of trust deterioration and breach, *The Electronic Journal of Knowledge Management*, vol. 12, no. 4, pp. 232–40.

Schilke, O. and Cook, K.S. 2013. A cross-level process theory of trust development in interorganizational relationships, *Strategic Organization*, vol. 11, no. 3, pp. 281–303.

Seligman, A. 1999. Trust and generalized exchange, in K. Ilmonen (ed.), *Sosiaalinen Pääoma ja Luottamus (2000)*, Jyväskylä: University of Jyväskylä pp. 39–54.

Sitkin, S. and George, E. 2005. Managerial trust-building through the use of legitimating formal and informal control mechanisms, *International Sociology*, vol. 20, no. 3, pp. 307–38.

Tyler, T.R. 2003. Trust within organizations, *Personnel Review*, vol. 32, no. 5, pp. 556–68.

Weibel, A. 2007. Formal control and trustworthiness: Shall the twain never meet? *Group & Organization Management*, vol. 32, no. 4, pp. 500–517.

Yukl, G. 2010. *Leadership in Organizations*, 10th edn, Upper Saddle River, NJ: Prentice Hall.

Zaheer, A., McEvily, B. and Perrone, V. 1998. Does trust matter? Exploring the effects of interorganizational and interpersonal trust on performance. *Organization Science*, vol. 9, no. 2, pp. 141–59.

PART III

Framing and stabilizing trust

9. Trust processes in inter-organizational relations: the role of imprinting

Anna Swärd

This chapter aims to contribute to the evolving literature on trust processes in inter-organizational relations by introducing the concept of imprinting. The concept of imprinting was first introduced by Stinchcombe (1965), referring to how an organization is affected by the industry conditions at the time of its founding and how these imprints persist over time. It has also been argued that imprints can be understood as experiences that determine subsequent social behaviour, but imprinting research has only partly addressed the dynamics of imprinting (Marquis and Tilcsik, 2013). This chapter argues that imprinting is a highly useful concept for understanding trust as a process in inter-organizational relations, because imprints are conditions or perceptions that are created during short, critical periods and remain stable over time. By understanding the trust imprints formed in inter-organizational relationships and how these imprints change over time, we gain an insight into which perceptions of trustworthiness are stable and enduring and which perceptions are more readily prone to change. Despite the numerous studies on imprinting, it remains to be discussed further in relation to trust processes and inter-organizational relations. This chapter offers insights into how we can understand imprinting in relation to trust – specifically, how trust imprints are created, how imprints persist and why imprints change.

Studies on alliance processes hint at an imprinting effect as relationships develop in stages (Das and Teng, 2002); initial conditions have an impact on the first interactions, while partners over time learn about each other, adjust and improve upon the initial conditions (Arino and De la Torre, 1998; Doz, 1996). Initial conditions are considered by some to be the starting point for understanding how a relationship evolves (Inkpen and Currall, 2004). Similarly, trust researchers hint at an imprinting effect in which trust – or a lack thereof – between partners during the initial stages of a partnership leaves strong imprints on later developments (Ferrin et al., 2008; Vlaar et al., 2007). It is widely accepted that trust develops over time and deepens as people learn about each other's intentions and qualities and observe consistent behaviours over time, and people tend to base their judgements of trustworthiness on various factors as relationships develop (Levin et al., 2006). In inter-organizational relations, the partners carry with them imprints from their organizations that affect how they approach a new partner. Further, expectations are based on prior experiences, reputation and third-party information, whereas perceptions of interactions will become more important over time (Ferrin et al., 2008). This shifting hierarchy of expectations supports the notion of trust building as a continuous and evolving process of information processing and learning (Möllering, 2012). However, this learning process is gradual and cumulative, and while some perceptions remain more stable over time, others change more easily.

The aforementioned studies show how events and conditions early in a relationship can initiate a positive or negative trust spiral, but it remains unclear how these initial conditions create imprints that remain stable and how and why these imprints may change or develop over time. Marquis and Tilcsik (2013) suggest that imprints result from conditions not only during the initial period, but potentially also during several sensitive periods or periods of transition in which new imprints are created. Marquis and Tilcsik (2013) offer an extensive review of imprinting studies but argue that there are very few *empirical* studies that consider the dynamic nature of imprinting. This chapter offers empirical insights that illustrate and support the notion of imprinting as a process and makes suggestions regarding how imprinting may also be useful for the understanding of trust as a process. The findings show how each individual forming an assessment of a partner's trustworthiness draws on early imprints, how new imprints are created during sensitive periods, how trust contributes to new layers of imprints and how some imprints remain stable and can resurface in periods of transition.

Insights into the imprinting process related to trust development are gained from an explorative study of two partners on a construction project that occurred in 2009–13. The partners involved in the project had no personal knowledge about each other prior to the first interactions. The project was followed in real time, from its inception to its completion, and offered valuable opportunities for studying periods of transition, how imprints are formed and in some cases remain stable and what makes them change. The chapter is organized as follows: the theory section presents insights into the concept of imprinting and relates these insights to trust processes in inter-organizational relations. The next section introduces the research design and the empirical fieldwork with a presentation of the illustrative case. The third section discusses the findings and then draws conclusions with implications for trust research and practice.

IMPRINTING AND TRUST PROCESSES IN INTER-ORGANIZATIONAL RELATIONS

The concept of imprinting has attracted interest in many fields and has a specific meaning beyond that of path dependence or the significance of history (Marquis and Tilcsik, 2013). Imprinting is not about long-term chains of events, but rather concerns how short, sensitive periods affect and are followed by periods of stability. Traditionally, imprinting research has focused on how environmental conditions early in an organization's life (Stinchcombe, 1965) or in the early career of an individual (Higgins, 2005) create lasting imprints. However, a recent paper argues that imprinting is most likely to be a dynamic process (Marquis and Tilcsik, 2013). Marquis and Tilcsik (2013) argue that imprinting has the following characteristics: (1) there are brief sensitive periods of transition during which the focal entity is more likely to be influenced by external conditions; (2) a process takes place by which the focal entity comes to reflect elements of the environment; and (3) imprints will persist despite subsequent environmental changes.

Imprinting in inter-organizational relations remains unexplored and is a context in which sensitive periods are readily observable due to the temporary character of these organizational forms (Bakker, 2010). Inter-organizational relations are likely to experience periods of transition as they are established and as new imprints are created or layered upon the imprints already present in each organization. The founding of a new inter-organizational relation could therefore be considered a 'sensitive period', as it is likely that the partners will carry with them imprints from their respective organizations that are likely to change as the partners go through a period of joint sensemaking. Some imprints prior to the inter-organizational relation will persist, while others will fade over time or become even more influential (Marquis and Tilcsik, 2013). Sensitive periods can be understood as periods of uncertainty during which one is more likely to be influenced by what occurs in the environment. It has been argued that individual-level transitions are seen as periods of anxiety, during which one strives to reduce uncertainty, and that one is more prone to being imprinted in such phases (Higgins, 2005). Individuals are likely to adopt new behaviours and norms during uncertain periods, and their behaviours following this period will reflect these imprints (Tilcsik, 2012). This also means that perceptions of trustworthiness are likely to change during periods of transition but are likely to persist after the sensitive period. For instance, people tend to carry with them the beliefs and behaviours formed during their early apprenticeships in their careers (Higgins, 2005; McEvily et al., 2012). Regarding trust, beliefs could entail that one is more prone to change one's perceptions about a partner's trustworthiness during sensitive periods; these perceptions may then remain stable in subsequent interactions before a new sensitive period occurs.

Trust has been defined and conceptualized in several ways, and the most commonly used definitions emphasize positive expectations of trustworthiness and willingness to accept vulnerability (Mayer et al., 1995; Rousseau, 1998). These definitions have been criticized for being too static, as they do not incorporate the dynamics of trust (Möllering, 2006; Nielsen, 2011). This chapter addresses how people learn about their partners and use various sources of information in their judgements of a partner's trustworthiness; as such, a more process-oriented definition is required. Möllering (2006) argues that trust manifests itself between reason, routine and reflexivity. People are constantly interpreting their relationships with others, trying to find reasons to trust, either in the context or in the actions of their partners. Interpretations lead to expectations about future behaviour. However, there will always be some uncertainty that one must suspend in order to trust; this suspension of uncertainty is known as a 'leap of faith' (Lewis and Weigert, 1985). The process of reducing uncertainty is important and often necessary for encouraging leaps of faith (Möllering, 2006). Trust is likely to be challenged throughout a relationship, and difficult phases may occur during which trust must be restored or strengthened again (Huemer, 1998). Trust thus involves a constant assessment of the other party's trustworthiness in varying situations. When deciding whether or not to trust, the trustee assesses the other party regarding ability, benevolence and integrity (Mayer et al., 1995). Ability refers to an evaluation of the other party's competencies, capacities and capabilities in a certain area. Benevolence is the tendency of the trustee to have good intentions and to want to act favourably towards the trustor (the individual determining whether to trust the trustee). Finally, integrity is adherence to the accepted principles and values (Mayer et al., 1995). Perceptions of trustworthiness will initially be based on prior interactions or a company's reputation, while more information can be gathered as partners start to interact (Lewicki and Bunker, 1996; Ring and Van de Ven, 1992).

Studies on alliances and trust hint at an imprinting effect and argue that there are certain initial conditions that are more or less favourable for initiating virtuous or vicious trust spirals (Ferrin et al., 2008; Vlaar et al., 2007). Relationships are known to develop in stages (Das and Teng, 2002), during which the initial conditions influence the first interactions, and over time the partners learn about each other, adjust and improve upon the initial conditions (Arino and De la Torre, 1998; Doz, 1996). Others argue that the initial conditions constitute the starting point for understanding how a relationship evolves (Inkpen and Currall, 2004). Relationships are restrained by the initial conditions, which can include a definition of the partnership objectives, design of the partner interface and governance systems, industry affiliation, culture, prior interactions and reputation (Arino et al., 2001; Doz, 1996). This effect means that the partners entering an alliance with another organization carry with them earlier imprints that affect their perceptions of their partners' trustworthiness. Imprints can be positive for trust; for example, a common understanding of the industry, routines and standard contracts can create a common framework as a basis for joint sensemaking. Initial perceptions have been found to be quite robust (Adobor, 2005), as people seldom seek information that is contradictory to their first beliefs (McKnight et al., 1998). Consequently, if the initial expectations are low, an actor is likely to interpret the actions and signals from the partner negatively, resulting in a negative trust spiral (Adobor, 2005). However, Adobor (2005) does not find evidence that initial expectations are determinants for the level of trust and suggests that the behaviours during the relationship phase might be just as important.

Trust is about prediction and interpretation (Möllering, 2006), and researchers have embraced the idea that the most important determinant of trust is what can be learned about a trustee by observing his or her behaviour (Ferrin et al., 2006). The actions performed by a partner will be one of the most important sources of information about trustworthiness as the partnership begins (Lewicki and Bunker, 1996; Lewis and Weigert, 1985; Rousseau, 1998; Six and Skinner, 2010). Early minor events and partners' initial moves have a strong impact on how trust develops (Doz, 1996; Ferrin et al., 2008). Partners may perform actions demonstrating goodwill in early encounters to see how the partner responds (Whitener et al., 1998). These goodwill actions include showing concern, good intentions or commitment (Bottom et al., 2002; Six and Sorge, 2008; Six et al., 2010). When the outcomes of these actions and reactions are positive, the process encourages larger leaps of faith that test trust and trigger deeper forms of trust. Thus, imprints are likely to be stable but may change as people learn (Doz, 1996) and make sense of their relationships (Weick, 1993). Consequently, it is unclear what kind of initial conditions and expectations create lasting imprints, why these imprints change and what remains of the imprinting effect from the initial conditions.

To gain an insight into the process of imprinting in relation to trust in inter-organizational relations, we must understand: (1) what a sensitive period is; (2) whether and how partners' trustworthiness perceptions change during sensitive periods – that is, how imprints are created; and (3) whether there are stable imprints after a sensitive period – that is, how persistent these imprints are. This line of inquiry suggests potential value in exploring whether there are multiple sensitive periods beyond the initial phase and whether some imprints will persist while others will fade over time (Marquis and Tilcsik, 2013).

EMPIRICAL SETTING, METHODS AND DATA SOURCES

This research relies on the case study method, because the aim is to understand relationship processes. The case study method allows for an in-depth analysis and understanding of complex social phenomena (Yin, 1994) and focuses on understanding the dynamics within single settings (Eisenhardt, 1989). Case studies enable researchers to investigate causal processes in more depth than is possible using statistical methods (Regin and Becker, 1992).

The two partners in the relationships under investigation were the private contractor (subsequently referred to as the contractor) and the Norwegian Public Roads Administration, which is responsible for all the roads in Norway (referred to as the client). These two partners have worked together on many previous projects, but because road projects are the responsibility of varying regional offices, very few individuals have actually worked together in the past. In this particular project, none of the individuals had previously worked together. It is common in the industry for the client to choose the contractor based on a competitive tendering process; thus, clients have limited advanced knowledge about the individuals with whom they will be coordinating for years to come.

The client team consisted of the project manager, two site managers, administrative personnel and several controllers. The project team on the contractor side consisted of the project manager, the site manager, several foremen and administrative personnel. Additionally, the contractor had hired a range of sub-contractors for specific tasks. During the construction phase, these teams worked separately from their main organizations and only reported to their headquarters on progress in terms of time and costs. The contractor team was located in a temporary facility next to the construction site, while the client team was located a few minutes away in another building.

The conflicts arising in these projects are often linked to disagreements regarding changes or incomplete clauses in the contracts. The contract specifies the exact operations necessary for completing the road project, and the contractor is asked to price each operation accordingly. Occasionally, specifications are found to be incomplete, or changes that cannot be anticipated occur on the sites. In these instances, contractors are compensated for any additional work necessary to complete the project. However, it is often unclear whether the additional work constitutes an actual change or addition to the contracts or whether there is simply a disagreement regarding the amount of compensation for additional work or inconvenience. Further, if the contractor does not receive the correct drawings from the client, the contractor can stop the work and demand compensation for the delay. There are few incentives for the contractor to finish on time or within the client's budget, as payment is based solely on the amount of work performed. Clients therefore monitor and inspect site work on a daily basis to protect themselves from opportunistic behaviour.

The reason for choosing this case and this setting was that it allowed for in-depth investigation and access to both sides of the dyad for an extended period of time. Due to the explorative nature of this study, it was initially unclear whether trust would be formed in this relationship or whether imprints would play a part – this understanding developed during the process of data collection and reviewing the existing literature. However, this setting proved to be ideal for studying trust and imprints, as the partners did develop trust despite some initial negative imprints. The absence of any previous interaction history enabled me to tease out the initial imprints and, subsequently, the imprints formed during interactions. This project was followed continuously in real time between 2009 and 2013. Observations in meetings took place every two weeks on average; these observations were the main sources of data, along with interviews and minutes from meetings. In total, 20 semi-structured interviews and 42 observations (160 hours) were conducted in addition to examining the minutes from 52 additional meetings. Table 9.1 shows when the data collection occurred in relation to the main four phases elaborated upon in the findings section.

Interviews were conducted with project managers, site managers, engineers and foremen from both organizations. A semi-structured interview guide was used that focused on how the partners perceived the relationship at the inception of the project, which information informed

Table 9.1   Data sources chronologically

Sensitive period 1	Sensitive period 2	Stable period	Sensitive period 3
Sept. 2009–Jan. 2010	Mid-Jan. 2010– June 2010	Sept. 2010–June 2011	July 2011–Nov. 2011
3 interviews	3 interviews	10 interviews	4 interviews
6 observed meetings 6 minutes from meetings	12 observed meetings 8 minutes from meetings	14 observed meetings 14 minutes from meetings	10 observed meetings 24 minutes from meetings

their assessments of the partner, how the relationship started and developed over time, which incidents contributed to better cooperation, which incidents and actions were harmful to cooperation, how the relationship was governed, whether any focus was given or specific action taken to improve cooperation, how and why conflicts arose and how the relationship was regarded at the termination of the alliance.

In research involving case studies, data analysis typically occurs simultaneously with data collection. I followed this approach by writing analytical memos as the data collection proceeded. The decision to order the field notes systematically as the data collection proceeded was important for the subsequent analysis. Pettigrew (1990) argues that data collection is about observations and verification, meaning that the data tell the story. During the interview process, I followed themes and trails that seemed to be significant to disconfirm or verify the preliminary patterns with further data. The ongoing analysis served as input for the subsequent interviews and observations. Concepts were seen as temporal until they emerged repeatedly in observations, interviews and documents (Corbin and Strauss, 1990). During the data analysis, I compared the emergent concepts with the relevant literature and searched for relationships between and among categories. The findings revealed three sensitive periods during which new imprints were created: the beginning of the project, the blast accident and the period near project termination. Between these sensitive periods, the trustworthiness perceptions remained stable. These findings will be further described below.

FINDINGS

Imprints Prior to the Project Start-up

The construction industry has standard contracts with which both the client and the contractor are familiar. These contracts are very specific and detailed, specifying each work operation as well as a well-defined meeting structure. Further, the industry has established roles with a project manager on each side, site manager, contractor foremen who oversee the work on the construction site and client controllers with engineering competence who monitor the construction work on a daily basis. There are also well-established procedures for the controllers to report any irregularities that they encounter during their inspections. Contractors, on the other hand, are required to report to the client whenever they experience that the work cannot be performed in accordance with the specifications in the contract, or when they anticipate that the work will be delayed. Actors in the industry emphasize trust as an important aspect of successful projects, because contracts are known to be incomplete, and unforeseen events often occur that are not covered in the contracts. However, many conflicts can arise with construction projects. The contractor and the client on this particular project carried imprints from the institutional context described above, as well as imprints from previous experiences with the involved firms (although the individuals had not previously worked together).

Because the project teams had not worked together in the past, some uncertainty surrounded the partners' expectations of the relationship apart from their mutual knowledge of each other based on reputation and previous encounters with the respective firms. The client team agreed that the contractor that won the bid was known to be capable and would certainly not have won the bid otherwise. Another perception among the client team was that contractors in general are known to charge excessively for additions and changes to the contract. Members of the contractor management team, on the other hand, had worked directly with the contractor organization or heard stories about the contractor organization – specifically, that it was often difficult to work with its personnel.

The contract between the partners was similar to other projects in the industry, with one major exception. The client specified the inclusion of a project development phase, during which the partners would sit together for the first two weeks and discuss any potential alternative approaches to the tasks that might save money. Any savings would be shared between the two partners. The members of the contractor team were suspicious about this new clause in the contract, because they were used to the client specifying the project approach in detail before both parties signed the contract.

In sum, the imprints carried into the relationship by each team included a well-known contract, clear distribution of roles and responsibilities, and experiences from previous projects. These imprints create a predictable context for the individuals entering the project and can thus create a common framework for joint sensemaking. However, changing these structures can lead to uncertainty about intentions, as evidenced in this situation.

The Beginning of the Project: The First Sensitive Period and the Evolvement of a New Layer of Imprints

The two partners first met at a start-up meeting in which the client project manager presented the contract and the intentions behind it. Both partners had the chance to express their concerns and their goals for the project. They later met again at the first project development meeting. The contractor project manager was surprised to find the client team sitting and waiting for the contractor team to present suggestions for cheaper solutions there and then. However, the contractor project manager and his site manager tried their best to come up with some initial suggestions that would be fruitful areas to explore. The client project manager stated that he found the contractor team to be dedicated to the task and behaving cooperatively.

> Well, we expected them to be competent, as they are one of the large contractors in the industry, and they are known to have good routines when it comes to health and safety issues. Apart from that, we didn't know much about the people involved. (Client manager)

> We have heard and also somewhat experienced that they have very rigid contracts and there are often conflicts in their projects. (Contractor manager)

The outcome of the first meetings was positive; both teams believed that the other team was making a genuine effort and would try its best to find solutions to which both parties could agree. The problem was that the project was predesigned; very few changes were possible, and the parties agreed that these meetings were useful in terms of becoming familiar with each other while the financial outcomes were limited. However, each side's perceptions based on the first interactions included perceived willingness to cooperate and genuine effort. This perception was evidenced by a decision from the contractor project manager and his team to relinquish compensation for the time spent in these meetings, because they felt that the meetings had been useful for everyone. The client team's perception of this action was that the contractor team was really trying its best to show its commitment to this project.

> They clearly show interest and commitment and treat us fairly; therefore, we need to act fairly in return. (Client manager)

> We found that the contractor team was really making an effort in starting off cooperatively; they really put time into finding other solutions. We were quite impressed. (Client manager)

As the actual construction work began, the contractor project manager conversed with the workers and specifically requested them to treat the members of the client team well because they were nice people. However, soon afterwards, the client controllers sent written complaints about the work not being performed in accordance with the contract, without first sharing this complaint with the workers on the site. The contractor project manager found this to be an unconstructive way to handle these issues and felt that it was inappropriate to submit complaints without even talking to the workers. He contacted the client project manager, who immediately spoke with the controllers about how to communicate with the contractor workers. The controllers were specifically asked to discuss issues directly with the workers on the site and document the agreed-upon solution when they returned to their offices.

> From other projects, we are used to the controllers sending written complaints, but sometimes this monitoring can be really annoying. It was not a surprise that they would do this here as well. (Contractor foreman)

> From other projects, we are used to things needing to be documented, so we did the same here. (Client controller)

After this episode, the controllers and the foremen spoke with each other several times each day and discussed how to solve difficult technical matters or improve the quality of the work being performed. A personal trusting relationship began to develop between controllers and foremen. One controller describes one of the contractor foremen as someone who always keeps his promises, is easy to talk to and is honest.

> They call us and ask us to come out to the site if they are uncertain about how to solve a problem. (Client foreman)

> It was really good that the project managers talked about how they wanted us to interact. After this we discussed openly with them and found that we could trust them to stick to the agreement. (Client controller)

The meetings between the managerial teams involved spending a significant amount of time and effort deciding and agreeing upon how to handle changes and additions, how to communicate with each other and how to solve issues of disagreement. As such, both partners needed to learn about each other's structures and routines. When the partners disagreed, they often referred to the contract but avoided engaging in conflict, rather postponing difficult issues for later meetings, allowing for more time to document and gather information.

The managers describe the relation in the following manner:

> These are honest and dependable people.

> They really try to solve issues and we can discuss with them openly.

In sum, during this period, due to favourable interactions during which the partners learned about each other's intentions, trustworthiness, structures and routines, new imprints seem to have developed gradually. However, we also see that the imprints preceding the project initiation still played a strong role. A new imprint was layered upon the established ones brought into the relationship by the parties. The new imprint did not replace the old ones, but rather created a new layer.

The Blast Accident – The Second Sensitive Period and Change in Imprints

About three months into the project, the contractor made a mistake when blasting for a new tunnel and rock fell onto the existing road. The traffic needed to be redirected and the rock cleared away. Additionally, a transformer station was hit and all the lights went off in the old tunnel, meaning that traffic could not pass until the problem was resolved. The client was surprised to find that the contractor readily accepted the blame for what had happened and anticipated negative reactions from the client. The client anticipated the contractor trying to blame it for insufficient planning or design. Conversely, the contractor team has experienced that when such things have arisen in other projects, the client issues fines or enacts other sanctions. The contractor management team, however, was pleased to find that the client refrained from sanctioning and rather cooperated in problem solving. The operational-level foremen and controllers worked efficiently together to open the road. Despite the difficulties, the blast accident was described as 'the turning point' for the relationship.

> We would have expected them to demand compensation. Instead of blaming us, they helped us out and did their best to solve the problems. The way it was handled made us believe that we could rely on these people. (Contractor manager)

> They readily took the blame for the blast accident and did their best to solve the matter. Instead of spending time debating economic matters, they worked together with us to open the road as soon as possible. (Client manager)

In sum, this second sensitive period created new imprints based on the high level of trust formed when trust was tested. Compared with the previous period, this was a real change that came from unsettling times and the client's decision to take a leap of faith by behaving cooperatively, something that was not expected by the contractor. This event was characterized by uncertainty for all the people involved as it was a situation in which one could not be sure about how the other party would behave. As such, the partners were more susceptible to new imprints during this time of uncertainty than they had been in the previous period.

Stability and Strengthening of the New Imprints

After this incident, individuals on both sides communicated and interacted on a daily basis. For instance, the foremen took the initiative to contact the controllers when they had a situation about which they were uncertain, and they approached the controllers more as discussion partners than as controllers. Discussions and disagreements were left to the managerial level, at which individuals reserved economic topics of conversation for separate meetings to avoid disrupting the project work.

The trusting relationship that developed was further tested approximately one year into the project, when the contractor found that a large amount of work had to be redone due to misspecifications in the design. The client showed great understanding of the contractor's frustration. In this situation, the contractor could have protested by refusing to continue working before the design was in place. However, the contractor decided to be helpful and act cooperatively. This decision was due partly to how the client had treated the contractor during the blast accident and partly to the trusting relationship that had developed during the blast accident.

> The contractor arranged for a series of extra meetings and really made an effort to make the best out of the situation. (Client manager)

They were very nice towards us when we had the blast accident. It was only fair that we would help them out this time. (Contractor manager)

Negotiating the Final Settlement: The Third Sensitive Period and the Resurfacing of the Initial Imprints

As mentioned previously, negotiations on economic settlements were saved for specific meetings. In these meetings, the managers strove to find an approach upon which both partners could agree. Issues often had to be postponed because an agreement could not be reached. The reason for this was often a lack of information. Closer to termination, the partners were accustomed to a higher frequency of conflict in these meetings, and although a trusting relationship had formed in the project, the partners were concerned about how the other would behave regarding the final settlement. Closer to termination, the use of language and the discussions in these meetings had an increasingly harsh tone. At the same time, the two project managers smoothed over much of the controversy expressed by the other managers and found ways to compromise on issues regarding which the other party had better arguments or better information. Additionally, over time, the contractor project manager found that it was productive to structure each meeting around an agenda that included negotiation around a mix of disagreements that the client had a greater chance of winning and cases that the contractor had a greater chance of winning. In this manner, both partners could leave a meeting with a feeling that they had won some and lost some. This way of handling the final settlement turned out to be productive, and the project finished on time and within budget.

> We were uncertain about how they would behave closer to termination, as we have had quite negative experiences with contractors in earlier projects. A trusting relationship is sometimes destroyed during the final economic negotiations. (Client manager)

> Closer to termination, we were uncertain about behaviours but found that they were trying to find solutions to which we both could agree. (Contractor manager)

On construction projects, it is common for conflicts to arise toward the end of the project despite work running quite smoothly up to that point. These late conflicts are mainly due to economic matters that have not been settled throughout the project.

The above interview extracts show how the early imprints resurfaced as uncertainties about the final settlement arose. Trust declined, but the imprints from the second period remained intact and trust was partly restored.

ANALYSIS AND DISCUSSION

The findings from the case confirm the importance of the early phase for understanding how trust develops (Doz, 1996); as such, the early phase can be characterized as the first sensitive period for the partners. In the early phase, uncertainty is high and information about trustworthiness must initially come from prior experience, reputation or third-party information. As such, both groups base their initial perceptions on how they view the organizations to which these individuals belong and assume that the partner group is representative of its organizations. The institutional context is important for the early perceptions, and the established structures and routines create predictability because the individuals involved know what to expect in terms of responsibilities. This predictability creates a common framework for joint sensemaking. Due to the competitive tendering procedure, the contractor is assumed to have significant ability. However, some negative background information is also present, such as a poor reputation and expected opportunistic behaviours. For instance, the contractor team had heard from others that the client was rigid and difficult to work with, and the client expected the contractor to take advantage of the lock-in situation by charging too much for additions and changes. This background information created imprints that affected how the partners behaved during the subsequent interactions.

The established structures and routines reduced uncertainty and created a common framework for joint sensemaking, as the partners knew what to expect when entering the project. However, the new clause in the contract, which stated that the partners were to sit together for the first two weeks and discuss alternative approaches, was not in accordance with these established imprints and gave rise to uncertainty. The findings show that the imprints discussed above made the partners suspicious about each other's intentions; for example, the contractor found it unusual for the client to be interested in hearing suggestions from the contractor regarding cheaper solutions. The findings also show that the partners initially behaved in accordance with the established roles and routines, such as when the controllers refrained from engaging in direct communication and rather sent written complaints about the work that had been performed. These behaviours can be attributed to imprints based on previous experiences, reputation and established roles and routines. However, the importance of these imprints faded as the partners began to interact and gain direct experience with each other. Early imprints have been found to have significant consequences as partners observe the other party and seek signs that confirm their first perceptions, such as a lack of competence or flexibility (Doz, 1996). However, it is widely acknowledged that trust changes as people interact and gain knowledge about each other (Lewicki and Bunker, 1996; Ring and Van de Ven, 1992). As such, we know that perceptions of trustworthiness change as new information about a partner emerges. Thus, developing trust can be considered a learning process during which initial imprints change as people gain positive experiences with one another incrementally over time. This process is also reflected in the findings from the case. The first meeting sequence between the management teams created positive expectations regarding trustworthiness. For instance, when the contractor relinquished compensation, this relinquishment was interpreted as willingness to cooperate and as a sign of trustworthiness. The findings also show that each partner's established structures and routines had to be adjusted to fit the intergroup demand. Additionally, the negotiation of structures and routines constituted an ongoing process that, over time, became institutionalized and strongly agreed upon. As such, favourable interactions and adjustments were incrementally layered upon the initial imprint in this phase.

The partners stated that the blast accident was the turning point in the relationship, because trust was tested and each partner could really experience that the other was trustworthy. The imprints were changed here for the first time and not only layered upon the initial imprint as in the first sensitive period. This finding is in line with others who have found that 'trouble' is not detrimental to trust building (Six and Skinner, 2010), but rather gives the partners a chance really to learn about the intentions of one another. By examining the interactions that followed, we see that the partners trusted each other in a deeper and more fundamental way than they had previously. This incident can be interpreted as a sensitive period during which the partners' assumptions and perceptions were altered in a fundamental way, and they found that their initial perceptions and imprints were not valid. In line with the reasoning by Marquis and Tilcsik (2013), it is fair to argue that a new imprint was created. It is evident that the new imprint guided behaviour during the problems related to drawings. In this instance, the partners behaved cooperatively based on the new imprint that was formed during the previous interactions and the testing of trust during the blast accident.

The findings show that imprints can resurface during periods of uncertainty, such as just before project termination. This shift can be interpreted as evidence of the existence of layers of imprints (Marquis and Tilcsik, 2013). In other words, although partners learn about each other through direct interaction and new bases of trust are formed, the first imprints remain in the background and can resurface later. In the case study in question, we see that the early imprint based on reputation, contract, roles and other factors resurfaced close to termination due to new uncertainties regarding the final settlement. The findings show that the partners in this situation referred back to the early imprint, which contained a perception that partners are likely to behave opportunistically when the relationship approaches termination. Interestingly, even though these imprints resurfaced, the imprint constituting a high level of trust gained through the interactions somehow remained and helped the partners reach an agreement.

CONCLUSION

The findings from this study offer an understanding of the process of imprinting related to trust. First, it offers an understanding of how early imprints affect behaviours during uncertain periods. Secondly, it provides an insight into how imprints remain stable and how new layers of imprints are created as partners interact with and learn about one another. Thirdly, it offers an awareness of how sensitive periods, during which trust is tested, give rise to new imprints that are quite persistent over time. Fourthly, it provides an understanding of how imprints can fade and resurface when new uncertainties arise. The findings show that the imprints that partners carry with them into a new relationship are important for determining the perception of trustworthiness early in a relationship and that the early phase also represents a sensitive period during which the partners are open to new imprints based on what they experience. In this manner, trust draws on imprints but also creates new imprints. These insights contribute to our understanding of trust as a process of learning, in which imprints are created and recreated through a learning process. It is thus confirmed that imprints affect trust, and it is also likely that relationships will undergo several periods of transition. The findings support earlier work that emphasizes the importance of initial conditions, but builds upon this understanding by showing how a learning process gives rise to new layers of imprints. Contributing to the understanding of the dynamics of trust imprints in inter-organizational relations not only benefits our understanding of trust as a process; it also contributes to the imprinting theory, as the imprinting concept has primarily been concerned with the organizational and individual levels (Marquis and Tilcsik, 2013) rather than the imprints formed in inter-organizational relations. Further, the study provides empirical insights into how imprints may change and develop over time.

These insights are preliminary in the sense that we cannot know with certainty that these effects are also valid for larger samples or in other contexts. Further explorative studies of how imprinting actually happens are needed. For instance, will some individuals be more predisposed towards imprints than others? If an imprint changes too easily, it may not have been an imprint in the first place. Further enquiry is needed to tease out the answers to these interesting questions. However, the aim of the chapter was to introduce the concept of imprinting into trust research and to illustrate how this concept can be beneficial in developing a clearer understanding of trust as a social learning process. This chapter suggests that the concept of imprinting is a promising concept to explore further in our quest for a deeper understanding of trust processes.

REFERENCES

Adobor, H. (2005) Trust as sensemaking: The microdynamics of trust in interfirm alliances. *Journal of Business Research*, 58 (3), 330–37.

Arino, A. and De la Torre, J. (1998) Learning from failure: Towards an evolutionary model of collaborative ventures. *Organization Science*, 9 (3), 306–25.

Arino, A., De la Torre, J. and Smith Ring, P. (2001) Relational quality: Managing trust in corporate alliances. *California Management Review*, 44 (1), 109–31.

Bakker, R.M. (2010) Taking stock of temporary organizational forms: A systematic review and research agenda. *International Journal of Management Reviews*, 12 (4), 466–86.

Bottom, W.P., Gibson, K., Daniels, S.E. and Murnighan, J. (2002) When talk is not cheap: Substantive penance and expressions of intent in rebuilding cooperation. *Organization Science*, 13 (5), 497–513.

Corbin, J. and Strauss, A. (1990) Grounded theory research: Procedures, canons, and evaluative criteria. *Qualitative Sociology*, 13 (1), 3–21.

Das, T. and Teng, B.S. (2002) Alliance constellations: A social exchange perspective. *Academy of Management Review*, 27 (2), 445–56.

Doz, Y.L. (1996) The evolution of cooperation in strategic alliances: Initial conditions or learning processes? *Strategic Management Journal*, 17 (Special Issue), 55–84.

Eisenhardt, K.M. (1989) Building theories from case study research. *Academy of Management Review*, 14 (4), 532–50.

Ferrin, D.L., Bligh, M.C. and Kohles, J.C. (2008) It takes two to tango: An interdependence analysis of the spiraling of perceived trustworthiness and cooperation in interpersonal and intergroup relationships. *Organizational Behavior & Human Decision Processes*, 107 (2), 161–78.

Ferrin, D.L., Dirks, K.T. and Shah, P.P. (2006) Direct and indirect effects of third-party relationships on interpersonal trust. *Journal of Applied Psychology*, 91 (4), 870–83.

Higgins, M.C. (2005) *Career Imprints: Creating Leaders across an Industry*. San Francisco, CA: Jossey-Bass.

Huemer, L. (1998) *Trust in Business Relations: Economic Logic or Social Interaction?* Umeå: Borea.

Inkpen, A.C. and Currall, S. (2004) The coevolution of trust, control and learning in joint ventures. *Organization Science*, 15 (5), 586–99.

Levin, D.Z., Whitener, E.M. and Cross, R. (2006) Perceived trustworthiness of knowledge sources: The moderating impact of relationship length. *Journal of Applied Psychology*, 91 (5), 1163–71.

Lewicki, R.J. and Bunker, B.B. (1996) Developing and maintaining trust in work relationships. In: R.M. Kramer and T.R. Tyler (eds), *Trust in Organizations: Frontiers of Theory and Research*. Thousand Oaks, CA: Sage, pp. 114–39.

Lewis, J.D. and Weigert, A. (1985) Trust as a social reality. *Social Forces*, 63 (4), 967–85.

Marquis, C. and Tilcsik, A. (2013) Imprinting: Toward a multilevel theory. *Academy of Management Annals*, 7 (1), 193–243.

Mayer, R.C., Davis, J.H. and Schoorman, F.D. (1995) An integrative model of organizational trust. *Academy of Management Review*, 20 (3), 709–34.

McEvily, B., Jaffee, J. and Tortoriello, M. (2012) Not all bridging ties are equal: Network imprinting and firm growth in the Nashville legal industry, 1933–1978. *Organization Science*, 23 (2), 547–63.

McKnight, D.H., Cummings, L.L. and Chervany, N.L. (1998) Initial trust formation in new organizational relationships. *Academy of Management Review*, 23 (3), 473–90.

Möllering, G. (2006) *Trust, Reason, Routine, Reflexivity*. Oxford: Elsevier.

Möllering, G. (2012) Process views of trusting and crises. In: R. Bachmann and A. Zaheer (eds), *Handbook of Advances in Trust Research*. Cheltenham, UK and Northampton, MA, USA: Edward Elgar Publishing.

Nielsen, B.B. (2011) Trust in strategic alliances: Towards a co-evolutionary research model. *Journal of Trust Research*, 1 (2), 159–76.

Pettigrew, A.M. (1990) Longitudinal field research on change: Theory and practice. *Organization Science*, 1 (3), 267–92.

Regin, C.C. and Becker, H.S. (eds) (1992) *What is a Case? Exploring the Foundations of Social Enquiry*. Cambridge: Cambridge University Press.

Ring, P.S. and Van de Ven, A.H. (1992) Structuring cooperative relationships between organizations. *Strategic Management Journal*, 13 (7), 483–98.

Rousseau, D.M. (1998) Why workers still identify with organizations. *Journal of Organizational Behavior*, 19, 217–33.

Six, F. and Skinner, D. (2010) Managing trust and trouble in interpersonal work relationships: Evidence from two Dutch organizations. *International Journal of Human Resource Management*, 21 (1), 109–24.

Six, F. and Sorge, A. (2008) Creating a high-trust organization: An exploration into organizational policies that stimulate interpersonal trust building. *Journal of Management Studies*, 45 (5), 857–84.

Six, F., Nooteboom, B. and Hoogendoorn, A. (2010) Actions that build interpersonal trust: A relational signaling perspective. *Review of Social Economy*, 68 (3), 285–315.

Stinchcombe, A.L. (1965) Social structure and organizations. In: J.G. March (ed.), *Handbook of Organizations*. Chicago, IL: Rand McNally, pp. 142–93.

Tilcsik, A. (2012) *Remembrance of Things Past: Individual Imprinting in Organizations*. Cambridge, MA: Harvard University.

Vlaar, P.W.L., Van den Bosch, F.A.J. and Volberda, H.W. (2007) On the evolution of trust, distrust, and formal coordination and control in interorganizational relationships: Towards an integrative framework. *Group & Organization Management*, 32, 407.

Weick, K.E. (1993) The collapse of sensemaking in organizations: The Mann Gulch disaster. *Administrative Science Quarterly*, 38 (4), 628–52.

Whitener, E.M., Brodt, S.E., Korsgaard, M.A. and Werner, J.M. (1998) Managers as initiators of trust: An exchange relationship framework for understanding managerial trustworthy behavior. *Academy of Management Review*, 23 (3), 513–30.

Yin, R.K. (1994) *Case Study Research: Design and Methods*. Thousand Oaks, CA: Sage.

10. Trust and distrust as cultural frames

Kevin Anthony Perry

This chapter explores trust and distrust as cultural frames.[1] The focus is on trust and distrust, which can be understood as cultural and social repertoires (resources) used by actors in social encounters to frame (define) social relations – a valuable approach to researching trust and distrust that is largely under-represented in the trust literature. Adopting this approach implies that culture influences action by shaping a 'tool-box' (repertoire) of 'habits, skills, and styles [resources] from which people construct strategies of action' (Swidler, 1986: 273). Through learning and hands-on experience, knowledgeable actors can develop and expand their cultural toolbox (Swidler, 1986) and through this develop culture. A frame is a mental construct used by social actors to perceive, place, identify and categorize people and situations (Goffman, 1974). Framing (applying frames) can be understood as a concept used to describe the mechanism by which individuals make sense of and organize the world around them. Actors use frames as a resource to zoom in on certain aspects of processes, events and people to disentangle them from the rest of the scene. Framing is an unconscious, individual activity whereby individuals draw upon resources such as prior experiences, education and culture to frame their experiences during social situations. While frames reflect the norms, values, culture and preconceived ideas of social groups serving as frames of reference (Goffman, 1974), they are not rigid. Frames guide individuals to define and organize others and situations over time and provide a course of action.

The chapter explores the relationships between a group of young men with diverse minority ethnic backgrounds (Palestinian, Turkish and Somalian), aged 17–25 years, and a team of youth (SSP) workers, a job consultant and a police officer (cop). The abbreviation SSP stands for the interdisciplinary collaboration between schools, social services and police, where the aim is to prevent crime and related risk behaviour among children and young people. SSP cooperation concerns preventing crime rather than investigating or bringing criminals to justice. The legislation states: '[...] an authority may disclose information about individuals to the police and other authorities involved in the cooperation [but] such information obtained in these forms of cooperation cannot be disclosed for the investigation of criminal cases' (Retsplejeloven, §115b). In other words, any information that comes to light during SSP cooperation cannot be used by the police to investigate or solve criminal cases. The majority of local authorities in Denmark have some form of SSP collaboration based on local resources. The team of youth workers focused on in this study is based at a youth club bordering a housing estate known as Sunset Boulevard; their participation in the local SSP cooperation is indicated clearly by the bold letters *SSP* imprinted on their work clothes. The youth workers' tasks involve managing the youth club, engaging young people in activities and positive relationships. In addition, they undertake outreach work in the local community, which includes working uninvited in the young people's neighbourhood and attempting to build trusting relationships – a prerequisite for further work.

In contrast, the job consultant's work involves administrating the rules governing unemployment and the labour market relating to the young men in her caseload. The key features of her job include enforcing work availability, active job seeking and improving the employability of benefit recipients. Applying the rules involves deducting social security benefits for failure to attend or comply with the system.

The police officer, armed with a Heckler & Koch Compact 9 mm pistol, baton, pepper spray, walkie-talkie and discretionary powers, operates in and around Sunset Boulevard. Often, his job brings him into contact and at times conflict with the young men. The approach, attitude and actions of these employees towards the young men determine whether the relationships develop into trusting or distrusting forms and have consequences for service delivery.

In this chapter, primarily from the perspectives of the young men, these relationships are explored, looking closely at how the young men frame and organize these professionals together with how they construct these frames. Fundamentally, the chapter explores how trust and distrust can be understood as cultural frames. First, the chapter examines some of the dominant logic in the current trust literature. Subsequently, through bringing Swidler (1986) and Mizrachi et al. (2007) into play, the chapter conceptualizes trust and distrust as cultural frames. Next, drawing on fieldwork data, the chapter shows how the young men frame the employees, before concluding.

METHODOLOGICAL DESIGN AND DATA COLLECTION

The data on which this chapter draws derive from nine months of fieldwork in two social housing complexes in Denmark. Between October 2009 and July 2010, I observed the interaction between two groups of young men with minority ethnic backgrounds and frontline public sector employees. During this period, I utilized different ethnographic methods, for example shadowing, participant observation and recorded interviews. I adopted an overt participant-observer role as the primary method of data collection. When attending *official* meetings between various employees, I employed observation–participation, which involved listening, observing interactions and taking notes – a fly on the wall with a notebook. Furthermore, I shadowed a number of employees during fieldwork while they carried out their jobs. Shadowing provides a direct, multidimensional picture of the role, approach, views and tasks of the person under observation (McDonald, 2005). While spending time in the community centres in the two neighbourhoods and a local youth club located on the outer edge of Sunset Boulevard I engaged in participant observation. Participant observation adds a critical aspect to the notion of observation, allowing the researcher to access the lived experiences of participants (Prus, 1996). The participant observation consisted of socializing and participating in various activities, such as table football and Thai boxing, as well as attending social gatherings. Partaking in social activities was valuable in relation to understanding salient issues faced by the young men and for following up on various observed events. Participating in these activities facilitated a mutual platform for initiating social relations and the trust-building process. During field research, it is crucial for researchers to provide opportunities for *locals* to evaluate them as people, to examine their attitudes and make sense of their presence in the setting. This testing of the researcher is salient and undoubtedly influences the outcome of the field research. Throughout this period, I recorded detailed field notes and a comprehensive research diary, describing experiences and observations together with initial reflections. During the analysis, I apply principles from Goffman's (1974) frame analysis and Lewicki and Bunker's (1996) trust development model. This melding uses a combination of the theoretical groundwork of the trust literature and secondary insights throughout, accounted for locally in the chapter.

EMPIRICAL AND THEORETICAL BACKGROUND

Empirical inquiry into dyadic interpersonal relationships ('A' trusting 'B'), typically researched within organizational contexts, dominates the literature on trust. The dominant logic behind most of this research is that trust is a *psychological condition* (Bachman and Inkpen, 2011; Rousseau et al., 1998), which enables people to take chances in the face of uncertainty and risk, while acknowledging vulnerability (Mayer et al., 1995; Rousseau et al., 1998). Although Lewis and Weigert (1985) initially reject the notion that trust decisions are reducible to individual psychology, in their functionalist approach they postulate that trust occurs *naturally* within established groups. However, their supposition implies that trust becomes entrenched within individual members of these groups, which indeed suggests individual psychology. They advance trust as a functional prerequisite for society, which otherwise would be 'chaos' encapsulated in 'paralysing fear' (Luhmann, 1979: 4). In his functionalist take on trust, Sztompka (1999) argues that cultural predispositions based on normative rules powerfully guide people when it comes to trusting or distrusting others. Sztompka's (1999) postulation implies that community members *go with the flow* within shared inflexible norms, which denotes a total lack of agency.

PROCESS PERSPECTIVE

Latterly, some researchers have recognized the value of embracing the process approach to understand trust (for example Khodyakov, 2007; Möllering, 2006; Nooteboom and Six, 2003). The process perspective goes considerably further than the dyadic and functionalist approaches to trust by acknowledging people as 'active creators of processes' rather than 'passive carriers of a process' (Möllering, 2006: 79). Trust involves creativity, mainly attributed to agency, whereby competent actors play a crucial role in initiating, shaping, sustaining and changing trust in the process of interaction with others (Möllering, 2006). Competent social actors purposely engage in 'extensive signalling, communication, interaction and interpretation in order to maintain the continuous process of trust constitution' (Möllering, 2006: 79). Khodyakov's (2007) process perspective encompasses reason, routine and reflexivity; people choose to trust others in the present, based on future expectations and the reputation of the other created in the past. When compared to the dyadic and functionalist approaches to understanding trust, through embracing the multidimensionality of relationships and a multitude of social processes, the process perspective provides a more convincing account of trust and trusting. Following Khodyakov's (2007) rationale, the same process must account for distrust decisions, where social actors choose to distrust others in the present based on future negative expectations and reputations created in the past. However, little is known about trust as reflexivity and as a process from a contextual perspective. In a rare work on the subject, Flores and Solomon (1998) conceptualize trust as a deliberate, dynamic, emotional, relational process which involves responsibility. Trust develops because of and within relationships through verbal and non-verbal communication; trust building becomes expressed through 'gestures, looks, smiles, handshakes and touches' (Flores and Solomon, 1998: 205). They discuss trust relations and how they evolve. What they do not consider and what can strengthen this discussion, is how trust is an instituted (cultural) resource for actors.

TRUST AND DISTRUST AS CULTURAL FRAMES

Mizrachi et al. (2007) propose a new theoretical perspective on trust called *trust repertoires*. Drawing heavily on Swidler (1986) and her concept of *culture in action*, they view culture as a repertoire of skills and practices used by knowledgeable actors in pursuit of goals rather than something that shapes their behaviour. According to Swidler (1986), culture provides actors with a 'toolbox' (repertoire) of habits, styles and skills which they use as 'strategies of action' (p. 273). In this way, another way of viewing trust and distrust is as cultural resources drawn upon by actors within a social context to organize action (Mizrachi et al., 2007; Swidler, 1986). In this perspective, three interrelated dimensions shape the practice of trust: agency (selecting and using strategies of trust in different contexts); culture (a collection of symbols and practices); power and politics (context influences the strategies selected) (Mizrachi et al., 2007). Rather than just observing and assessing other actors and situations, actors take a step further and *actively* determine the variation of trust to use in response to the situation and react accordingly to meet changes in circumstances (Mizrachi et al., 2007). Accordingly, 'doing' trust requires broad social skills, cultural knowledge and mindfulness, enabling actors to assess situations, understand the broader social context and evaluate viewpoints of the actions of others and the nuances and gestures of trust performance (Mizrachi et al., 2007). Culture shapes action, with knowledgeable actors using cultural repertoires skilfully, and creatively deciding upon different courses of action to suit the situation – actors use culture as a resource to direct action.

Nonetheless, during cross-cultural encounters, problems can occur when actors from different cultures misunderstand the intentional and unintentional signs and symbols conveyed by the other. Branzei et al. (2007) argue that '"trust-warranting signs" form attributions of trust-worthiness to unfamiliar trustees in collectivist versus individualist cultures' (p. 61). Following their line, it is in signs that one sees trust and trustworthiness, and '*sign reading*' is a fundamental part of deciding whether or not to trust (Bacharach and Gambetta, 2001, as cited by Branzei et al., 2007). Branzei et al. (2007) find that the effectiveness of dispositional and contextual signs varies systematically depending on the truster's national culture. Both intentional and unintentional signs given off by trustees are more easily picked up and correctly interpreted by individuals who share similar cultural norms, values and expectations (Doney et al., 1998). However, in cross-cultural encounters, the absence of trust-warranting signs can lead to misunderstandings and hinder trust (Branzei et al., 2007).

Following the above, another way of considering trust and distrust is to view them as tools whereby knowledgeable actors utilize social and cultural forms of trust and distrust in social contexts to frame social relations. In other words, trust and distrust are resources that social actors use to define relationships and facilitate organized social action.

Mizrachi et al. (2007) show how trust is a constant reflexive process used to delineate boundaries around social relations. Drawing on Goffman (1974), one could go further and argue that trust and distrust are strong cultural (institutional) frames used by actors to organize relationships. In this perspective, trust and distrust as frames are not only used to organize social relations, they are also a method of interpreting and labelling social events that reflect institutionalized relationships. While Mizrachi et al. (2007) tend to portray social relations in a post-modern way (culture can be used in an unrestricted manner), the concept of framing underlines that not all repertoires are available to social actors, which is also in accord with Swidler's (1986) original analysis. Along these lines, the frame provides a bridging construct (Floyd et al., 2011) between an interpersonal-relational and institutional approach to trust as a resource. Floyd et al. (2011) define a bridging construct as 'A concept which combines different ideas and elements related to a specific phenomenon' (p. 11). Bridging constructs connect different streams of research that can be distinguished conceptually at various levels of analysis in a coherent and operational way (Floyd et al., 2011: 3). Instead of speaking of trust in terms of a resource used freely, I view it as a resource that can be used as a strategy in the given situation by actors in its different institutionalized variations.

DEFINITION OF TRUST AND DISTRUST

Following Goffman's (1974) concept of framing, I define trust and distrust as cultural and social resources used by actors in social encounters to frame social relations – the frame being an institutionalized resource. This definition denotes a dialectical process between social structure and human agency. Trust in this chapter means 'confident positive expectations' and distrust means 'confident negative expectations' (Lewicki et al., 1998: 439). First, this implies that there are many dimensions and variations of trust. Second, this means that knowledgeable social actors use the different sides of trust and distrust to frame (define) individuals and social relations. Third, this means that trust and distrust are not static; rather, they are dynamic with a repertoire of variations used to fit the situation. Accordingly, social actors draw upon a range of interactional repertoires that they use to negotiate their way through daily encounters. Social actors draw on accessible resources and practices that have a deeper meaning with regard to people over time in the context. In other words, while being sensitive and reactive to changes in face-to-face displays, attitudes and behaviour, actors are entangled in structured (institutional) configurations. The concept of framing expresses a dialectical relationship between social structure and social actors, whereby social actors shape the environment and the environment shapes them.

DISTRUST FRAMING: EXAMPLES FROM FIELDWORK

The following section presents some contextual examples from the fieldwork that illustrate distrust and trust as cultural frames and tools used to construct these frames. The section looks at how the young men frame the employees and organize their relationships with them. As encountered during the fieldwork for this study and underpinned by the accounts of the youth workers, the relationships between these workers and the young men can best be described as hostile. While the youth workers defined the young men as dangerous criminal troublemakers, the young men framed the youth workers in terms of distrust and suspicion. Effectively, this became operationalized through labelling the youth workers the *Super Snitch Patrol*.

SUPER SNITCH PATROL

Surprisingly, I heard about the Super Snitch Patrol on my first day of fieldwork in Paradise Way, some 20 miles away from their base bordering Sunset Boulevard. On that occasion, I was shadowing Maria (SSP youth worker). We were returning to the clearly marked local authority car when a man shouted 'Heyyy what's the local authority doing here?' The question initiated an encounter in which the man (Hassan) asked about the abbreviation SSP. After Maria explained, Hassan smiled and said he had heard about SSP from some of his friends over in Sunset Boulevard. Hassan explained that the word on the street was that SSP workers were not trustworthy as they were police collaborators. Maria responded in a friendly, courteous manner but downplayed Hassan's remarks. However, while driving back to the office, Maria acknowledged some truth in Hassan's account. The following extract from my research diary is illustrative:

> 'Oh but [Sunset Boulevard], it's much worse there than here, they are crazy [laugh], did you know they call the SSP workers the Super Snitch Patrol?' Maria laughed and said she had heard that rumour before. Maria later explained that some of the young people in [Sunset Boulevard] have lost confidence in some of the local SSP workers because they give too much information to the police. According to Maria, many young people simply don't trust SSP workers and turn their backs on them (Research Diary, October 2009).

This short excerpt exemplifies how Hassan frames the relationship between the SSP workers and the young men in terms of distrust. Moreover, from a process perspective, it reinforces the notion that impressions and reputation matter to trust and distrust, while demonstrating how reputation travels over distance. Reputation represents a perceived identity, reflecting a mishmash of individual traits, behaviours and impressions revealed over time (Ferris et al., 2004, as cited by Lewicki and Brinsfield, 2011: 125). In addition, it illustrates that information about others obtained from *reputable* second-hand sources strengthens the reputation of others. Finally, it indicates that the SSP employees are aware of the trust predicament, giving credence to Hassan's utterance.

SUNSET BOULEVARD

I entered the community centre in Sunset Boulevard one Friday evening in January 2010 with the purpose of determining its suitability as a site for future data collection. Immediately, I observed many young men from minority ethnic backgrounds engaged in various table-based activities – I got the impression that all eyes were on me. I approached a service area, bought a cup of coffee and went to sit down. A young man approached, held out his hand in the way of greeting and introduced himself. Asad, a young man of Palestinian heritage, worked at the community centre. He said he had noticed me entering the building and subtly enquired about my reason for being there. During the encounter, it became apparent that Asad was, in a friendly way, sizing me up. Asad seemed satisfied with my account and invited me to accompany him to the kitchen. Upon entering, Asad introduced me to Kazim, a young man of similar age and ethnicity. While drinking tea, they asked about my research, which led to an animated exchange:

Kazim: Which local authority employees are you looking at?
KP: Social workers, SSP workers and others who work with young people.
Asad: SSP [raised voice], we only ever see them down here with the police when there's trouble.
Kazim: SSP workers, we hate them.
KP: Can you tell me why you hate SSP workers?
Kazim: They spy for the police, and they are grumpy.
Asad: Yeah we call them the *Super Snitch Patrol.*[2]
Kazim: They spy for the police; well apart from [Adem] he is ok.
KP: Can you give me an example?
Kazim: They are really bossy and impolite; I used to go to the youth club over there [Institution], the adults are not nice, they are unjust and they talk down to you, it's like you shouldn't be there.
Asad: One of my friends was in trouble, so I asked [Margret] for some advice, a couple of days later the police came to my house to ask questions, I told them nothing. Anyway my friend got arrested, she went behind my back [...] I lost all confidence in her she is a snitch and I want nothing more to do with her.

During the short exchange, they spoke passionately about the youth workers; their narratives embraced emotions such as disappointment, resentment and treachery. Such a passionate response transpires in relations that once have been close. This may well be the case in this instance as during fieldwork a few of the youth workers explained how their relationship with the young men had once been close but had deteriorated over a couple of years. Perhaps this partially accounts for this emotional response and the feeling of betrayal. Solomon and Flores (2001) shed light on the emotional aspects of trust and distrust and maintain that powerful emotions are at play in both trusting and distrusting. Trust involves feelings such as affection, anxiety, hope and gratitude, whereas distrust involves suspicion, resentment, dread and paranoia (Solomon and Flores, 2001).

Asad's statement about only seeing the youth workers together with the police when there was trouble is consistent with the youth worker accounts. For example, when Margret (youth club manager) explained her team's practice, she told of an agreement they had with the emergency services:

> There have been many container fires and stones thrown at the fire brigade and the police, so we have a deal that if there is a fire alarm [they] phone us, AND it's pissing funny when we drive down there [raised voice], because it's a joke the fire brigade are parked behind the police at the entrance [...] waiting for us [...] and [they] follow us in and then take care of their jobs, putting out fires that the youths have started (Interview: Margret).

During the kitchen encounter, Kazim expressed hatred towards all bar one of the youth workers, which suggests anger and intense dislike towards the Danish youth workers. Rempel and Burris (2005) maintain that *hate* embraces the essence of passionate experiential conditions between people almost as often as does love. Kazim gave two reasons for his strong dislike of the youth workers: (1) they were police spies; (2) they were grumpy. When providing an example, Kazim talked about an experience of visiting the youth club where the staff unjustly acted condescendingly towards him and made him feel unwelcome. During the encounter, Asad endorsed and reinforced Kazim's claim that the youth workers were police collaborators. Asad's statement referring to the youth workers as the *Super Snitch Patrol* reinforces Hassan's account above. In addition, Asad disclosed an example in which he had approached Margret and asked for advice that could help one of his friends. Subsequently, the police visited his house to question him and later arrested his friend. Potentially, this could have had serious ramifications for Asad because he was the one who revealed his friend's name to Margret. Snitching, in this sense, goes beyond reporting someone to the authorities; it involves betraying the trust of friends and neighbours. In addition, it involves exposing oneself and those closest to danger (Yates, 2006). Based on his experience, Asad frames Margret in distrust and excludes her from future interaction, which is in harmony with Maria's account above. Furthermore, Asad's account is consistent with Margret's narrative concerning her cooperation with the police:

> Ermmm, I am employed by the local authority, sometimes I have to [...] report things that they don't want me to go further with, it can be in

connection with the SSP cooperation with the police, I talk to the police, they are my co-operational partners, I don't cover for them, if I know the youths have committed crime and the police ask, then I don't lie or try to conceal crime, I would never dream of that (Interview: Margret).

The basis of Asad's and Kazim's distrust of the youth workers is knowledge through experience of interaction and subsequent sensemaking processes. Through a series of interactions, over time, they have learned to have *confident negative expectations* towards these workers, whose behaviour is predictable. Comparable to Khodyakov's (2007) articulation of the trust process perspective, these social actors have chosen to distrust others in the present, based on future negative expectations of potential harm. Storytelling in the context creates a reputation for the SSP workers which spans distance and time, shaping the views of others about them.

SNITCHING

Evidently, not snitching and deterring snitching is part of the social code of the young men and at the same time a powerful cultural tool for organizing relationships with others. Defining another person as a snitch places a high distrust frame around him or her; this can have serious consequences, such as excluding people from interaction or, in extreme cases, forcing them out of the community. In most communities, people stigmatized as snitches face dangerous consequences if they do not leave (and sometimes even if they do). However, in this case, unless the youth club is relocated or the youth workers find new jobs, they are forced to stay.

The youth club borders Sunset Boulevard and sometimes the youth workers accompany the police into the neighbourhood where they meet a hostile reception. During fieldwork, some youth workers said they were disappointed with certain police officers because they told individual youths that the information leading to their arrest came from the youth workers, which caused unnecessary aggression. This hostility towards the youth workers was apparent throughout the fieldwork and culminated with an arson attack on the youth club.

There is a wealth of research that underscores the serious nature of snitching and the implications attached to it. Yates (2006) found that the labels 'grassing' (snitching) and 'grass' were widely used to describe individuals who inform the authorities about other community members. The grass stigma signifies untrustworthiness, which can have negative consequences for the individual involved and his or her family (Yates, 2006). Wieder (1975), in his research in a half-way house (an institution that bridges the gap between prisons and community), identified six maxims of the 'Convict Code' in which snitching plays a leading part. Wieder (1975) found that participants had learned the code on the street long before their prison experiences, which implies interplay between the institution and the individual.

INJUSTICE AND JUSTICE

During an interview with Salim, a 25-year-old man of Palestinian heritage, I asked him why the young men disliked the youth workers. Salim said there could be many reasons as there was much water under the bridge. Salim explained that most of the bad feelings could be attributed to 'unjust' actions. Salim said the Danish employees at the youth club were 'horrible and unjust', spoke abruptly and imposed unjust sanctions in which the punishment usually outweighed the violation of youth club rules. In Salim's account, the young men look out for one another, especially in times of trouble, and adhere to a cult of honour and loyalty. For example, if someone outside the group attacks a group member, all will rush to defend. This group identification and loyalty that Salim spoke of are the stuff from which Lewicki and Bunker's (1996) identification-based trust derives. Group-based trust linked to group membership develops as individuals identify with the goals adopted and supported by the group (Kramer, 1993, as cited by Lewicki and Bunker, 1996).

The notion of *injustice* is central to Salim's narrative concerning the distrust of the youth club workers, which is consistent with other accounts from Sunset Boulevard. In addition, I observed that *locals* consistently relied on words like 'unjust' and 'just' when talking about others in terms of trust or distrust. Injustice and justice are meaningful notions for distrusting/trusting decisions in this context, constituting primary cultural tools relied on to construct frames around others. During some interviews with youth workers, they expressed views consistent with the young men's narratives. For example, during one interview, a youth worker talked about the young men in derogatory terms, labelling them 'shit' and calling for their forced removal from the street:

> So I said to [the police officer] why don't you take a big van, drive it down to the newsagents and take all the shit, put them into the van and drive all the shit out of there [laugh] nothing would happen (Interview: Bente).

Being unjust, according to Salim, involves the youth workers sanctioning young people unreasonably, that is, the penalty outweighing the crime. According to Salim's account, if the penalty is not in proportion to the crime, resentment and anger arise. This is in tune with Foucault (1991), who argued:

> The prison also produces delinquents by imposing violent constraints on its inmates; [...] when he sees himself exposed in this way to suffering, which the law has neither ordered nor envisaged, he becomes habitually angry against everything around him; he sees every agent of authority as an executioner; he no longer thinks that he was guilty: he accuses justice itself (p. 266).

While the prison is a far cry from the youth club, Foucault's message is still valuable here and illustrates a clear link between injustice and anger. Perhaps this helps explain some of the bitterness and hatred expressed by Kazim and others in Sunset Boulevard towards the youth workers. Furthermore, the concept of injustice can be used as is a powerful tool for organizing collective social action against individuals and organizations (Miller, 2001). As Miller (2001) concludes, a personal injury labelled as injustice becomes a shared injustice, and settling a score becomes a defence of the honour and integrity of the whole community. In other words, the cry of injustice transforms the personal into the public and suggests an action strategy (Miller, 2001). Therefore, framing individuals, groups or institutions as unjust indicates a cultural tool used to trigger collective social action against identified others. Framing persons or groups in terms of injustice constructs distrust frames around them. During the fieldwork, it became apparent that there were some employees with majority ethnic backgrounds whom the young men trusted. Below, I explore how the young men talk about and frame two professionals with majority ethnic backgrounds and compare this to relevant literature on trust.

TRUST FRAMING: THE JOB CONSULTANT

During the interview with Salim, I wondered if he was prejudiced against the Danish youth workers. Therefore, I asked him if all Danish local authority employees were unjust in their dealings with the young men:

Salim: Naaaa I don't think so, I don't really know, it's mostly them from the club and some of those grumpy bastards from the housing association [laughs].

KP: Can you tell me which Danish workers you consider to be fair or just?

Salim: I can only think of two, [Linda] she is a *sagsbehandler*, what's that in English?

KP: A social worker or a case manager.

Salim: Yeah she is just [fair] and the boys like her, I like her and you can trust her.

KP: Why is she trustworthy?

Salim: Because she treats you with respect, speaks with you and not down to you.

KP: Anything else?

Salim: Yeah she listens and you can see that she cares about you, you can see that in her face.

KP: How can you see that?

Salim: [Laughs] I don't know, you just can, you can see it and you can feel it.

KP: You said that you can think of two Danish employees, who is the other one?

Salim: Hmmm the other one I think is just is [Dennis] and he's a cop [laughs].

KP: Ok, in what way is [Dennis] just?

Salim: Hmmm he is fair, he listens to you and meets you with respect, even if you are in the wrong.

KP: Anything else?

Salim: Yeah he dares to come here and talks with the boys, he is the only cop who dares to come down here and talk with the boys, the others are rude and racists [laughs] [...] with [Dennis] you know where you have him and you can trust him [...].

KP: Can you give me an example?

Salim: Yeah if he says he will bust you for doing something next time he catches you, you know he will [...] he is a man of his word.

When talking about which Danish employees he considers *just* or *fair*, trust becomes linked to *fairness*. This reinforces the link between fairness and trust advanced by Lind (2001). In Salim's statement, he associates *grumpiness* with the idea of being unjust and puts listening and communicating on an equal footing with being just. When considering Danish employees who are just, Salim gave the names Linda (job consultant) and Dennis (police officer). Salim considers Linda trustworthy because she is fair, treats people with respect and communicates on an *equal* footing. After a prompt, Salim added that Linda signals that she *cares*; this relates to ideas such as benevolence, integrity, goodwill and compassion, considered by some researchers as belonging to the broad heading of *strong* trust (Maguire and Philips, 2008). Maguire and Philips (2008) define trust as: 'the expectation that some other will act with predictability and benevolence', which according to them is the basis of strong trust

(p. 374). Strong trust involves a *leap of faith* (Möllering, 2006) based on expectations of the benevolence of the other. This variation of trust is what Mizrachi et al. (2007) refer to as *normative*, maintaining that it occurs in 'informal, emotionally charged personal relationships, such as friendships, families, and communities' (p. 145). However, in this case, Salim is talking about a job consultant employed by the local authority. Salim's explanation for trusting Linda fits with notions of strong trust rather than weak trust, which most of the literature suggests should be the case between a *service user* and a *service provider*.

During fieldwork, other interactants organized their relationships with both Linda and Dennis applying similar frames to Salim. For instance, while talking with Omar (recently released from prison) about his future work prospects, a car drove past and the driver [Linda] waved – this triggered a dialogue:

Omar:	Look there's my contact person [points], do you know what a contact person is?
KP:	Yes, I know […] what is she like?
Omar:	She is ok; she has helped me a lot, her name is [Linda].
KP:	Oh right, I have met her.
Omar:	Cool […] she is really good to talk to and treats people fair […].
KP:	In what way is she fair?
Omar:	She listens and gives you a chance, she doesn't just take your money if you don't turn up.
KP:	Ok that sounds fair, how has she helped you?
Omar:	Errrr she helped me to get sorted out when I came out of prison, she is the one who helped me get a place on the bricklayer course.
KP:	Excellent.
Omar:	When you have problems you can always phone her, and then arrange to meet.
KP:	She sounds reliable.
Omar:	Yeah, you know you can trust her.
KP:	How do you know you can trust her?
Omar:	You just do, she keeps her word and you know her heart is in the right place, you can see that she likes you.
KP:	How can you see that?
Omar:	She smiles and shows she cares, she phoned me on my birthday and congratulated me, she reminds me of my mother.

Comparable to the interpretations outlined earlier, perceptions around justice/fairness are important to Omar's account. While Omar is unsure about Linda's job title, he is sure about the impression she gives and gives off. Linda listens, signals respect and is caring, fair and dependable. In Omar's explanation, he connects the significant life event of prison release with receiving support from Linda, something that has helped him to move on with his life. Through experience, Omar has learned that Linda keeps her word, is reliable and cares and therefore is worthy of his trust. According to Omar, Linda reminds him of his mother, which suggests strong trust.

TRUST FRAMING: THE COP

According to Salim, Dennis meets people with respect and listens even when they are committing an offence; this suggests consistent behaviour and makes his actions predictable. In addition, Dennis dares to go into Sunset Boulevard and talk to the boys, which may be rather unusual in the neighbourhood. Perhaps this perceived daring behaviour adds to Dennis's reputation and the respect he is accorded. Lewicki and Bunker's (1996) knowledge-based trust offers a satisfactory explanation for this, namely that Dennis has built up knowledge of the young men over an extended period and can therefore predict how they will receive him. The data strongly reinforce the latter aspect, showing that Dennis is decidedly calculating during policing and does not seem to leave anything to chance.

During fieldwork, I only ever observed the police driving around Sunset Boulevard. However, I observed Dennis interacting with the young men on a number of occasions during sporting activities. My observations at the time left me with the impression that the majority of the young men respected and trusted him. In addition, Salim said that with Dennis people know what to expect because he keeps his word; this implies that Dennis behaves consistently, which adds to his predictability. Salim's interpretation of Dennis fits with Lewicki and Bunker's (1996) definition of knowledge-based trust in which predictability is a key feature.

While observing/participating in a discussion in the community centre, a police car drove past, which triggered an automatic response from those sitting around the table. In unison, they gave 'the finger' to the passing car while shouting obscenities. During the subsequent exchange, Ibrahim said 'all police are bastards they don't give a fuck about us'. I took this opportunity to ask about Dennis.

KP:	So are all police bastards?
Ibrahim:	They are fucking pigs.
Aadil:	They are racist bastards who hate us.
KP:	Ok, but what about [Dennis]?
Ibrahim:	Yeah, he is OK [OK means trustworthy].
KP:	So why is he OK?

Aadil:	He is just, keeps his word and you can count on him.
KP:	What do you mean by just?
Muhammad:	He treats us with respect and is fair.
KP:	In what way is he fair?
Ibrahim:	He is not like the others; he speaks politely to us and explains things.
KP:	OK ... anything else?
Muhammad:	Yeah ... he likes us you can see it in his eyes.
Aadil:	When he meets us he smiles and shakes hands, he is a good man.
Ibrahim:	Yeah but he can be hard sometimes [laughs].
KP:	How?
Ibrahim:	If you don't keep your promise then he gets mad.
KP:	What happens then?
Ibrahim:	He tells you off or gives you a fine.

This framing of Dennis during the group encounter has many similarities to those illustrated above. Notions of justice and injustice play a significant role in deciding between who is trustworthy and who is not. According to this account, whereas other police officers are unjust, Dennis is OK because he keeps his word, explains things, is reliable, meets the young men with respect and speaks politely – all the signs of fairness. Similar to Salim's account, this implies that the young men frame their relationship with Dennis in a variation of trust which primarily involves predictability, with a hint of deterrence. The relationship between Dennis and the young men can best be described as a mix between knowledge-based and calculus-based trust. Furthermore, this account implies that Dennis is successful in his communication and impression management when interacting with the young men.

The narratives above that name and frame Linda and Dennis are in tune with Whitener et al.'s (1998) research on *perceptions of trustworthiness*. Although their work primarily deals with relationships between managers and employees, it shows how action/interaction influences perceptions of trustworthiness and is therefore useful to explain why the young men perceive Linda and Dennis as trustworthy. Whitener et al. (1998) developed a typology of five categories of managerial trustworthy behaviour, of which two are useful here: (1) behavioural consistency and (2) behavioural integrity.

Behavioural consistency involves reliability over time and across situations, which allows employees to predict the future performance of managers, in turn increasing confidence in expectations. Consistent, positive behaviour promotes and reinforces the level of trust in the relationship. Behavioural integrity involves walking the walk and talking the talk (Goffman, 1959), confirming consistency. Through observations, employees evaluate the moral character, honesty and integrity of managers by matching what they say to what they do and thereby making inferences about their trustworthiness. Dasgupta (1988, as cited by Whitener et al., 1998) identified two behaviours central to judgements about integrity: telling the truth and keeping promises. Both behavioural consistency and integrity fit well with the young men's narratives about Linda and Dennis and help to explain why they perceive them as trustworthy.

DISCUSSION AND CONCLUSION

Stepping back from the street-level accounts reveals a larger story of tension, conflict, suspicion and distrustful relations. This unfolding story of antagonism illustrates a difficult challenge to employees worldwide who work in similar contexts and use comparable methods of operation in which building trusting relationships is critical to successful service delivery. Nonetheless, despite the tension and suspicion, the narratives illustrated above show that trust is available in the same contexts – if the police officer and the job consultant can win the respect and trust of the young men, so can others.

This chapter carefully explores how the young men frame individual employees and how they construct these frames. Overall, the data suggest that the relationship between the young men and youth workers developed over time from amicability to mutual distrust. Through a series of perceived hostile encounters with the youth workers, the young men excluded them from interaction and the neighbourhood. Within the same rationale of the process perspective, the data reported here show that distrust arises through a history of interaction within a given context. Through a history of interaction, the young men built an intimate knowledge of the youth workers' modus operandi and consequently chose distrust as a strategy for dealing with them. The data reported here are in harmony with Mizrachi et al. (2007), who show how actors interchangeably rely on different variations of trust as strategies to demarcate social relations to fit changing situations. However, in their study they only consider trust as a resource to delineate social relations and not distrust. This chapter shows how distrust is a powerful tool in stigmatizing and socially excluding individuals and groups from social interaction. Distrust becomes a powerful means of initiating collective social action against identified common enemies. Nonetheless, the young men interchangeably use both distrust and trust to organize their relationships with those around them, which indicates knowledgeable actors who carefully observe and evaluate the other before deciding on a strategy of action.

The fundamental question that the chapter addresses is how trust and distrust can be understood as cultural frames. The data imply that the young men in this case use distrust as an approach towards the youth workers because of their attitude and modus operandi. Conversely, they use trust as a strategy towards the job consultant and the cop because of their particular approaches and attitude. In this sense, trust and distrust can be understood as cultural frames, used as strategies in the environment by knowledgeable actors to respond to unfolding events and to organize relationships with others. Notions of injustice and justice are important underlying cultural tools used to organize relationships with others. These become key concepts in understanding how some workers manage to negotiate cultural frames in the area. The data show that trust is available and that cultural frames are open to negotiation, so that trust can be achieved by thinking outside or by expanding cultural toolboxes.

IMPLICATIONS FOR FUTURE RESEARCH

In the trust literature there is a tendency to distinguish between interpersonal and institutional-based trust. This study shows that distrust and trust emerge at the micro level in the encounter between people through a history of interaction. Nonetheless, during encounters, underlying structural and cultural discourses are at play that can undermine the trust-building process. This study shows how people use cultural tools to frame and organize their relationships with the *other* as either distrust or trust. These frames become counteracted by other frames from others as strategies of action. The implication is that we need studies of trust that combine an institutional and an interpersonal approach. We need more focus on the institutional powers that lead to the erosion of trust at the micro level. This indicates the need for research that takes into account structural and cultural dimensions of power and prejudice which actors rely on to frame others and which can be counterproductive to trust and trusting.

STUDY LIMITATIONS

This study gives in-depth insights into the distrusting and trusting relationships between a group of young men with minority ethnic backgrounds and a number of professionals within a particular context.

Therefore, it can only give a glimpse of what was happening between those social actors at that time and no grand generalizations can be made based on this single fieldwork study. Nonetheless, this study can be indicative of what may be occurring in similar contexts between professionals and young men, especially where workers use similar methods of operation. Due to ethical considerations, all people and places are given pseudonyms. Hence, ethical considerations are on a par with reliability and validity. Therefore, identical research with these interactants cannot be replicated unless by chance. However, identifying people and places is no guarantee of study replication as it is impossible to freeze time in a social setting (LeCompte and Goetz, 1982). Ethnographic research is by nature a personal endeavour in which the researcher uses himself or herself as a tool to negotiate the field and build trusting relationships and it is thus difficult to replicate. However, a similar research project in a similar area in Denmark with a similar focus could yield similar findings.

NOTES

1. The chapter utilizes key findings and data from the PhD Dissertation *Framing Trust at the Street Level – An Empirical Interpretative Study of Distrust and Trust between Frontline Public Sector Employees and Young Men with Minority Ethnic Backgrounds in Denmark* (Perry, 2012).
2. The term 'snitch' is used to denote someone who provides information in an underhand manner, commonly about criminal activity, to the authorities.

REFERENCES

Bacharach, M. and Gambetta, D. (2001) Trust in signs. In: Cook, S.K. (ed.) *Trust in Society*. New York: Russell Sage Foundation, pp. 148–84.

Bachmann, R. and Inkpen, A.C. (2011) Understanding institutional-based trust building processes in inter-organizational relationships. [Online] Available from: http://epubs.surrey.ac.uk/178684/2/rev_rev_rev_OS-subm__27_Sept_2010.pdf (Accessed 11 May 2015).

Branzei, O., Vertinsky, I. and Camp, R.D. (2007) Culture-contingent signs of trust in emergent relationships. *Organizational Behavior and Human Decision Processes*, 104, 61–82.

Doney, P.M., Cannon, J.P. and Mullen, M.R. (1998) Understanding the influence of national culture on the development of trust. *Academy of Management Review*, 23, 601–20.

Flores, F. and Solomon, R.C. (1998) Creating trust. *Business Ethics Quarterly*, 8, 205–32.

Goffman, E. (1959) *The Presentation of Self in Everyday Life*. New York: Doubleday Anchor Books.

Floyd, S.W., Cornelissen, J.P., Wright, M and Delios, A. (2011) Processes and practices of strategizing and organizing: Review, development, and the role of bridging and umbrella constructs. *Journal of Management Studies*, 48, 933–52.

Foucault, M. (1991) *Discipline and Punish: The Birth of the Prison*. London: Penguin Books.

Goffman, E. (1974) *Frame Analysis: An Essay on the Organisation of Experience*. Lebanon, NH: North Eastern University Press, New England.

Khodyakov, D. (2007) Trust as a process: A three-dimensional process. *Sociology*, 41 (1), 115–32.

Kramer, R.M. and Tyler, T.R. (eds) (1996) *Trust in Organizations: Frontiers of Theory and Research*. Thousand Oaks, CA: Sage Publications, pp. 114–39.

LeCompte, M.D. and Goetz, J.P. (1982) Problems of reliability and validity in ethnographic research. *Review of Educational Research*, 52, 31–60.

Lewicki, R.J. and Brinsfield, C. (2011) Framing trust: Trust as a heuristic. In: Donohue, W.A., Rogan, R.R. and Kaufman, S. (eds) *Framing in Negotiation: State of the Art*. New York: Peter Lang Publishing, pp. 110–35.

Lewicki, R.J. and Bunker, B.B. (1996) Developing and maintaining trust in work relationships. In: Lewicki, R.J., McAllister, D.J. and Bies, R.J. (1998) Trust and distrust: New relationships and realities. *Academy of Management Review*, 23 (3), 438–58.

Lewis, D.J. and Weigert, A. (1985) Trust as a social reality. *Social Forces*, 63, 967–85.

Lind, E.A. (2001) Fairness heuristic theory: Justice judgements as pivotal cognitions in organisational relations. In: Greenberg, J. and Cropanzano, R. (eds) *Advances in Organisational Justice*. Stanford, CA: Stanford University Press, pp. 56–88.

Luhmann, N. (1979) *Trust and Power*. Chichester: John Wiley.

Maguire, S. and Phillips, N. (2008) Citibankers at Citigroup: A study of the loss of institutional trust after a merger. *Journal of Management Studies*, 45 (2), 372–401.

Mayer, R.C., Davis, J.H. and Schoorman, F.D. (1995) An integrative model of organisational trust. *Academy of Management Review*, 20, 703–34.

McDonald, S. (2005) Studying actions in context: A qualitative shadowing method for organisational research. *Qualitative Research*, 5 (4), 455–73.

Miller, D.T. (2001) Disrespect and the experience of injustice. *Annual Review of Psychology*, 52, 527–53.

Mizrachi, N., Drori, I. and Anspach, R.R. (2007) Repertoires of trust: The practice of trust in a multinational organisation amid political conflict. *American Sociological Review*, 72, 143–65.

Möllering, G. (2006) *Trust: Reason, Routine, Reflexivity*. Bingley: Emerald Group Publishing.

Nooteboom, B. and Six, F.E. (eds) (2003) *The Trust Process in Organisations: Empirical Studies of the Determinants and the Process of Trust Development*. Cheltenham, UK and Northampton, MA, USA: Edward Elgar Publishing.

Perry, K.A. (2012) *Framing Trust at the Street Level – An Empirical Interpretative Study of Distrust and Trust Between Frontline Public Sector Employees and Young Men with Minority Ethnic Backgrounds in Denmark* (PhD dissertation). Roskilde University, Denmark.

Prus, R. (1996) *Symbolic Interaction and Ethnographic Research*. New York: State University Press.

Rempel, J.K. and Burris, C.T. (2005) Let me count the ways: An integrative theory of love and hate. *Personal Relations*, 12, 297–313.

Retsplejeloven [Rights Procedure Act], chapter 11, § 115 stk. 2. https://www.retsinformation.dk/Forms/R0710. aspxid=157953 [Accessed 11/05/2015].

Rousseau, D.M., Sitkin, S.B., Burt, R.S. and Camerer, C. (1998) Not so different after all: A cross discipline view of trust. *Academy of Management Review*, 23 (3), 393–404.

Solomon, R.C. and Flores, F. (2001) *Building Trust: In Business, Politics, Relationships, and Life*. New York: Oxford University Press.

Swidler, A. (1986) Culture in action: Symbols and strategies. *American Sociological Review*, 51, 273–86.

Sztompka, P. (1999) *Trust: A Sociological Theory*. Cambridge: Cambridge University Press.

Whitener, E.M., Brodt, S.E., Korsgaard, M.A. and Werner, J.M. (1998) Managers as initiators of trust: An exchange relationship framework for understanding managerial trustworthy behaviour. *Academy of Management Review*, 23 (3), 513–30.

Wieder, D.L. (1975) Telling the code. In: Turner, R. (ed.), *Ethnomethodology*. Victoria: Penguin Education.

Yates, J. (2006) You just don't grass: Youth crime and grassing in a working class community. *Youth Justice*, 6, 195–210.

11. Expectations matter when studying trusting as a process: developing trust based on expectations between investment managers and entrepreneurs

Uffe Kjærgaard Hansen, Maria Bosse and Mette Apollo Rasmussen

This chapter introduces expectations as an element of trusting and develops a sensitive framework for studying expectations from a micro-process perspective. Trust is part of most organizing practices of organizations today. Research shows that the benefits of organizing inter-organizational relationships on trust are numerous. In general, trust can be seen as a social phenomenon emerging in repeating interactions among actors in an organizing setting. Though there is no generally accepted definition of trust (Möllering, 2006), most conceptions highlight the role of positive expectations regarding the behaviour of others (Adobor, 2005; Blomqvist and Snow, 2010; Dirks and Ferrin, 2001; Ellonen et al., 2008; Jagd, 2008; Kramer and Lewicki, 2010; Luhmann, 1979; Mayer et al., 1995; Mayer et al., 2007; Möllering, 2006; Zaheer, 2008).

Overall, we find a lack of theoretical frames for studying trusting as it emerges through social interactions in microprocesses. We argue there is a need for tangible theoretical terms to focus qualitative research on trusting.

We stress that trusting should be grasped as a process, since static terms and quantitative measurements are unable to answer the question of how trust fluctuates and changes (Möllering, 2012). The contribution of this study to the trust literature is a theoretical framework, which sheds light on expectations as a means of exploring trusting. By focusing on expectations, instead of the entire concept of trusting, researchers can produce descriptions that explain how trusting develops and changes over time. In this chapter, we unfold what happens when expectations are challenged and how this affects joint action.

By applying the thoughts of Blumer (1969) and Mead (1934), the theoretical framework described in this chapter provides an insight into how expectations change through the ongoing adjustment between people. When people incorporate their expectations about the other into their own behaviour, mutual adjustment takes place. Qualitative descriptions can provide insights into this process, when the descriptions are sensitive to the ways people adjust to each other, by grasping the position of the other.

The research question is: 'How can trusting be described and understood through expectations emerging in social interaction?'

We have chosen to include a case to illustrate how our proposed framework can be applied when studying trusting. We have selected an episode, taking place between actors from two organizations, in which expectations are negotiated and changed.

THE RESEARCH CONTEXT

The case takes place in an investment company, INV, which places risk capital in start-up companies and regional SMEs. INV helps entrepreneurs to raise the necessary capital. INV invests in 6 to 8 companies annually and has about 20 feasibility studies and about 40 inquiries running. INV ended 2012 with a profit of DKK 2.7 million and strengthened equity, which now represents DKK 22.4 million. INV plays an active role in promoting growth and development in Region Zealand. These activities are funded by the Region Zealand and EU regional fund and work for companies and organizations in Region Zealand to increase the share of funding from national and international funds. INV has a Managing Director and a Head of Administration, who have close cooperation in the overall management and daily operations of the company. The board of directors, consisting of five people, has the crucial approval authority when investing in new projects or companies. INV has six investment managers, who manage a portfolio of companies, receive new inquiries, screen cases, undertake feasibility studies, due diligence, intent and contracts and have a share in the board of directors in their portfolio companies. Each investment manager has responsibility for a segment or an industry, such as ICT, life science, cleantech, industrial innovation, experience technology and games.

CHAPTER STRUCTURE

The remainder of the chapter proceeds as follows. First, a brief review is conducted of trusting, how expectation is acknowledged as a key issue of understanding trusting and how the negotiation and changing of expectations can be studied as part of trusting in social interactions. Second, we argue and illustrate that trusting should be studied from a process perspective to produce answers to the question of how trusting fluctuates. Subsequently, we show how elements of symbolic interactionism can be used as a theoretical framework focusing on the microprocesses in which expectations are at play. In the fourth section, we show the potential of the theoretical framework by applying it to an empirical study, in which expectations are negotiated and changed. The chapter concludes with a discussion of the theoretical framework of symbolic interactionism's new insight into how expectations explain the fluctuating nature of trusting.

THEORETICAL BACKGROUND

Trusting and Expectations

In this section, we briefly review work arguing that expectations are acknowledged as an element of trusting. Then, we propose that the negotiation and change of expectations can be applied as a means to understand how trusting fluctuates. We develop an understanding of how expectations are negotiated and changed as part of trusting.

The trust concept is rich in meaning in everyday life and it is used daily in descriptions of relationships among people in organizing practices. Though there is no generally accepted definition of trust (Möllering, 2006), most conceptions highlight the role of positive expectations regarding the behaviour of others and vulnerability to that behaviour.

In Table 11.1 we draw on the trust literature to show our understanding of trusting and define expectations as a key element of trusting.

As shown by the table, expectations are central to trust definitions; trust is formed in relationships and a central element is mutual expectations about others' intentions and actions; trust is considered a condition that reaches beyond the content of formal contracts and job descriptions; uncertainty regarding others' actions must be borne in mind; and, in social relationships, people have expectations about what others choose to do. Expectations are related to the future, when there will be an evaluation of whether the other person's intended action is appropriate (Bachmann and Inkpen, 2011; Van Ees and Bachmann, 2006). With

Table 11.1   Trust and expectations

Authors	Trust and expectations
Mayer, Davis and Schoorman	'trust is the willingness of a party to be vulnerable to the actions of another party based on the expectations that the other will perform a particular action important to the trustor, irrespective of the ability to monitor or control the other party' (Mayer et al., 1995: p. 712).
Rousseau, Sitkin, Burt and Camerer	'trust is a psychological state comprising the intention to accept vulnerability based upon positive expectations of the intention or behaviours of another' (Rousseau et al., 1998: p. 395).
Lewicki, McAllister and Bies	'confident positive expectations regarding another's conduct' (Lewicki et al., 1998: p. 439).
Maguire and Phillips	'the expectation that some other will act with predictability and benevolence' (Maguire and Phillips, 2008: p. 374).
Zaheer	'When actors involved in an exchange share a set of expectations constituted in social rules and legitimate processes, they can trust each other with regard to the fulfilment and maintenance of those expectations. By the same token, actors can only trust those others with whom they share a particular set of expectations. Either way, trust hinges on the actors' natural ability to have a world in common with others and rely on it' (Zaheer, 2008: p. 358).
Möllering	'trust as favourable expectation regarding other people's actions and intentions' (Möllering, 2001: p. 404).
Luhmann	'Whoever wants to win trust must take part in social life and be in a position to build the expectations of others into his own self-representation' (Luhmann, 1979: p. 62).

Luhmann's understanding of trusting and expectations, we discuss and unfold how expectations can be used to understand trusting as a collective and social phenomenon.

   The uncertainty of the future relates strongly to mutual expectations, because how can trust be established based upon the unknown? Luhmann considers the future beyond the imagination of human potential, which problematizes trust, because the future involves more options than the ones that are obvious in the present (Luhmann, 1979). Luhmann notes: 'To show trust is to anticipate the future. It is to behave as though the future were certain' (Luhmann, 1979: p. 10). Luhmann considers familiarity and trust as different modes of emphasizing expectations (Luhmann, 2000). He describes familiarity as a routinized way of socializing. One could say that trust is not needed in a familiar world. Trusting presupposes a situation of changing expectations and 'The path to trust is by way of entering into the expectations of others in a very general, loose, way: one can fulfil them better than expected, or in a different way' (Luhmann, 1979: p. 62). However, trusting relations contain a certain kind of familiarity, since familiarity is needed as a precondition for trust (Luhmann, 1979: p. 19). Thus, familiarity provides guidelines to our way of socializing and thereby familiarity is the first step towards trusting. Nevertheless, it is when familiarity is no longer enough and expectations are changing that trusting emerges and can be followed.

Trusting and Expectations Studied in a Process Perspective

Process studies have the ability to explore microprocesses that occur in situated interactions. Process studies can explore phenomena or clarify aspects of phenomena that are less explainable through rational means because they take into account the development over time. We agree with Möllering, who suggests:

> A shared point for highlighting the process character of trust could be to speak of trusting, not trust, in order to express that the objective of study is not just a measurable outcome (i.e. attitude or behaviour) but the particular way such outcomes are produced and used while acknowledging that the 'product' of trust is always unfinished and needs to be worked upon continuously. (Möllering, 2012: p. 1)

Möllering (2012) argues that applying a process perspective will produce research that can answer how trusting fluctuates. Trusting should be studied as a phenomenon in relationships, developed and created in intersubjective relations and studied when people 'engage in extensive signaling, communication, interaction and interpretation in order to maintain the continuous process of trust constitution' (Möllering, 2006: p. 79). Within the organizational trust literature, trusting in and between organizations is considered a sensitive matter and a difficult phenomenon to study (Möllering, 2012). Trust has often been studied as a static phenomenon despite applying a qualitative perspective. Methods of studying trust have previously been the subject of research (Lyon et al., 2012; Möllering, 2006, 2012), involving different methods, qualitative as well as quantitative, to broaden our understanding of trust – and of course to 'encourage trust researchers to reflect on the methods they use' (Lyon et al., 2012: p. 1). These contributions have enriched the field with various methods of studying trust, but many of the methods, even the ones with a qualitative starting point, tend to measure and quantify rather than to explore and unfold trusting, because they are limited by their theoretical framework. It is important for the study of trusting that the analytical framework chosen to support the analysis is well suited to describing how expectations are negotiated and changed. Studying the temporal nature of trusting also influences how the research should be approached epistemologically: 'Process research is concerned with understanding how things evolve over time and why they evolve in this way' (Langley, 1999: p. 692). However, it is important to include the distinction made by Van de Ven and Poole (2005) and Welch and Paavilainen-Mäntymäki (2014) between the weak and the strong process approach. The main divide is ontological and concerns whether organizations are viewed as things that change (weak) or whether it is more productive to talk about organizing processes that create structures, which we then label as organizations (strong) (Van de Ven and Poole, 2005). In our case, we are concerned with describing how the phenomenon, trusting understood through expectations, is negotiated and changed in organizing processes. Organizing can be described as the process through which people try to reduce the uncertainty or ambiguity that they experience through interaction, and the structure that is named the organization emerges when routinized patterns of interdependency are established in this process (Weick, 1979). As such, we position ourselves within the strong process perspective.

These ontological assumptions also provide an idea of how to approach the study of expectations epistemologically. We need to gain access to the actual interactions in which people reduce uncertainty and establish meaning, both reliant on trusting. When seeking an answer to *how* trusting changes, it is necessary to apply a strong process perspective, because it is concerned with exactly those 'how' questions.

CONCEPTUALIZING THE FRAMEWORK FOR STUDYING TRUSTING: UNFOLDING THE PROCESS OF EXPECTATIONS

Luhmann argues that, 'The possibilities for action increase proportionately to the increase of trust – trust in one's own self-presentation and in other people's interpretation of it' (Luhmann, 1979: p. 40). When researching trusting, we argue that the understanding of how people adjust to each other is relevant, because 'Whoever wants to win trust must take part in social life and be in a position to build the expectations of others into his own self-representation' (Luhmann, 1979: p. 62). Hence, it is in this process of adjustment, or, as Mead (1934) describes it, 'taking the attitude of the other', that expectations are negotiated and changed. When expectations of others are built into the self-representation, it changes. This happens through interaction and at the same time changes the interaction; in turn, the expectations of others regarding one's own behaviour change as well. Luhmann draws on the thoughts of Mead in his description of this process (Luhmann, 1979):

> The organization of the self is simply the organization, by the individual organism, of the set of attitudes toward its social environment – and towards itself from the standpoint of that environment, or as a functioning element in the process of social experience and behaviour constituting that environment – which it is able to take. (Mead, 1934: p. 91)

In the above, Luhmann and Mead address the process of grasping the expectations of others and integrating them into one's conception of others. It is noteworthy that the expectations of others and the expectations of oneself are integrated into the concept of the generalized and the specific other. They both contain a conception of the expectations of others regarding oneself and the expectations of oneself regarding the actions of others.

In the following, we take the theoretical turn towards symbolic interactionism[1] (Blumer, 1969; Denzin, 1969; Mead, 1934), unfolding the process of expectations. Mead's and Blumer's theories on interaction are relevant because they deal with exactly how people maintain and change their mutual expectations and therefore they allow us a better understanding of how expectations, as part of trusting, are negotiated and changed. Symbolic interactionism sheds light on the fragile and contextual character of trusting and indicates that trusting is at the same time a result of social interaction and a precondition of interaction. We introduce three key concepts from their theories, which are relevant when discussing expectations:

- gesture response;
- taking the attitudes of the other;
- joint action.

Gesture Response

The gesture response process is how Mead describes interaction (Mead, 1934), and it is one of the main concepts for a symbolic interactionism approach to interaction. He distinguishes between what he calls significant and what he calls non-significant symbols. These symbols are the means of interaction. For gestures to be significant, they must have similar meanings for multiple individuals (Mead, 1934). The significant symbol implies that the gesture calls forth the same response in the individual acting as in the one receiving. This allows for adjustment to the response, but also for mutual sensitivity in the interaction (Mead, 1934). Significant symbols allow us to see actions as others might and repeatedly change the roles that we adopt in different contexts. 'Only in terms of gesture as significant symbols is the existence of mind or intelligence possible; for only in terms of gestures which are significant symbols can thinking – which is simply an internalized or implicit conversation of the individual with himself by means of such gestures – take place' (Mead, 1934: p. 47).

Mead describes how people, when they make a gesture to others, at the same time make it to themselves. In addition, they respond to their own gesture and expect how others will respond, in such a way that they put themselves in the position of the other (Mead, 1934). The adjustment of the conception of the specific or generalized other occurs when there is a mismatch between the expected response and the one that is given. In the gesture response process, not everything is negotiated; norms, language and structural elements are taken for granted and reproduced and only become visible in the conversation if they are questioned or challenged by the participants. We see this as the shared familiar world, which is a precondition for trusting as described by Luhmann (1979).

Taking the Attitudes of the Other

Mead (1934) builds his theory about social interaction on the idea that the individual identity is a social process of internalizing the response of others. Through the process of internalizing reactions experienced in interaction, people both establish conceptions of specific others and imagine the reactions of groups of people, the generalized other. Mead provides an understanding of how people grasp the direction of the acts of others, stating that, '... those gestures which in affecting us as they affect others call out the attitude which the other takes, and that we take in so far as we assume his role' (Mead, 1934: p. 97). This is relevant when we want to examine expectations as part of trusting in interaction, because they are concerned with how people adjust their perception of others through the process of gesture and response. The concept of expectations is not explicitly present in Mead's theory, but it is in the process of taking the attitude of the other that expectations become tangible in interaction.

The conception of the specific or generalized other influences the behaviour of the individual, because an action by the individual will call forth the same or a similar response in him or her as in the other.

However, when there is a mismatch between the response that is expected and the one that is experienced collectively, mutual conceptions and expectations of others are adjusted (Mead, 1934). These conceptions contain the expected reactions of both the specific and the generalized other, and as such they become central to the study of expectations. To understand how people adjust their conceptions or expectations of each other, we need to focus on the interaction in which these are shaped (Mead, 1934). It is in interaction that people actively apply their conceptions of each other to adjust their behaviour to the given situation. This interaction is also where people adjust their conception of each other based on the response to the gesture made. As such, the generalized other and specific other encompass the expectations of the future actions of the other and they change through interaction based on the gesture response process.

Joint Action

Denzin draws on Mead (1934) to develop a better understanding of the process of grasping the direction of the acts of others. When Denzin describes joint action, he argues that it is through the lodging of self in interaction and the generalized other of the others in the interaction that stable definitions of self and identity emerge. In this process of defining the situation, each other and themselves, people develop preliminary 'rules of conduct' (Denzin, 1969). 'While participants may initially agree on definitions, rules of conduct, and images of self, these definitions may be so vague as to permit conflicting points of view to later emerge to challenge the entire basis of joint action' (Denzin, 1969: p. 924).

Denzin condenses Blumer's (1966) assertion in the following way: 'Joint actions, which represent the generic form of all interaction, rest on the ability of the human to grasp the direction of the acts of others' (Denzin, 1969: p. 923). Denzin focuses on how interaction and joint action require the actors to understand and incorporate mutual interpretations and expectations of others into the definition of the situation and their own course of action. A break from expectations would require a negotiation or at least a reinterpretation of the expectations of the others for joint action to continue.

The mutual expectation of how to act and engage in daily practice is, as Blumer describes, 'grasped' in the relations and enables shared actions. Blumer writes that individuals and groups continually attend to the contexts of their situation, interpret those contexts and select a plan of action based on the interpretation (Blumer, 1969). Those situations in

which the mutual expectations become tangible to researchers in interaction occur when someone or something does not live up to the
expectations of the other and expectations have to be adjusted. These
situations are bound to occur because:

> However carefully we plan the future it always is different from that which
> we can previse, and this something that we are continually bringing in and
> adding to is what we identify with the self that comes into the level of our
> experience only in the completion of the act. (Mead, 1934: p. 203)

As such, the negotiation of expectations is ongoing, since 'One makes
contracts and promises, and one is bound by them. The situation may
change, the act may be different from that which the individual himself
expected to carry out, but he is held to the contract which he has made'
(Mead, 1934: p. 203). Since expectations should be understood as
something that changes through ongoing interaction, they serve as a
relevant focal point for studies of trusting as a microprocess.

Similarly to Luhmann, Blumer and Mead focus on how interaction and
joint action require the actors to understand and incorporate the interpretations and expectations of others into the definition of the situation and
their own course of action. The mutual expectation of how to act and
engage in daily practice is, as Blumer describes, grasped in the relations
and enables shared actions. As Denzin puts it, 'The meaning of an object
resides not in the object itself but in the definitions brought to it, and
hence must be located in the interaction process' (Denzin, 1969: p. 923).
Paraphrasing Denzin, one could say that the expectations of the other do
not reside in the individual expecting, but are located and maintained in
the interaction process.

METHODOLOGY

In the following, we apply the concept of expectations from the literature
on trust combined with insights from symbolic interactionism to the case
previously presented. The data are taken from two-year-long ethnographic field research carried out as participative observation. The
empirical research was conducted by one of the authors, and it is
presented as a first-person narrative. The event was selected because it
represents a process of negotiating and changes of expectations in an
inter-organizational context. The narrative is presented chronologically,
but is broken into pieces to discuss the theoretical issues analytically
when relevant. As such, the empirical analysis includes an illustration of

how to apply the framework presented above. The research was conducted in Danish and translated into English. The translation of quotations has been conducted as faithfully as possible to the original Danish, maintaining the meaning of the phrases.

Setting the Scene

The narrative on which we zoom in concerns a particular meeting between the investment manager and the entrepreneurial company. When we enter the collaboration, the investment manager has worked with the entrepreneurial company for six months, negotiating and defining a possible investment. Out of the investment manager's three current investment prospects, this company is the one that he has deemed most promising, with high expectations of the experienced entrepreneurial team. The entrepreneurial company is seeking co-financing capital for a product that has already been developed and is waiting to meet the market. The entrepreneurial team consists of three men, who have worked together for many years in other companies and started up four years ago on their own. The investment manager, with a long career as an engineer, has recently been employed by INV. His approach to the particular entrepreneurial company is very optimistic in terms of investing risk capital and creating a success.

The narrative describes the interactions between the investor and the entrepreneurs and is an example of an ongoing social process in which trusting is negotiated and changed. Trust between an investor and an entrepreneur is essential for their ability to perform and collaborate until the collaboration is formalized. The situation takes place when the collaboration is just about to be formalized. Up until now, it has been an informal relationship working towards an investment. As such, the participants are vulnerable to each other, because there are no legal consequences if choosing to end the collaboration. Up until now, the participants have been vulnerable and maintained positive expectations of each other's future actions, and they have developed a relationship based on trust. However, as we will show, these expectations, and thus trusting, are challenged and then negotiated for the collaboration to continue.

Gesture Response: Uncertainty and Failed Expectations

It was a winter morning and I was at the office at INV, to meet investment manager John. Later that day, we were driving together, heading for a meeting with a small SME company. We were meeting at their new location half an hour's drive from INV. This meeting was set up to discuss the entrepreneurs' newly developed business plan.

Entering John's office, I immediately sensed that something was wrong; John seemed very upset. He told me that he had sent a term sheet[2] to the company the day before, and he had received a reply that made him furious. Mark, the directing entrepreneur from the company, replied that he found the content of the term sheet unreasonable. Mark wanted to start the meeting by discussing the term sheet. To gain a second opinion, John asked me to read the email from Mark:

> Dear John,
>
> I will suggest that we begin [the meeting] by going through the term sheet. We have read it and find it quite unreasonable. But maybe we have misunderstood the different sections. Thus, I will suggest that you explain the sections, so that we are sure we understand the meaning behind them correctly. I think this is the most efficient way to do it, so that we don't waste each other's time with the presentation, etc.
>
> We look forward to meeting you.
>
> Best regards, Mark.

After reading the email, I looked at the term sheet. I realized that some of the sections could be understood as offensive because they relate to how the power should be distributed between the investor and the entrepreneurs. I could imagine how this document could seem frightening if I was to engage in a deal with a 'big investor' trying to 'take' something from the small entrepreneur.

I returned to John's office to tell him how I viewed the situation. Perhaps the entrepreneur reacted in a moment of conflicting feelings, and maybe it was too soon to jump the gun.

John carried on, with tears in his eyes: 'I have spent six months on helping them, and this is how they thank me?'

He was more than furious, and he deliberately chose not to answer the email because he was worried that it would make things worse. I said to John that maybe his reaction at this moment was exactly the same reaction as the entrepreneur had when he read the term sheet. John agreed that emotions had completely taken over and that was why he did not dare to answer the email.

In the car heading for the meeting, we talked about the face-to-face meeting as being the best way to solve the emotional clinches. John made it clear to me that anything could happen; he expected that the meeting could go both ways. Either their roads were to split and everything was lost or they could make sense and proceed in a good way.

Initially, the narrative describes how both John and Mark experienced each other's actions as contradictory to the expectations developed through the ongoing collaboration. At this time, there was a high degree of uncertainty regarding the continuation of the collaboration. Despite ongoing fruitful collaboration, John and Mark seemed to disagree regarding the understanding of the term sheet. Mark interpreted the term sheet as a way for John and INV to take control of his company. He found this unacceptable and reacted firmly in his email to John. It is clear from his reaction that he did not expect this from John, and Mark implicitly questioned the continuation of the cooperation in the email. What was at stake here was a break with the way in which Mark had previously experienced the collaboration with INV, which for him became a break with the expectations that they had developed mutually. The email with the term sheet was not in line with Mark's conception of a specific other, in this case John.

John's reaction to Mark's email shows that he did not expect that response to the term sheet template. He suddenly felt as if he had wasted six months working with the company and described the situation as one in which the collaboration could come to an end.

Consequently, both Mark and John were internalizing the response of the other to their gesture and thereby changing their conception of each other, but also imagining the reactions of the generalized other. John was expecting a certain reaction from 'the other' and, due to the mismatch, continued collaboration was in jeopardy, caused by the experience of failed expectations by the people involved. As became clear in the subsequent interaction, the term sheet is a routine procedure for John and, as such, he expected a different response to it from Mark. John had previously expressed a positive expectation towards the company, because he described it as the most promising of his prospects. Luhmann (1979) describes how familiarity is central to trusting, and since there seemed to be a disagreement concerning the understanding of the term sheet, this established a challenge for continuing the collaboration in a trusting manner.

Taking the Attitude of the Other: Emerging Adjustments

When we reached the IT company, we were welcomed by Mark, Tom and Paul; they showed us around their newly rented, spacious offices. According to the business plan, the company was supposed to grow from 3 to 30 employees in two years. Mark, the Directing Entrepreneur, had a big corner office with a large meeting table, red leather furniture and a view of the seashore. The two Technical Entrepreneurs, Tom and Paul, shared an office down the hall, with plain office furniture and a large amount of computer gear.

We gathered round the meeting table filled with lavish amounts of snacks and goodies. John took the initiative to start the meeting and stated without any filter how he felt about the email from Mark. He did not hide his frustration and feelings; thus, the atmosphere was very tense. At one point, he said that Mark, with his behaviour, was 'digging his own grave' and that 'he should weigh every word he used'. John seemed ready to take on the fight with no return possible. It seemed as if everyone was holding their breath. Mark acted in just as upset a manner and replied: 'Yes, I was furious too, because we feel like you take too much of the company!'

Meanwhile, I observed that Tom was giggling about what Mark had said, and John continued: 'But I gain nothing from this, it is INV.'

With a determined voice, John continued with a longer speech explaining the background of a term sheet: why INV makes one, that it was only a draft and why a term sheet is important in the investment process. He argued that a term sheet minimizes discussions and that INV wanted to be the minority to secure that the entrepreneurs had an incentive. Still, INV needed to secure the capital that it had invested by, for instance, entering the board.

Mark nodded and continued:

> Mark: It was perceived as if you could 'push us around' and you must understand that you are talking about my 'lifeblood' and that is why I reacted as I did. I am fully capable of running this business without you!
>
> John: Me too; you don't have to mark your territory.
>
> Mark: I just feel hurt, but of course you should protect your investment.
>
> John: I could easily run off, but you still want the investment, right?
>
> Mark: Yes, of course.

What took place here was that John was trying to adjust his response to clarify whether their collaboration had a future, although it is obvious that John was still furious. It is clear that the email confused John at first. Hearing Mark's worries regarding the control over the company, John began adjusting his conception of Mark's attitude toward himself and thereby changed his understanding of Mark's concerns regarding the term sheet. What happened was that John responded to a gesture from Mark, and in doing so, he adjusted his conception of Mark by incorporating his response into the conception of the specific other.

John took the perspective of Mark and interpreted the term sheet and his own actions, which provided meaning to Mark's understanding about John as personally striving to assume control of the company. John said, 'But I gain nothing from this, it is INV'; with that gesture, he was attempting to clarify that he held no personal ambition to take over the company. John was trying to clarify diverse understandings; thus, expectations were changing and negotiated in an ongoing process.

Joint Actions: Negotiating Expectations as an Ongoing Process

When John, in his interaction with Mark, realized that his email, with the term sheet attached, had given Mark a negative experience about their collaboration, he took the attitude of Mark to negotiate mutual expectations of the future. John tried to see the world through Mark's eyes and adjust his behaviour towards Mark. The following shows that negotiating and changing expectations are an ongoing process.

They agreed to run through the term sheet to clarify the ambiguities. Mark ran the discussion; Tom and Paul were still surprisingly quiet. John explained the sections that they were not clear about and he made clear that they had the opportunity to suggest changes to the terms. John raised the issue of INV needing to be able to pull the plug and get its investment back, as some sort of 'fire escape'.

The discussion at one point took place as follows:

John: Our interest is only to be successful [...] I think your interests are the same as ours!

Mark: Yes, I agree, but we lose power.

Paul: But Mark, we already are bound to sell in the constellation we have now [co-sale obligation].

John: You will not be able to block a good trade.

Tom: Yes, you [INV] should be able to get your investment back.

John: This is our emergency exit.

Mark: Then we could lose the company?

John: Yes!

John continued by explaining that the term sheet is a routine element of the investment process for INV and pointed out all the beneficial qualities of the document. John was attempting to establish the term sheet as part of a familiar world, but it was only familiar to him. In this gesture towards Mark, John was emphasizing that the term sheet should not be seen as a threat and that all entrepreneurs who receive capital experience the same. John was trying to establish a rational explanation of the term sheet. This did not, however, change Mark's interpretation of the situation, and his response remained the same, thinking that the term sheet would lead to a transfer of control. As the familiar world was not shared by all in the interaction, John's reference to it was ineffective. Mark stated that they did not need the investment to run their business. John did not address the failed expectations of Mark, and as such Mark continued to bring up the subject.

John apparently struggled to explain this balance between being a minority in shares and still having some rights. The discussion entered the more detailed financial aspects, Tom and Paul took over somewhat and Mark was 'pushed' to the side, but he kept trying to hang in there. As Paul discussed the formalities in the term sheet with John, I realized that he was actually trying to understand the meaning of them, and he was not as emotionally affected as Mark. John and Paul went through the sections in a very constructive way. Sometimes, Mark interjected with statements such as: 'We can lose the company if we sign this, and we need to deal with the worst-case scenario to protect ourselves!'

Then, John adjusted his gesture again, by running through the questioned paragraphs in the term sheet, emphasizing that they were open to discussion. Again, it seemed as if John was interpreting Mark's opposition as a sign of him not understanding the investment process. However, this adjustment did not bring about a change in Mark's response; instead, he continued to oppose the term sheet. John attempted to renegotiate the meaning of the term sheet and establish a common goal by saying: 'Our interest is only to be successful ... I think your interests are the same as ours.' John was attempting to underline that they had a shared interest and a shared future. Again, this was not enough to furnish the term sheet with meaning for Mark. Instead, he raised the issue about control again, making it clear that his concerns and failed expectations had not yet been addressed. The term sheet actually constituted a transfer of power, at least with regard to a potential sale of the company. However, Mark's two co-entrepreneurs entered the discussion and appeared to be more forthcoming than Mark. Thus, although Mark may have seemed disagreeable, his interpretation of John's behaviour was accurate. The term sheet was a document that was intended to transfer control, and this contradicted his expectations of the investment process. At this point, John's attempts to talk about a shared future were not explicitly fruitful.

Next, John went through the financial aspects of the term sheet, and Paul and Tom were active in discussing the different elements; however, Mark continued to say that he feared they could lose the company. It was clear that the mutual expectations had not been re-established yet. During the discussion of the financial terms, John repeatedly talked about shared goals and a shared future. The positive reactions of Tom and Paul seemed to play a part in the negotiation of expectations. Paul actively explained different financial elements to Mark, and this seemed to bring forth a change in the interaction. This situation shows that the involvement of Paul and Tom led to Mark taking a more positive perspective on the continuation of the collaboration. When Mark realized that they were not nervous about the term sheet, he adjusted his actions.

Changing Expectations and Establishing Joint Action

John tried to calm Mark down, saying that a common goal was important. Paul also calmed Mark down by explaining and simplifying the sections in the terms; Paul helped the process by making sense of the ambiguity.

When they had examined the entire term sheet, John asked them: 'What about the business plan I made, do you like it? Do you see yourself in it?'

All replied at once: 'Yes, we do.'

They explicitly praised the business plan, with no objections, and they thanked him directly for his work. After this, the meeting proceeded for another hour, with other subjects on the agenda.

By engaging continually in the social processes of negotiation and changing expectations, Mark and John reached new meanings about the written interaction, which initiated the renegotiating of the failed expectations. The analysis shows that they use the conception of the other to adjust their behaviour and establish mutual expectations of the ongoing collaboration.

Joint actions were made possible by John, Mark, Tom and Paul when they, over time, adjusted their actions towards one another and established a useful interpretation of each other. At the end of the narrative, John asked the entrepreneurs, 'What about the business plan I made, do you like it? Do you see yourselves in it?' John was asking the entrepreneurs whether his description of their common future, the business plan, was recognizable to them. The question addressed whether John had sufficiently understood them and their business and thus put himself in their position. The entrepreneurs agreed and talked very positively about the business plan. It becomes clear that the business plan and John's continued efforts to talk about a shared future were important when negotiating expectations. During the meeting, expectations of the collaboration were negotiated and changed, and the analysis shows the centrality of the idea of taking the attitude of the other to understanding how this process unfolds.

On the way home in the car, we talked about what had happened at the meeting. John was pleased with the outcome. We talked loosely about the need for competencies in the company, but John found the team to be very strong and he believed that they had what was necessary to run the company.

A couple of days later, John told me that the IT company had been assessed by the internal evaluation staff of INV, who were very impressed with the entrepreneurial team. The evaluation recommended an investment in the company. The negotiated term sheet was sent to the company's lawyer, and John was very satisfied and said: 'Now we just need to look forward and not look back!'

After the meeting, and one more positive interaction, with the team, John had rebuilt his trust in the entrepreneurial team. In addition, John was clear about his positive expectations of the future joint action. The narrative shows how expectations change and end up as mutual expectations, providing a direction for the future collaboration.

DISCUSSION

Pros and Cons of the Illustrated Study

The analysis illustrates John and Mark's initial response to the term sheet and the email. The interaction at the meeting is an example of a situation in which trusting fluctuates. However, through the discussion of the term sheet and the email, the expectations towards one another change. The actors are vulnerable to each other's actions while they are negotiating their future collaboration, in which money and reputation are at stake. While no contractual formality, at this stage, binds the actors together, the glue consists of negotiated trusting. The empirical setting shows that trusting enables joint actions in a situation without contractual bindings. Another situation of negotiating trusting might bring forward a more explicit picture to exemplify the core phenomenon. An example outside an organizational setting, in which it is not only money that is at stake, but security or even lives, could be self-explanatory. Imagine ethnographic research on the relation and interaction between a hitchhiker and the driver picking up a stranger. No one would argue that this is not a situation in which trusting matters.

Conceptual Contribution

The above narrative analysis illustrates that the framework of symbolic interactionism provides an insight into how expectations change. At first, the joint action was challenged due to expectations, on both sides, not being met. Then followed the interaction at the meeting during which the continued collaboration was explicitly questioned. Both John and Mark stressed that they were not vulnerable to the other, by stating that they could make it on their own; however, their agitation belied this. After this, John began to adjust his conception of Mark by attempting to take the perspective of Mark and calm him down. This was when conception and thus expectations changed; however, as the narrative shows, it was a process that moved through several adjustments to re-establish expectations and allow the joint action to continue. John referred several times to a mutual future collaboration. He was attempting to reaffirm the mutual expectations and seeking confirmation from the others that his description of the expectations of the mutual future was appropriate.

What the example shows is that a focus on expectations sheds light on the interactional negotiation that occurs when joint action and trusting are challenged by failed expectations. It is a process that, in this case, moves from initial agitation through explicit negotiation of expectations to the re-establishment of mutual expectations, achieved through a focus on a shared future. As such, the framework, when used to analyse this narrative, provides an insight into the way in which expectations are negotiated and changed. We contribute to the discussion on process views on trusting gathered by Möllering (2012) by making the concept tangible in interaction through the perspective of symbolic interactionism.

Implications for Further Research on Trusting

When theoretically framing a study as suggested above, aiming to study trusting as a microprocess, there are certain methodological aspects that need to be considered. First of all, this perspective calls for a qualitative approach, because the object of study is interaction between people. To capture interaction and understand how expectations are negotiated and changed, it would be relevant to apply participative observation, securing the researcher access to everyday interactions (Alvesson and Sköldberg, 2009). To oblige these conditions, one data collection method could be to produce written field notes, audio or video recordings, and so on, enabling the researcher to describe change in expectations through narratives (Watson, 2011).

Observations of meetings provide an opportunity to study joint actions and to identify how trusting fluctuates and changes. Observations of interactions can reveal the dynamics of joint actions and thus how and when expectations are challenged and negotiated. At the same time, observations offer an opportunity to explore gesture responses in inter-actions.

Informal conversations and qualitative interviews can be valuable as an empirical approach to access actors' conception of mutual actions. However, because the gesture responses comprise actions, verbal as well as non-verbal, data collected by conversation and interviews should extend the observations and field notes by asking questions.

Interpretation and reflexivity in the process of engaging with the phenomenon of study are already made explicit in the work of Blumer (1969) and are necessary here as a way to approach the empirical field.

CONCLUSION

'How can Trusting be Described and Understood Through Expectations Emerging in Social Interaction?'

By unfolding expectations, as part of trusting, through the concepts of the generalized other, gesture response and joint action put forth by symbolic interactionism, we extend the knowledge of trusting in two ways. First, we offer an approach whereby expectations can be grasped as an element of interaction, which makes this integral element of trusting tangible in empirical descriptions. Through the ongoing adjustment required for joint action, mutual expectations are frequently expressed and discussed in interaction. We argue that when expectations are approached with con-cepts from a symbolic interactionism perspective, which offers a rich interactional vocabulary, they provide an understanding of how expect-ations change. By viewing expectations as the conception of the other, it becomes possible to describe and analyse how they change through the interactional process of gesture and response.

Second, the applied approach allows researchers to understand how trusting changes in a given interaction. By applying the suggested framework to our case, we came to see how trusting is an important element for the continued joint actions between actors in organizations in which formalities are lacking. The framework shows how expectations, and thus trusting, fluctuate, are constantly negotiated and constitute the basis for joint actions, making organizational interactions successful.

In conclusion, we argue that the suggested theoretical framework of symbolic interactionism can contribute to the further understanding of trusting as dependent on the ongoing negotiation of expectations.

NOTES

1. Blumer was a student of Mead and the one who coined Mead's work under the notion of symbolic interactionism (Blumer, 1969: p. 1).
2. The 'term sheet' is the document that outlines the material terms and conditions regarding the investment process.

REFERENCES

Adobor, H., 2005. Trust as sensemaking: The microdynamics of trust in interfirm alliances. *Journal of Business Research*, 58(3), pp. 330–37.

Alvesson, M. and Sköldberg, K., 2009. *Reflexive Methodology: New Vistas for Qualitative Research*. London: Sage Publications.

Bachmann, R. and Inkpen, A.C., 2011. Understanding institutional-based trust building processes in inter-organizational relationships. *Organization Studies*, 32(2), pp. 281–301.

Blomqvist, K. and Snow, C.C., 2010. High-performance trust in the global knowledge economy. Paper presented at the 5th EIASM Workshop on Trust Within and Between Organisations, 28–29 January, Madrid.

Blumer, H., 1966. Sociological implications of the thought of George Herbert Mead. *The American Journal of Sociology*, 71(5), pp. 535–44.

Blumer, H., 1969. *Symbolic Interactionism: Perspective and Method*. Englewood Cliffs, NJ: Prentice Hall.

Denzin, N.K., 1969. Symbolic interactionism and ethnomethodology: A proposed synthesis. *Synthesis*, 34(6), pp. 922–34.

Dirks, K.T. and Ferrin, D.L., 2001. The role of trust in organizational settings. *Organization Science*, 12(4), pp. 450–67.

Ellonen, R., Blomqvist, K. and Puumalainen, K., 2008. The role of trust in organisational innovativeness. *European Journal of Innovation Management*, 11(2), pp. 160–81.

Jagd, S., 2008. Tillidsbaseret ledelse: En ny udfordring for ledere? *Leadership*, December, pp. 1–31.

Kramer, R.M. and Lewicki, R.J., 2010. Repairing and enhancing trust: Approaches to reducing organizational trust deficits. *The Academy of Management Annals*, 4(1), pp. 245–77.

Langley, A., 1999. Strategies for theorizing from process data. *Academy of Management Review*, 24(4), pp. 691–710.

Lewicki, R.J., McAllister, D.J. and Bies, R.J., 1998. Trust and distrust: New relationships and realities. *The Academy of Management Review*, 23(3), p. 438.

Luhmann, N., 1979. *Trust and Power.* Chichester: John Wiley.

Luhmann, N., 2000. *Familiarity, Confidence, Trust: Problems and Alternatives.* Oxford: Blackwell.

Lyon, F., Saunders, M.N.K. and Möllering, G., 2012. *Handbook of Research Methods on Trust.* Cheltenham, UK and Northampton, MA, USA: Edward Elgar Publishing.

Maguire, S. and Phillips, N., 2008. 'Citibankers' at Citigroup: A study of the loss of institutional trust after a merger. *Journal of Management Studies*, 45(2), pp. 372–401.

Mayer, R.C., Davis, J.H. and Schoorman, F.D., 1995. An integrative model of organizational trust. *Management*, 20(3), pp. 709–34.

Mayer, R.C., Schoorman, F.D. and Davis, J.H., 2007. An integrative model of organizational trust: Past, present, and future. *The Academy of Management Review*, 32(2), pp. 344–54.

Mead, G.H., 1934. *Mind, Self, & Society: From the Standpoint of a Social Behaviorist.* C.W. Morris, ed., Chicago, IL: University of Chicago Press.

Möllering, G., 2001. The nature of trust: From Georg Simmel to a theory of expectation, interpretation and suspension. *Sociology*, 35(2), pp. 403–20.

Möllering, G., 2006. *Trust: Reason, Routine, Reflexivity.* Oxford: Emerald Group Publishing.

Rousseau, D.M., Sitkin, S.B., Burt, R.S. and Camerer C., 1998. Not so different after all: A cross-discipline view of trust. *Management*, 23, pp. 393–404.

Möllering, G., 2012. Process views of trusting and crises. In Bachmann, R. and Zaheer, A. (eds) *Handbook of Advances in Trust Research.* Cheltenham, UK and Northampton, MA, USA: Edward Elgar Publishing, pp. 285–306.

Van de Ven, A.H. and Poole, M.S., 2005. Alternative approaches for studying organizational change. *Organization Studies*, 26(9), pp. 1377–404.

Van Ees, H. and Bachmann, R., 2006. Transition economies and trust building: A network perspective on EU enlargement. *Cambridge Journal of Economics*, 30(6), pp. 923–39.

Watson, T.J., 2011. Ethnography, reality, and truth: he vital need for studies of 'how things work' in organizations and management. *Journal of Management Studies*, 48(1), pp. 202–17.

Weick, K., 1979. *The Social Psychology of Organizing.* New York: McGraw-Hill.

Welch, C. and Paavilainen-Mäntymäki, E., 2014. Putting process (back) in: Research on the internationalization process of the firm. *International Journal of Management Reviews*, 16(1), pp. 2–23.

Zaheer, A., 2008. *Handbook of Trust Research.* Cheltenham, UK and Northampton, MA, USA: Edward Elgar Publishing.

12. Process dynamics of trust development: exploring and illustrating emergence in the team context

Taina Savolainen and Mirjami Ikonen

Within organization and management research, the research on intra-organizational trust in workplace relationships has proliferated during the last ten years. Trust, facilitating social coordination and collaboration, belongs to the fundamental social processes in organizations. This chapter aims to advance the current theoretical discussion and empirical research on intra-organizational processes of trust by focusing on the dynamics of the trust development process in the team context. The purpose is to meet the existing need for a more dynamic conceptualization of the process and its emergence by employing a qualitative approach to studying trust. The development of trust is seen as a relational, stage-wise and process-oriented phenomenon characterized by collaborative dynamic interaction between organizational actors, for example leaders, followers and team members. In work relationships, some of the main forms of interaction that characterize trust building involve communication, knowledge sharing and collaborative actions (for example Burke et al., 2007).

This study aims to elaborate and advance a process approach to studying trust development in interpersonal work relationships by examining the aspects of emergence in the trust-building process in the team context. As enrichment of methodological diversity has been called for in recent years in the field (Lewicki et al., 2006; Möllering, 2006), it is our intent to illustrate the dynamics and forms of emergence of the development process through qualitative interview data from two teams. We do not intend to be exhaustive in this chapter (within the scope of a single article). However, as qualitative empirical research on intra-organizational trust development in work relationships, from a process perspective in particular, is largely lacking and needs more attention

(Schilke and Cook, 2013), we aim to explore and add to the current knowledge of trust as a dynamic multiple process between individuals and within dyads and groups by focusing on the interactions and activity of workplace trust in the team context. There is no doubt that the research problem and setting are highly complex, but this does not mean that the research is not worth pursuing. The empirical investigation also endeavours to produce findings, ideas and insights regarding a process view of trust at the micro level for further research.

The theoretical framework of the study draws upon the current theoretical discussion and models of trust development – mainly on dimensional and stage-based models (Dietz and Den Hartog, 2006; Lewicki and Bunker, 1995; Lewicki et al., 2006). The study suggests *a way to study* trust development as a process and an emergence of process. The empirical study is conducted within two teams: a sports team, consisting of hired coaches and members, and a multi-professional team, consisting of a leader and members in a third-sector work organization. Furthermore, metaphors are used in *a theory-constructive way* in the analysis and description of the empirical findings. The innovative and generative power of metaphors is utilized in theorizing about the empirical findings (Boyd, 1993; Knudsen, 2003).

THEORETICAL BACKGROUND

Concept and Nature of Trust

Trust plays multiple roles within organizations (Fulmer and Gelfand, 2012; Möllering et al., 2004), enabling more open interpersonal communication at different levels of organizations. Trust has been identified as one of the most frequently examined constructs in the recent organizational literature (Burke et al., 2007). Trust is seen as an essential element of intra- and inter-organizational social systems. It contributes to information and knowledge sharing in various types of relationships between actors (Savolainen, 2008). Different conceptualizations and levels of trust exist in interpersonal relations, for example, trust among peers, among team members, between supervisors and subordinates and at managerial and organizational levels (Möllering, 2006). In our knowledge era, trust is also important as a human, intellectual, intangible asset and skill in workplaces and has an influence on the innovative organizational culture (Anderson et al., 2014; Savolainen and Lopez-Fresno, 2013). Trust generates social capital, affects the organizational climate and fosters organizational learning (for example Lewicki et al., 2006). In the literature, trust is acknowledged to be *a relational phenomenon* and is seen as evolving gradually over time in interactions between trustor and trustee (Mayer et al., 1995).

Interpersonal, Relational View of Trust

While different definitions of the nature of trust in interpersonal relations exist, ambiguous and complex issues related to the context and dynamics of relationships are not well understood (Atkinson, 2004). Early trust researchers Deutsch (1962) and Rotter (1967) refer to trust-related behaviour in relationships (dyadic and group), which comprises a person's beliefs and expectations of whether the trustee's behaviour or, more specifically, the word, promise, verbal or written statement can be relied upon. Mayer et al. (1995: p. 712) define trust as involving vulnerability and the inability to control the other party. Pertaining to trust in *relationships*, Mayer et al.'s model contains the factors of trust formation in a relational context between trustor and trustee, but the model works unidirectionally. Therefore, it does not involve the dynamic and reciprocal nature of interaction in relationships and, hence, process orientation, which is the focus of this study. Recent studies of reciprocal trust formation have investigated dyadic relationships (see, for example, Brower et al., 2000; Ikonen, 2013; Savolainen, 2009), yet the dynamics and processes of trust development in interpersonal work relationships remain largely unexamined, even though trust at the individual level can predict several outcomes, such as job satisfaction, organizational commitment, turnover and job performance (Dirks and Ferrin, 2002; Lewicki et al., 2006: p. 992).

As we study trust building in a reciprocal interaction process within a team, the leader–member exchange theory, LMX (Graen and Uhl-Bien, 1995), adds to our conceptual understanding of trust as a process in team relationships. The LMX model is about 'leadership making' between dyadic partners developing relationships (Uhl-Bien, 2006; Graen and Uhl-Bien, 1995). Thus, LMX provides a more in-depth understanding of trust in the team leader–member relationship. The leader develops a one-to-one exchange relationship with each follower over time, and both parties bring some value to it (Yukl, 2010).

Process Perspective on Studying Trust Development

Prior trust research has presented some perspectives and models on which to draw in developing a process-oriented approach. To the early theoretical models of trust development belongs Zand's (1972) *spiral model of reinforcing trust*, which describes the strengthening of trust by interactions in a process based on actors' expectations and actions. The recent and widely known models are based on stage-wise development of trust (Lewicki and Bunker, 1995, 1996). According to Lewicki and Bunker (1996), trust develops in three stages and bases of trust: *calculus-*, *knowledge-* and *identification-based trust*. The models appear progressive in nature, with a tendency for linear development. They propose, for example, that the better the other party is known, the deeper the relationship between the parties will become over the course of time. To be more exact, the stage-based models may not represent 'genuine' process models from the point of view of organization and management research, as they do not involve the main elements used in the process studies, such as the time, dynamics (interaction), context (environment), tensions and contradictions that drive development (Langley et al., 2013; Pettigrew, 1990; Van de Ven and Poole, 1995) and the emergence of a process. However, the prior models of trust development provide this study with ideas and advice representing 'the initial seeds sown' to increase our understanding of process orientation.

When abstract issues and concepts such as trust development are studied empirically, the focus is on evolving phenomena. The current trust research needs to reveal the dynamics of trust development in greater depth. For this, a process approach to examining social inter-action processes is needed (Fulmer and Gelfand, 2012; cf. Langley et al., 2013; Savolainen, 2011b). However, the process view on trust develop-ment has scarcely been discussed or explored empirically (Savolainen, 2011b; Schilke and Cook, 2013). Process studies in the organization and management field focus the attention on *how and why things develop, emerge, grow or terminate over time* (Langley et al., 2013).

Characterizing elements in process studies
In organization and management research, specifically concerning organ-izational change, *the process perspective* has been discussed and process theory developed over the two decades since the publication of a widely quoted work by Van de Ven (1992), with the study by Van de Ven and Poole (1995) and the work of Pettigrew (for example 1990) also contributing to the issue. Following Langley et al. (2013: p. 1, italics added) on the nature of process studies in organization and management, (they) 'take *time* seriously, illuminate the role of tensions and contra-dictions in driving *patterns* of change, and show how *interactions* across levels contribute to change. They may also *reveal the dynamic activity*

underlying the maintenance and reproduction of stability.' The main characterizing features are temporality (time), dynamics (interaction) and context.

Time is a fundamental feature in studying processes (Langley et al., 2013). Time and timing have played a more or less visible role in organizations and management, and in the entire organizational world, temporal lenses have been used through the ages. Recently, time has captured the attention in organization studies, with emerging alternative views of time (Orlikowski and Yates, 2002). Time in human activity – of organizations in particular – is not necessarily considered explicitly or is considered in a limited fashion as 'clock-based' (chronological, quantitative, independent of man, measurable and objective) rather than 'event-based' (qualitative, constructed, not of measurement but of human activity and opportunity, and shaped by actors) (Orlikowski and Yates, 2002). Beside the fundamental dichotomy of objective–subjective in time, an alternative third view of time is suggested in a recent work by Orlikowski and Yates (2002: p. 686) as 'experienced in organizational life through a process of temporal structures and structuring that characterize people's everyday engagement in the world'. Temporal structures are understood as both shaping and being shaped by ongoing human action and, more generally, simultaneously enabling and constraining. By recognizing the view of time and its influence on shaping human workplace practices, the process view and study of social processes may increase and deepen our understanding of the dynamics of trust development in the interactions and activity of workplace actors and within their relationships. The process approach thus adds to scientific knowledge beyond what is produced in dominantly quantitative, static and generalization-oriented research (Langley et al., 2013; cf. Lewicki et al., 2006).

The second characterizing feature is *interaction*. Trust can be seen as an interactive, ongoing process over time (Jagd, 2010). In trust development, interactions between people occur via compatible words and actions (Lewicki and Bunker, 1996; Mishra, 1996: p. 268) and via an active role played by actors when undergoing social change, gradual growth, contradictions, failure or the restoration of trust (Langley et al., 2013; Möllering, 2006). The concept of *active trust* captures actors' involvement and something about the nature of trust development as a continuous building process in dynamically changing *contexts*, which is the third feature when studying processes. Even the early work by Zand (1972) refers to a process view, with a spiral dynamically reinforcing trust. A few quite recent empirical findings of explorative studies on the nature of the trust development process show that the process is complex – appearing in multiple or diverse forms, not merely progressive in nature; instead, it seems that the process emerges as a kind of diverging pattern, as a kind of 'wavelike' move forward and backward (Ikonen, 2013; Ikonen and Savolainen, 2010; Laaksonen, 2010; Savolainen, 2011a).

Studying the Emergence of the Development Process

Emergence has typically been assumed to be a process that is too complex to be studied directly and thus has hardly been examined directly. The *dynamics* of emergence has been scarcely considered so far, while, in quantitative research, emergence has been measured as a static rather than a dynamic phenomenon. In this chapter, we face the challenge of attempting to capture some aspects of the dynamics of emergence in the team trust-building process. As Kozlowski and Klein (2000: p. 55) define it: 'A phenomenon, say trust, is emergent when it originates in the cognition, affect, behaviours, or other characteristics of individuals, is amplified by their interactions, and manifests as a higher level, collective phenomenon'. Trust is emergent, as it originates in affect and cognition by individuals and is amplified by their interactions manifesting at multiple levels, as a dyadic-, group- and organization-level phenomenon.

Emergence as a multilevel process has received limited research attention among micro-level organizational processes, due to the scarce conceptualizing available and the fact that it is a highly complex subject to study. Kozlowski and Chao (2012), discussing and studying emergence as a bottom-up, micro- and multi-level process and illustrating it in team phenomena (cognition and cohesion), attempt to advance a more dynamic, process-oriented conceptualization. According to them, three issues have received little attention: emergence is dynamic, it manifests in different idealized forms and it can vary in form over time; emergence is considered to be manifested in certain *forms*: convergent, homogeneous and composition phenomena; and individual interactions in teams potentially create shared perceptions that form a common understanding (homogeneous, composition emergence) while different perceptions in teams fragment (heterogeneous, divergent, compilation emergence) (Kozlowski and Chao, 2012). Dynamic *processes of convergence or divergence* are inherent in both the composition and the compilation form of emergence. Compilation forms of emergence, as dynamic processes, have been very scarcely explored. However, forces for differentiation may prevail and need attention in organizations. This suggests a complementing move from agent-based to human actors (Kozlowski and Klein, 2000).

Studying Trust in the Team Context

Teams are widely spread and rooted in practice when organizing and performing work: 'Teams are complex dynamic systems, exist in a context, develop as members interact over time, and develop and adapt as situational demands unfold' (Kozlowski and Ilgen, 2006: p. 78). The group level is a highly interesting one for studying the trust development process. The relational dynamics within a team emerges from dynamic individual interaction, interaction between members and interaction with the team leader. Teams are the crucial test for emergent phenomena in organizations (Kozlowski and Chao, 2012). They are situated at the crossroads of 'authentic emergence', which means that they are rooted at the micro level, at which individual-level processes interact, intersect and manifest over time as collective team qualities and are influenced by the higher (macro) level *context* (Hackman, 2003). We believe that a team is a fertile entity and level for studying trust building as a dynamic, emergent process. According to Kozlowski and Ilgen (2006: p. 80; cf. Gehman et al., 2013), teams are embedded in a multilevel system, having individual-, team- and organizational-level aspects; they focus on task-relevant processes and involve temporal dynamics with episodic tasks and developments. Team processes as emergent phenomena unfold in a proximal task or social context in which teams are involved while also being part of a larger organization system or environmental context.

While the importance of trust at the group level in teams has been recognized (Costa et al., 2001: p. 226), trust research has largely been carried out at the individual level (Serva et al., 2005: p. 626). However, both levels are relevant. The team leader is expected to build trust in the team members (peers) as well as dyadic relationships between the leader and the members. Studying trust in a team requires the acquisition and increasing of knowledge of the dynamics of multilevel and multi-form relationships. In team behaviour and action in trust building, emergence is manifested in collaboration. Bedwell et al. (2012: p. 130) define collaboration as 'an evolving process whereby two or more social entities actively and reciprocally engage in joint activities aimed at achieving at least one shared goal'. Collaboration involves key elements of emer-gence: *process-oriented* (dynamic exchanges that influence and are influenced by the individual actors involved); *multilevel* (manifested at the group level and influenced by individual- and dyadic-level inter-actions of actors); and *temporally sensitive* (requiring time to develop) (Kozlowski et al., 2013).

Lewicki et al. (1998) discuss the key role that trust plays as a foundation for effective collaboration, and they offer multiple motives that shape collaborative behaviour. The authors discuss a 'new' view of relationships that are multifaceted and multiplex. They point out that the varied views that individuals hold of each other may be temporary and transitional. This means that the state of balance and consistency in relationships at the cognitional level of actors varies and affects relationships. In work relationships, organization members need to develop the capacity to know when, in what respect and in what ways to trust or be trusted (or when possibly to control others or protect themselves).

In previous team research, a shared common vision is seen to facilitate leaders' and team members' focus on a common goal (Gillespie and Mann, 2004: p. 602).

Trust has important effects on behavioural outcomes, such as higher-level cooperation (Dirks and Ferrin, 2002; Lewicki et al., 1998). The cohesion of the group has a stronger impact on performance in sports teams than in other working teams (Mach et al., 2010). Regarding sports teams, Dirks (2000) finds that trust in the leader has a significant effect on team performance, but at the same time trust in teammates has no effect at all. Sports teams are often hierarchically ordered and directly managed. Dirks (2000) presents self-directed work teams as a possible example in which a member is more reliant on peers than on the leader, who may or may not be officially named. Thus, trust involves multi-role behaviours that affect intra-group-level relationships. Trust is seen as a necessary requirement for team cohesion and functioning relationships (Brower et al., 2009; Burke et al., 2006; Kozlowski and Chao, 2012; Savolainen, 2008).

In summary, in the empirical study, individuals, dyads and group are the analysis levels for studying the process dynamics and emergence (forms/types) in trust building. At the team level, trust shapes collaborative behaviour manifested in individual and dyadic interaction and involving collaboration in relationships. These need to be studied to identify and understand the team's multiple levels, events, episodes, activities, communication, knowledge and emotion sharing and negotiation, to mention the most important of them.

Suggesting a Framework

We suggest a *conceptual, analytical framework* (Figure 12.1) based on the idea of synthesizing the two models (stage-based and LMX) explained above. As the prior models involve some dynamics and process orientation, assuming progression in development (cf. Van de Ven and Poole, 1995), we suggest a framework that will make the *dynamic perspective* on trust as a process and the *emergence* of trust development

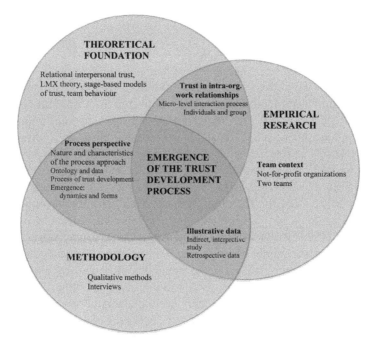

Figure 12.1   Framework for studying the emergence of the trust development process

potentially 'studiable' and understandable with the supporting qualitative methodology (Savolainen, 2011b). The framework is supported by recent qualitative empirical findings (for example Ikonen, 2013; Ikonen and Savolainen, 2010). These findings tentatively suggest that the process of trust development may emerge in a multiple pattern (and not in a linear or merely progressive form) and appear in varying forms of development ('rich', diverse and multi-directional by nature). The conclusions, tentative as they may be, are also supported by recent theoretical discussion meant to advance the research designs for capturing the dynamics of emergence (Kozlowski and Chao, 2012; Kozlowski et al., 2013). In qualitative studies, analytic frameworks are used. These frameworks comprise linked theoretical concepts and views used *to understand the underlying process* (that is, a sequence of events, episodes, interactions or constructs and how they relate), in this case, the dynamic phenomenon of emergence in the team trust-building process.

METHODOLOGY

Adopting a Qualitative Approach

Trust research has moved in a more empirical direction in recent years. As the quantitative methodology has dominated in empirical studies, methodological diversity and a qualitative approach and techniques in particular have been called for as complementary methods (Fulmer and Gelfand, 2012; Lewicki et al., 2006; Möllering et al., 2004) 'to meaning-fully capture changes and dynamics in trust development over time' (Lewicki et al., 2006: p. 1015; see also Fulmer and Gelfand, 2012; Langley et al., 2013). The empirical research on interpersonal trust development in work relationships in general, and from the process perspective in particular, is at an early stage. The reason for the scarce research lies in the highly complex research problem. The study attempts to meet the challenge, filling in the methodological gap by choosing a qualitative approach. There are two main reasons for this: due to the scarce qualitative empirical research on the dynamic process, a per-spective on trust development exists for developing theoretical concepts and for the topic, and there is a need to study the process perspective with empirical qualitative studies, as process studies following an in-depth qualitative approach unfold the dynamics and patterns of processes better (Savolainen, 2011b). So far, Atkinson's work (2004) represents a rare example among the explorative, qualitative, empirical studies of trust in work relationships, focusing on the top-management-level peers. Other examples of qualitative studies on process can be found in the context of the Nordic trust research network (Häkkinen, 2012; Ikonen, 2013; Savolainen, 2009, 2013; Savolainen and Lopez-Fresno, 2013; Savolainen et al., 2014).

Emergent design in the tradition of qualitative research suggests a process that is not predetermined, that is, the process is not finalized at the outset but often begins with guiding questions (Miles et al., 2014). An analysis of the data and their interpretation are important to describe and gain an understanding of the *perceptions* of individuals and groups studied in real-life situations. Ontologically, interpretive research assumes that organizations are socially constructed realities. Trust development is clearly a social process (cf. Fulmer and Gelfand, 2012). Therefore, the reality in which trust is built can be investigated from multiple points of view, one not excluding another. Following a social constructionist epistemology, we consider individuals' perceptions (expressions) as socially constructed and representing only one 'truth' that cannot be regarded as the ultimate truth. From the process perspective, when the dynamics of trust development is in focus, the questions of *how* and *why* trust develops in the way that it does are used as typical questions in process studies. They contribute to producing contextual *know-how* knowledge of the underlying patterns or constructs of process development (Langley et al., 2013; Savolainen, 1997) instead of the 'know-what' produced in quantitative studies.

Our focus is on exploring collaborative team behaviour and actions and illustrating how dynamic interaction between team members emerges in trust building. At a meta-theoretical level, differing approaches to examining emergence are suggested by Kozlowski and Klein (2000). Positioning our approach in respect to the study of emergence, the study represents a qualitative, indirect approach. It should also be noticed that this study is contextual, and contexts (environment) and their differences influence the *kinds of processes that emerge and how* (Kozlowski and Chao, 2012; Savolainen, 1997) and, thus, what unfolds. Retrospective data are collected, analysed and interpreted to make an inference about the process of emergence *after* it has occurred, but the *process is implicit and assumed* since direct, real-time assessment is not possible. Retrospective data involve past events, episodes and so on. We also partly use real-time data containing interviewees' perceptions of 'the present day', that is, at the time of interviewing. Qualitative research tends to develop and yield a holistic understanding of an emergent phenomenon. Description is rich and interpretive, meant for theory building, but tends to be challenging in replication and generalization. Despite the challenges, qualitative research has been the primary methodology for studying emergent phenomena to understand process dynamics and emergence, which correlational and experimental methods can reveal in a limited way (Kozlowski et al., 2013).

Data Collection and Analysis

In a study that is explorative in nature, the empirical qualitative data and their analysis may play an *illustrative role* (cf. Orlikowski and Yates, 2002), as in this study. This means that the interview data and their interpretation in the form of a 'thick' written description of the findings are used to illuminate *the development of a process and its emergence in the micro-level interaction process of trust building*. In other words, we aim to analyse data, produce a description using interview excerpts (quotes) and make interpretations to identify 'patterns' of the process of trust development in the team. We attempt to capture dynamic aspects of emergence unfolding in the process. This very purpose of illustration through the interview data of two teams is related to the issue of 'thick' or 'thin', that is, *the amount of data* needed and the amount gathered in the study. While two teams are involved and some of the team members are interviewed, the amount of data is considered to fulfil the purpose of this descriptive study in contributing new empirical findings. We also aim to present findings, ideas and insights for the benefit of further research. It is noteworthy that it is not our purpose to generalize the findings but instead to produce contextual, *know-how* knowledge from a real-life team case.

The data were gathered from a sports team and a team of professionals in a third-sector organization during in-depth thematic and open-ended face-to-face interviews. Eight in-depth interviews were conducted with informants, of whom six were team members (players and professionals) and two were leaders (a coach and a team leader). The sports team, remaining anonymous in the study, represents a common ball-game team at the highest national league level. As the sports team members are hired employees, the trust-building situation is assumed to be similar to that in the context of a work organization. The sports team comprises thirteen members and two coaches, who lead the team. The access was gained on the basis of prior knowledge of and contact and familiarity with the team (Laaksonen, 2010). These circumstances facilitated the building of trust between the researcher and the informants selected for the study (Lyon et al., 2012). In the professional team, the data were gathered from the team members and the leader in a not-for-profit organization that provides social services organized in multi-professional teams. Each team has its performance level set, as future funding opportunities for new projects depend on the achieved performance.

A thematic in-depth interview method was selected as the most appropriate for gaining the interviewees' views (expressions, experiences, beliefs, feelings) on how trust is built. As trust may be a delicate matter for the informants, an informant-centred procedure allowed the researcher to listen to expressions concerning unanticipated but closely related issues that would be particularly important to the informants. Typically, for a qualitative study, the how and why (and 'when') types of questions were presented to the informants to find out about trust-building process-related behaviours and actions. As for temporality and time in the process study, the interviews contained mainly retrospective but also real-time data, as explained above. This allowed us to analyse the data by sequencing the events and organizing them in a temporal order. The interviews were collected on the organizational sites, and the duration of the eight interviews (leaders and team members) varied between 45 and 75 minutes. All the interviews were recorded, transcribed and then translated from Finnish into English.

Data are analysed holistically in qualitative research. During the analysis, attention was paid to essential issues and details based on the ideas and concepts in the analytic theoretical framework (Figure 12.1) and on the research questions. *Thematic content analysis* was used as a method of analysis. In the analysis of the interviews, we concentrated on the interviewees' perceptions (expressions of interaction, that is, experiences, feelings, beliefs) and expressions of activities and events. This method enabled us to capture *meanings* in a particular situation while allowing us to understand the perspective of trust building as a process. Typically, in qualitative research with interpretive and constructionist assumptions, several possible interpretations of the same data may be produced, but all the interpretations are *potentially meaningful* (Eriksson and Kovalainen, 2008).

The focus of the analysis, from a process ontological perspective, was on the process and dynamics of developments. Thus, the interest in the data analysis when exploring unfolding processes lay in the *flowing* (*moving*), that is, team interaction, activity and events as processes in which actors, chains of activity and events are in continuous and mutually interacting *flux* (Langley et al., 2013). This facilitated the analysis in unfolding the emerging development of trust. An in-depth process type of data gathered from a series of events and activities is challenging, due simply to the large volume of words. Thus, in analysing interview data, a mass of information exists and may create the sensation of 'drowning' (Langley, 1999). Therefore, the handling of data requires proper coding, organizing and thematizing of the interview material. The analysis in the process study meant recognizing and identifying 'logic' patterns behind the trust-building process by looking at the unfolding dynamics of their emergence. In the analysis, this required 'under the surface', in-depth investigation and understanding of the data, interpretation of the data and making a 'thick' description of them. While developments (principally activities, events and interactions) may be more or less complex, the final aim was to reveal how the process of development emerges.

KEY FINDINGS

On the basis of the data, the findings of the key elements and process features are illustrated by the telling metaphors of seed and shell, sprout and growing plant. Quotes from the interviews are used to illustrate the findings and to help the reader to find the link between the interviewee's expression and the researchers' interpretation of the data.

Initially, trust is tentatively created at the beginning of a relationship. At first, the individuals do not know each other; their interaction frequency is low, and a tendency to be at a 'distance' and searching for a contact appears. Information is rarely shared, and communication is fairly poor. The metaphor describing these interactions' activities is considered to be that of a *seed and shell that contains all the opportunities (potential) for growth*.

> Trust does start from some kind of feeling of being off the stage, when everyone is looking around and making observations and forming opinions of others and of what they can do. (Player)

> Well, in the beginning usually it's like people looking around and seeing what they and other people think they are and what they can do. (Player)

The metaphor of a *seed* is used to describe the fragile nature of initial trust. A seed shows the delicate nature of early trust building in which sensitivity and courage are needed to take steps forward. Initial trust building within teams involves knowledge sharing to become familiar with the fellow team members, forming a general impression or, if known early enough, deepening the knowledge about the team members. When feeling as if they are distant outsiders who are only observing the events, activities and people, individuals may behave defensively, protect themselves and *remain in their 'shell'*. When this occurs, tensions, paradoxes and contradictions are implicit (cf. Langley et al., 2013). In both teams, individuals showed a tendency to protect their emotions as they were 'still in their shell'. This was manifested in decreasing interaction by remaining more formal. Individuals did not come out of their shell, as they were not courageous enough to overcome their suspicions and take the risk of being betrayed (cf. the leap of faith, Möllering, 2006).

However, as the members of the team came to know each other better, the emergence of trust was formed by time and interaction. A metaphor that describes this is the *sprout*. Opening up is described in the cited interviews as follows:

> Trust building definitely takes time. To me it's obvious, because you just can't have trust overnight. (Coach)

> In my opinion, you should be able to talk about the stuff openly. Especially if the other person is sorry. Or of course it can also happen that you don't see that and cause harm by carelessness. (Player)

> What I have found a good thing among us is that people do dare to say aloud what they think in our team. ... We have made strong progress in these issues as a team. (Team leader)

Individuals, like a plant, open their shell, that is, they let others come closer, their personality and character become more recognizable and interaction less formal. Due to this more flexible and open sharing of information, the individual members feel safe and are courageous enough to share more at the personal level; individuals are more active and willing to deepen their relationships, and they require a certain level of commitment from the other person.

> We were somehow forced to express ourselves aloud, and the space was given for that. Everyone had to talk aloud about their thoughts. It was a kind of wake-up. By this, I don't mean a launcher or initiator itself, but we got some embryos, you know, for a new culture of discussion in our organization. (Team member)

The quote above describes how trust building was initiated in interaction by mutual understanding and shared information. Here the leaders and team members communicated on a regular basis without avoiding disagreeable issues. Discussing and sharing thoughts more openly than at the beginning can be seen as the emergence of strengthening trust. In addition, common procedures, instructions and behavioural rules are formed and shared, indicating how work is to be carried out rigorously and carefully. Moreover, work-related issues of developing 'rules of the game', that is, common ways for performing tasks rigorously and carefully, come under the spotlight. Within a team, trust building seems to include this type of interaction (talking) and activity.

Opening up may manifest as a diverging 'pattern' of development in the way described in the quote below:

> I have to admit that it is easier to build deeper trust with some team members, just through experience from the beginning. You have to work harder with the younger ones to get info on their motives and skills. Some in the team are 'old hands', and you just can trust them. (Coach)

Based on the interviews, team members and their leader influence, as individuals, as dyads and as a group, the formation of trust in relationships in their particular ways and forms that differ between new team members and 'old hands' (cf. Kozlowski and Chao, 2012 on team cohesion). Furthermore, trust building seems to be influenced by self-confidence and a sense of equality. These may also be shared and spread, emerging at the team level as quoted below:

> Self-esteem must be right: you can't be too insecure. Insecurity spreads to others. (Player)

> In a team, you need to feel equal in order to develop and maintain trusting relationships. It does not necessarily mean equal salary; it is more important how you get along with each other and what attitude you have got. (Player)

Opening up as a team seems to include the types of interaction shown in the quotes above. The role of trust seems to be important in motivation and team relationships. In moving forward, the individuals become willing, courageous and ready to develop trusting relationships. They are more in contact with each other, and interaction becomes *more open*, while communication is less formal and more personal. Dyads are loyal to and willing to help each other by giving feedback, which builds up trust and a higher level of commitment.

Nevertheless, backward moves may appear, for example, through different challenges encountered. The sports team's performance during that particular season did not meet the expectations, and in the other team, a large organizational change was in progress. The interviews revealed issues that may put trust to the test in the team's leader–member relationships. This was expressed in the data as follows.

> It's too bad, but there are disappointments with some players. It's obvious that if the coach doesn't trust the players and the players don't trust each other, it is manifested in something – in this case, in the results. No trust, no potential for results. This means trust in general, like trust in the team organization and each player. (Coach)

> When you start to work for a common goal, different personalities are the issue that affects the team a lot. In a situation where no-one agrees or even tries to listen, it is extremely hard to express your own opinions. (Coach)

> Well, I think it has been different in our team – I'm not saying easier … but anyway – to start. We didn't have the kinds of strong tensions as the [name] department had. So, it has been clearer for me, you know somehow to get … but on the other hand, these tensions within the organization can't be there without affecting the whole organization. (Team member)

In our interpretation, the following interactions describe *emerging tensions* manifested in critical words, a lack of appreciation, self-centredness and negative feelings. However, the quotes below suggest that, after testing, trust – like a plant – can grow and become stronger than trust that has never been tested, at least to some extent.

The process of trusting may also involve a kind of 'downward spiralling'. The best way to describe this is as 'splashes and calms'. Trust may stay stable or go down a little. Sometimes it is 'the downs', in fact, that strengthen trust. (Coach)

Trust doesn't always just move forward, I think. You know, sometimes bad experiences strain trust for a time, but in the long run they may be the ones that make it stronger. (Player)

In our interpretation, the quotes above reveal the dynamics of emergence in the trust-building process. These are shown in the data as a downward spiral as well as splashes and calms, manifested both at the individual and the dyadic level as well as at the collective team level, where it is manifested as a tentative notion. When a trusting relationship dynamically develops 'becoming growing' (cf. Langley et al., 2013, who use this applicable concept, not explicitly with trust but with a process approach), it is more likely to deepen into an emerging 'opening-up pattern' in the trust-building process. It may also occur that a trusting relationship will not grow, but remain stable.

To summarize, the initial trust building (shell) and opening up (seed) emerge in the process involving initiative and collaborative actions, time, interaction (talk), self-esteem, know-how and experience, and 'control' of fellow team members. The descriptions of the findings with supporting quotes, as shown above, create an understanding of how trust was built in the teams and enable us to discuss the dynamics and unfolding forms of emergence in the process (described later metaphorically in Figure 12.2). The dynamics of the trust-building process in the team unfolds as *the growing plant*. The plant and *emergence as growth* are manifested first in initial trust building involving the moments of breaking the shell. This describes the time for team members and the leader/coach to begin to get to know each other, and second by 'opening up', that is, 'becoming growing' through increasing interaction, collaborative activity ('training for play' sessions) and richer communication.

In the findings, *the paradox and the kind of contradiction* between change and stability appear in the very first steps of the trust-building process in which both *protection or defensive behaviour* and *willingness to proceed* with courage emerge. When discussing a process approach, Langley et al. (2013) consider paradoxes, tensions, dialectics and contradictions as implicit emerging driving patterns in the unfolding of processes and changes in their qualities. The dynamics of trust building unfolds as both suspicions and risk-taking calculations and appear as 'dawning' moments for trusting relationships to begin to *sprout*. This sub-metaphor (process pattern) shows a tendency of stability in moving into a *growing 'mode'*. When individuals express the desire to grow and take risks, relationships may ripen and become 'fruitful'. Further, the dynamics of the trust development process unfolds as tensions between the episodes of 'splashes and calms' occur. These are manifested, for example, in backward spirals in trusting, tentatively related to the 'depth', that is, the intensity, of development.

More interestingly, each of the members is perceived to affect the nature of the dynamics and the process, which 'takes' or follows its own pace and intensity in progressing or regressing (down- and backward spirals). The question concerns the *speed and intensity with which growth 'becomes' (changes of growth or declines occur)*. Illustrated as the plant metaphor, plants may be cut down to grow better afterwards; withering leaves and flower buds may exist at the same time, describing the pace and intensity of growth. As for the *temporality* in the process, interestingly, for some time, the process may remain stable in 'getting to know' or it may remain on a stranger stage and stable level of knowing about the peer or leader. If the potential for growing is not seen in the 'opening up', it means that trust in relationships will not begin to sprout. Thus, in this case, trust is not created or strengthened, even though time and effort have been invested in its building by the trust team members.

In summary, the dynamics of the process in teams' trust building emerges in multiple developments of stability, progress (sprout/growth) and backward spirals within individual and dyadic team relationships. The dynamics of emergence in the process unfolds as *forward and backward motion in development*, which reflects and tentatively suggests a diverging pattern or form of emergence (Kozlowski and Chao, 2012). The process features, patterns and dynamics of emergence are illustrated in Figure 12.2 with the help of the 'plant metaphor'.

Summary of the Key Findings

The dynamics of trust development unfolds in multiple developments. The shaping of the process appears to be a complex, multi-featured, multi-directional and diverging form rather than a form of a linear type (Figure 12.2). The process pattern *involves a kind of constant 'flux'*. Tensions, contradictions and paradoxes emerge and are related to the intensity (depth and pace) and direction (backward/forward) of the developments in trust building. Tensions between stability and growth appear in progressions of developments or in stagnating and even declining (backward) directional moves. The process pattern exhibits the paradox in the very first development steps in the trust-building process, in which both defensive protection and willingness to proceed seem to

Figure 12.2 Trust development process: dynamics and emergence in the team context, illustrated as the growing plant metaphor

appear. Time and interaction play a role in the progression and shaping of the process of 'the growing plant'.

In the shaping of the process, the 'calm', peaceful periods in trust development can be seen as a fruitful time for deepening the formation of trusting relationships. Active efforts and, on the other hand, more passive and stable time in the relationship dynamics appear. Trust development is voluntary and freedom-based in nature. Trust does not develop or strengthen by obligation or under pressure. The dynamics of trust seems to relate to the atmosphere, and the team climate seems to play an important part. Functioning interpersonal relationships support trust building in teams (Savolainen, 2008 on project group relationships).

To summarize, the trust development process can be described with the help of *the plant metaphor* with its three metaphoric features ('branches') of *seed*, *sprout* and *growing plant*. The seed, generating the 'shell', involves the dynamics of initial development and is manifested in protection and suspicions. This development may remain 'in the shell' or emerge as the 'opening up' in the progression of building trust. To reach this fruitful 'moment', the shell state seems necessary for the team: initially, they have to become familiar with each other and grow in courage to go ahead while considering the risks; occasionally, they might have to remain in a suspicious and/or defensive state. In this way, if at all, the opening-up moment of building trust will be reached. However, it seems that non-progressive development may be in the driver's seat (low growth), stagnating, breaking off or even declining. An interesting paradox emerges in the process, featuring tensions between stability and growth, that is, seed and sprout, emerging in suspicions vs. opening up.

SUMMARY AND CONCLUSIONS

This chapter contributes to process studies on trust development by exploring how the dynamics of development in the trust-building process emerges and unfolds in a team. Applying the theorizing of studying processes and drawing on the conceptualization of the dynamics of emergence by Kozlowski and Chao (2012), Kozlowski and Klein (2000) and Kozlowski et al. (2013), the empirical study has produced more in-depth findings and understanding of the emergence of the trust development process in a team. The study makes a contribution to the current trust research in several ways: first, by adding to the empirical process studies on intra-organizational trust development within work-place relationships; second, by developing and suggesting a conceptual way for studying trust development empirically from a process per-spective; third, by enriching the methodological diversity with the use of a qualitative approach to explore the dynamics of trust development and the emergence of the process; and fourth, by producing new empirical findings and insight into further research.

The findings reveal that the process of trust development emerges by presenting features and patterns of the development process. The study provides tentative 'sprouts' of unfolding dynamics and forms of the emergence of the process. Moreover, the process pattern of the trust-building process is suggested and illustrated through the 'growing plant' metaphor. The study increases our understanding of the complexity of the trust development process and of how to study the dynamics of its emergence. We would like to emphasize that our illustrative exploration needs and deserves further consideration and scrutiny in continuing studies.

As a practical implication, the findings reinforce the importance of training managers to help them to understand their crucial role in leadership and in the process of trust development. For example, a team leader's support and regular interaction from the very beginning could be one of the essential elements of trust building.

Limitations of the Study

The study targeted two teams in a non-profit sector with only part of the team members involved, which is a limitation of the study. Further, when studying the dynamics of the emergence of the process *indirectly and using qualitative methods*, the underlying mechanisms cannot actually be scrutinized; therefore, it is the interpretation of the researchers on which the reader has to rely. This is also related to the issue of construct validity (Kozlowski and Chao, 2012) and further concerns the retrospective, indirect type of study in question. By applying Kozlowski's ideas and theorizing of emergence mentioned above, the purpose of this study is not to develop a more advanced theoretical model of emergence but rather to make a contribution by producing new *contextual* empirical, richer and in-depth knowledge of the process of trust development by illuminating the way in which the process emerges in the team context. Moreover, qualitative data may bring practical challenges to studying emergence, that is, what emerges from data and how. This may be influenced by several issues, for example access to its study and the phenomenon as such, as well as individual, interpersonal and contextual issues (proximate and external environment).

The study makes a 'rich' description of the trust-building process, presenting the findings on process dynamics, but it does not propose any substantive meaning as a higher level construct; it rather suggests a 'configurational' idea of a team-level pattern in the trust-building process and emergence (Figure 12.2). In this contextual study, generalizations cannot be made, and more research is needed. The starting point for this study is *explorative, and the data play an illustrative role*, meaning that the empirical data describe and illuminate a complex topic that has scarcely been studied empirically. This is a limitation justifying the amount of interview data used and our 'playing' with rich qualitative data. In further research, the qualitative data need to be extended to involve more multiple contexts. This study produces contextual findings; however, contexts differ and, thus, influence the kinds of processes that emerge and how (Kozlowski and Chao, 2012; Savolainen, 1997) and what unfolds. Moreover, with the purpose of contributing to the empirical process studies of trust development, the study produces findings and insights that will be utilized in further research. The chapter suggests that trust development from the process perspective needs to be studied empirically in various contexts and longitudinally at different levels of analysis. Employing qualitative methodology and methods would enrich and stimulate further research to address the questions that remain unanswered.

REFERENCES

Anderson, N., Potočnik, K. and Zhou, J. (2014) Innovation and creativity in organizations. A state-of-the-science review, prospective commentary, and guiding framework. *Journal of Management*, 40 (5), 1297–333.

Atkinson, S. (2004) Senior management relationships and trust: An exploratory study. *Journal of Managerial Psychology*, 19 (6), 571–87.

Bedwell, W.L., Wildman, J.L., Diaz-Granados, D., Salazar, M., Kramer, W.S. and Salas, E. (2012) Collaboration at work: An integrative multilevel conceptualization. *Human Resource Management Review*, 22, 128–45.

Boyd, R. (1993) Metaphor and theory change: What is 'metaphor' a metaphor for? In: Ortony, A. (ed.), *Metaphor and Thought*. Cambridge: Cambridge University Press, pp. 481–533.

Brower, H.H., Schoorman, F.D. and Tan, H.H. (2000) A model of relational leadership: The integration of trust and leader–member exchange. *Leadership Quarterly*, 11 (2), 227–50.

Brower, H.H., Lester, S.W., Korsgaard, M.A. and Dineen, B.R. (2009) A closer look at trust between managers and subordinates: Understanding the effects of both trusting and being trusted on subordinate outcomes. *Journal of Management*, 35 (2), 327–47.

Burke, C.S., Sims, D.E., Lazzara, E.H. and Salas, E. (2007) Trust in leadership. A multi-level review and integration. *Leadership Quarterly*, 18, 606–32.

Burke, C.S., Stagl, K.C., Klein, C., Goodwin, G.F., Salas, E. and Halpin, S.M. (2006) What type of leadership behaviors are functional in teams? A meta-analysis. *Leadership Quarterly*, 17, 288–307.

Costa, A.C., Roe, R.A. and Taillieu, T. (2001) Trust within teams: The relation with performance effectiveness. *European Journal of Work and Organizational Psychology*, 10 (3), 225–44.

Deutsch, M. (1962) Cooperation and trust: Some theoretical notes. Reprinted in: Bachmann, R. and Zaheer, A. (eds) (2008) *Landmark Papers on Trust. Vol. I.* Cheltenham, UK and Northampton, MA, USA: Edward Elgar Publishing, pp. 3–47.

Dietz, G. and Den Hartog, D.N. (2006) Measuring trust inside organisations. *Personnel Review*, 35 (5), 557–88.

Dirks, K.T. (2000) Trust in leadership and team performance: Evidence from NCAA basketball. *Journal of Applied Psychology*, 85, 1004–12.

Dirks, K.T. and Ferrin, D.L. (2002) Trust in leadership: Meta-analytic findings and implications for organizational research. *Journal of Applied Psychology*, 87, 611–28.

Eriksson, P. and Kovalainen, A. (2008) *Qualitative Methods in Business Research*. London: Sage.

Fulmer, C.A. and Gelfand, M.J. (2012) At what level (and in whom) we trust: Trust across multiple organizational levels. *Journal of Management*, 38 (4), 1167–230.

Gehman, J., Trevino, L. and Garud, G. (2013) Values work: A process study of the emergence and performance of organizational values practices. *Academy of Management Journal*, 56, 84–112.

Gillespie, N. and Mann, L. (2004) Transformational leadership and shared values: The building blocks of trust. *Journal of Managerial Psychology*, 19, 588–607.

Graen, G.B. and Uhl-Bien, M. (1995) Relationship-based approach to leadership: Development of leader–member exchange (LMX) theory of leadership over 25 years: Applying a multi-level multi-domain perspective. *Leadership Quarterly*, 6 (2), 219–47.

Hackman, J.R. (2003) Learning more by crossing levels: Evidence from airplanes, hospitals, and orchestras. *Journal of Organizational Behavior*, 24, 905–22.

Häkkinen, S. (2012) *Towards a Trust-Based Model of Leadership within the Leader–Member Exchange Theory Framework. A Qualitative Study of Leaders' Trustworthiness in SME Context*. Dissertations in Social Sciences and Business Studies, 45. Joensuu: Publications of the University of Eastern Finland.

Ikonen, M. (2013) *Trust Development and Dynamics at Dyadic Level. A Narrative Approach to Studying Processes of Interpersonal Trust in Leader–Follower Relationships*. Dissertations in Social Sciences and Business Studies, 53. Joensuu: Publications of the University of Eastern Finland.

Ikonen, M. and Savolainen, T. (2010) Trust in team leadership: Linearity or wavelike development? In: *Proceedings of ISLC Conference*. Lund: Lund University.

Jagd, S. (2010) Balancing trust and control in organizations: Towards a process perspective. *Society and Business Review*, 5 (3), 259–69.

Knudsen, S. (2003) Scientific metaphors going public. *Journal of Pragmatics*, 35, 1247–63.

Kozlowski, S.W.J. and Chao, G.T. (2012) The dynamics of emergence: Cognition and cohesion in work teams. *Managerial and Decision Economics*, 33, 335–54.

Kozlowski, S.W.J. and Ilgen, D.R. (2006) Enhancing effectiveness of the work groups and teams. *Psychological Science in Public Interest*, Michigan University, 7 (3), 1–48.

Kozlowski, S.W.J. and Klein, K.J. (2000) A multilevel approach to theory and research in organizations: Contextual, temporal, and emergent processes. In: Klein, K.J. and Kozlowski, S.W.J. (eds), *Multilevel Theory, Research and*

Methods in Organizations: Foundations, Extensions, and New Directions. San Francisco, CA: Jossey-Bass, pp. 3–90.

Kozlowski, S.W.J., Chao, G.T., Grand, J.A., Braun, M.T. and Kuljanin, G. (2013) Advancing multilevel research design: Capturing the dynamics of emergence. *Organizational Research Methods,* 16 (4), 581–615.

Laaksonen, P. (2010) *Luottamusprosessin Luonne ja Luottamuksen Kehittyminen Tiimissä – Tapaustutkimus Kolmannen Sektorin Organisaatiossa* [*The Nature of the Process of Trust and Development of Trust in the Team – A Case Study in a Third Sector Organization*]. Master's Thesis, UEF, Department of Business.

Langley, A. (1999) Strategies for theorizing from process data. *Academy of Management Review,* 24 (4), 691–710.

Langley, A., Smallman, C., Tsoukas, H. and Van de Ven, A.H. (2013) Process studies of change in organization and management: Unveiling temporality, activity, and flow. *Academy of Management Journal,* 56 (1), 1–13.

Lewicki, R.J. and Bunker, B.B. (1995) Trust in relationships: A model of trust development and decline. In: Bunker, B.B. and Rubin, J.Z. (eds), *Conflict, Cooperation, and Justice.* San Francisco, CA: Jossey-Bass, pp. 133–73.

Lewicki, R.J. and Bunker, B.B. (1996) Developing and maintaining trust in work relationships. In: Kramer, R.M. and Tyler, T.R. (eds), *Trust in Organizations.* Thousand Oaks, CA: Sage, pp. 114–39.

Lewicki, R.J., McAllister, D.J. and Bies, R.J. (1998) Trust and distrust: New relationships and realities. *Academy of Management Review,* 23, 438–58.

Lewicki, R.J., Tomlinson, E.C. and Gillespie, N. (2006) Models of interpersonal trust development: Theoretical approaches, empirical evidence, and future directions. *Journal of Management,* 32 (6), 991–1022.

Lyon, F., Möllering, G. and Saunders, M.N. (2012) Introduction: The variety of methods for the multi-faceted phenomenon of trust. In: Lyon, F., Möllering, G. and Saunders, M.N. (eds), *Handbook of Research Methods on Trust.* Cheltenham, UK and Northampton, MA, USA: Edward Elgar Publishing, pp. 1–15.

Mach, M., Dolan, S. and Tzafrir, S. (2010) The differential effect of team members' trust on team performance: The mediation role of team cohesion. *Journal of Occupational and Organizational Psychology,* 83, 771–94.

Mayer, R.C., Davis, J.H. and Schoorman, F.D. (1995) An integrative model of organizational trust. *Academy of Management Review,* 20 (3), 709–34.

Miles, M., Huberman, M.A. and Saldana, J. (2014) *Qualitative Data Analysis. A Methods Sourcebook.* 3rd edn. Thousand Oaks, CA: Sage.

Mishra, N. (1996) Organizational responses to crisis: The centrality of trust. In: Kramer, R.M. and Tyler, T.R. (eds), *Trust in Organizations.* Thousand Oaks, CA: Sage, pp. 261–87.

Möllering, G. (2006) *Trust: Reason, Routine, Reflexivity.* Oxford: Elsevier.

Möllering, G., Bachmann, R. and Lee, S.H. (2004) Introduction: Understanding organizational trust – foundations, constellations, and issues of operationalization. *Journal of Managerial Psychology,* 19 (6), 556–70.

Orlikowski, W.J. and Yates, J. (2002) It's about time: An enacted view of time in organizations. *Organization Science,* 13 (6), 684–700.

Pettigrew, A. (1990) Longitudinal field research on change: Theory and practice. *Organization Science,* 1 (3), 267–92.

Rotter, J. (1967) A new scale for the measurement of interpersonal trust. Reprinted in: Bachmann, R. and Zaheer, A. (eds) (2008) *Landmark Papers on Trust. Vol. I.* Cheltenham, UK and Northampton, MA, USA: Edward Elgar Publishing, pp. 48–62.

Savolainen, T. (1997) *Development of Quality-Oriented Management Ideology. A Longitudinal Case Study on the Permeation of Quality Ideology in Two Finnish Family-Owned Manufacturing Companies.* Research Series in Computer Science, Economics and Statistics, No. 37. Jyväskylä: University of Jyväskylä.

Savolainen, T. (2008) Sharing tacit knowledge in a project-based organization: Perspective of trust. In: Kujala, J. and Iskanius, P. (eds), *Proceedings of the 13th ICPQR, International Conference on Productivity and Quality Research,* Oulu.

Savolainen, T. (2009) Trust development in leader–follower relationships. Paper presented at the Scientific International Conference on Economics and Management, April, Kaunas University of Technology, Kaunas.

Savolainen, T. (2011a) Luottamusjohtajuus Inhimillisen Pääoman Uudistamisessa [Leadership by trust in renewing human intellectual capital]. In: Puusa, A. and Reijonen, H. (eds), *Aineeton Pääoma Organisaation Voimavarana.* UNI Press, pp. 117–41.

Savolainen, T. (2011b) Inter-personal trust development between actors within organizations: From linearity to multiplicity. Discussion paper presented at the *First Seminar of the Nordic Research Network on Trust within and between Organizations.* Joensuu, UEF. [Online] Available at: http://trust.ruc.dk/internal.

Savolainen, T. (2013) Change implementation in intercultural context: A case study of creating readiness to change. *Journal of Global Business Issues,* 7 (2), 51–8.

Savolainen, T. and Lopez-Fresno, P. (2013) Trust as intangible asset: Enabling intellectual capital development by leadership for vitality and innovativeness. *Electronic Journal of Knowledge Management,* 11 (3), 244–55.

Savolainen, T., Lopez-Fresno, P. and Ikonen, M. (2014) Trust–communication dyad in inter-personal workplace relationships: Dynamics of trust deterioration and breach. *Electronic Journal of Knowledge Management,* 12 (4), 232–40.

Schilke, O. and Cook, K.S. (2013) A cross-level process theory of trust development in interorganizational relationships. *Strategic Organization,* 11 (3), 281–303.

Serva, M.A., Fuller, M.A. and Mayer, R.C. (2005) The reciprocal nature of trust: A longitudinal study of interacting teams. *Journal of Organizational Behavior,* 26, 625–48.

Uhl-Bien, M. (2006) Relational leadership theory: Exploring the social processes of leadership and organization. *Leadership Quarterly,* 17, 654–76.

Van de Ven, A.H. (1992) Suggestions for studying strategy process: A research note. *Strategic Management Journal,* 13, 169–88.

Van de Ven, A.H. and Poole, M.S. (1995) Explaining development and change in organizations. *Academy of Management Review,* 20 (3).

Yukl, G. (2010) *Leadership on Organizations.* 10th edn. Upper Saddle River, NJ: Prentice Hall.

Zand, D. (1972) Trust and managerial problem solving. Reprinted in: Bachmann, R. and Zaheer, A. (eds) (2008) *Landmark Papers on Trust. Vol. I*. Cheltenham, UK and Northampton, MA, USA: Edward Elgar Publishing, pp. 3–47.

PART IV

Interplay of trust-processes

13. Trusting in the change of new public management

Margit Neisig

As described in the public administration literature (for example Klausen, 2013; Osborne, 2010; Pollitt and Bouckaert, 2011), the new paradigm of public management seems to be gaining ground. The once-so-vital position of new public management (NPM) increasingly seems to be taken over by new public governance (NPG). The proliferation of NPM from the late 1970s onwards transformed the Weberian public administration, in which the key elements were a focus on setting and administering rules and guidelines, a central role for the bureaucracy in policy making/implementation and the hegemony of the professional in the service delivery system (Osborne, 2010). With the emergence of NPM, the hegemony of the professional declined and private-sector management gained ground as an ideal. As part of the managerial tools there was an emphasis on input–output control and evaluation. Performance management and audits, marketization, competition and contracts were implemented as tools for resource allocation.

However, NPM has been severely criticized for its intra-governmental focus in an increasingly plural world and for its adherence to the application of outdated private-sector techniques (Osborne, 2010).

Osborne (2006) describes NPG as opposed to NPM. While the latter is a child of neoclassical economics and particularly of rational/public choice theory, NPG is rooted firmly within organizational sociology and network theory and acknowledges the increasingly fragmented and uncertain nature of public management in the twenty-first century. It taps into a more contemporary stream of management theory, concerned with the 'relational organization', than the output and intra-organizational focus of NPM does.

The transformation of the public sector, however, also relies on the transformation of trust/control paradigms. Bouckaert (2012) refers to three different types of trust – 'institutional trust', 'calculus-based trust' and 'relational trust' – that become relevant as a context and driver of public-sector reform (Van de Walle, 2011).

Institution-based trust refers to broad support systems that guarantee that risk levels will be acceptable and trust cultures will remain. Calculus-based trust is grounded in rational choice and economically defined exchange. Relational trust is based on information from within a relationship and is therefore sometimes labelled affective or identity-based trust, which also refers to good faith in a relationship. 'We' becomes an important concept. In general, this trust is closely based on identification with desires, intentions, mutual understanding, groupthink and shared objectives of these groups and their organizations.

Bouckaert (2012) matches these three types of trust to models of governance: for institutional trust, it is hierarchy or the (neo) Weberian state (NWS); for calculus-based trust, they are performance and market or new public management (NPM); and for relational trust, they are networks or new public governance (NPG). In transforming the public sector from NPM to NPG, the process of transforming the mode of trusting therefore becomes an issue of interest.

To understand this transformation of the process of trusting as inter-twined with public sector reform is a very complex issue, and for that purpose this analysis applies the framework developed by Möllering (2013) in a case study of a free municipality trial at a Danish job centre. A process view of trust*ing* is also thoroughly explained in the introductory chapter in this book (Jagd and Fuglsang, this volume). Understanding the change of NPM in terms of transforming the process of trust*ing* might contribute to avoiding the reduction of the change process to a simple matter, as for example creating new methods of management and measurement or exploring isolated municipal experiments. By taking a trust*ing* perspective, more complex process dynamics are explored.

Möllering sets out a framework based on five process views of trusting, which have been interpreted as five distinct perspectives that can also be seen as separate scholarly traditions. However, this study may contribute to unfolding the understanding of the five perspectives as a layered – or at least a partly layered – model (described below). This layered understanding may explain major obstacles in the process of changing the way of trusting while transforming public sector administration from NPM to NPG.

The case explores how the different stages of trusting, as shown in Möllering's framework (understood as a layered model), build upon each other and how obstacles to the trusting at lower stages might impose great difficulties on reaching good results in trusting at higher stages.

THE PROCESS OF TRUSTING IN NPM VERSUS NPG – AND WHAT IS AT STAKE IN THIS CASE STUDY

Before entering into more detail with a layered understanding of Möllering's framework as a framework to explain the obstacles to reaching more profound new ways of trusting, an understanding of the public sector reform, being a trust reform as well, is needed. Furthermore, a brief presentation of the case of the Danish job centre and the intentions of the analysis will be provided.

Put simply, in the traditional NPM service delivery model, the citizens are treated as consumers of public programmes and services, and civil servants conformingly deliver standardized modules of public services that the citizens, in flexible compositions, are eligible to receive. Ideally, the citizens have a choice of different public or private service providers or they can make their voices heard through user committees, advisory bodies, strengthened complaint channels, user surveys, benchmarking and so on.

However, neither the citizens nor the civil servants are co-*designing* the services to any great extent, even though they may be co-producing the services. Therefore, this kind of service delivery system is characterized as transactional (Lenihan and Briggs, 2011) in the sense that a citizen pays tax and the public service provider delivers a service according to standardized norms.

Trust and control play intertwined roles as the citizen (the trustor) is vulnerable to whether the service meets the standards. However, the trustworthiness of the system (the trustee) is based on control or managerialism by which actors are made 'accountable' and processes 'transparent' through management models based on documentation and evaluation. If the standards are not met, the citizen can take other actions (complaining or finding another service provider). In that way, trust and control (based on managerialism and market mechanisms) rely on each other as a duality, as thoroughly explained by Möllering (2005).

However, a paradigm of co-design is emerging involving a participatory *partnership*. Long-term interactive relationships allowing the development of professional knowledge of cross-disciplinarily engaged civil servants as well as the resources from the citizens (users) and the civil society are required to solve complex and wicked[1] issues effectively. The shift is a transition from NPM to NPG (Klausen, 2013; Osborne, 2010; Pollitt and Bouckaert, 2011).

As explained by Edelenbos and Eshuis (2012), this also implies a shift in the trust/control duality from the NPM paradigm, relying heavily on control, to the NPG, with a stronger emphasis on trusting, rooted in interpersonal engagement and not only transactional systemic inter-relations. This means that relationships need to be redefined as engaging service partnerships (Lenihan and Briggs, 2011). A new welfare delivery reform thus also has to be a trust reform. The new paradigm requires trust rooted in a greater 'we' and citizenship, not only based on managerialism and customer satisfaction. As this chapter shows, control still plays an important part in the new paradigm, particularly in the social learning of the new trust relationship. Thus, a new role of controlling also has to be learned.

The empirical part of this chapter concerns a job centre trying to substitute a highly detailed process intervention with a management system based on impact objectives and evidence-based knowledge. This should allow more freedom in conducting the local tasks compared with the process interventions and an emphasis on trust and responsibility of the employees' professionalism.

The overwhelming documentation, evaluation and registration resulting from the extensive process control of the job centres in Denmark have burdened the employees' core tasks with administrative work (Holt et al., 2009: p. 10).

The free municipal trials were launched in the Danish Finance Act 2011 by the former government (Local Government Denmark, 2012). The aim was to enable municipalities to test new ways of controlling their own task solutions, including management methods (Ministry of Interior and Health, 2010: p. 1). This also implied the rethinking of the national regulation, including regulatory exemptions.

Many studies have investigated the Danish employment service; however, this study gains insight into the microprocesses and the different interpretations that are at play when the state regulation is rolled back in a free municipal trial and the local authority tries to establish its own alternative management model.

The study shows that, despite the release from state regulations and the visionary support from the local top management, the trial ended up quickly reinstating a local process regulation similar to the state regulation just rolled back. That is, the number and frequency of the job centre's contact conversations with unemployed people were re-established as an indicator of efficiency instead of measuring the effectiveness of the job centre in placing people in employment (impact measurement). Focusing on the impact would allow other processes, for example contact with employers or coordinated social and health efforts, to count as equally important as just contact conversations with unemployed citizens. Many unemployed people manage well in searching for a job with less frequent contact with a job centre, so the resources might be more effectively spent on more complex clients. This analysis focuses on the dynamics that may explain why the trial did not fulfil its intentions; the analysis also suggests some learning points from the trial based upon a layered understanding of Möllering's framework of trusting.

The case contains multiple organizational layers. Within the job centre, the Director of Labour Market has the administrative responsibility and refers to the local politicians. The head of the job centre has the daily responsibility for running the job centre according to the political and legislative conditions. The team leaders are responsible for coaching their teams and the employees for serving the unemployed according to the legislation, political priorities and managerial framework set forth locally as well as nationally. The IT systems also play a major role as process regulation.

The local municipality is subjected to external political and legislative conditions. Local Government Denmark (LGD) represents all the 98 municipalities before the national government, and it conducts cross-municipality projects such as IT architecture projects. The Ministry of Interior and Economic Affairs (MoI&EA), the Ministry of Finance (MoF) and the Ministry of Labour Market (which is not touched upon in this analysis) play a role related to the job centre. Finally, the government has the overall political responsibility. In addition, the mass media participate, for instance, in agenda setting. These are just the major actors, as other parties also play roles.

The focus is on how this case may help in understanding how the change from NPM to NPG is dependent on the social learning of new trust/control relationships in these complex, multilayered settings and which obstacles are met in this process.

MÖLLERING'S FIVE PROCESS VIEWS

The underlying assumption in this chapter is that a layered approach to Möllering's framework may guide a faceted understanding of how to handle or cope with obstacles throughout the change process from NPM to NPG.

Even though the five process views, labelling trusting as (1) continuing, (2) processing, (3) learning, (4) becoming and (5) constituting, have been interpreted as five distinct perspectives and scholarly traditions, Möllering (2013) also states that the views 'to some extent build

264 	Trust, organizations and social interaction

onto each other and develop from relatively moderate to more pro-nounced notions of process' (Möllering, 2013: p. 289). However, this layered connectedness has been under-researched and is thus explored in this chapter. The assumption is that lower stages of trusting have to be reached for higher stages to be achieved. In the case study, the extent to which unsolved obstacles at lower stages in the framework hinder successful trusting processes at higher stages is revealed. The case study also reveals the importance of understanding the social construction and learning of a new role of controlling as an intertwined process of trusting (Möllering, 2005).

The first view, *continuing*, represents not only trusting's temporal dimension, but also the fact that it has to be created and recreated over and over again. It has to be understood as a phenomenon in which the past, present and expectations of the future act together, for instance through critical events. This continuing flow shapes the practical implementation of an intervention that changes the way in which people trust.

The second view, *processing*, is related to the idea that trust involves information processing. However, Möllering digs into how information becomes a preliminary state of trust as trustworthiness is perceived subjectively, people misjudge and miscalculate, and trust is characterized by insufficient information and emotionally enabled leaps of faith (Möllering, 2006). He underlines that the social information processing is shaped by social processes of communicating and sensemaking as well as by organizational and institutional contexts.

The third view, *learning*, focuses on how trusting enables learning and vice versa and how trust processes draw on familiarity to facilitate familiarization. Trust, control and learning develop in a dynamic co-evolving relationship, and the mental and social processes of trusting produce *trust histories*, which are shared by actors within their relevant communities. Trusting as learning potentially also changes the trustors and trustees themselves. This leads to the fourth view: becoming.

The following question is also highly relevant to this case: to what extent can the learning process of trust be started without a trust basis but with the aim of developing trust? Möllering mentions 'trusting as testing' and recalls Axelrod's (1984) tit-for-tat strategy, Luhmann's (1979) idea of trust as a risky, supererogatory investment and Hardin's (1993) concept of 'as-if trust'. This 'testing' involves willingness to be vulnerable, as is typical for trust, but lacks the element of positive expectations.

The fourth view, *becoming*, focuses on the *actors'* identities. Möllering acknowledges that identity-based trust has been highlighted as a particu-larly interesting form of trust in organizations, for example by Kramer

(2001). However, with the process approach, Möllering is moving 'away from the idea that "trust" is a kind of end-state shaped by the identity (and social identification) of the actors involved, toward a process view that presents "trusting" as part of the actors' continuous becoming' (Möllering, 2013).

The fifth view, *constituting*, builds on the idea of social constitution, as laid out, for example, in structuration theory (developed by Giddens, 1979, 1984), which emphasizes social structures rather than actors, though the whole point is that structuration encompasses agency. In this respect, trusting as constituting emphasizes trusting as 'practice', which also distinguishes this approach from the previous one, which focused on the actors' 'identity'.

The assumption is that the five views are to be understood as layers. Constituting is difficult to reach without becoming, which is difficult to reach without learning, which is difficult to reach without processing, and all forms of trusting are intertwined with the continuous flow of the creation and recreation of trust.

The case study unfolded below has a double purpose: (a) to explore the layered nature of Möllering's framework and determine how the perspectives in the framework constitute layers of trusting; and (b) to ascertain how an understanding of this layered nature of trust*ing* helps to guide the change process of transforming NPM into NPG.

CASE BACKGROUND

The current structure of the Danish employment service was formed by a structural reform in 2007. Ninety-one municipal job centres were established, and the national employment service (AF) was closed and brought into this structure. The employment service makes up a large budget item in the Danish Finance Act.

As described by Holt et al. (2009), the core tasks in the job centres have shifted from personal contact and counselling to registration, evaluation and documentation. The civil servants are free to organize their day, but the working content is relatively laid out around legal requirements and procedures for registration.

Contact conversations with unemployed citizens consist of statutory conversations (National Labour Market Authority, 2013). The first statutory conversation with the unemployed citizen is the CV conversation. It should take place within the first three weeks of unemployment. Every unemployed citizen should be scheduled for a statutory contact conversation no later than every three months.

The management of the municipality needs to control the contact cadences to be observed, because the reimbursement from the state to the municipality depends among other things on the timeliness and compliance with these procedural rules. These are now easily controlled by the IT portal, Jobindsat.dk, in which the civil servants register what is needed.

The idea of the experiment is to provide citizens with more flexible and better-coordinated help in finding a job, especially citizens with complex problems. In these situations, the experiment is about more flexibility across the municipal organization regarding who is allowed to do what, employees of the job centre or those in the social service being responsible for services targeting citizens who have physical or psychological disabilities or who are socially vulnerable. The social service is in charge of shelter, housing, efforts towards abuse and so on, and the idea of the trial is for example to let civil servants in these other parts of the social services have employment conversations with citizens with whom they already have contact.

Under the heading *Focus on impact rather than process*, the idea is also to achieve more flexibility in the timing of contact conversations and in the form and content of the conversations. The objective is to use the budget and staff resources better according to the needs of individual citizens.

Rather than a detail-oriented regulation of the work processes, the idea is to create some leeway locally and rely on professionalism to a greater extent.

CASE STUDY: METHOD

The case was chosen as it provides an opportunity to study many dimensions in this complex process of social creation and recreation of (dis)trust and control through an inter-organizational process of transition, displacing NPM in favour of NPG.

The organizational levels of the analysis are:

(a)   government (trustor)–municipality (trustee);
(b)   ministry (trustor/trustee)–ministry (trustor/trustee);
(c)   municipal leaders (trustor)–municipal employees/citizens/media (trustee).

Not all relevant aspects of all the organizational levels are included in the analysis due to limited time and space. The chosen episodes of focus elucidate the dynamics at play in the highly complex transition process, which is the aim of the analysis.

The empirical study is based on two parts:

1. semi-structured qualitative interviews with the managerial hierarchy and employees at the job centre;
2. document analysis of written documents, such as political addresses, selected governmental documents concerning the legal framework and other types of official documents, as well as selected journal articles.

Interviews were conducted with the Director of Labour Market, the head of the job centre, one team leader and two employees.

Each interview included an interviewer, an informant and an observer and lasted for 40 minutes. The informants had all been employed within the public sector for five to ten years and had the relevant education and experience required for their position.

The interview guide was created from an interest in the changes brought about by the experiment. The point of departure was questions on the motive for the change, the involvement of the employees and the potential contained by the experiment. The issues of trust emerged spontaneously in the interviews as trust relations in the public sector were a major issue in the reason for establishing the free municipality trials, as explained below.

The interviewees were selected through a hierarchical process, but to judge from the interviews, all the interviewees felt free to express themselves and they were not chosen to represent any kind of loyalty towards their managers.

The written documents represent a period of time before and after the interviews at the job centre. The analytical idea is to gain an understanding of the political and institutional settings of the studied free municipality trial and the way in which these settings are also part of a social learning process of trust*ing* in a complex multilayered political environment.

The documents chosen for the analysis represent relevant parts of political rhetoric documenting the semantic shifts from a longitudinal perspective. Through selected documents and journal articles, the use of semantics was studied in the articulation of four themes: the free municipality programme; the trust relationships in public sector management; the public sector productivity; and the IT architecture. These semantic themes were chosen as they penetrate the communication across all systems at play and form a shared semantic reservoir. The themes were found as patterns through the semantic analysis.

The empirical data were analysed in a hermeneutic process to understand the dynamics of trust*ing* and social learning of new types of trust relationships addressed by the five process views explained by Möllering (2013). In this analytical process, the interviews as well as the documents were coded to determine the semantic themes, and the construction and reconstruction of the themes were followed from a longitudinal perspective to reveal the dynamism in the way in which (dis)trust and control are articulated from a process perspective.

Finally, Möllering's five views on trust as process were applied to see which kind of understanding this could generate to grasp whether or not the five perspectives were 'building onto each other' or just separate perspectives.

It turned out that the trust*ing* process is blocked and does not reach more advanced levels. Therefore, all five views have not been equally applied. The last two views – trust as becoming and trust as constituting – were only briefly analysed, as these stages were not fulfilled. As this actually shows the layered connectedness of Möllering's five process views, building on each other, all five views were included in the analysis anyway.

CASE STUDY: ANALYSED BY MÖLLERING'S FRAMEWORK

Trusting as Continuing

To understand 'trust as continuing' in relation to this case, having many organizational levels and being interlinked with the practice of NPM in the overall public sector, a multilevel longitudinal perspective is relevant.

To start with level (a), the free municipality trials were created against a background of distrust between the national government and the municipalities taken as a whole. This seems to have influenced the local trial, in which old trust relations are recreated and not qualitatively changed according to the goal.

The idea of establishing the Danish free municipal experiments in the period 2012–15 was formulated against the political background that public debt needed to be reduced. The goal was to ensure confidence in public finances in the wake of the global financial crisis. For several years, problems with violated municipal budgets (Ministry of Finance, 2010) had created distrust in the management of public budgets.

In parallel, the local municipalities criticized the increasing governmental micro management of the municipalities' task performance (Institute of Local Government Studies, 2009). The idea of the free municipality trials was formulated against this background of distrust (see the later quote by Thulesen Dahl at the Danish People's Party's annual meeting in 2010). The experiments are to be regarded as testing the extent to which mutual trust might be established.

In other words, the trials were not part of an overall innovation strategy for public welfare, which also explains why no national support systems were in place to back up the individual trials. Therefore, the individual trials were vulnerable to the media if their productivity declined. Trust as continuing would show up as 'distrust as continuing'.

This situation affects the local level (c). In this distrusting atmosphere, the influence of the press on the trial in the job centre is, amongst others, expressed by a team leader:

> We are much more exposed, also management-wise, and it appears every time a story is in the media, our local media and so on, well, then we have to go out and find data and find new ways to generate data, and then we are in a bit of a cross field, right ... (Interview, team leader)

This quotation shows that the job centre is 'forced' by the media not to break the social norms of being productive, which is part of trusting as continuing – the old form of control has to continue to create public trust. Municipal leaders (trustor) cannot trust the media (trustee) without providing the old form of data/control. This was an argument to maintain cadence measurements of contact conversations, even though the aim was to stop process intervention.

To return to level (a), as the government in 2011 changed from a right-wing to a centre-left-wing government, a trust reform was announced as part of the new governmental programme:

> The government, in cooperation with the municipalities and the regions, will implement a reform with a focus on trust, leadership, professionalism and less bureaucracy. This is to ensure that public tasks are more focused towards performance – efficiency, quality and service – and to lesser extent in meeting the process requirements. Increased focus on results will create space for more professional responsibility and make room for modern management and increased innovation. (Danish Government, 2011)

In other words, the rhetoric changed and the intention was now to create a new governance dialogue, partnerships between the state and the municipalities and what has been termed a trust reform for the public sector. This is a very different framework from the context in which the examined trial was born.

The approach to the free municipality trials also changed. In the late summer and autumn of 2012, relevant ministries collaborated on the development of new interdisciplinary studies within six general trial themes. The aim was to contribute *jointly* to recreating the task performance in key areas of the public sector and to conducting comparable experiments in several free municipalities to achieve a wider base of experience and improved systems of interaction. One of the six trial themes was 'Rethinking the active employment effort' (Ministry of Interior and Economic Affairs, 2013). In other words, the experiments turned into a more coordinated innovation of the welfare production. This also reduced the vulnerability towards the press, as single experiments could be balanced by other trials and backed by ministerial support.

However, neither the investigated case nor the new interdisciplinary experiments can be characterized as radical innovations in their content, orientation or trust relationships compared with the current regulation or organization. They can be considered as learning by experiments of an incremental nature, and hereby trust is recreated as the future is created in the light of the past. In November 2012, the announced comprehensive trust reform of the public sector was, if not ceded, reduced by the Minister of Interior and Economic Affairs, Margrethe Vestager: 'The reality has dawned on me in the sense that a trust reform is such a package, that it is difficult to find a ribbon that is long enough to reach around' (Avisen.dk, 2012).

This chapter returns to reflecting analytically on this in the next sections related to the second and third process views referred to earlier. However, from the perspective of *trusting as continuing*, the trust relations have *evolved* from the hostile political environment in which the trial was born. However, the absence of a comprehensive trust reform still underlines the need to end distrust by reducing the unnecessary rules one by one, a process that had already begun under the previous government, which launched a debureaucratization programme (Danish Government, 2008, 2009). Throughout this process, talks have resulted in a mini tripartite agreement on seven principles for a trust reform (Government et al., 2013) laying out a foundation for cultural change.

Using the notion of 'trusting', the connection of different states of trust at different points in time is considered. The focus is on trying to grasp how the practical implementation of the trial is influencing the way in which people trust – not only the trust level at different points in time. The conclusion is that trust relations have not changed qualitatively;

however, the attitudes ended up being more constructive but also disappointed and hesitant, and the old familiar control paradigm still exists as a foundation for trusting – created and recreated.

An interesting question is: what was the missing part that led to the withdrawal of an overall trust reform as well as to the reproduction of the process intervention in the free municipality experiment? Furthermore, what can be learned in terms of the preconditions required to reach a qualitative shift in trust relations all the way from the national government to the municipal leadership–employee relations to entail participatory non-transactional engagement of the citizens? The answer is to be sought in the next process view.

Trusting as Processing

Of the utmost relevance in this study are processes concerning how trustors and trustees generate and 'process' (that is, handle) information to produce the outcome of trust. As mentioned, due to NPM, trusting is now based on concepts of making actors 'accountable' and processes 'transparent' through management models based on documentation and evaluation. These management models emphasize *detailed process interventions and regulation* as an intertwined *part of trusting* in 'the system'.

An important part of this case study shows that a new paradigm of information processing – a new language of control – is emerging incrementally. However, as it is not yet institutionalized, both the free municipality trial at the job centre and the political trust reform have missed that fundamental brick.

This also appears in the tension of agendas of the MoF and the MoI&EA regarding modernization of the public sector in general. Here, level (b) analysis is relevant. The modernization agenda initiated by the MoF aims at budget management and goal compliance, yet it focuses more on impact objectives and less on process intervention (MoF, 2013). Against this, the MoI&EA provides the trust reform, which lacks some content that can be measured in economic terms. In other words, there are two different 'languages' or ways to generate and 'process' (i.e. handle) information to produce the outcome of trust.

Even before the Minister of Interior and Economic Affairs ceded or reduced the total trust reform, she hoped for support from the Danish Productivity Commission:

> I hope that the commission will help us to become better at talking about what productivity in the public sector is, and provide us with a language and tools to stick to. There are many dimensions of being productive in the public

sector and I think we often end up with discussions that are very superficial because it is not included, what kind of a quality that is being delivered. (Margrethe Vestager, in Lindholm and Bendix, 2012)

Considerable potential for higher levels of efficiency and quality in the public sector was later suggested by the Productivity Commission. It identified four key factors to increase productivity in the public sector: clear leadership, motivated staff, clear performance requirements and *more autonomy in how to solve the tasks* (Productivity Commission, 2013).

The Productivity Commission dealt with the difficulties of measurement in the public sector and pointed out the requirement to use impact objectives (instead of process intervention), which were also aimed for in the studied free municipality trial (Productivity Commission, 2013: pp. 26–32). The Productivity Commission also indicated an inherent tendency for bureaucracy to increase bureaucracy (Productivity Commission, 2013: p. 9). From this perspective, the studied municipal trial is an interesting illustrative case. The issues touched upon are not just those of the ceded or reduced trust reform, but also apply to the productivity in the public sector in general.

The Productivity Commission recommended a method to create a new management dialogue consistent with the studied experiment, allowing more autonomy in task performance. However, the problem for the free municipality trial was that this management dialogue was not clearly defined; thus, commitment and trust were not established.

This level (b) analysis shows that trust as processing is shaped by social sensemaking processes as well as by organizational and institutional contexts. The two ministries have to create a common managerial language to shape new paradigms of trust as well as control.

Another challenging aspect of the public system is found in their computer systems – an aspect that criss-crosses all the organizational levels of this analysis. The Director of Labour Market at the job centre expresses a visionary need for an overall digital package, allowing the employees to extend a better service towards the citizens (Interview, Director of Labour Market). This is a precondition enabling a holistic administrative process and attaining an early and interdisciplinary coordinated employment effort.

In practice, many barriers prevent an interdisciplinary and cross-organizational effort at the municipal level. Some of these barriers are a result of national regulation and personal data security. Others are due to the division of the municipal organization and the sectoral nature of the IT systems.

A recurring theme in the examined case was the IT systems maintaining specific workflows and constituting a process intervention. Neither holistic management nor impact objectives are promoted in this way. To cope with this, Local Government Denmark published *Proposals for an Impact Based Business Architecture in the Field of Employment* (LGD, 2013a), addressing some of the challenges mentioned.

The proposals focus on results and impacts and a desire and need to involve and encourage citizens to take ownership of their search for employment. Further, they aim to improve the efficiency of the administration. This implies common public standards for data to ensure mutual understanding and alignment across organizations.

With these proposals, the architectural strategy is for each discipline to have ownership of its own terms of language and *mutually to recognize each other's terms* (LGD, 2013a). Thus, IT across 'silos' enables the creation of evidence for best practices towards different conditions (LGD, 2013a).

In other words, both the studied free municipality trial and the trust reform have been in a situation without the fundamental data and basic IT tools necessary to support their visions. This IT architecture has only now been drafted as a proposal (LGD, 2013a). Thus, the data foundation to create a new paradigm of control as a basis for new trusting relationships has not yet been available across sectors.

Such architecture also implies extensive ethical evaluation concerning how transparent personal data should be across the public sector to protect the privacy of citizens. Hence, to proceed further along this line, new trust relationships have to be built regarding the public sector and civil society.

To sum up, trusting as processing seems to be a key issue. A new dialogue and way of measuring are emerging but are still very fragile and not institutionalized. As these elements were and are missing, people are processing 'as usual' from their own perspectives.

Trusting as Learning

One of the questions that Möllering calls interesting and unduly peripheral in trust research concerns the extent to which the learning process of trust can be started without a trust basis but with the aim of developing trust. This question is particularly relevant to this case study. As previously explained, the free municipality trials were born in a very hostile political climate concerning trust at level (a). The idea of the free municipality trials was conceived by the Danish People's Party (governmental parliamentary supporting party):

> We will create a trial in which we say to the municipalities that if you truly
> believe, that you can solve tasks better if you get a freer framework, let's take
> the municipalities at their words ... You have the responsibility to show that
> you can get money to last longer, and that you can get the money to ensure a
> better quality to the citizens. If the trial becomes a success ... it must of
> course be extended to a national level ... if it shows to be a failure, we are
> back and we must declare that it does not work with the free framework for
> local authorities. (Thulesen Dahl, 2010)

The trials are to be regarded as a learning process testing the extent to
which mutual trust might be established. Even though no money was
granted to the trials, more than one in five (22 out of 98) municipalities
applied for the status of free municipality and it was decided to grant the
status to nine municipalities instead of only five (Ministry of Interior and
Health, 2011). Despite the criticism regarding the short time in which to
apply, the lack of money to finance the trials and a pending conflict
between the national government and Local Government Denmark
regarding who should decide on the applications, the engagement in
gaining a freer framework was shown by the many applicants.

In other words, the question that Möllering poses on whether actors
engage in interaction to gain experience with others actually took place
in this case study. He asks: 'What would be the status of this kind of
"trusting as testing"?' He addresses trust as 'testing' involving willingness to be vulnerable, as is typical for trust, but states that it lacks the
element of positive expectations in the face of uncertainty, which is
another important element of trust definitions. Therefore, he asks: 'is this
"testing" already "trusting"?'

In this case, the answer may be an ambivalent 'yes/no'. The applying
municipalities wanted a freer framework and were willing to invest to
obtain it, by being vulnerable as well. That was the reason why so many
municipalities applied. They have visionary leaders, as in this case study,
for example the Director of Labour Market, who wanted to test ideas. At
the same time, they are trying to reduce their vulnerability, sometimes so
much that it hampers the goal of the trial. It is an ambiguous answer, not
yes or no. In some cases, success will be achieved if the local conditions
and engagement are in place; other cases will not succeed, simply
because of this ambiguity, and many such cases, like this case, will lead
to a decoupling, saying one thing and doing another.

As Möllering underlines, these mental and social processes of trusting
are producing *trust histories* shared by actors within their relevant
communities. As we saw in this case, the trust history shared among the
employees is expressed by an employee:

So it may well be in theory, that 'we' have an idea that we are a free municipality, but in fact we must have the same number of conversations as we had before. This is the fact ... what we can learn from this, is that we must certainly not go down in cadences [of contact conversations]. (Interview, employee no. 2)

If this quote shows the trust history, the employees all know that their daily leader, the head of the job centre, has no willingness to undertake a risky, supererogatory investment (Luhmann, 1979) and not even an 'as-if trust' (Hardin, 1993), in which trust is feigned willingly to trigger the information that might allow the development of a proper basis for trust. The daily head of the job centre simply does not trust the trial at all and leaves no further space for trusting as learning. This shows that the top management has not rooted the trial in the organization. There is simply a decoupling – the organization is saying one thing and doing another.

The same trust history might be the case at the political level. The trust reform was part of the election programme and part of the government programme. The ceding or reduction of the reform contributed to a trust history of the government not keeping its election promises. This is a trust history that the right-wing opposition has been successful in maintaining.

The learning may also be that trusting takes much more than just one trial and that it is not realistic to make one big political trust reform. A new public paradigm moving from transactional NPM service delivery to broad partnerships engaging the citizens (users), the civil society as well as cross-disciplinary and cross-organizational cooperation (NPG) clearly is not *a package, for which you can find a ribbon that is long enough to reach around.* In other words, it is not possible to create a top-down trust reform. It took 20 to 30 years to create the NPM that we have today. A new paradigm is emerging incrementally, from many different sources, but it may take another 10 to 20 years to reach a fully elaborated, institutionalized new paradigm.

However, the case also shows that not having successful trusting as processing in place makes learning difficult, as it may foster decoupling.

Trusting as Becoming

As neither the decoupling of the trial nor the reduced trust reform leave much room for trusting as becoming, I will not elaborate much on this part of trusting. However, several actors in this case *identify* with the struggle towards a trust-based, freer paradigm. This identification is also trusting as part of the actors' *continuous becoming.*

For the time being, the public trusting is intertwined with 'accountability', 'transparency' and a huge amount of regulation: 'The employment area is steeped in rules and bureaucracy. The law alone is 22,408 pages ...' (Local Government Denmark, 2013b).

In this case, trusting as becoming seems to mean identifying with a new public agenda *shaping an alternative* to the still-very-vital NPM bureaucracy, while keeping legal certainty as the good side of control. Legal certainty is what makes citizens trust the public administration. The identification with a new public agenda may evolve into *a social movement* shaping what will emerge – a movement in which actors are identifying. Seen from that perspective, the Director of Labour Market, the Minister of I&EA, the labour market parties contributing the seven principles of a trust reform (Government et al., 2013), the Productivity Commission and a very wide group of Danish researchers who have jointly contributed a discussion paper on future management (Andersen et al., 2012) are sending trusting signals and confirming the actors' willingness to *belong* to *this collective*. In this analysis, this is seen as a form of trusting as becoming. However, it does not involve the identity of civil servants.

Trusting as Constituting

Pilot experiments may be a way of creating a new kind of practice. However, as the decoupling took place and the practices were not developed, the supporting IT architecture was only a proposal, the Productivity Commission only made a report, the researchers only contributed a discussion paper and the tripartite agreement only contributed seven principles, the practices are still very limited. In this case, the point is that the social structures of the alternative NPG paradigm are still weak. Nevertheless, one could say that the NPM paradigm to a large extent is (re)producing the rules and resources in which it is embedded.

DISCUSSION AND CONCLUSION

The case shows the problems involved in conducting isolated trials in the public sector, because so many circumstances spread their influence across sectors and hierarchies.

The Möllering-inspired analysis of trusting underlines the social process and this case study contributes an understanding of how successful trusting at lower stages seems to be a precondition for achieving trust at higher stages:

1   Trust as Continuing

The temporal dimension of trust in this case showed up as a development of the political environment in which the trial took place from hostile to more supportive, but the old, familiar control paradigm as a foundation for trusting was created and recreated.

2   Trust as Processing

Inter-organizational trust as processing fails due to premature tools for a new controlling paradigm. This was evident in the struggle to create a new public dialogue, a new 'language' of governance, a new IT infrastructure and so on. The aim is to create 'a new kind of' accountability and transparency that is not so dependent on process interventions and detailed regulation. A new controlling paradigm tends to leave local actors more flexibility in creating partnerships across sectoral demarcations. This enables the design of public services across silos and according to local conditions. As this new controlling paradigm was premature, trusting as processing was unsuccessful and therefore caused trouble with trusting at higher stages.

3   Trusting as Learning

The social learning produced in this case is the ambiguity of the trial, the ambivalence of the participants, the mechanism of decoupling within the organization and the negative trust histories developed by the employees. One conclusion may be that to substitute the NPM paradigm developed over 20 to 30 years and to enable a *new paradigm* (NPG) to *emerge*, it takes much more than just a pilot experiment and a top-down political reform. However, the second conclusion is that not having successful trusting as processing in place makes trusting as learning difficult, as decoupling is fostered.

4   Trusting as Becoming

Identity-based trust, sending trusting signals that confirm the actor's willingness to belong to *a collective* – in this case, *a social movement* trying to *shape an emerging alternative* to the still-very-vital NPM bureaucracy – is the outcome of trusting as becoming. However, as lower stages of trusting had not been successful, trusting as becoming did not involve civil servants' identity.

5   Trusting as Constituting

Pilot experiments may be a way of creating trusting as 'practice'. However, in this case, a decoupling took place and the practices did not change.

To return to the layered connectedness of Möllering's five process views, this case study indicates that lower stages of trusting have to be reached for higher stages to be achieved. It also shows the importance of understanding the social construction and learning of a new role of controlling as an intertwined process of trusting (Möllering, 2005). In this case, it is an *integrated part of* trusting as processing.

Not having the *relatively moderate* layers of trusting in place proved in this case to be a hindrance to reaching *more pronounced notions* of the trusting process. The perspectives in Möllering's process views transformed into layers as the trust process simply became blocked at the lower levels of trusting. Decoupling and trusting as testing took place at the learning stage instead of social learning processes leading to a new stage of 'becoming'. At the stage of 'becoming', the only type of new identity to evolve was the identity of being a change agent. No new civil servant identity emerged. In addition, at the level of trusting as constituting, no new practices were constituted due to the decoupling taking place, blocking the social learning process of becoming. Thus, this case illustrates that constituting is difficult to reach without becoming, which is difficult to reach without learning, which is difficult to reach without processing, and that all forms of trust are intertwined with the continuous flow of creation and recreation of trust.

The conclusion is also that to gain success in constructing a new paradigm of public management, a broad multilevel process perspective on trusting – and the intertwined controlling – is needed, structurationally speaking. This regards the creation of a new language, information processes, partnerships, mindsets and so on. While the above processes are being reconstructed, new roles and identities will *incrementally* be created at the individual, organizational and systems levels. It is not possible to rush to a high level in the trusting process without solidly building the lower levels of trusting in the first place.

As it took decades to build trust in the prevailing paradigm, it will take much more than a pilot experiment, or a top-down political reform, to build trust in a new paradigm. However, based on trusting as becoming, the study indicates that a collective movement is gaining ground in trying to *shape an emerging alternative* to the still-very-vital NPM bureaucracy. Here, proliferation of ideas and identification occur.

The process approach of understanding trust*ing* contributes to explaining the difficulties in achieving results in the many attempts to change the NPM paradigm. However, besides broader social learning of new forms of trusting, new forms of *controlling* also have to come into place and to be learned. These are to leave more flexibility in fostering trust relationships and partnerships across multiple inter-organizational levels. Initiatives based on isolated experiments or variables neglect the process as a social phenomenon of trusting.

Therefore, this case study contributes in the same way as the introductory chapter (Jagd and Fuglsang, this volume) in calling for research on how all these change initiatives are part of, and have to be conceived as, a multilayered, multi-stage processual social learning of new ways of trust*ing* in the public sector.

ACKNOWLEDGEMENT

I would like to express my deepest appreciation to all those who provided me with the opportunity to write this chapter and provided helpful support. Special gratitude is due to the students who have been involved in gathering and analysing the empirical data from the job centre: Helle Glimø, Catrine Granzow Holm, Joan Gestelev Jacobsen and Sisse Lykke Linde. Last but not least, many thanks to the reviewers and editors who have invested effort and provided helpful comments and advice that have improved the chapter.

NOTE

1. Wicked problems have no definitive formulation, no criteria upon which to determine 'solving', and to which solutions are not true or false, only good or bad. Every wicked problem is a symptom of another problem, and no solution of a wicked problem has a definitive, scientific test (Rittel and Webber, 1973).

REFERENCES

Andersen, L.B., Greve, C., Klausen, K.K. and Torfing, J. (eds) (2012) An innovative public sector that generates quality and shared responsibility: Manifesto for public sector reform in Denmark. (Online). Available at: http://www.forvaltningspolitik.dk/ (accessed 13 November 2014).

Avisen.dk (2012) *Vestager: Virkeligheden er gået op for mig*. Copenhagen, 23 November.

Axelrod, R. (1984) *The Evolution of Cooperation*. New York: Basic Books.

Bouckaert, G. (2012) Reforming for performance and trust: Some reflections. *NISPAcee Journal of Public Administration and Policy*, 5 (1), 9–20.

Danish Government (2008) *Afbureaukratisering – Mere tid til service og omsorg.* October, Copenhagen.

Danish Government (2009) *Mere tid til velfærd. Regeringens plan for mindre bureaukrati i kommuner og regioner.* October, Copenhagen.

Danish Government (2011) *Et Danmark, Der Står Sammen.* Copenhagen: The Government Program.

Edelenbos, J. and Eshuis, J. (2012) The interplay between trust and control in governance processes: A conceptual and empirical investigation. *Administration & Society*, 44 (6), 647–74.

Giddens, A. (1979) *Central Problems in Social Theory: Action, Structure and Contradiction in Social Analysis.* London: Macmillan.

Giddens, A. (1984) *The Constitution of Society.* Berkeley, CA: University of California Press.

Government, Danish Confederation of Professional Associations (Akademikerne), Danish Regions, FTF-Confederation of Professionals in Denmark & Organisations of Public Employees (OAO) (2013) *Principper for samarbejde mellem parter på det offentlige arbejdsmarked om modernisering.* June, Copenhagen.

Hardin, R. (1993) The street-level epistemology of trust. *Politics & Society*, 21 (4), 505–29.

Holt, H., Hvid, H., Grosen, S.L. and Lund, H.L. (2009) IT, Køn og Arbejdsmiljø – i administrativt arbejde. *SFI*, 9(11). Copenhagen, SFI – The National Research Center for Welfare. (Online) Available from: http://www.sfi.dk/Files/Filer/SFI/Pdf/Rapporter/2009/0911-It_koen.pdf (accessed 5 November 2013).

Institute of Local Government Studies (2009) Staten spiser af det kommunale selvstyre. *AKT Nyt*, 1. Copenhagen. (Online) Available at: http://www.kora.dk/udgivelser/udgivelse/i7372/Staten-spiser-af-det-kommunale-selvstyre (accessed 5 March 2015).

Klausen, K.K. (2013) Public administration, new PA, NPM, NPG: What's in a name? In: Busch, T., Heichlinger, A., Johnsen, W., Klausen, K.K. and Vanebo, J.O. (eds), *Public Management in the Twenty-First Century.* Oslo: Universitetsforlaget, Chapter 2, pp. 44–57.

Kramer, R.M. (2001) Identity and trust in organizations: One anatomy of a productive but problematic relationship. In: Hogg, M.A. and Terry, D.J. (eds), *Social Identity Processes in Organizational Contexts.* Philadelphia, PA: Psychology Press, pp. 167–80.

Lenihan, L. and Briggs, D. (2011) Co-design: Toward a new service vision for Australia? *Public Administration Today*, 25 (January–March), pp. 35–47.

Lindholm, M.R. and Bendix, H.W. (2012) *Vestager varsler opgør med offentlig ledelse.* Copenhagen, denoffentligesektor.dk, 30 May. (Online) Available at: http://www.denoffentlige.dk/nyheder/vestager-varsler-opgor-med-offentlig-ledelse (accessed 5 March 2015).

Local Government Denmark, LGD (2012) *Frikommuneforsøg.* (Online) Available at: http://www.kl.dk/Fagomrader/Okonomi-og-dokumentation/Frikommuneforsog/ (accessed 5 March 2015).

Local Government Denmark, LGD (2013a) *Forslag vedrørende en resultatorienteret forretningsarkitektur på beskæftigelsesområdet.* Version 1.0, Copenhagen.
Local Government Denmark, LGD (2013b) *KL ser frem til hovedrengøring af beskæftigelsesområdet.* Copenhagen, 2 February. (Online) Available at: http://www.kl.dk/Beskaftigelse-og-integration1/KL-ser-frem-til-hovedrengoring-af-beskaftigelsesomradet-id120222/?section=132442 (accessed 5 March 2015).
Luhmann, N. (1979) *Trust and Power.* Chichester: Wiley.
Ministry of Finance (2010) Massiv budgetoverskridelse i kommunerne i 2009. Press Release, 18 May, Copenhagen.
Ministry of Finance (2013) Aftale om kommunernes økonomi for 2014 – viljen til reformer styrker velfærden. Press Release, 13 June, Appendix 3: Principles on municipal–state collaboration. (Online) Available at: http://www.fm.dk/nyheder/pressemeddelelser/2013/06/aftale-om-kommunernes-oekonomi-for2014/~/media/Files/Nyheder/Pressemeddelelser/2013/06/KL%20aftale/Bilag%203.Principper%20for%20kommunal-statsligt%20samarbejde.pdf (accessed 5 March 2015).
Ministry of Interior and Economic Affairs, MoI&EA (2013) Nye frikommuneforsøg udviklet i samarbejde mellem frikommuner og ministerier, 11 February. Appendix to: Press Release: Frikommunerne udfordrer især Jobcenter-regler, 11 February.
Ministry of Interior and Health (2010) Til alle Kommuner. Letter from the Ministry of Interior and Health, 22 December. (Online) Available at: http://www.kl.dk/ImageVaultFiles/id_46172/cf_202/Indenrigs-_og_sundhedsministerens_brev_til_kommune.PDF (accessed 5 March 2015).
Ministry of Interior and Health (2011) Her er de ni frikommuner. Press Release, 7 April. Copenhagen.
Möllering, G. (2005) The trust/control duality. *International Sociology*, 20 (3), 283–305.
Möllering, G. (2006) *Trust: Reason, Routine, Reflexivity.* Amsterdam: Elsevier.
Möllering, G. (2013) Process views of trusting and crises. In: Bachmann, R. and Zaheer, A. (eds), *Handbook of Advances in Trust Research.* Cheltenham, UK and Northampton, MA, USA: Edward Elgar Publishing.
National Labour Market Authority (2013) *Kontaktforløb.* Copenhagen, National Labour Market Authority. (Online) Available at: http://ams.dk/da/Viden/Indsatser/Kontakt-og-aktivering/Kontaktforlob.aspx (accessed 5 December 2013).
Osborne, S.P. (eds) (2010) Introduction. In: *The New Public Governance? Emerging Perspectives on the Theory and Practice of Public Governance.* New York: Routledge.
Pollitt, C. and Bouckaert, G. (2011) *Public Management Reform: A Comparative Analysis: New Public Management, Governance, and the Neo-Weberian State.* 3rd edn. New York: Oxford University Press.
Productivity Commission (2013) *Produktivitet i den offentlige sektor – hvor er problemerne?* Working paper, June.
Rittel, H. and Webber, M. (1973) Dilemmas in a general theory of planning, *Policy Sciences*, 4, 155–69.

Thulesen Dahl, K. (2010) *Kristian Thulesen Dahls tale ved Dansk Folkepartis Årsmøde i Herning 2010*. (Online) Available at: http://www.danskfolkeparti. dk/Kristian_Thulesen_Dahls_%C3%85rsm%C3%B8detale_2010 (accessed 5 March 2015).

Van de Walle, S. (2011) NPM: Restoring the public trust through creating distrust? In: Christensen, T. and Lægreid, P. (eds), *The Ashgate Research Companion to New Public Management*. Farnham: Ashgate, pp. 309–20.

14. Trust, control and public sector reform

Steen Vallentin and Niels Thygesen

The Danish government platform of October 2011 speaks of a pressing need to de-bureaucratize the public sector. It suggests that centralized government control and detailed regulation should be replaced with more modern forms of governing that allow for local self-management while maintaining a strong sense of responsibility and accountability toward a common purpose. A trust reform is thus in the making and it comes with urgent calls for leadership and adherence to professional values: efficiency, quality and service. Controls that do not directly benefit the purpose of providing value for citizens should be abandoned and this should leave more room for trust to develop and be an asset (Den danske regering, 2011).

Although the Danish government has been widely criticized for failing to live up to these promises of decentralization, underpinned by more trusting modes of governing, our starting point is that the trust reform *has* developed beyond the articulation of broad governmental aspirations and *is* starting to make a difference in the public sector. Hence, trust and related concepts, such as social capital and self-management, are debated across the landscape of public organizations, reaching into central administrative functions as well as decentralized institutions. Municipalities and regions are increasingly addressing the trust issues that pertain to how they are governed and how they govern themselves and labour organizations are promoting trust as a means of breaking the shackles of the new public management (NPM) paradigm and liberating public employees from controls run rampant.

In this chapter we provide an analysis of such reform efforts from the point of view of the trust–control nexus (Bijlsma-Frankema and Costa, 2005; Das and Teng, 2001; Möllering, 2005). With this focus, we are tapping into one of the main queries in the trust literature: whether trust and control should be considered substitutes or in more complementary or mutually constitutive terms (Bijlsma-Frankema and Costa, 2005; Das and Teng, 1998; Inkpen and Currall, 2004; Khodyakov, 2007; Möllering, 2005; Sitkin, 1995; Sitkin and George, 2005; Zucker, 1986). We argue that a complementary view has particular value and relevance for an understanding of reform processes in the public sector. Thus, we will argue for the value of considering trust reform not as a matter of replacing control with trust, but as a matter of reconfiguring intricate relationships between trust and control. In process terms, what we will be concerned with is not the making of trust per se. It is the effects that de-bureaucratization has on relations between trust and control. Hence, we concur with Edelenbos and Eshuis (2012), who argue that 'one-sided attention to either control or trust does not do justice to the complexity of the practice of public management. In practice, public managers have to deal with the complex interplay between trust and control all the time' (p. 651).

For empirical analysis, we turn to the area of *home care* within the Municipality of Copenhagen (*Københavns Kommune*). Home care refers to health care or supportive care provided in the user's/citizen's home by home care professionals. This is a noteworthy case for several reasons. First, home care has often been singled out as the very epitome of NPM run amok, that is, a low-skilled service area besieged by management control, documentation requirements and monitoring. Second, concrete steps have been taken in the municipality, as part of the trust agenda, to give more freedom to employees in home care and give them more room to exercise their professional expertise and judgement at work. Third, the case is a vivid example of trust–control interplay as reform efforts are moulded within a standard NPM model that is usually associated with a controlling mindset. Finally, the case illustrates the importance of considering the reconfiguration of trust and control as a process that takes place over time.

Our analysis is an exploratory case study providing a broad outline of developments in home care. We give an early account of a reform process that is still in the making. In terms of how we approach 'process' as such, we apply what Chia and Langley (2004) have referred to as a 'weak view' (see also Welch and Paavilainen-Mäntymäki, 2014). This means that we treat process as important, but as being, ultimately, reducible to the action of things. According to a weak view, processes form part of the world under investigation, whereas according to a strong view, the world *is* process (Hernes, 2008, p. 23). We find additional inspiration in Hernes' effort to overcome the separation between process and entity (substance). Instead of asking whether something is process or entity, we should ask 'how it came to take on entitative properties and, furthermore, how those properties feed into processes in turn' (Hernes, 2008, p. 30). This involves an assumption 'that something is stable for the sake of analysing it, while allowing for it to become something else' (Hernes, 2008, pp. 30–31). Hence, we will treat the reform effort in question as a mode of de-bureaucratization that we can speak about meaningfully in its own right (as an entity) while at the same time showing how its modus operandi and various relational effects must be considered in process terms. Following Möllering's (2013) categorization of process views (see introductory chapter in this volume), our analysis will, in particular, emphasize *learning* and *becoming* features of trust building – as we show how public sector reform is a social learning process that produces new identities and relationships.

Overall, we aim to contribute to the general discussion of relationships between trust and control, while also making a call for more studies to address specifically trust/control issues in public sector management and development. Overall, our concern is to show *how trust reform in the public sector is a process involving an interweaving of trusting and controlling mindsets and practices.* Theoretically, we apply a socio-analytical lens to the workings of trust and control in organizational settings, drawing in particular on the sociological trust literature (Bachmann, 2006; Lewis and Weigert, 1985; Luhmann, 1979) and Foucauldian notions of power (Foucault, 1980, 1982; Grey and Garsten, 2001). In terms of methodology, we make use of qualitative data from home care, including interviews and written materials. Next, we present our theoretical approach to matters of trust and control in relation to public sector management. This is followed by a brief note on methodology and our analysis of trust reform in home care.

THE TRUST–CONTROL NEXUS

As an analytical starting point, we concur with Luhmann (1979) and Lewis and Weigert (1985) when they argue that trust must be considered 'an irreducible and multidimensional social reality' (Lewis and Weigert, 1985, p. 967). To apply a socio-analytical lens is to insist that trust is a property of collective units and applicable to relations among people rather than psychological states taken individually (Lewis and Weigert, 1985). This means that we emphasize relational and situational (as opposed to dispositional) antecedents of trust; that is, we consider how trust (or distrust) is a product of past direct and indirect experiences between different parties and how the development of trust is contingent upon the uncertainties and risks that are involved in situational encounters (Gargiulo and Ertug, 2006).

Although closely intertwined with control, trust is different from control in terms of how it reduces complexity. Trust reduces complexity – and enables action – by making a bet on a positive future outcome and excluding negative possibilities from consideration (Luhmann, 1979). Control, on the other hand, reduces complexity by regulating and reducing the number of possible outcomes (Edelenbos and Eshuis, 2012). Supporting a substitution perspective, some research has shown that formal control mechanisms, involving the codification, monitoring and safeguarding of social relations, can undermine or chase out trust (Bijlsma-Frankema and Costa, 2005; Khodyakov, 2007), while other contributions have pointed to situations in which trust seems to remove the need for control. However, there are equally many examples of trust and control being complementary (Bachmann, 2001) and this has been reflected in theorizing as well as in empirical studies (Bijlsma-Frankema and Costa, 2005; Das and Teng, 1998; Inkpen and Currall, 2004; Khodyakov, 2007; Möllering, 2005; Sitkin, 1995; Sitkin and George, 2005; Zucker, 1986). Möllering suggests that trust and control be considered a duality, arguing that 'each assume the existence of the other, refer to each other and create each other, but remain irreducible to each other' (2005, p. 284). It is increasingly recognized that trust and control both serve to enable the effective functioning of individuals, teams and organizations and that both constitute essential features of organizational life (Costa and Bijlsma-Frankema, 2007). Furthermore, it has been argued that not only informal – social – modes of control (Bradach and Eccles, 1989) but even formal control mechanisms can be conducive to trust building, the latter 'by providing people with objective rules and clear measures on which to base their assessments and evaluations of others' (Bijlsma-Frankema and Costa, 2005, p. 270; see also Das and Teng, 1998; Long and Sitkin, 2006; Weibel, 2007).

We proceed without making strong assumptions about the positive value of trust or control. Gargiolu and Ertug (2006) have suggested that the trust literature has an optimistic bias. Certainly, the trust discourse as it relates to organizational development embodies a multitude of potential benefits related to liberation of individuals and individual competencies, higher commitment and job satisfaction (accompanied by lower levels of conflict), better communication and stronger interpersonal and inter-organizational relationships, lower transaction costs etc. (Gargiulo and Ertug, 2006). Our way of challenging this implied optimism is to argue that the turn to trust is not about rolling back control as much as it is about negotiating or reconfiguring intricate relationships between trust and control. It may be more about subtle changes than radical shifts. This means that we need to question the extent to which concrete modes of trust-based reform are actually able to deliver on the ostensible benefits put forward in the trust literature. Empirical analyses form a necessary part of such an endeavour.

TRUST, CONTROL AND PUBLIC SECTOR MANAGEMENT

The turn to trust in organizations can be considered part of a cross-sectorial emergence of post-bureaucratic modes of organizing. Among the principal features of post-bureaucracy are the reduction of formal levels of hierarchy, an emphasis on flexibility rather than rule following, the achievement of consensus through institutionalized dialogue (as opposed to acquiescence to authority) and reliance on shared values and a shared sense of mission – all creating a high need for internal trust (Grey and Garsten, 2001). However, we notice a dearth of research that explicitly addresses the trust–control nexus as it relates to public sector management and organization. In relation to the public sector specifically, the role of trust has to be understood in light of the prevalence of different governance paradigms. To simplify, following Osborne (2006), we distinguish here between three archetypes: the classical model of public administration, new public management (NPM) and new public governance (NPG) (see also Edelenbos and Eshuis, 2012).

The classic, bureaucratic model of public administration is a product of the political studies discipline. Its main concern is the workings of the unitary state and it considers policy making and implementation as vertically integrated within government. By comparison, NPM is rooted in neoclassical economics, in particular rational/public choice theory. It envisions a disaggregated state in which policy making and implementation are at least partially disengaged and in which implementation is taking place through a number of independent service units that are ideally in competition with each other – in a horizontally organized market place that is supposed to enable effective cost and performance management through the use of contracts. Finally, NPG is rooted in the disciplines of organizational sociology and network theory, while also being indebted to the literature on organizational social capital. It acknowledges the fragmented and uncertain nature of modern public management and taps into recent developments in management theory that are concerned with creating 'the relational organization'. It puts emphasis on the forging of strong and enduring intra- and inter-organizational relationships and the governance of processes, making room for trust and relational capital to act as core governance mechanisms (Osborne, 2006).

As Grey and Garsten (2001) argue, trust does not figure explicitly in the ideal-type Weberian bureaucracy with its reliance on professional rules and values, formal procedure and role-based responsibilities. While this is the ideal of the classic, hierarchical model, NPM subscribes to an economic understanding of trust as embedded in effective contracting mechanisms. It is only with the turn to NPG that the benefits of social (interpersonal) trust, as opposed to rules and contracts (as manifestations, if you will, of systemic trust), are embraced. In practice, however, most public organizations contain elements from all three archetypes (while not being reducible to any archetype or any combination of archetypes of course). This means that the conditions for social trust have to be seen as closely intertwined with the use of rules and contracts. The appeal to trust thus emerges as one component or concern among others in the management of public organizations. Edelenbos and Eshuis (2012) similarly argue that trust and control co-evolve over time in public organizations; that is, they influence and reinforce each other in a reciprocal relationship. Note also how Osborne (2006) speaks of trust as a governance mechanism.

To embrace the tenets of NPG is not to abandon entirely a systemic view of trust as something that can be enabled by the use of rules and contracts. It is to recognize their respective limitations and to work towards enabling social trust in those spaces and relations in which the governance provided by rules and contracts does not suffice and/or fails to be productive. However, such efforts also have a systemic edge as they take place through the promotion of governance models and uses of management technologies that are conducive to social trust and to the promotion of relational capital as an organizational and individual asset.

Trust-based forms of management are still efforts to manage people and therefore they must, no different from other forms of management, be considered in light of how they affect and/or are supposed to affect people and the technical means by which they strive to do so. Applying a Foucauldian lens, Grey and Garsten (2001) argue that trust can be considered 'a specific form of power', which is not to say that all exercise of power can be understood in terms of trust, but rather 'that no instances of trust can be understood as separate from power' (p. 232). This follows from a Foucauldian understanding of power as being omnipresent in social relations, relational and dispersed. Power cannot, in this view, be reduced to a form of repression that operates in the negative form of commands or prohibiting rules. It can also be a positive and productive force that enables action and empowers individuals (Foucault, 1980, 1982). This view of power as being omnipresent brings us back to the point we made initially about trust and control as complements.

Seeing them as such is to emphasize their temporal and spatial simultaneity, that is, how trust and control are interwoven and mutually defining features of social relations in organizations.

With regard to the public sector and public sector management, this is ultimately a matter of avoiding a polarized view of the trust–control nexus that gives primacy to the social benefits of trust while neglecting the value and necessity of control, documentation, monitoring and so on. This polarized view has gained currency as a legitimate counter-reaction to the success, if you will, of the new public management (NPM) paradigm. With regard to the provision of welfare services, it has been discussed as a conflict between, on the one hand, the values and warm hands of the caring profession and managerialist tendencies sustained by a market ethos on the other (Clarke and Newman, 1997; Gilbert, 2005). However, we find it imperative to maintain that in spite of urges to repair the damages to trust supposedly incurred by NPM, control needs to be thought of as a part of the solution – not just as the problem that is to be solved by means of trust. The question is not whether or not to control, but *how* to remodel or transform control: how to get rid of unnecessary or meaningless controls that do not contribute to the creation of value, fail to motivate employees and so on. In other words, we need to accommodate not only the repressive but also the potentially productive features of control (cf. Grey and Garsten, 2001).

This boils down to a balanced view of trust as an ongoing and dynamic effort to create strong professional relations and mutual commitments in organizations. We now turn to the case of home care in the Municipality of Copenhagen.

NOTE ON DATA AND METHODOLOGY

The following qualitative analysis of trust reform in home care serves as an exploratory case study. In our short account, we provide an outline of how trust reform has been implemented, with a particular focus on the content of reform activities and how they have been communicated internally. As mentioned, we treat the reform effort in question as a mode of de-bureaucratization that we can speak about meaningfully in its own right (as an entity), while at the same time showing how its modus operandi and various relational effects must be considered in process terms. Hence, we apply our 'weak' process view both to the process implications of de-bureaucratization and to implementation as a process comprising a variety of actions. Apart from various internal documents and presentations, along with informal conversations, the analysis builds on seven interviews with managers and consultants at higher administrative levels. This includes interviews with the mayor, two home care managers, two internal consultants, one group leader and one local head of visitation. In the interviews, we have strongly emphasized process issues and obtaining multiple perspectives and critical opinions about the reform and its effects. Our approach in interviewing can be described as critical and constructive in the sense that we have sought to challenge ideal notions of the function of trust on the one hand and have aimed to provide a productive input to the understanding of what makes or breaks efforts to promote trust in modern public sector management on the other. In line with our socio-analytical approach, our focus has been on trust as a social and relational phenomenon related to, among other things, the organization/governance of home care. Getting people to speak freely about their experiences of the reform and their concerns about its effects has been relatively unproblematic as trust is not seen as a panacea to all problems in home care, but rather as one reform element among others to which the organization is subjected or which it is working towards implementing. Likewise, our questions concerning trust *and* control were not a stretch for interviewees, who generally confirmed the analytical relevance of this problematic and showcased a high level of process awareness. In the following pages, we proceed to outline the reform and reflect on process aspects, mainly based on managerial depictions of what the reform is supposed to accomplish and how, as well as managerial experiences of the reform so far.

TRUST REFORM IN THE MUNICIPALITY OF COPENHAGEN

The Municipality of Copenhagen is Denmark's largest in terms of citizens, budget and employees and is so far leading the way among public organizations when it comes to addressing the relevant trust issues in a programmatic fashion. Hence, in its budget agreement for 2013 the political leadership vows to 'remove all unnecessary controls and bureaucracy' and give employees more freedom and time to carry out their core tasks (instead of filling out forms and documenting their activity for control purposes and so on) (Københavns Kommune, 2012, p. 69). According to this document, the Municipality of Copenhagen is setting a trust agenda and striving to create rule-free areas and trustful spaces for its managers to manage and its employees to self-manage (aims that have been reaffirmed in the budget agreement for 2014 and in other communications). However, it is also clearly stated that the turn to trust is not about removing all rules and control requirements. The purported aim is to get rid of 'unnecessary controls' – however they may be defined and separated from supposedly 'necessary' ones. Home care is an area in which considerable efforts have been made to do that.

MAKING ROOM FOR TRUST IN HOME CARE

Home care in the Municipality of Copenhagen provides health care or supportive care to people in need, in particular senior citizens (aged 65+). Home care has approximately 1200 employees, is organized into five units covering local boroughs and 40 operational groups, and makes 8700 visits to users per day. Home care operates under the auspices of The Health and Care Administration (*SUF – Sundheds- og Omsorgsforvalt-ningen*), and the turn to trust was initially driven by an urge of the incumbent mayor (political head of the administration) to curb the detailed regulations and the control mentality associated with many years of rule according to the principles of NPM (the mayor, representing the Socialist People's Party, in 2009 used the reform of home care as an election promise when running for office). Although the trust agenda involves a wider range of ambitions relating to both managers and employees, the pivotal reform activity has been to implement a new governance model for home care, which, as mentioned, has been known to represent NPM run amok.

Provision of home care is organized through an NPM model that creates an internal market place by separating the *ordering* and the *delivery* of services in order to benefit *receivers*. Home care services are ordered by a *visitation* function that has the task of assessing the needs of users. Visitation thus serves as the public authority which decides the services to which individual users are entitled, and operations (or other, private service providers) then makes the delivery. The new governance model does not tinker with this basic principle. Instead, it reduces the number of specific units (work tasks) designated in the management of home care while introducing *visiting blocks* as a more open and trusting means of steering.

Before the reform, the management of home care specified no less than 79 individual units/deliveries and home care professionals had to register, on a handheld computer (a so-called PDA – Personal Digital Assistant), their check-in time for work, their coming and going for each user's home and their lunch time. In internal communications, the new govern-ance model has been presented as a radical administrative simplification, and the transition has been framed as putting an effective end to the 'time and control tyranny' in home care. The time tyranny *has* ended in the sense that home care professionals no longer have to register how they spend their time. They have been relieved of this administrative burden and this should better enable them to be mentally present, caring and attuned to the individual needs of users – apart from actually having more time for the core task of delivering care. Internally, the end of time registration is generally considered as a welcome farewell to an 'unnecessary' control mechanism. Although a lot of time registration was taking place in the old system, it was unclear to many, ranging from the current mayor to employees, how or whether the resulting documentation actually served a practical purpose.

The new governance model is centred on visiting blocks rather than specific services. Visiting blocks embrace the whole service encounter and this means that home care professionals have been given more freedom to manoeuvre and exercise their professional expertise and judgement. Visiting blocks basically refer to the time of day when service is delivered: morning, middle of the day and evening. However, depending on the needs of users, the content stipulated in visiting blocks can be 'light', 'moderate' or 'comprehensive'. Moreover, the new governance model also distinguishes between 'early' and 'late' evening and makes it possible to specify special needs for support in visiting blocks (particularly for elderly people suffering from dementia or other cognitive ailments). When all is accounted for, the new model defines 19 visiting blocks. Included in visiting blocks are services such as helping the user get dressed and move around, personal hygiene, toilet visits, baths, light cleaning and waste disposal, serving of breakfast and other meals, along with help in eating and drinking. On top of this, a number of services are given specifically to users (that is, they are not integrated in visiting blocks). There are 21 of these in all and they include help with medicine (taking of medicine and opening of medicine bags), transportation outside the home, shopping and social visits and telephone calls. In addition, many of the deliveries included in visiting blocks can also be given as specific services if users have additional needs that cannot be accommodated within the time span of visiting blocks. What has been accomplished, in sum, is akin to a 50 per cent reduction in managed units: from 79 (services) to 19 (visiting blocks) + 21 (services) = 40.

The focus on visiting blocks along with the lack of time registration means that home care professionals are given considerable leeway with regard to how they spend their time in users' homes: they can choose to prioritize one task over another, or they can choose to spend more time with one user at the cost of others on any given day. In all, however, they have not been given more time to do their job, which arguably puts pressure on their ability to manage their own time, avoid giving favourable treatment to particular users and so on. Instead of time registration, home care professionals now have to make a daily and weekly work plan and coordinate this with users based on their needs. This reflects how the new model is also meant to accommodate better user dialogue and inclusion of citizens. The work plan is an administrative burden, but serves an important professional purpose as it should make it easier for temporal workers to do a good job, that is, one that is attuned to the needs and expectations of the individual user. Importantly, the new model also puts new professional demands on home care professionals as they are now saddled with the task – and responsibility – of documenting and communicating the changing needs of users and negotiating with visitation in order to ensure that these needs can be met and accommodated within the existing budget.

While the new governance model opens up considerable space for home care professionals to self-manage and prioritize their own time and effort within visiting blocks, it is misleading to think of this as providing a control-free space or associating the implied view of trust with some radical notion of autonomy. Trust reform appears as a matter of degrees rather than a radical overturning of home care management – even if, in terms of numbers, it involves a considerable de-bureaucratization. The new governance model makes use of supposedly more productive forms of control that aim to establish more trusting relations, but still within clearly defined parameters. Trust reform is about loosening/remodelling, but not relinquishing, the control associated with structures, rules and regulations.

BALANCING TRUST AND CONTROL IN HOME CARE

Trust reform is, in other words, about finding new ways to balance trust and control. Control is maintained, formally and structurally, by the NPM model within which these developments are moulded. As mentioned, it is a model that builds on the ideal of an internal market place. It installs an economic principal–agent relation – and thus an internal division of labour – by separating the *ordering* and the *delivery* of services to benefit the *receivers*. It thus tends to create opposite interests and corresponding control needs in the organization – in contrast to the cooperative mindset that we most often associate with trust. Visitation is, of course, an ongoing process as the needs of users change and must be reassessed continuously, but at any given time it is the visitation function that is responsible for determining the services to which home care users are entitled. The new governance model has maintained this basic principle (which is meant to keep the supply side – operations – from driving up costs), but it has had an immediate effect in the sense that visitation is now a more open task. The focus on visiting blocks means that visitation does not have the same detailed control over exactly what services are provided and how. The 'how' is to a larger extent determined by operations, that is, home care employees. In this sense, visitation has to rely more on trust.

The new model has meant that the needs of approximately 9000 users of home care have had to be transferred into a new governance scheme. A complete reassessment of needs has not been necessary; instead the task has been to translate the provision of 79 special services into the new scheme, consisting of 19 visiting blocks and 21 additional services. Importantly, this has not in itself been a cost-cutting exercise. We are talking about a home care budget of approximately DKK 700 million before and after the reform. The expected benefits are related to the provision of better services in the future.

The trust reform has meant that home care is subjected to a more open and less detailed control regime. It is part of an effort to make control more meaningful and transparent. There has always been a considerable element of trust involved in home care as employees are sent out, on their own, without a manager looking over their shoulder, to do work in people's homes. With the trust reform, however, the elements of trust and self-management have been made more explicit. Making it work according to plan, however, is no simple matter.

PROCESSES OF TRUST AND CONTROL IN HOME CARE

The Health and Care Administration, of which home care is a part, has 10 000 employees in all and an annual budget of approximately DKK 6.3 billion (2012). It is a large organization, with considerable administrative (central planning) resources that have been put to use in the implementation of the new governance model. However, instead of a traditional top-down approach to implementation, a pilot project was established in one of the local areas to provide overall guidance. The pilot project involved the local home care manager, two group leaders, the leading person from visitation, a couple of labour representatives, a couple of employees and a controller. Together, in collaboration with the two work groups involved, they came up with a model for implementing and communicating the new scheme. As a next step, this model was tested in two other work groups from the same local area.

The approach chosen shows an attentiveness to process and the challenges involved in properly embedding this new initiative in the organization, namely by engaging operations and not leaving the planning to central administrative staff. Although the process has been initiated and coordinated by a central unit with formal responsibility, this unit has regarded its role as being more that of a facilitator than a primary driving force. This, again, is a sign of a trusting mentality because it has to a considerable extent meant forgoing control over the process. The attentiveness to process also applies to the expectations regarding the outcomes of this initiative. It is strongly emphasized by interviewees that the easiest part of trust reform is implementing a new structure. The hard part has to do with the process of cultural change that must follow. This is not only a matter of home care professionals adjusting themselves to a new, more self-managing mindset. It is also a matter of redefining what the management of home care is about, particularly in operations. In other words, it involves creation of new managerial and employee identities. The trust reform is supposed to allow managers to focus less on administrative tasks, including routine planning and documentation, and have more of a professional focus. It is supposed to free them up to engage more in professional dialogue with employees. This is an important part of the new governance model, considering its increased reliance on professional judgement calls and the uncertainties and responsibilities associated with it. As part of this effort, managers are supposed to engage more closely with employees and how they do their job. This includes occasional observation of how home care is being carried out in users' homes. Ideally, employees should perceive this supervision as part of a professional dialogue, but it can also be seen as undue interference, signalling distrust and an unwelcome need to look over the shoulder of employees. The important point is that efforts to create more trusting relationships can have the opposite effect. There is a challenge here for managers to (re)assert themselves in terms of their professional expertise – after many years in a system preoccupied with administrative paperwork, documentation and control. Part of the learning process has to do with creating a new, more professional dialogue between managers and employees that is based on trust and a mutual understanding of the new governance model and its possibilities.

The process of implementing the new governance model is still in its early stages and it is bound to proceed differently in different parts of the organization. As mentioned, home care consists of five local units and 40 operational work groups with 40 group leaders. The local units cover different boroughs and the different work groups and their leaders and employees to some extent reflect the different cultures found in different parts of a big city. No central efforts are made to streamline – or control – how different managers cope with the challenges related to trust in regard to their employees and there is an acceptance that there can be strength in diversity.

With regard to internal resistance to trust initiatives, the new governance model can generally be considered a success story, both politically and in the organization, as it represents a welcome softening of the stronghold of NPM that comes with promises of better performance, better care and happier and more motivated employees. However, scepticism has been detected among some employees, whose reaction is related to negative experiences of prior reform efforts. This is another indicator that trust-based forms of management may not be experienced as such and may not be successful in creating trust. The reform has also shown signs of increasing tensions between visitation and operations by tipping the scales and altering the power balance between the two. Arguably, the trust reform makes it more legitimate for operations not only to call for more time to do a proper job with users, but also to challenge the NPM-dictated authority of visitation in home care altogether. This problematic must be seen in light of a tendency in recent years for many municipalities to abandon this type of NPM model in favour of more holistic and relational models of governance.

Many unanswered questions remain. How can visitation maintain a sense of proper control under the new regime? Will the new model actually produce superior results in terms of quality and/or efficiency measures? And how will this affect the continued political support for this endeavour? How much support will employees need under the new working conditions? And will the support given be considered a sign of trust or distrust? How will managers, particularly in operations, respond to the new managerial challenges and the push for more professional dialogue and leadership? Will there still be room for employees who are not comfortable with the demand that they should be self-managing, or is there a social exclusion mechanism involved in the turn to trust? This is an important consideration with regard to home care as it is a low-skilled service area in which many employees may need structure to feel comfortable in the work situation. These are some of the questions we can ask with regard to future developments in home care.

CONCLUSION

Following Costa and Bijlsma-Frankema, 'it would be wrong to assume that trust is a panacea to all problems in contemporary organizational relations' (2007, p. 393). In this chapter we have set out to explore how trust reform in the public sector is a process involving an interweaving of trusting and controlling mindsets and practices. Using the case of home care, we have shown how our understanding of such reform efforts can benefit from a balanced view of the trust–control nexus. This approach has allowed us to question what it is that is produced through reform efforts associated with the term 'trust'. Instead of being preoccupied with the potential benefits of trust, our analysis has provided a basis for questioning whether trust reform – in the form of de-bureaucratization – necessarily produces more trust or more trusting conditions in public organizations. This is not a matter of substituting the optimistic bias of the trust literature with a pessimistic view of the practical limitations of trust. We find it important to challenge the dominance of the new public management paradigm and see trust as a vital part of such an agenda. Nuanced accounts of how trust reform actually works are needed in order to gain a better understanding of the complexities involved in making trust work – alongside control. This is our positive contribution.

Our analysis of developments in home care suggests that trust reform can produce a variety of things, of which trust is only one. It can produce new managerial and employee identities, new freedoms and new responsibilities at the same time. It can alter power balances and affect relationships between organizational functions and actors in a variety of non-obvious ways. It can involve new processes of learning and its success may partly depend on participants' past experience of other reform efforts (or, for that matter, their current experience of the impact of other reform agendas). We need to understand such processes better and thus the working conditions of more trusting forms of governing in the public sector. Trust forms an integral part of the new public governance paradigm with its focus on relational organization. But more studies are needed to venture beyond programmatics and to look into the empirical nitty-gritty of how and to what effect trust and modes of governance associated with trust are brought to bear in public organizations. We have argued that the trust–control nexus provides a productive means of entry to such studies. Studies of public sector reform hold great potential with regard to contributing to the literature on trust and control. Furthermore, the focus on trust and control not only provides us with a sound basis for theorizing managerial challenges in the public sector, it is also a perspective, we argue, that is well aligned with the practical challenges ahead.

ACKNOWLEDGEMENT

The authors wish to thank Rasmus Hagedorn-Olsen (MSc, Copenhagen Business School) for his contribution to the gathering of empirical data for this study.

REFERENCES

Bachmann, R. (2001) Trust, power and control in trans-organizational relations. *Organization Studies*, 22 (2), 337–65.

Bachmann, R. (2006) Trust and/or power: Towards a sociological theory of organizational relationships. In: Bachmann, R. and Zaheer, A. (eds) *Handbook of Trust Research*. Cheltenham, UK and Northampton, MA, USA: Edward Elgar Publishing, pp. 393–408.

Bijlsma-Frankema, K. and Costa, A.C. (2005) Understanding the trust–control nexus. *International Sociology*, 20 (3), 259–82.

Bradach, J. and Eccles, R. (1989) Price, authority, trust and control: From ideal types to plural forms. *American Review of Sociology*, 15, 97–118.

Chia, R. and Langley, A. (2004) The first Organization Studies summer workshop: Theorizing process in organizational research (call for papers). *Organization Studies*, 25 (8), 1486–8.

Clarke, J. and Newman, J. (1997) *The Managerial State*. London: Sage.

Costa, A.C. and Bijlsma-Frankema, K. (2007) Trust and control interrelations: New perspectives on the trust–control nexus. *Group & Organization Management*, 32 (4), 392–406.

Das, T.K. and Teng, B-S. (1998) Between trust and control: Developing confidence in partner cooperation in alliances. *Academy of Management Review*, 23 (3), 491–512.

Das, T.K. and Teng, B-S. (2001) Trust, control, and risk in strategic alliances: An integrated framework. *Organization Studies*, 22, 251–83.

Den danske regering [The Danish Government] (2011) *Et Danmark, der står sammen. Regeringsgrundlag, oktober 2011*. (Online) Available at: http://www.stm.dk/publikationer/Et_Danmark_der_staar_sammen_11/Regeringsgrundlag_okt_2011.pdf (accessed 1 December 2014).

Edelenbos, J. and Eshuis, J. (2012) The interplay between trust and control in governance processes: A conceptual and empirical investigation. *Administration & Society*, 44 (6), 647–74.

Foucault, M. (1980) Truth and power. In: Faubion, J.D. (ed.) *Power. Essential Works of Foucault 1954–1984*. New York: The New Press, pp. 111–33.

Foucault, M. (1982) The subject and power. In: Faubion, J.D. (ed.) *Power. Essential Works of Foucault 1954–1984*. New York: The New Press, pp. 326–48.

Gargiulo, M. and Ertug, G. (2006) The dark side of trust. In: Bachmann, R. and Zaheer, A. (eds) *Handbook of Trust Research*. Cheltenham, UK and Northampton, MA, USA: Edward Elgar Publishing, pp. 165–86.

Gilbert, T.P. (2005) Trust and managerialism: Exploring discourses of care. *Journal of Advanced Nursing*, 52 (4), 454–63.

Grey, C. and Garsten, C. (2001) Trust, control and post-bureaucracy. *Organization Studies*, 22 (2), 229–50.

Hernes, T. (2008) *Understanding Organization as Process: Theory for a Tangled World*. London: Routledge.

Inkpen, A.C. and Currall, S.C. (2004) The co-evolution of trust, control, and learning in joint ventures. *Organization Science*, 15, 586–99.

Khodyakov, D. (2007) Trust as a process: A three-dimensional approach. *Sociology*, 41 (1), 115–32.

Københavns Kommune [The Municipality of Copenhagen] (2012) *Budget '13*. Copenhagen: Københavns Kommune.

Lewis, J.D. and Weigert, A. (1985) Trust as a social reality. *Social Forces*, 63 (4), 967–85.

Long, C.P. and Sitkin, S.B. (2006) Trust in the balance: How managers integrate trust-building and task control. In: Bachmann, R. and Zaheer, A. (eds) *Handbook of Trust Research*. Cheltenham, UK and Northampton, MA, USA: Edward Elgar Publishing, pp. 87–106.

Luhmann, N. (1979) *Trust and Power*. New York: John Wiley.

Möllering, G. (2005) The trust/control duality. *International Sociology*, 20 (3), 283–305.

Möllering, G. (2013) Process views of trusting and crises. In: Bachmann, R. and Zaheer, A. (eds) *Handbook of Advances in Trust Research*. Cheltenham, UK and Northampton, MA, USA: Edward Elgar Publishing, pp. 285–305.

Osborne, S.P. (2006) The new public governance. *Public Management Review*, 8 (3), 377–87.

Sitkin, S. (1995) On the positive effect of legalization on trust. *Research on Negotiation in Organisations*, 5, 185–217.

Sitkin, S. and George, E. (2005) Managerial trust-building through the use of legitimating formal and informal control mechanisms. *International Sociology*, 20 (3), 307–38.

Weibel, A. (2007) Formal control and trustworthiness – Shall the twain never meet. *Group & Organization Management*, 32 (4), 500–517.

Welch, C. and Paavilainen-Mäntymäki, E. (2014) Putting process (back) in: Research on the internationalization process of the firm. *International Journal of Management Reviews*, 16, 2–23.

Zucker, L.G. (1986) Production of trust: Institutional sources of economic structure, 1849–1920. In: Bachmann, R. and Zaheer, A. (eds) *Landmark Papers on Trust, Vol. 1*. Cheltenham, UK and Northampton, MA, USA: Edward Elgar Publishing, pp. 74–132.

15. From bank to business: contextual change and transformation of trust bases

May-Britt Ellingsen[1]

BACKGROUND

Grounded theory is the methodological basis for this chapter. Thus, this study is not about testing hypotheses, but it explores social processes and grounds theories and concepts in empirical findings. Here the focus is on the social foundation of trusting and the social construction of mutual understanding, an unexplored perspective in trust research, and the chapter aims to reduce this gap in the knowledge.

When the Norwegian bank crisis was at its peak, one of Norway's biggest newspapers stated that 'The credit market was deregulated. The image of banks as social institutions was pushed aside and their new role as competing businesses came to the fore' (*Aftenposten*, 17 February 1991). One of the effects of this process was a loss of general trust. Trust is perhaps one of the most precious assets for a bank; as Einar Forsbak, manager of the Norwegian Savings Banks Association, stated: 'There is an equally serious problem for banks that they lose trust as that they lose money. Banking is based on trust' (*Aftenposten*, 15 July 1991). A well-functioning economic system is dependent on trust in money, in the monetary system and in banks (Qvigstad, 2014). 'Declining general trust in the banking industry threatens the foundations of the economy', stated Minister of Finance Sigbjørn Johnsen in a report to the Parliament concerning the banking crisis (Johnsen, 1991). Securing stability and trust in the financial system is therefore an important governmental function (St. Prp. nr. 16, 1991–92).

Deregulation introduced market competition into savings banks and led to a transformation of banks from prudent local institutions administering credit regulations to competitive and risk-taking financial actors (Eitrheim et al., 2004; Sandal, 2004; Vale, 2004).[2] This process, combined with banking mismanagement, resulted in a banking crisis and a loss of trust (Nordnes, 1993; Vale, 2004). However, few customers chose to exit from their bank and trust was restored after some years.

This chapter explores how change in economic organization can affect trust processes. The analysis is based on grounded theory methodology and suggests a process perspective on trust. Trust is analysed as a process of sensemaking and social construction, here as a leap of faith triggered by a sense of mutual understanding. The empirical example is an in-depth study of how the social construction of trust between customers and a Norwegian savings bank was eroded by deregulation. This is also an example of how trust processes at the micro level can be affected by changes in macro structures.

The erosion and restoration of trust are general social processes. The chapter contributes to the process perspective on trust by exploring a sense of mutual understanding as a trigger for the leap of faith. Mutual understanding will be defined further below. The suggestion here is that mutual understanding is dependent on sharing social bases as these are the social world in common (Berger and Luckmann, 1991). The social bases of mutual understanding can be categorized as pre-contractual, relational and structural. The bases are dynamic, flexible and maintained in continuous, ongoing processes. Change in the social bases will affect the maintenance and erosion of trust.

The chapter starts with a presentation of a perspective on trust as a dynamic process of social construction; thereafter follows a presentation of the methodology and data. The third section analyses the transformation of trust bases and is followed by a conclusion.

THE SOCIAL CONSTRUCTION OF TRUST

Möllering (2013) suggests analysing trust as a dynamic and continuous process, as *trusting* and not as a static outcome. 'Process views of "trusting" emphasize that trust is always "in process" and is even a process in itself' (Möllering, 2013: p. 287). Trusting can be examined as social or mental processes or as a dynamic between these dimensions. To examine trust as a process, Möllering suggests five process views of trusting. To some extent, these views build on each other; they describe and emphasize different processes and 'develop from relatively moderate to more pronounced notions of process' (Möllering, 2013: p. 290). The five processes also represent a gradual development towards more complex perspectives on analyses of trusting and they can be considered as steps in the development of studies on trust as a dynamic and continuous quality. The five process labels are: (1) trusting as continuous and as a development from phase to phase; (2) trusting as processing of information, as input and outcome; (3) trusting as learning; (4) trusting as becoming and identity formation; and (5) trusting as constituting. According to Möllering, practice as reflexive reproduction of social patterns is a key element of trusting as constituting. The work here is an extension of trusting as constituting. The chapter suggests a dynamic, grounded theory-based perspective on trust *as a process of social construction*. This means analysing trust as a complex and multilevel process, as practices in context and reflexive sensemaking, as interaction and relational processes and as structuration of social patterns. This chapter contributes a dynamic process perspective that analyses how sensemaking, relations and social structures shape the trust process.

Trust in banks and banking is made up of several elements: face-to-face interaction and experience, reputation and trust in the formal structures and regulations that secure financial transactions. Trust is sensemaking (Fuglsang and Jagd, 2013). It is a feeling triggered by mutual understanding and compounded of pre-contractual, relational and structural elements (Ellingsen, 2015), it is multilevel and it includes processes on the micro, meso and macro levels (Fulmer and Gelfand, 2012). This chapter analyses trust in savings banks as sensemaking in a compound and dynamic multilevel process of social construction.

There is no common definition of trust; it is multifaceted and relational. Scholars have emphasized different facets in their definitions and research, providing a multitude of perspectives (Fulmer and Gelfand, 2012). Trust is a personal feeling based on individual disposition and socialization, influenced by both personality and social system, and cannot be exclusively associated with either (Luhmann, 1979). Trust is a social construction (Lewis and Weigert, 1985) that reduces social complexity and suspends social risk, uncertainty and vulnerability (Barber, 1983; Giddens, 1993; Lane, 1998; Luhmann, 1979, 1990; Möllering, 2006; Rousseau et al., 1998). It is a relational quality that is generated and maintained through social interaction (Flores and Solomon, 1998; Misztal, 1996; Seligman, 2000; Möllering, 2006) and a structural quality that is institutionalized through formal, legitimate structures (Bachman and Inkpen, 2011; Zucker, 1986). To trust is to make oneself vulnerable 'based upon positive expectations of the intentions or behaviour of the other' (Rousseau et al., 1998: p. 395). It is to make *a leap of faith* and surrender one's vulnerability to the trustee (Giddens, 1993; Möllering, 2006). The leap of faith is a suspension of doubt and perceived risk and makes us act as if the risk is solved or manageable (Möllering, 2006). The leap of faith is triggered by an anticipated or acknowledged tacit social contract that there is a *mutual understanding* between trustor and trustee (Ellingsen, 2015).

The analytical perspective here is that the social construction of trust is anchored in mutual understanding and a social platform with pre-contractual, relational and structural elements that function as a base for expectations and the leap of faith into trusting. The development and maintenance of trust – trusting – is a dynamic social interplay between sensemaking and social interaction framed within a social context (Wright and Ehnert, 2010) unfolding at the personal, relational and structural level. Trusting is an ongoing process created through human agency and sensemaking in a temporally embedded process that includes the past, the present and the future (Emirbayer and Mische, 1998: p. 963). The study of trust between bank and customer illustrates trust dynamics both as a long-term process and as an event of social construction in the present.

Mutual understanding means believing that one shares relevant social definitions in the particular social situation and that the other will act as expected (Gambetta, 1990) and in line with the presented and socially visible personality (Luhmann, 1979). It is neither a total identification with the other nor a comprehensive agreement, but mutual consent (Weber, 1978) related to a particular context and this can include a belief in the other's benevolence, integrity and ability (Mayer et al., 1995). I hold that the development of mutual understanding is the process whereby doubt is turned into trusting, and it is developed through step-by-step communication with mutual acceptance and confirmation of each other's definition of the situation and sufficient agreement on the intention to act in accordance with these. These processes lead to suspension of doubt and when one has the sense of confirmed mutual understanding, the leap of faith from doubt to trusting is triggered (Lewis and Weigert, 1985; Möllering, 2006). If the anticipated mutual under-standing is confirmed, trust is maintained. This is more than a rational cognitive process. It is also an emotion generated from interpretations of the social bases of trust. I suggest that a study of the development or erosion of trust should focus on the social basis: the elements that are shared by those involved in a trust process. This is the foundation for expectations and for the development of mutual understanding and subsequent trust that the expectations will be fulfilled.

Expectations are the key to social predictability, interaction and trust (Barber, 1983; Luhmann, 1979). They guide social behaviour and the development of mutual understanding. Expectations are complex; they are about what *to do* and about what *not to do*. They can be tacit and/or explicit and can concern a particular situation or general background expectations (Zucker, 1986). Actors make assumptions and expectations about future actions and act as if the other can be trusted (Luhmann, 1979; Möllering, 2006). Action confirms the anticipated mutual understanding on which trust is based and this maintains trusting. As long as the expectations and anticipated mutual understanding are confirmed, everything works as expected and trust is maintained, but the trust process remains invisible. If the expectations are broken, trust erodes and one becomes aware of the lack of trust. Studies of the development, erosion, maintenance and repair of trust require further examination of the mutual understanding of expectations and how they are fulfilled.

I hold that analytically the social platform for developing mutual understanding can be divided into pre-contractual, relational and structural bases as a common ground for social action and expectations. These bases are not mutually exclusive; they can be complementary and support each other. A study of trust processes means here an exploration of how the transformation of the social bases of expectations and mutual understanding influence the social construction of trust. I suggest that this is a dynamic process of perception and interpretation and of sensemaking, interaction and confirmation of mutual understanding.

Social construction is deeply rooted in a series of habitual, taken-for-granted assumptions about common norms and rules of action and interaction (Berger and Luckmann, 1991). This is an assumed common stock of knowledge and a basis for *pre-contractual* trust. Actors need confidence in the belief that others in the same setting share this knowledge to some extent and that they will, accordingly, behave reasonably (Brenkert, 1998; Luhmann, 1990; Misztal, 1996; Sztompka, 1999; Weber, 1978). The trust in others' willingness to keep to the social script is pre-contractual trust, a taken-for-granted form of trust established over time through socialization and experiences. We learn to take it for granted that numerous tacit promises will be kept; this is a tacit social contract. The basis for pre-contractual trust is recreated through social experience and learning as a continuous process inherent in everyday life. The analysis of the customer and bank data indicates that social and organizational change is transformation of the pre-contractual basis for trust. After deregulation, the banks changed the tacit social contract and the pre-contractual basis for the relationship; thus, the taken-for-granted platform for expectations had to be redefined.

Relational trust is based on familiarity and develops in social processes through communication and interaction. Relational trust bridges the barrier between oneself and the other; it is based on personal relationships and reciprocity, face-to-face interaction and relationships in which those involved know each other and have the reassurance of sharing common rules and norms (Giddens, 1993; Luhmann, 1979; Misztal, 1996; Sztompka, 1999; Zucker, 1986). Relational trust is the quality that we probably perceive intuitively as 'trust' in our everyday language. The study indicates that the trust between customers and banks had a relational basis that was maintained through interaction and confirmation of mutual understanding. When the banks started to act differently after deregulation, the relational basis had to be renegotiated step by step.

Structural trust refers to non-personal and generalized trust. This form of trust is also referred to as institution-based trust, generalized trust, system trust, trust in abstract systems and macro-level trust (Giddens, 1993; Lane and Bachmann, 1996; Luhmann, 1979; Misztal, 1996; Sztompka, 1999). An institution is a complex and ambiguous concept. The question of 'how and when institutions matter with regard to trust building is one of the least understood areas within trust research', according to Bachmann and Inkpen (2011: p. 282). My point is that the concept of structural trust refers to formal structures and systems as bases of trust, while the concept of pre-contractual trust refers to meaning systems as bases of trust. Structural bases of trust, I suggest, are platforms for the generalization of trust between strangers and over time and distance. These bases are generated through formal structures, such as the judicial system with laws, property rights, business regulations and contracts, systems that are backed by legitimate sanctions. The development of bases for structural trust is closely interwoven with the institutionalization of a legitimate nation state, expert systems or supranational institutions. The possibility of sanctions from a legitimate power serves to safeguard the trustor; it brackets out the risk and the formal structure functions as a basis for mutual understanding. Structurally-based trust is trust in the system of sanctions and arbitrary sanctioning; alternatively, a lack of legitimate, formal structures means a lack of structural bases of trust. The data in the customer–bank study indicate that the deregulation removed part of the structural bases of trust in banks, but did not remove the arrangements that secured customers' deposits – which are the structural bases of trust in the banking system.

Trust is socially constructed and individually stored in the customers' memory (Wright and Ehnert, 2010). As a temporally embedded process (Emirbayer and Mische, 1998), the *pre-contractual* is informed by the past but shapes the present, which is the *relational* process taking place here and now embedded in a *structural* context. Both the relational and the pre-contractual process affect the imagination of the future towards which the leap of faith is directed. The relational process is influenced by the pre-contractual basis of trust and feeds back on this basis. I therefore hold that social change and change in the level of trust are about change in the bases of trust.

The main finding in the study of the bank–customer relationship is that the deregulation of savings banks was also a deregulation of the trust relationship with their customers. Deregulation changed the bases of mutual understanding and the common platform for making the leap of faith had to be rebuilt to restore trust. An analysis of trust processes involves making the various elements in the process visible and establishing relationships and causality among the elements to explain how processes unfold.

METHODOLOGY AND DATA

Qualitative studies are well suited to identifying causal sequences and tracing the processes involved in the enactment of change (Campbell, 2004: p. 79). The empirical basis of the analysis is a qualitative, in-depth study of the trust relationship between customers and savings banks when the bank crisis was at its peak. The informant data provide unique material from personal customers and savings bank employees in a turbulent period of transformation.

The data were interpreted, categorized and analysed through the grounded theory methodology, an inductive methodological approach for explorative studies, exploring micro-level processes and discovering social patterns. The method provides thick descriptions, hypotheses, concepts and theory based on empirical data (Glaser and Strauss, 1967). Thus, this study is not about testing hypotheses, but explores social processes and grounds theories and concepts in empirical findings. A grounded theory generates categories and concepts that are related in an explanatory framework for the studied phenomenon. The grounded theory is a dynamic and ever-developing framework as new data can specify, expand and develop the theory. The theory presented here is one conceptualization of the social construction of trust and shows a perspective that is hardly studied in trust research.

The aim of the data collection was to gain insights into the informants' sensemaking and experiences of the relationship with the bank, including their general trust in banks and banking, and to explore how deregulation and the subsequent bank crisis influenced the trust relationship between a particular savings bank and its customers. Important data sources were open, in-depth interviews supplemented with the informants' narratives of the experiences that they considered relevant to understanding their trust in banks and banking. The key informants were 10 personal customers, 5 of each gender, aged 25–50, with a medium income and a bank relationship of a minimum of 10 years. The customers' answers were surprisingly congruent independent of their gender, age and geography (Nordnes, 1993). These data were supplemented with about 100 cross-checking talks/interviews over a period of 10 years. These data were collected as conversations, purpose-based interviews and requests for narratives from people whom I met in various social arenas. People were eager to talk about banks when they heard about the study. The cross-checking was conducted to prevent bias and selective perception of only the elements that fitted in with the existing observations and thoughts (Altheide and Johnsen, 1998; Denzin, 1998: p. 327). News articles and letters to the editor about banks during the period 1989–92 were additional sources of customer data.[3] The viewpoints in the newspaper were rather congruent and supported the findings of the interviews and the cross-checking. The analyses of these data provide an insight into why a loss of trust was reported in the national surveys and internal bank surveys. The aim of the data collection was also to gain knowledge of how bank employees experienced the transformation of banking after the deregulation and crisis and how they perceived the banks' strategies to achieve the customers' trust in the new bank market (Ellingsen, 1998). Ten bank employees with more than 10 years of experience in banking (clerks and management) were interviewed in 1990–91.[4] In 1996–99, the data material was extended with 100 hours of structured interviews with bank managers and clerks and observation data from several meetings with the top management.[5] The bank informants were from the head office and two local branches of a Northern Norwegian savings bank group, which was severely hit by the crisis. As a contrast, two management and three employee interviews were collected from a small, local independent savings bank in Trøndelag, which was almost unaffected by the crisis and had fewer than 10 employees.

All the quotations referred to are from the two sets of data; they represent strong tendencies in the material and were translated by the author. The interview data are supplemented with internal material produced by the banking group, such as internal customer surveys, internal evaluations, plans, strategies, reviews and employee studies, various internal information documents and advertisements. The bank data provide an understanding of how the bank worked to adapt to the market competition and how practices were transformed. Analysed together with the interview data, the bank material provides insights into how the bank perceived the situation, the values and aims it was guided by, how it constructed meaning and thus its pre-contractual basis for trust. The document studies also include the bank history and official

Norwegian reports about the deregulation of Norwegian banking and governmental measures to handle the bank crisis, material that views this bank and the banking crisis from outside. The researcher's background and her views can be considered as a resource in the research process, but this demands reflexivity and openness about her background (Olesen, 1998). My background provided a network into the bank and clues about what to look for and whom to ask. If there was any bias, my sympathy, as researcher, was with the customers and front-line clerks.

An exploration of the trust consequences of deregulation demands an insight into the social basis for the trust relationship between banks and customers *before* deregulation and the changes afterwards. This had to be constructed retrospectively based on the available data, which consisted of a few bank documents from the late 1950s, such as letters to customers, advertisements and annual reports. The interview data, such as memories and narratives from experienced bank employees, including my work experience as a bank clerk in the mid-1970s and customers' memories and narratives, supplemented the document data.

The focus in this part of the interviews was on actions and expectations and on how trust was constructed. The retrospective recalling of these experiences was of course coloured by the informants' recent experiences; it was a reinterpretation of the past through a co-reflection with an interviewer. The pre-contractual platform for customer trust is thus constructed from data collected a few years *after* deregulation (1989–92) and is based on the researcher's interpretation of customers' stories about their expectations and experiences *before* deregulation and their experiences and expectations *after* deregulation.

The analysis of retrospective data can indicate what people used to expect from their bank and how they perceive this to have changed – thus, how the pre-contractual, relational and structural bases for mutual understanding have changed. Memories are not fixed, objective and measurable entities; they are dynamic social constructions and are subject to change retrospectively. They are the past brought into the present trust process and thus projected into the future as present actions are directed towards the future (Emirbayer and Mische, 1998; Wright and Ehnert, 2010). However, there was a large convergence in the interview data, and even though the official reports about customers are scarce, they support the qualitative data material. When empirical findings, including memories, were presented to customers and the bank, they recognized them. In grounded theory, recognition from the field is an indication of reliability and validity, as well as a sign that the concepts work and fit. The questions of validity and reliability are addressed differently in grounded theory methodology as questions of conceptual work and fit, and I will return to this below. Work and fit mean that the concept makes implicit social processes visible and that the concept and grounded theory have explanatory power with regard to the empirical processes in question (Glaser and Strauss, 1967; Glaser, 1978).

The next sections analyse the empirical data and discuss how the bank crisis led to the erosion of trust and the role of mutual understanding and dynamic social bases in this process.

THE PRE-CONTRACTUAL BASIS FOR TRUST: RATIONING AND REGULATION

Banks and customers build a history and a capital of trust through interaction and other experiences. These relational processes shape the pre-contractual basis for trust: the customers' tacit and explicit expectations about how a bank ought to perform its role, how it should operate and which norms and values it should practise. The Savings Bank Act, governmental regulations on banking and other laws and regulations are the structural context for the relationship between banks and customers. As a whole, the pre-contractual, relational and structural elements shape the social platform for developing mutual understanding and trust. The data indicate that the trust capital is a reflexive and dynamic capital; customers have an account of trust that is filled up or reduced through every interaction and other experiences with the bank. Interaction generates, maintains or erodes relational trust; if the bank performance fulfils the customers' expectations acceptably, there is mutual understanding and the interaction process runs as usual – relational and pre-contractual trust are maintained without much reflection. The data indicate further that unilateral transformation of an expected common foundation for mutual understanding – such as a new practice – eroded trust; the account of trust was overdrawn when the expectations were repeatedly broken.

From the post-war period until the deregulation, the Norwegian regulation system was very comprehensive and economic stability through regulation was an important policy instrument (NOU 1992: 30; Rapport nr. 17 (1997–98)). The interest level was fixed, low, steady and predictable (Berg and Eitrheim, 2009; NOU 1986: 5; Knutsen, 2012) and it was taken for granted by the customers that the interest was not subject to negotiation (Nordnes, 1993). The most noticeable elements of the regulated bank practice for the customers were credit rationing, a lack of competition in the bank sector, the low and fixed interest rate and having a local bank (Eitrheim et al., 2004; Sandal, 2004; Vale, 2004).[6]

The banks' main task was to disperse credit to the most trustworthy customers and to attract deposits (Rapport nr. 17 (1997–98)). The traditional role of a savings bank was designed to distribute credit to a local community in accordance with politically determined aims for a politically set price (NOU 1992: 30; Nordnes, 1993). According to Rapport nr. 17 (1997–98: p. 57), 'Traditionally the bank culture in Norway was characterized by formal procedures, requirements for good documentation, hierarchical management and distinctly risk aversion. Credit assessment was thorough; the attitudes were conservative and collateral good. This bank culture was adapted to a situation of rationing and economic stability.' Savings banks were local banks; they almost had a monopoly and were familiar with the local context and local customers. Bank practices were based on stability, familiarity and prudence and their attitude was imprinted with cautiousness and meticulousness, responsibility and equality (Nordnes, 1993). An experienced manager in the small and independent savings bank made these observations:

> In the old days, bank work went on in traditional ways, there were no demands of profit or allocations to fund or reserves, and the profit was what it was. Our concern was that we were the local savings bank; that was our mission. We did not consider the market, profit and those matters. We thought in line with tradition and our work went on year by year. (Experienced manager)

These values were instituted as elements of the pre-contractual basis of customers' trust and governed the development of relational trust. The bank culture and regulation regime are elements of the pre-contractual basis for trust and a framework for the relationship. This shaped the customers' perceptions and expectations of the bank and was what they all took for granted in the relationship prior to and in the first phase of deregulation.

In practice, regulation meant that the Government and the Ministry of Finance set strong restrictions to limit the total credit supply and distribution. Each bank had a quota of loans dedicated to credit purposes and had to report this to the National Bank. When the quotas were filled up, the banks were obliged to stop providing credit (NOU 1986: 5; NOU 1992: 30; Rapport nr. 17 (1997–98)). Savings banks did not take risks and credit was approved after thorough assessment of the loans' purposes and the customers' security, background and payment ability. A good relationship with the bank was necessary to be entrusted with credit. The customers therefore expected that credit, as a scarce resource, was quite fairly distributed among them and that each customer was treated equally and thoroughly. As one customer said after deregulation: 'I thought the bank treated us customers equally, but no, the bank looks at each of us as a profitable transaction; this is a huge discrepancy between expectations and reality' (male customer). Another customer pointed out:

> If it is so that all customers are treated differently, but believe that there is equal treatment, whereas the reality is that the bank every time it enters into an agreement with a customer considers this as an isolated transaction to ensure profitability, then there is a tremendous gap between the customer's expectations and the realities. (Male customer)

Rationing meant that customers were rarely allowed to borrow as much as they requested, and they became accustomed to the practice that the bank, rather than their request, decided the amount of credit. This reinforced the paternalistic image of savings banks as institutions working for the benefit of the customer and the local community (Nordnes, 1993). One customer said: 'I thought that the bank meant well and would work to do the best for me. There I was wrong. They [the banks] just think about their own profit. Now they provide loan approvals without consideration of the consequences for the customer's wallet' (male customer).

To sum up, the customer data supported by the official reports indicate that stability, predictability, risk aversion, prudence, fixed interest, free services and limited access to credit were prevalent elements of the pre-contractual basis of trust in the bank–customer relationship. Deregulation changed this.

TRANSFORMATION OF THE RELATIONAL BASIS FOR TRUST: DEREGULATION, BANK CRISIS AND LOSS OF TRUST

The aim of the regulations was first and foremost to secure economic stability and governmental control of the credit supply (Eitrheim et al., 2004). In addition, they had trust effects. The regulations and the Norwegian Banks' Guarantee Fund constituted a structural framework for the credit supply; they safeguarded the customers' deposits and were a structural base for trust. Deregulation targeted control and allocation effects, but as regulations had trust effects, the deregulation created unintended trust effects, such as the erosion of trust, because the common bases of mutual understanding changed rather suddenly. The banks behaved unpredictably for the customers; by taking high prices, the tacit social contract was violated and profit and risk taking were unfamiliar behaviour.

A political and ideological shift took place throughout the Western world during the 1980s. Banking was deregulated; political control and regulation gave way to market competition. Economic liberalization resulted in a banking and financial crisis that hit the Western economy throughout the 1980s until the mid-1990s (Knutsen, 2012; Reinhart and Rogoff, 2008). In Scandinavia, the crises were protracted. Sweden and Finland were harder hit than Norway (Heffernan, 1996), where several of the largest savings and commercial banks were put under public adminis-tration (NOU 1992: 30; Sandal, 2004; Steigum, 2004). The Norwegian Banks' Guarantee Fund had to act to secure customers' deposits (Vale, 2004). Economic history indicates that financial liberalization is followed by crises in banking and finance (Kaminsky and Reinhart, 1999; Kindle-berger and Aliber, 2011; Reinhart and Rogoff, 2011). Crises can spread to the rest of the economy (Heffernan, 1996) and lead to a severe loss of customers' trust in their bank and the general public's trust in the financial system (NOU 1992: 30; Rapport nr. 17 (1997–98); St. Prp. nr. 16 (1991–92)). An exploration of how bank crises can lead to the erosion of trust at the micro level, among bank customers, has general interest.

There was a political consensus about the necessity to deregulate the finance system as the regulations no longer functioned as intended. Deregulation was also expected to be a means to improve competition and efficiency in the financial sector (NOU 1980: 4, 1986: 5, 1989: 1, 1992: 30). When the direct regulation of savings banks' and commercial banks' lending was repealed on 1 January 1984, the credit demand was high and a credit boom followed (Sandal, 2004).[7] Restrictions on capital movement were deregulated, resulting in an extensive inflow of foreign capital, and banks and other finance companies expanded into new markets as geographical restrictions were removed. To compete, banks engaged in far more risk taking and in 1988 the banking crisis emerged (Eitrheim et al., 2004; Moe, 2004; NOU 1992: 30; Rapport nr. 17 (1997–98); Sandal, 2004; St. meld. nr. 39 (1993–94); Vale, 2004). The increased inflow of money triggered banks' expansion; they took greater risks to compete for customers but were not ready for this. Neither management nor employees had sufficient competence in risk evaluation and the banks were not prepared organizationally for market competition (Johnsen, 1991; NOU 1992: 30; Rapport nr. 17 (1997–98); Reve, 1990; St. meld. nr. 39 (1993–94); Vale, 2004). Financial crises are aggregated effects of bank failures, managerial misjudging of risk, missing signals of trouble and general managerial deficiency (Heffernan, 1996; Knutsen, 2012), in addition to system mechanisms (Johnsen, 1991; NOU 1992: 30; Rapport no. 17 (1997–98)). The crisis is also an effect of the change in bank attitudes and working procedures, and I hold that it is an indication of changes in the social bases of trust.

The crisis in banking and finance peaked in 1991 (Kaminsky and Reinhart, 1999). Major economic losses occurred that resulted in bank mergers, depreciation of banks' share capital and/or being subjected to public control for a period. The national survey data show that trust in banks dropped considerably after deregulation and reached its lowest point in 1991; see Table 15.1. The table is a summary of the figures from the MMI Tiltrobarometer (Market and Media Institute Trust Barometer) produced by the former MMI, now the NF (Norwegian Financial Barometer).[8] The MMI answers were scaled from 1 to 4 and the NF scale is from 1 to 6, where 6 is *very little* and 1 is *very high*. To create comparable data between the MMI and the NF, categories 2 and 3 in the NF survey are merged into *pretty good trust*. Generally, Norwegians have a high level of trust in organizations and public bodies (Wollebæk et al., 2012). In 1985, banks were among the most trusted organizations in Norway. Six years later, this trust had been sharply reduced.

Table 15.1   Trust in Norwegian banks 1985–2012

Year	Pretty good trust	Very high trust	Trust (sum)
1985	66%	10%	76%
1991	28%	1%	29%
1999	65%	10%	75%
2012	74%	10%	84%

The survey indicates that in 1985, the first year after the deregulation, 76 per cent of the respondents trusted banks. In 1991, this figure was only 29 per cent. After 8 years, in 1999, trust in banks was restored to the same level as before the crisis. In 2012, trust seems to have grown even stronger; 84 per cent now trust banks and the percentage of respondents with *very high trust* is steady, at 10 per cent. The variation in trust on the aggregate level indicates that trust in banks is crisis-sensitive, but can be restored.

The banks' juridical framework was deregulated and the changes in the structural bases of trust transformed banking and the pre-contractual basis of trust. The pre-contractual basis of trust includes the banks' attitude, which is how people in the bank think and work, the image of the bank as an institution – as a set of values in practice and the expression of these values in practical work – and the tacit social contract. The main characteristics of the savings bank were changed; there were 'pronounced cultural changes in banking', according to Rapport nr. 17 (1997–98: p. 57). The bank and customer data indicate that the face-to-face interaction across the bank counter acquired a new focus on profit and the bank operated with new procedures, which changed the relational basis of trust.

After deregulation, credit should be allocated through demand, price and competition, and the new aims were competition and profit. To compete meant to treat the customers differently. The banks started to charge for previously free services; the credit interest was differentiated between customers and increased frequently without warning. The intro-duction of pricing and negotiation made customers feel that the bank was dishonest and cheating them:

> I thought the others had the same terms as me. When you deal with a social institution such as the bank, you expect fairly the same conduct as when you deal with the public bureaucracy, namely equal treatment. This principle is beyond question when it comes to banks I expect. I hold that it has to do with honesty. (Male customer)

Among customers, the price variation was perceived as a serious vio-lation of their pre-contractual expectations and for a majority of the informants equal conditions were an indication of honesty: 'I thought everyone had to pay the same high price on loans – but that is not so. The bank has different prices. I didn't know until I talked to my neighbour about this. The bank is not fair. I feel that they are fooling me' (female customer). According to the data, the charging for previously free services and the differences in interest were important reasons for the erosion of trust in the relationship with the bank, in addition to the new risk-taking attitude.

Deregulation was the institutionalization of new bank practices and values. The banks did not act predictably; the practices and attitudes were unfamiliar to the customers – and the common basis of mutual under-standing had crumbled away. In addition, the risk taking and excessive financial loss represented a risk of losing deposits and bankruptcy. The administration of credit in accordance with political aims was replaced with aggressive market competition: 'Loans had become a commodity for sale' (Rapport nr. 17 (1997–98): p. 57). One bank manager stated that: 'Now we have to do business, we have to take the market into consideration, which is today's popular way of thinking' (experienced bank manager). The transition from careful savings bank to business and market competition was not only unfamiliar for the customers. The savings banks were not prepared for the market, for new practices and for new aims. The deregulation changed the structural frames for the relationship with the customer; this affected the pre-contractual basis of trust and led to new practices and values in the relational platform for trust processes between bank and customer.

A NEW ACCOUNT OF TRUST: THE DEREGULATED BANK – COMPETITION, RISK AND PROFIT

One aim of deregulation was to create equal conditions for competition in the financial sector, but within a few years, the effect was aggressive marketing of loans, a lack of risk assessments, huge economic losses and the financial crisis. Hard competition, easy access to expensive capital and a high interest level characterized the new credit situation (NOU 1992: 30; Rapport nr. 17 (1997–98); Vale, 2004) and the politicians called for creative and daring banking enterprises (Imset and Stavrum, 1993; Nordnes, 1993). For instance, addressing the Norwegian Bankers' Association, the Industry Minister Johan Peder Syse stated:[9] 'We have noticed a somewhat tepid attitude from the banks when it comes to taking on risk projects. Let us now have some efforts here that show that there still is bravery and engagement in the bank palaces. Show yourself as pioneers, not as hesitating clerks promoting temperance.' Syse demanded a shift in attitudes and practice. Even though the banks were positively disposed towards deregulation, they were poorly prepared culturally to handle their new role as competitive businesses (Nordnes, 1993; NOU 1992: 30; Rapport nr. 17 (1967–98); Reve, 1990; Vale, 2004).

Profit aims and expensive credit funds made it necessary for the banks to charge the highest possible interest and to promote a risk-seeking credit policy. The high risk should be compensated for by high interest; this was risk pricing. Risk pricing is an approval of subprime loans (Knutsen, 2012) and high prices should make a good profit and compensate for the risk, as some losses could be tolerated, as a bank manager explained: 'We have to take risk to expand and make profit, but we charge high interest on risky credit. That's how we can earn money' (experienced bank manager).

After deregulation, the savings banks could expand beyond the municipality and approved many risk projects that proved not to be viable. Several risky customers had no plans to pay back the credit, regardless of the interest that they were charged. These were high-risk customers who had previously not been granted credit, but when the

banks expanded into new places and new markets, they were unfamiliar
with the customers. Fierce competition and growth ambitions made
expanding banks accept customers whom local banks had turned down
(Rapport nr. 17 (1997–98)). In addition, the banks did not consider risk:
'it was a lack of management and control' and 'the banks even considered control to be unimportant', according to Rapport nr. 17 (1997–98)
(p. 58). The interview data from bank managers supported this attitude.
Most banks lent out far more money than their equity capital ratio
allowed and a disproportionately large part of the loans was lent out to
customers without the ability to repay. In addition, most of the savings
banks had a low or lacking level of competence in credit work, as their
focus and education had been on deposits (Nordnes, 1993; NOU 1992:
30; Rapport nr. 17 (1997–98)).

The losses became far greater than the banks were able to cover with
their equity capital. The earnings were simply too low to cover the risk
and the effect was a severe banking and financial crisis. Customers
questioned the banks' honesty, ethical standards and competence, and
both local and national newspapers (see note 3) wrote frequently about
the erosion of trust. Banks' management and politicians were concerned
about the loss of trust and the consequences of this for the trust in
the financial system (Johnsen, 1991; NOU 1992: 30; Rapport nr. 17
(1997–98)).[10]

According to the new bank strategies, profit and growth should
consolidate the competitive power. Credit was the main source of profit
in addition to charges and the banks had to compete to attract credit
customers (NOU 1992: 30; Rapport nr. 17 (1997–98)). Profit-seeking
banks advertised, offered and virtually requested their customers to take
out loans with high interest: 'they were selling loans' (Rapport nr. 17
(1997–98): p. 51). The data indicate that the banks' eagerness to lend
money made customers question the banks' responsibility; as one customer stated: 'How can the savings bank send me letters offering credit?
Their task should be to urge me to save my money!' (female customer).

The customers were used to the careful savings banks that promoted
saving in schools, in advertisements, through their practice and even
through their name, *savings banks*. The deregulated banks' practice was
hardly recognizable and many customers perceived this new, risk-seeking
credit policy as a violation of their expectations about serious bank
practice; as one said: 'I became sceptical when the bank just gave me the
credit, they didn't ask any questions, even though we had not become
customers yet' (male customer). As pointed out above, customers' trust
was based on expectations of stable interest, limited access to credit and
careful consideration of creditworthiness. The savings banks' role was to

be responsible and act with prudence. From the customers' point of view, the deregulated bank practice was governed by unfamiliar values. Risk taking and a profit focus were a shift in attitude and practice that was also new to the bank clerks; as one said: 'Previously we had no focus on earning money; we didn't hear anything about that. We just had to do our job' (experienced female clerk). Many of the experienced clerks worried about the risk and credit expansion: 'The best ones among us, the management assert, are those lending out most. Doesn't our management see the risks this involves?' (experienced male clerk).

With hindsight, the 'worriers' were right. A number of banks proved to have operated in a financially grey zone and sometimes outside what were legal transactions in the 1980s. The banks were 'characterized by lenient handling of the regulations' (Rapport nr. 17 (1997–98): p. 58) and violation of the reporting rules concealed the loss and excessive lending. The banks did not perceive the risks: 'it was a lack of management and control' (ibid.: p. 57), and 'the banks even considered control to be unimportant' (ibid.: p. 58). Internal control mechanisms and competence were weak and partly absent when it came to new and complicated financial transactions (ibid.; Nordnes, 1993; NOU 1992: 30; Sandal, 2004).

The customers' lack of trust was an effect of change in the pre-contractual and relational bases of trust. Risk-seeking banks did not perform the expected prudence, and the interaction with customers was characterized by an unfamiliar profit-maximizing attitude and unpredict-able interest. The tacit contract was violated as the banks had redefined their role as profit-seeking businesses in a financial market and appar-ently expected their customers suddenly to transform from ordinary people dependent on the bank into profit-seeking and selective actors in a bank market.

UNAFFECTED STRUCTURAL-BASED TRUST

The interview data indicate that the erosion of trust was a complex phenomenon and that the informants distinguished between relational and structural-based trust, that is, between trust in their bank and trust in the financial system. Trust in the financial system was unchanged. Even though general trust eroded, very few customers chose to exit and withdraw their bank deposits.

In a market, *exit* is the solution for discontented customers (Hirschman, 1970), but in real life, exit is not always an option because there is no real competition or real market. Bank customers' voice said low trust, but their behaviour was characterized by loyalty. They experienced that there was no real competition, the price variation was between customers and not between banks, it was difficult and expensive to change bank and most customers lacked information about prices and bank services. They felt exploited by the banks, as one customer explained: 'They say that there is competition among banks, but that is not the case. The banks have a monopoly on money, they have similar prices and as a customer you are at their mercy' (male customer). Being at the banks' mercy was not a new situation, but the economic consequences were harder now because of the banks' strong emphasis on profit. Bank customers' loyalty could also be an effect of relational and structural trust providing the bank with a trust capital that was huge enough to contain the loss of pre-contractual trust. The ties of loyalty and the inconvenience of changing banks generated slack: a reservoir of trust that provides a higher threshold for customer exit despite high prices or a general loss of trust. Trust capital is developed over time; it can provide the bank with strong glue to the customer and a buffer against exits in situations of trust violation. An additional reason for the lack of exits is probably the high level of trust in formal structures in Norway.[11] The customers trusted that their deposits were safe and protected by the Norwegian Banks' Guarantee Fund. This was trust in Norwegian laws and in the Government rather than in the banks, and it turned out that this trust had a solid structural foundation. Securing general trust in the financial system was the aim of the governmental actions in the banking crisis (Johnsen, 1991; NOU 1992: 30; Rapport nr. 17 (1997–98); St. Prp. 16 (1991–92)).

In retrospect, one can conclude that the crisis functioned as a reinforcement of the structural-based trust in the banking system because the Government acted as expected and the deposits and customers' money remained safe.[12] The banking crisis caused an erosion of the pre-contractual trust in banks, but not in the pre-contractual trust in the financial system as such.

Formal structures can be changed with the stroke of a pen; changes in social meaning systems and in sensemaking are long-term processes. In 1999, the aggregate level of trust in banks was restored to the level before deregulation (MMI Trust Barometer).[13] Restored trust indicates that a new, common basis for pre-contractual trust and the development of mutual understanding between banks and customers has been established. There is also a new generation of customers who are not accustomed to prudent savings banks with a community spirit – their expectations are adapted to the competitive, profit-seeking banks. Bank prices are fairly differentiated, market information is better and swapping banks has become easier. Customers still remain loyal to their bank; for instance, 88 per cent of the respondents expected to have the same bank next year (Sparebankforeningen, 2003) and in 2009 only 4 per cent of the customers swapped banks (FNO, 2010). Even though the customers seem to be very loyal, the transition to market relations means that there is always a risk of customers' exit. The study of trust processes between banks and customers indicates that to establish and maintain trust, the banks have to fulfil the expectations and create a common basis for mutual understanding. This does not mean that there has to be total agreement between the two, but that the customer experiences the bank as predictable and reliable. To maintain trust and a common platform for mutual understanding, banks have to communicate values and visions, products and services; they have to market a platform for customer expectations and the development of mutual understanding.

CONCLUSION

To sum up, deregulation was a comprehensive transformation of practices and values in the relationship between banks and customers. The familiar platforms for mutual understanding eroded when the pre-contractual and relational bases of trust were undergoing transformation as the bank redefined the tacit social contract. Customers did not know what to expect from the bank; to be trusted requires behaving as expected and confirming the anticipated mutual understanding on which trust is based. Deregulation and transformation of the bank organization were planned changes, but changes in the trust bases were unintended social effects and unnoticed as *trust* effects. However, unnoticed does not mean that they are invisible. On the contrary, changes in trust may appear in many disguises, for instance as exits, silent (or open) resistance, a lack of cooperation or voices of disappointment and complaints. Social change transforms social organization and social perception – the way things are done and the way we think about them, the tacit perceptions and taken-for-granted patterns, on what we trust, where we place our trust and how stable the trusting is. More precise knowledge of what and where we place our trust will provide better insights into the social construction of trust.

Introductorily, I stated that the analysis of deregulation as a transformation of trust bases is an extension of trust as constituting. As the chapter has demonstrated, the exploration of the bases and development of mutual understanding demand a multilevel and process-based approach to studying how social patterns are reconstructed. This perspective examines the trust process from a holistic perspective, as social construction based on sensemaking and reflexivity and as interaction and production and reproduction of social patterns situated in particular social contexts and within particular structural frames. Studies of the development of mutual understanding and maintenance of trust as a dynamic process represent a multilevel, holistic and long-term approach that includes the reproduction and recreation of social patterns as well as the creation of new patterns.

The contribution of this study is a holistic analytical tool for exploring the social construction and reproduction of trust as an ongoing social construction process. The exploration of the social bases of trust and the dynamics between bases provides insights into social change and the relationship between change and trust. This process perspective opens up the possibility of studying the social construction of trust as a particular event in the present, as construction of mutual understanding and for studying the long-term maintenance of trust as dynamics and transformation of trust bases on the micro, meso or macro level. The trust perspective has proved its general relevance to studying trust processes, for instance in regional development, in female entrepreneurship, in gender cultures in the Norwegian army and in regional industrial readjustment.[14]

The practical consequences of this study are that to avoid a loss of trust in situations of social change, it is necessary to become more aware of the trust bases and trust effects. These social constructions are mainly taken for granted, but have to be made explicit to understand how trust is affected by unfulfilled expectations, social change and transformation. As one of the preparation measures for planned and intended social change, it is recommended to examine which trust bases will be affected and how to prepare to avoid a loss of trust or restoration of trust. This can for instance be achieved through making elements of the pre-contractual basis of trust explicit and creating arenas for developing new bases of mutual understanding through continuous dialogue, not as one-sided and unexpected change, such as in the bank case. Other measures can include enhancing the possibilities of developing relational trust or strengthening structural trust bases.

Trust is a personal feeling with a social basis and the dynamics between the social basis and the individual sensemaking is fundamental to the process of developing and maintaining trust. An exploration of the dynamics between the social basis of trusting and the individual sensemaking provides a richer understanding of trust as a social phenomenon and trusting as a social process. This dynamic is a key to the social construction of trust and it is necessary to explore it in the social construction of trust.

NOTES

1. This text is based on the analyses in chapter 13 of Ellingsen (2015).
2. For linguistic reasons, the word 'bank' is used interchangeably with 'savings bank'.
3. Local papers: *Nordlys* and *Tromsø*. National papers: *Dagbladet, VG, Dagens Næringsliv* and *Aftenposten* in 1990–91.
4. The management informants were male and the clerks were female, reflecting the gendered pattern in the bank.
5. The gender pattern was the same, but some of the informants had less than ten years' bank experience.
6. Geographical expansion outside the municipality was in practice prohibited as expansion demanded concession, which was not consented (NOU 1992: 30).
7. The deregulation period lasted from December 1977 until summer 1990 as laws and regulations were repealed and partly reintroduced for a shorter time during this period. The date 1 January 1984 is often used as a defining moment for the deregulation (St. meld. 39 (1993–94)) as the repeal of credit restriction was one of the conditions for the later crisis (NOU 1992: 30).
8. Table 15.1 is a summary of figures from the MMI Trust Barometer and figures from the NF. The MMI Trust Barometer is included in the Norsk Monitor (The Norwegian Monitor), which is a series of surveys conducted every second year since 1985. These surveys are not a public service; they are paid for and there is limited access to the results for non-customers. The Norwegian Monitor is based on a representative sample of 4000 respondents from the population in Norway aged over 15. The respondents answer a battery of questions, among which is a question about trust in various organizations and public bodies. The figures up to 2005 are from the MMI and those from 2006 are from the MMI-Synnovate. The NF is based on 3000 respondents from the Norwegian population aged over 18. The respondents answer a battery of questions about financial services. The MMI respondents were asked the following question (my translation): 'I will now read the name of some of the institutions in the Norwegian society. Will you please state for each of the names I read whether you have very high trust, quite high trust, little trust or no trust at all.' The 2012 data are from the NF and the respondents were asked the following question (my translation): 'To what extent do you have trust in banks in the Norwegian market?'
9. J.P. Syse addressed this in a meeting on 9 April 1984 at the Norwegian Bankers' Association (*Den Norske Bankforening*), which is an employers' organization. Quoted from Økonomisk Revy 84/5, in Rapport nr. 17 (1997–98: p. 51).
10. This fear is also expressed in St. meld. nr. 16 (1988–89), St. meld. nr. 24 (1989–90), St. meld. nr. 39 (1993–94) and St. Prp. nr. 16 (1991–92).
11. Norway is among the countries in the world with the highest level of general trust (Skirbekk and Skirbekk, 2012).
12. The ones who lost money directly because of the banking crisis were those who had invested in banking shares and investors co-financing risk projects.
13. See note 10.
14. The studies referred to are from applied research projects at Norut and published in Norut reports: Ellingsen (2003/11), Ellingsen (2005/10), Ellingsen (2013/08), Ellingsen et al. (2008/15) and Ellingsen and Lotherington (2008).

REFERENCES

Books and articles

Altheide, D.L. and Johnson, J.M. (1998) Criteria for assessing interpretive validity in qualitative research. In: Denzin, N.K. and Lincoln, Y.S. (eds), *Collecting and Interpreting Qualitative Materials*. Thousand Oaks, CA: Sage, pp. 283–312.

Bachman, R. and Inkpen, A.C. (2011) Understanding institutional-based trust building processes in inter-organizational relationships. *Organization Studies*, 32 (2), 281–301.

Barber, B. (1983) *The Logic and Limit of Trust*. New Brunswick, NJ: Rutgers University Press.

Berg, S.A. and Eitrheim, Ø. (2009) Bank regulation and bank crisis. Working Paper 2009/18. Oslo: Norges Bank.

Berger, P. and Luckmann, T. (1991) *The Social Construction of Reality*. London: Penguin Press.

Brenkert, G. (1998) Trust, morality and international business. In: Lane, C. and Bachmann, R. (eds), *Trust Within and Between Organizations: Conceptual Issues and Empirical Applications*. Oxford: Oxford University Press, pp. 273–97.

Campbell, J.L. (2004) *Institutional Change and Globalization*. Princeton, NJ: Princeton University Press.

Denzin, N.K. (1998) The art and politics of interpretation. In: Denzin, N.K. and Lincoln, Y.S. (eds), *Collecting and Interpreting Qualitative Materials*. London: Sage Publications, pp. 313–44.

Eitrheim, Ø., Gerdrup, K. and Klovland, J.T. (2004) Credit, banking and monetary developments in Norway 1819–2003. In: Eitrheim, Ø., Klovland, J.T. and Qvigstad, J.F. (eds), *Historical Monetary Statistics for Norway*. Occasional Papers 35. Oslo: Norges Banks skriftserie, pp. 377–408.

Ellingsen, M-B. (1998) *Kompetanse – Lønnsom Investering eller Trendy Tiltak?* Norut rapport SF 04/98. Tromsø: Norut.

Ellingsen, M-B. (2003) *Fortellinga om Kompetansesamfunnet – om Tillit og Risiko i et Regionalt Utviklingsprosjekt*. Rapport IV i prosjekt 'Kunnskap og Næring' i Kyst-Finnmark, – samarbeid om kompetanseutvikling i små kommuner. Tromsø: Norut rapport 08/2003.

Ellingsen, M-B. (2005) *Å Slå en Sprekk i Statens Vegg? Sluttevaluering av Prosjektet 'Bindende Avtaler Mellom Kommune, Fylke og Stat – et Instrument i Regional Utvikling'*. Tromsø: Norut rapport 10/2005.

Ellingsen, M-B. (2013) *Båtsfjord i Omstilling: Tillitsbasert Nærings- og Samfunnsutvikling. Sluttevaluering av Båtsfjord i Omstilling 2007–2012*. Tromsø: Norut rapport 01/2013.

Ellingsen, M-B. (2015) *The Trust Paradox – An Inquiry into the Core of Social Life*. Doctoral thesis. Tromsø: University of Tromsø – The Arctic University of Norway.

Ellingsen, M-B. and Lotherington, A-T. (2008) Network credit: The magic of trust. In: Aaltio, I., Sundin, E. and Kyrö, P. (eds), *Women Entrepreneurship and Social Capital: A Dialogue and Construction.* Copenhagen: Copenhagen Business School Press, pp. 121–46.

Ellingsen, M-B., Karlsen, G-R., Kirkhaug, R. and Røvik, K-A. (2008) Monolitt eller mosaikk? Pilotundersøkelse og programutkast for undersøkelser av kultur i Forsvaret. Tromsø: Norut rapport 15/2008.

Emirbayer, M. and Mische, A. (1998) What is agency? *American Journal of Sociology*, 103 (4), 962–1023.

Flores, F. and Solomon, R.C. (1998) Creating trust. *Business Ethics Quarterly*, 8, 205–32.

Fuglsang, L. and Jagd, S. (2013) Making sense of institutional trust in organizations: Bridging institutional context and trust. *Organization*, published online before print, 1 August 2013.

Fulmer, C.A. and Gelfand, M.J. (2012) At what level (and in whom) we trust: Trust across multiple organizational levels. *Journal of Management*, 38, 1167–230.

Gambetta, D. (ed.) (1990) *Trust: Making and Breaking Cooperative Relations.* Oxford: Basil Blackwell.

Giddens, A. (1993[1990]) *The Consequences of Modernity.* Cambridge: Polity Press.

Glaser, B.G. (1978) *Theoretical Sensitivity.* Mill Valley, CA: Sociology Press.

Glaser, B.G. and Strauss, A.L. (1967) *The Discovery of Grounded Theory.* New York: Aldine de Gruyter.

Heffernan, S. (1996) *Modern Banking in Theory and Practice.* Chichester: John Wiley and Sons.

Hirschman, A.O. (1970) *Exit, Voice and Loyalty.* Cambridge, MA: Harvard University Press.

Imset, G. and Stavrum, G. (1993) *Bankerott: Det Norske Bankvesens Vekst og Fall.* Oslo: Gyldendal.

Johnsen, S. (1991) *Redegjørelse til Stortinget om situasjonen i Kreditkassen mm. Forhandlinger i Stortinget nr. 18, 17.10.1991, kl. 18.00* [Report to the Parliament Regarding the Situation in Kredittkassen etc. no. 18, 17 October 1991, at 6 p.m.].

Kaminsky, G.L. and Reinhart, C.M. (1999) The twin crises: The causes of banking and balance-of-payments problems. *American Economic Review*, June, pp. 473–500.

Kindleberger, C.P. and Aliber, R. (2011) *Manias, Panics, and Crashes.* 5th edn. Hoboken, NJ: Wiley, pp. 1–37.

Knutsen, S. (2012) Why do banking crises occur? The American subprime crisis compared with the Norwegian banking crisis 1987–92. Working Paper 03/12. Oslo: Norges Bank.

Lane, C. (1998) Introduction: Theories and issues in the study of trust. In: Lane, C. and Bachmann, R. (eds), *Trust Within and Between Organizations: Conceptual Issues and Empirical Applications.* Oxford: Oxford University Press.

Lane, C. and Bachmann, R. (1996) The social constitutions of trust: Supplier relations in Britain and Germany. *Organizations Studies*, 17 (3), 365–96.

Lewis, J.D. and Weigert, A. (1985) Trust as social reality. *Social Forces*, 63 (4), 967–85.

Luhmann, N. (1979) *Trust and Power.* Chichester: John Wiley and Sons.

Luhmann, N. (1990) Familiarity, confidence, trust. In: Gambetta, D. (ed.), *Trust: Making and Breaking Cooperative Relations*. Oxford: Basil Blackwell, pp. 94–107.

Mayer, R.C., Davis, J.H., Schoorman, F.D. (1995) An integrative model of organizational trust. *Academy of Management Review*, 20 (3), 709–34.

Misztal, B.A. (1996) *Trust in Modern Societies*. Cambridge: Polity Press.

Moe, T.G. (2004) Extract from Report No. 17 (1997–98) to the Storting on the Norwegian banking crisis. In: Moe, T.G., Solheim, J.A. and Vale, B. (eds), *The Norwegian Banking Crisis*. Occasional Papers 33. Oslo: Norges Banks skriftserie, pp. 209–23.

Möllering, G. (2006) *Trust: Reason, Routine, Reflexivity*. Oxford: Elsevier.

Möllering, G. (2013) Process views of trusting and crises. In: Bachmann, R. and Zaheer, A. (eds), *Handbook of Advances in Trust Research*. Cheltenham, UK and Northampton, MA, USA: Edward Elgar Publishing, pp. 285–305.

Nordnes, M-B.E. (1993) *Konto for Tillit*. Hovedoppgave i samfunnsplanlegging og lokalsamfunnsforskning. Tromsø: University of Tromsø.

Olesen, V. (1998) Feminist qualitative research in the millennium's first decade: Developments, challenges, prospects. In: Denzin, N.K. and Lincoln, Y.S. (eds), *The SAGE Handbook of Qualitative Research*. London: Sage, pp. 129–46.

Qvigstad, J.F. (2014) On institutions: Fundamentals of confidence and trust. In: *On Institutions – Fundamentals of Confidence and Trust*. Occasional Papers 47. Oslo: Norges Bank skriftserie, pp. 7–28.

Reinhart, C.M. and Rogoff, K.S. (2008) *Is the US Sub-prime Financial Crisis so Different? An International Historical Comparison*. Working Paper 13761. Cambridge, MA: National Bureau of Economic Research.

Reinhart, C.M. and Rogoff, K.S. (2011) From financial crash to debt crisis, *American Economic Review*, 101 (5), 1676–706.

Reve, T. (1990) *Bankkrisen, hva gikk galt?* SAF rapport, nr. 3. Bergen: SAF.

Rousseau, D.M., Sitkin, S.B., Burt, R.S. and Camerer, C. (1998) Not so different after all: A cross-discipline view of trust, special topic forum on trust in and between organizations. *Academy of Management Review*, 23 (3), 393–404.

Sandal, K. (2004) The Nordic banking crises in the early 1990s. Resolution methods and social costs. In: Moe, T.G., Solheim, J.A. and Vale, B. (eds), *The Norwegian Banking Crisis*. Occasional Papers 33. Oslo, Norges Banks skriftserie, pp. 77–116.

Seligman, A.B. (2000[1997]) *The Problem of Trust*. Princeton, NJ: Princeton University Press.

Skirbekk, H. and Skirbekk, G. (2012) Tillit og mistillit i Norge og Sicilia. In: Skirbekk, H. and Grimen, H. (eds), *Tillit i Norge*. Oslo: Res Publica, pp. 59–83.

Steigum, E. (2004) Financial deregulation with a fixed exchange rate. Lessons from Norway's boom–bust cycle and banking crisis. In: Moe, T., Solheim, J.A. and Vale, B. (eds), *The Norwegian Banking Crisis*. Norges Bank's Occasional Papers, no. 33, Oslo, pp. 23–75.

Sztompka, P. (1999) *Trust: A Sociological Theory*. Cambridge: Cambridge University Press.

Vale, B. (2004) The Norwegian banking crisis. In: Moe, T.G., Solheim, A.J. and Vale, B. (eds), *The Norwegian Banking Crisis*. Occasional Papers 33. Oslo: Norges Banks skriftserie, pp. 1–22.
Weber, M. (1978) *Economy and Society*, Roth, G. and Wittich, C. (eds). Berkeley: University of California Press, Vols I and II, pp. 22–86, 212–384, 583–90, 635–1110, 1301–81.
Wollebæk, D., Enjolras, B., Steen-Johnsen, K. and Ødegård, G. (2012) Tillit i Norge etter 22. juli. In: Skirbekk, H. and Grimen, H. (eds), *Tillit i Norge*. Oslo: Res Publica, pp. 29–58.
Wright, A. and Ehnert, I. (2010) Making sense of trust across cultural contexts. In: Saunders, M.N.K., Skinner, D., Dietz, G., Gillespie, N. and Lewicki, R.J. (eds), *Organizational Trust: A Cultural Perspective*. Cambridge: Cambridge University Press, pp. 107–26.
Zucker, L.G. (1986) Production of trust: Institutional sources of economic structure, 1840–1920. *Research in Organizational Behavior*, 8, 53–111.

Official Norwegian Reports

NOU 1980:4 Rentepolitikk (Interest policy).
NOU 1986:5 Konkurransen på finansmarkedet (The competition in the financial market).
NOU 1989:1 Penger og kreditt i en omstillingstid (Money and credit in a time of readjustment).
NOU 1992:30 Bankkrisen (The banking crisis).
Rapport nr. 17 (1997–98) til Stortinget om den norske bankkrisen (Report no. 17 (1997–98) to the Parliament on the Norwegian banking crisis).

White Papers

St. meld. nr. 39 (1993–94) Bankkrisen og utviklingen i den norske banknæringen [The banking crisis and the development of the Norwegian banking industry].
St. meld. nr. 24 (1989–90) Om Kredittilsynets, Norges Banks og Finansdept. behandling av Sparebanken Nord-Norge i 1989 [The Financial Supervisory Authority, The Norwegian Bank and the Ministry of Finance's handling of Northern Norwegian Savings Bank in 1989].
St. meld. nr. 16, (1988–89) Om Kredittilsynets, Norges Banks og Finansdept. behandling av Sparebanken Nord og Tromsø Sparebank [The Financial Supervisory Authority, The Norwegian Bank and the Ministry of Finance's handling of the Northern Savings Bank and Tromsø Savings Bank in 1989].
St. prp. nr. 16 (1991–92) Om bevilgning til Statens Banksikringsfond, Statens Bankinvesteringsfond og Sparebankenes sikringsfond [Allocation to the State Bank Guarantee Fund, the State Bank Investment Fund, Savings Banks' Guarantee Fund].

Web References

Edelmaninsights (2013) (Online) Available at: www.slideshare.net/Edelman insights/global-deck-2013-edelman-trust-barometer-16086761 (accessed May 2014).
FNO (2010) (Online) Available at: http://www.fno.no/Hoved/Aktuelt/Presse meldinger/Pressemeldinger-2010/Farre-bytter-bank/ (accessed May 2014).
Norsk Finansbarometer (2012) (Online) Available at: http://www.fnh.no/Hoved/ Aktuelt/Sporreundersokelser/Finansbarometeret1/Finansbaromteret-2012/Finans barometeret-2012/ (accessed May 2014).
Norwegian Banks' Guarantee Fund (2014) (Online) Available at: http://www. bankenessikringsfond.no/en/Main/About-us/ (accessed May 2014).
Sparebank foreningen (2003) (Online) Available at: http://www.sparebank foreningen.no/id/3438.0 (accessed May 2014).

Newspapers

Aftenposten, 17 February 1991.
Aftenposten, 15 July 1991.

16. Trust as process within and between organizations: discussion and emerging themes

Søren Jagd and Lars Fuglsang

In this chapter, we discuss the contributions in the previous chapters and suggest themes for further studies of the intertwining of trust and process. The goal of this book is to bring forward new knowledge on trust and processes from two distinct perspectives. First, exploring *how trust is formed* through processes of social interactions in which social actors observe, reflect upon and make sense of trust behaviour and its meaning in an organizational and social context and, second, exploring *how trust forms a constitutive element in social processes* more generally in organizations.

Process studies address questions about 'how and why things emerge, develop, grow, or terminate over time, as distinct from variance approaches dealing with co-variation among dependent and independent variables' (Langley et al., 2013). Process studies have been scarce in trust research, but have started to receive attention in recent years (Lyon et al., 2015). However, process studies in trust research may tend to be less theoretically ambitious than process studies in theories of organizing (Nikolova et al., 2015: 234). Most of the process studies in the trust literature tend to be so-called 'weak' process studies focusing on stages of trust development. They are seldom 'strong' process studies concerned with process as ontology. The present volume does not, however, position itself directly in this discussion of weak and strong process views, even if it is sympathetic to the strong process perspective. It contains studies of trust that seek to capture how trust emerges in specific empirical settings. It contributes to the process view of trust by providing case analysis of trust-building processes as they unfold in practice. The book therefore has a more empirical focus, trying to explore and theorize through case studies how trust is formed by or is forming social processes.

The contributions of the book show that trust and distrust are produced and reproduced in a complex interplay with social processes and practices. One contention of the book is that trust forms part of a living meaningful experience (Schütz, 1967) rather than being a state of mind or an organizational feature. From the perspective of process studies, it is explored how trust is intertwined with practices that evolve over time rather than trust being an entity which is linked to persons or organizations. From this perspective, instead of asking how trust may be measured or how it is a resource for managers, we should inquire into how trust is unfolding and how managers are intertwined with and caught up in trust processes.

TRUST AS A SITUATIONAL AND CONTEXTUAL PHENOMENON

Many studies of trust can be found that seek to define trust and trustworthiness as a state of mind, for example as 'a psychological state comprising the intention to accept vulnerability based upon positive expectations of the intention and behaviour of another' (Rousseau et al., 1998). Such definitions, important as they are not least for quantitative research, tend nevertheless to move attention away from the practising and production of trust. Studies of trust as process and practice create an alternative perspective of trust. Trust is seen as related to people's presence and engagement in practice. To fully appreciate these contextual aspects of trust, and the impossibilities of completely 'instrumentalizing' trust either for research or for practitioners, more contextual and qualitative studies are needed. As has been demonstrated in process studies of organizing, they may be linked to philosophical and phenomenological perspectives in social and human sciences (cf. Hernes, 2014).

As argued in the first section of this book, trust may therefore be highly contingent on the sense made of the specific situation and of the context in which trust is experienced and enacted by actors. As argued by Johansen, Espedal, Grønhaug and Selart (Chapter 2) different situations may call for different forms of actions corresponding to different dynamics of trust-building. Alwood, Berbyuk-Lindström and Johansson (Chapter 4) show in their case study that trust is a dynamic relational process that varies with the specific circumstances. These studies illustrate in different ways that we cannot speak of trust and trusting as having general features. Instead we may, as argued by Cohn (2015), see trust as 'something which only emerges from specific practices in particular situations', thereby being a 'quality potentially attributed by people to particular assemblages of people and things' (Cohn, 2015: 3). By stressing the contextual situatedness of trust, we may promote sensitivity towards what distinguishes the particular situations according to actors involved instead of focusing on the general features of trust. A question for further trust research could be to explore the relation between different situations and different ways of understanding and enacting trust.

TRUST AND TIME: TIMEWORK ON TRUST?

Trust is widely accepted as having a temporal dimension by connecting past, present and future (Nikolova et al., 2015), but as shown in Frederiksen's (Chapter 3) elaboration of Luhmann's (1979) distinctions between event temporality and continuity temporality, the relation between trust and related concepts and time may be complex and in need of further study. Tor Hernes (2014) draws a distinction between 'periodic temporality', which does not confer agency upon the passing of time, and 'ongoing temporality', implying that actors are seen as always being in the present. From the perspective of ongoing temporality, 'past and future are not temporal elements distinct from the present, but dimensions of the present experience' (Hernes, 2014: 45). With the passing of time we are continually thrown into situations in which we may recreate past and future. We may focus on particular experiences in the past, thereby giving these particular experiences importance for the present, while we may forget or overlook other experiences in the past which may or may not seem relevant for us. According to Hernes, to the extent that the future is open, so also is the past. This perspective opens up for an understanding of 'the past being open to re-interpretation, and therefore consequential for the anticipation of future acts' (Hernes, 2014: 46).

In relation to trust research, the perspective of ongoing temporality invites us to study actors' re-interpretation of the past and the future as part of their ongoing trust work. It means that trust is not an entity that may be stored and used whenever needed, but that the character and use of trust is dependent on collective reflections on past, present and future. Trust is not 'one thing', but comes in many shapes and is emotionally evaporating. Pockets and spaces of common reflections where participants can interpret the past, present and future are critical for how trust evolves in an organization, as explained by Hansen, Bosse and Rasmussen (Chapter 11) and Swärd (Chapter 9).

TRUST AS AN EMERGENT QUALITY OF SOCIAL RELATIONS

Following the weak process perspective, we may pose questions about the building, maintenance and the destruction of trust. This trust 'building' metaphor may support an understanding of trust as a relative stabilized phenomenon. By instead pointing to trust as an emergent quality of social practice (Cohn, 2015), we may direct attention to trust as being in recurrent processes of emergence. Every encounter changes trust, quantitatively and qualitatively. Trust may be reproduced but at the same time it cannot stay the same. Reproduced trust may be stronger, more complex trust, meaning that we gain additional knowledge about the trustee, about situations that condition our mutual trust, about limits of trust and so on. In this sense trust is always in a state of becoming (Tsoukas and Chia, 2002), always changing to something different.

Again, this perspective of trust cautions against treating trust as a specific resource that can be used for a specific purpose. Trust is rather accumulating and changing over time. Trust may in this sense be understood as a basic characteristic of life, an ontology of Being in the sense of Heidegger (compare, for example, Tomkins and Simpson, 2015), which shows up in many different ways in concrete situations without being ever fully captured by its specific manifestations. Every new situation requires new manifestations of trust, and these manifestations of trust may even oscillate towards distrust. When, for example, a manager performs a trustful act by helping an employee to solve a problematic situation, thus showing signs of ability, benevolence and integrity (Mayer et al., 1995), this may soon be experienced as an act of control and distrust requiring different, new actions of the same manager.

TRUST AND SOCIAL PROCESSES

How is trust involved in social and organizational processes? Some chapters of the volume take a sensemaking perspective on trust as a starting point (for example Chapter 5 by Näslund, Chapter 6 by Mogensen, and Chapter 11 by Hansen, Bosse and Rasmussen). This perspective is inspired by micro-sociological approaches such as symbolic interactionism. Following this perspective, organizational and social life is driven towards deriving meaning from social interaction. While trust in a basic sense may be seen as constitutive of such social interactions that enable meaning and sensemaking, this perspective of trust also implies that the meaning of trust itself must be derived from collective sensemaking processes. Along these lines, trust becomes an act of engagement and reflection within a social and organizational environment. Weick (1995: 170) has argued that the enactment of sensemaking takes place through four processes of arguing, expecting, committing and manipulating. Expecting has been treated in one of the chapters as an agent of sensemaking (Chapter 11). This means that the various manifestations of trust are in a constant flux. They can never be fully learned, appropriated, imitated, exploited or inscribed into organizations.

Thus, the result of a book taking a process perspective may be somewhat disappointing for those who expect to learn what trust is and how it can be performed. Rather than delivering a perspective of trust as a ready-made tool that can be learned and adopted, we suggest that any interference that is supposed to create trust is part of a wider search for trusting as a social process that can never be accomplished in any concrete context. Does this mean that there is no way to build or prompt trust by manipulating organizational structures? No, we don't think so. As is shown by the different chapters in the book, organizations must provide conceptual and physical spaces and cues for trust. As demonstrated in Chapter 7 by Gausdal, various interventions can be made to facilitate trust processes, requiring all participants to be active by sharing, reflecting on, and having dialogues about experiences and challenges within an organization.

Emphasizing processes of negotiation of meaning and relationships in trust research can be a way to move beyond dominant models of management such as new public management or other types of performance management. It is not the performance but the basic social and human constitutive conditions of organizing that become focal points for research. At some point, such an approach to trust would have to involve a perspective of governance as well. Negotiations of meaning, relationships and trust presume that people have the opportunity to say no, and this again is dependent on governance structures. Thus we suggest that further research may revitalize institutional and political studies and explore their potential contribution to understand the democratic aspects and governance of trust and trusting.

REFERENCES

Cohn, Simon. 2015. '"Trust my doctor, trust my pancreas": trust as an emergent quality of social practice', *Philosophy, Ethics, and Humanities in Medicine*, 10(9), 1–9.

Hernes, Tor. 2014. *A Process Theory of Organization.* Oxford: Oxford University Press.

Langley, Ann, Smallman, Clive, Tsoukas, Haridimos and Van de Ven, Andrew H. 2013. 'Process studies of change in organization and management: Unveiling temporality, activity, and flow', *Academy of Management Journal*, 56(1), 1–13.

Luhmann, N. 1979. *Trust and Power: Two Works by Niklas Luhmann.* New York: John Wiley and Sons.

Lyon, Fergus, Möllering, Guido and Saunders, Mark N.K. 2015. *Handbook of Research Methods on Trust.* 2nd edn, Cheltenham, UK and Northampton, MA, USA: Edward Elgar Publishing.

Mayer, R.C., Davis, J.H. and Schoorman, F.D. 1995. An integrative model of organizational trust. *Academy of Management Review*, 20(3), 709–34.

Nikolova, Natalia, Möllering, Guido and Reihlen, Markus. 2015. 'Trusting as a "Leap of Faith": Trust-building practices in client–consultant relationships', *Scandinavian Journal of Management*, 31, 232–45.

Rousseau, D.M., Sitkin, S.B., Burt, R.S. and Camerer, C. 1998. Not so different after all: A cross-discipline view of trust. *Academy of Management Review*, 23(3), 393–404.

Schütz, A. 1967. *The Phenomenology of the Social World.* London: Heinemann Educational Books.

Tomkins, L. and Simpson, P. 2015. Caring leadership: A Heideggerian perspective. *Organization Studies*, 36(8), 1013–31.

Tsoukas, Haridimos and Chia, Robert. 2002. 'On organizational becoming: Rethinking organizational change', *Organization Science*, 13(5), 567–82.

Weick, K.E. 1995. *Sensemaking in Organizations.* Thousand Oaks, CA: Sage.

Index